New Edition

Navigating Special Education Law and Policy

Dixie Snow Huefner
Cynthia M. Herr

IEP

IDEA

FERPA

ADA

IEP
RESOURCES

Navigating Special Education Law and Policy
New Edition

Authors: Dixie Snow Huefner and Cynthia M. Herr
Editors: Joan Donovan and Tom Kinney
Graphic Design: Sherry Pribbenow

An Attainment Publication

Attainment Company, Inc.

P.O. Box 930160
Verona, Wisconsin 53593-0160 USA
1-800-327-4269
www.AttainmentCompany.com

ISBN: 1-57861-782-0

Credits

Every effort has been made to contact copyright holders for permission to reproduce borrowed material where necessary. We apologize for any oversights and would be happy to rectify them in future printings.

The map of the Federal Court Circuits is reprinted from West's Federal Reporter 3d with permission of Thomson Reuters. The FERPA case scenario in Appendix C is reprinted from the Education Law Reporter with permission of West Group.

The description of functional behavioral assessment is used with permission of Rob O'Neill, PhD, Professor, University of Utah, Salt Lake City.

Dedication

This book is dedicated to all the educators and parents who help children with disabilities lead meaningful lives and contribute to the society in which we live.

Contents

(Short Chapter Synopses)

Part I An Overview of Federal Special Education Law

An introduction to special education law: legislation, regulations, and the federal courts; special education terminology; the organization of the book; and legal references.

The evolution of federal special education law from the 1960s to 2011.

An introduction to the meaning of disability under the major civil rights statute affecting the rights of all individuals with disabilities in the public schools.

An introduction to the scope of the nation's most extensive civil rights statute for individuals with disabilities and the extent to which it is being used to reinforce the rights of students with disabilities in public and private educational settings.

Part II The Individuals With Disabilities Education Act

Which students are eligible for special education under IDEA, and issues concerning eligibility.

Requirements for comprehensive assessment of a child's need for special education services, and ongoing assessment issues that involve general and special educators, other qualified professionals, and parents.

The purpose, scope, and specific contents of individualized education programs (IEPs) and the important role of the team members (including general and special educators and parents) who develop IEPs.

The meaning of due process of law and the legal rights extended to parents of IDEA students, including the extent to which parents of children with disabilities are permitted and encouraged to participate in special education decisions affecting their children.

Expanded Contents

Part I An Overview of Federal Special Education Law

Part II The Individuals With Disabilities Education Act

Part III Section 504 of the Rehabilitation Act of 1973

List of Tables and Figures

Tables

Figures

Acknowledgments

Just as it takes a village to raise a child, according to the African proverb, so it takes a village or at least a professional family to raise up a book. Special thanks go to colleagues and students, who, over the years, have helped us keep current and accurate. Thanks are also due to our editors at Attainment Company, Inc., for much encouragement and support. Any errors or misunderstandings, of course, are our responsibility, not that of others.

Reflecting on influences that helped to shape this book, Dixie is struck by how many educators and lawyers are on her family tree. She adds: Like my father, however, I chose not to practice law, and I have been happy to combine education and law in the service of special education. My high school vice-principal was the first to tell me that I should consider becoming an educator. Some twenty years later, I took him seriously. My interest in political science, education, law, and individuals with unique and special needs and talents combined to create mid-life career opportunities in special education law. I thank my gene pool, my environmental circumstances, and the values and support of my family for the instincts, incentive, and ability to pursue my interest in special education law over the past three decades.

Cindy is, first of all, honored and grateful to Dixie for the opportunity to collaborate on this third edition. She adds: I have used this book, from the first edition on, as a text in my Law & Special Education class. It has provided many graduate students in special education with a firm understanding of both the spirit and the letter of special education law. I also thank Dr. Barbara Bateman for providing me with my first introduction to special education law many years ago when IDEA was very new. In the years since, Dr. Bateman is the "expert" to whom I have turned whenever I have questions about the law. I am grateful to her for so many years of mentorship, and for her abiding friendship.

Introduction

This book is about special education law and children with disabilities who are of public school age. It is written primarily as a textbook for educators-in-training and is suitable for an undergraduate or a graduate text in colleges and universities. It is also suitable as an introduction to special education law for practitioners: special and general education teachers, principals and superintendents, special education directors, school psychologists, social workers, school board members, board attorneys, parents, and others who have reason to understand special education issues and do not yet have many years of experience dealing with them. Higher education instructors, especially those who teach graduate students, will want to supplement this book with actual court cases, journal articles, case studies, and the statutes and regulations themselves.

The book is designed to provide a framework for understanding why educators are asked to serve children with disabilities in so many specific ways. It also attempts to indicate how special education law has evolved over the years. It is not a primer or a cookbook with quick and easy recipes for particular troubles, although it does suggest strategies to prevent problems. The overall intent is twofold: (a) to provide a conceptual foundation for the expansion over the past 40 years of federal law affecting children with disabilities, and (b) to help educators and parents be informed about their vital roles and the roles of multiple professionals in educating children with disabilities and steering federal and state policies. The law keeps changing, and those who were exposed to the law in earlier years need to understand the developments that have occurred over the past decade.

With this, the third edition, the final IDEA regulations of 2006 have been integrated into the text. Important court cases decided after the second edition have likewise been included, along with updated statistical information on IDEA students. Additional relevant No Child Left Behind Act regulations have also been incorporated, along with the 2008 amendments to the Americans with Disabilities Act and Section 504 of the Rehabilitation Act and the 2008 amendments to FERPA regulations.

Readers will discover that we spend more time on legislation and regulations than on judicial decisions. It is important to understand that, in the special education arena, as in other areas of law, legislation has primacy and establishes the basic legal standards. Regulations follow to help clarify the intent of the legislation and guide its implementation. Court interpretation comes last, after ambiguities in the law create issues that require judicial resolution.

Readers may find that they want to read the book from start to finish. On the other hand, Part I provides an overview for those who simply want a basic understanding of the three major statutes affecting students with disabilities. Part II, the longest part of the book, describes the major issues that have arisen under IDEA. Part III describes the nondiscrimination requirements of Section 504 for those who wonder what Section 504 does that the Individuals With Disabilities Education Act (IDEA) does not.

We hope that, whatever use you make of the book, you will understand more completely the rights of children with disabilities; the complexities of the legal relationships between federal and state governments; the relative contributions being made by legislation, regulations, and court decisions; and the ultimate responsibility that rests with parents and teachers to make appropriate education a reality for children with disabilities.

Dixie Snow Huefner and Cynthia M. Herr
Spring 2011

About the Authors

Dixie Snow Huefner

Dixie Snow Huefner is professor emerita in the Department of Special Education at the University of Utah. One of the few professors of special education with a law degree, her training and perspective have given her an unusual advantage in teaching and writing about special education law. With an undergraduate degree in political science from Wellesley College and graduate degrees in special education and law from the University of Utah, she has been a close observer and sometime-participant in politics and public policy in Massachusetts, Utah, and Washington, DC. After completing law school and being admitted to the Utah State Bar, she served a prestigious clerkship with the Honorable Stephen H. Anderson, U.S. Court of Appeals for the Tenth Circuit, before joining the Special Education Department as a full-time faculty member.

Professor Huefner's teaching and writing have focused on areas of special education law; home, school, and community partnerships; and disability law and policy. Her articles have appeared in leading education and law journals. In addition to earlier editions of *Navigating Special Education Law and Policy* (formerly titled *Getting Comfortable With Special Education Law*), she co-authored *Education Law and the Public Schools: A Compendium*, published by Christopher-Gordon Publishers. While a full time faculty member, she was a frequent presenter at national and regional conferences and training institutes and a member of the Board of Directors of what is now known as the Education Law Association. During 2004–2005, she was the chair of the board of directors of the Utah Parent Center. She continues her interest and involvement in public policy at all levels of government.

Cynthia M. Herr

Cynthia M. Herr is an assistant professor/research associate in Special Education at the University of Oregon. She has directed and taught in personnel preparation programs in special education for over 25 years. She currently directs a grant-funded personnel preparation program in autism. Dr. Herr has taught children and adults with a wide variety of disabilities in elementary school, community college, and the UO during her 37 years in special education.

Dr. Herr is a nationally recognized author and expert in special education law. She has consulted with school districts and has also served as an advocate for parents of children with disabilities. She has conducted workshops on IEP development as well as social skills training for community agencies. Dr. Herr has published in the areas of special education law, autism, and secondary transition.

In her free time Dr. Herr enjoys reading mysteries and relaxing with her Bernese Mountain Dog, Hershey, and her African Grey Parrot, Akilah.

Common Acronyms Used in Special Education Law

[Acronyms are pronounced as independent alphabet letters unless other wise indicated.]

ADA	Americans with Disabilities Act
ADD / ADHD	Attention Deficit Disorder / Attention Deficit Hyperactivity Disorder (sometimes used synonymously)
APSE (ăp-sē)	Average per student expenditure
BIP (bip)	Behavioral intervention plan
C.F.R.	Code of Federal Regulations
EAHCA	Education for All Handicapped Children Act (also known as Public Law 94-142), enacted in 1975 as Part B of the Education of the Handicapped Act (since renamed the Individuals With Disabilities Education Act)
ED (ĕd)	U.S. Department of Education
EHA	Education of the Handicapped Act, the precursor to IDEA
ESEA	Elementary and Secondary Education Act
ESY	Extended school year
FAPE (fāpe)	Free appropriate public education
FERPA (fer-pa)	Family Educational Rights and Privacy Act
FBA (fooba)	Functional behavioral assessment
HCPA	Handicapped Children's Protection Act (part of IDEA)
HOUSSE (house)	High, objective, uniform state standard of evaluation
IAES	Interim alternative educational setting
IDEA	Individuals With Disabilities Education Act
IDELR	Individuals With Disabilities Education Law Report
IEE	Independent educational evaluation
IEP	Individualized education program
LEA	Local educational agency (includes a school district, an intermediate educational unit, a public charter school)
LEP	Limited English proficiency
LoF	Letter of Findings issued by the Office for Civil Rights (OCR)
LRE	Least restrictive environment

M-D	Manifestation Determination
NCLB	No Child Left Behind Act
OCR	Office for Civil Rights in the U.S. Department of Education
OSEP (o-sĕp)	Office of Special Education Programs in the U.S. Department of Education
OSERS (o-surs)	Office of Special Education and Rehabilitative Services in the U.S. Department of Education (OSEP is a subdivision of OSERS)
PBS	Positive behavioral supports
SEA	State educational agency
Section 504	A brief paragraph in the Rehabilitation Act of 1973 prohibiting discrimination against otherwise qualified persons with disabilities in programs or activities receiving federal money
U.S.C.	United States Code

Table A.

Comparison of IDEA, Section 504, and ADA
in Education Settings

	IDEA	SECTION 504	ADA
Nature of Statute	Funding grant and civil rights statute	Civil rights statute	Civil rights statute
Statutory Reach	States and school districts accepting money under the statute	Public and private schools (preschool through grade 12) and higher education institutions accepting federal money	Public sector and parts of private sectory (e.g., secular private schools and day-care centers)
Protected Groups	Students with IDEA disabilities	Students, parents, and employees with Section 504 disabilities	Service recipients (e.g., students, parents) and employees with ADA disabilities
Definition of Disability	13 specific disabilities, if the disability adversely affects the child's education to the extent that special education and related services are needed (developmental delay allowed for younger children)	Functional definition (mental or physical impairment that substantially limits a major life activity, record of such, or regarded as having such an impairment)	Functional definition (essentially the same as Section 504)
Age Ranges	Part B: 3 through 21 Part C: Birth through 2	(Birth to death, depending on program or activity)	Same as Section 504
Program Requirements	Free appropriate public education (FAPE) in the Least Restrictive Environment (LRE) with an Individualized Education Program (IEP)	Nondiscrimination (FAPE) for school-age children Reasonable modifications (programs and services) Reasonable accommodations (employment) Accessible facilities	Same as Section 504 ADA Accessibility Guidelines
Enforcement	Administrative complaint mechanisms Private right of action in court	Administrative complaint mechanisms Inferred private right of action in court	Administrative complaint mechanisms Private right of action in court
Implementing Agencies	OSEP within ED	OCR within ED Equal Employment Opportunity Commission (EEOC)	OCR EEOC Department of Justice (for Title III)

Part I

An Overview of Federal Special Education Law

Chapter 1

The Multiple Sources of Special Education Law

Chapter Outline

Background

Multiple Sources of Law: Constitutions, Statutes, Regulations, and Court Cases

An Introduction to Our Federal Court System

Special Education Acronyms

The Three Parts of This Book

Footnotes and Paragraph Insets

      Citations to Federal Court Cases

      Citations to Federal Statutes and Regulations

      Citations to Administrative Rulings and Documents

Conclusion

Review

References

Selected Supplementary Resources

Background

Before the 1970s there was no such thing as a body of special education law. In fact, prior to 1954 and the U.S. Supreme Court's *Brown v. Board of Education* (1954, hereafter *Brown*) school desegregation decision, there was not much of a body of general school law, either. Education is not mentioned in the U.S. Constitution, and in colonial times education was largely the responsibility of individual families and communities. During the nineteenth century, with the advent of mass compulsory education, it became largely the responsibility of the states. State constitutions created state education systems, and state legislatures delegated authority to state and local boards of education to run those systems with minimal interference. The few existing court decisions came primarily from state courts; these concerned curriculum content and the process by which schools could discipline and exclude students.

Two important interpretations of the U.S. Constitution by the U.S. Supreme Court in the early 1920s resulted in the recognition of parental and private school rights that states had sought to curtail. One case prohibited the states from requiring parents to place their children in public school, recognizing that parents had the right to select a private school education for their children (*Pierce v. Society of Sisters*, 1925)). The other case recognized the right of a private school teacher to instruct elementary school students in a foreign language (*Meyer v. Nebraska*, 1923).

These early cases implicated the constitutional boundaries of public control over private education but not student and teacher rights in the public schools. Rights that we now take for granted were not litigated until after the *Brown* decision. For instance, until the last half of the twentieth century, there were no cases addressing the right of students to be free from unreasonable searches and seizures by school officials. No cases interpreted the free speech rights of students or teachers, or the right to be protected against discrimination based on race, gender, or disability. In most matters, school employees and students were subject to all school district rules, as long as those rules were not considered arbitrary or irrational.

In the aftermath of the desegregation decision in *Brown*, successful cases were brought in which the individual rights guaranteed under the Bill of Rights and the Fourteenth Amendment to the U.S. Constitution were held to apply to students and teachers in school situations. These rights were embedded in the equal protection and the due process clauses, both of which will be discussed in detail in the chapters that follow. As a result of the expansion of these rights to new populations, the number of discrimination claims against school districts grew. Disability rights issues emerged in the wake of expanded federal court involvement in education issues, the larger civil rights movement, and the philosophical "deinstitutionalization" movement within the disability community. The rights of students with disabilities not to be discriminated against, and to receive an appropriate education, were largely the result of accelerated political lobbying and lawsuits in the 1960s and early 1970s. This book addresses these rights and the concomitant responsibilities of general education teachers, special education teachers, school administrators, school psychologists, social workers, other auxiliary personnel, and parents to work together for the benefit of children with special needs.

Many educators and parents have not had the opportunity to understand the legal sources of the rights of children with disabilities or the limits of those rights. Often they read too much into legal decisions, thinking that the decisions are more independent of the facts than they are, or that they reduce the sound discretion of school officials more than is actually the case. One intent of this book is to dispel some of these misunderstandings while also empowering those who work with students to advocate for children with disabilities.

Before launching into the most essential material about special education law, readers need to understand more basic material about (a) the sources of the laws they must obey, (b) special education terminology, and (c) the organization of this book. The remainder of this chapter deals with these three topics.

Multiple Sources of Law: Constitutions, Statutes, Regulations, and Court Cases

Readers may recall from their high school civics classes that the U.S. Constitution is the fundamental source of law in the United States. It sets the framework for our form of democracy and establishes the basic principles that guide our federal government and its relationship to the states. In turn, state constitutions establish the basic framework for state and local government within the respective states.

The United States is a federal republic divided into three *levels* of government: federal, state, and local. The federal government has been given limited powers under the Constitution. Powers not given to the federal government are retained by the states or the people. The balance of power between federal and state governments is called *federalism*. In school law, as in many other areas of law, tensions exist between state and federal levels of government over who should do what, and how much power should reside at each level.

Tension also exists between the local level and each of the other two levels. Technically, however, local governments are creations of the states because each state government decides whether and how to divide the state into cities, counties, school districts, and so forth. Because a state's legislature or constitution delegates various responsibilities to these local government units, ordinary citizens often think of these units as operating with independent authority. In actuality, however, the authority can be constrained or reshaped by the state government. Nevertheless, for day-to-day operating purposes, we speak of three levels of government: federal, state, and local.

Within each government level are three *branches* of government: legislative, executive, and judicial. These branches are created by federal and state constitutions and create what is known as a government with separation of powers. Each branch has its own set of government duties and functions. Nonetheless, the branches have overlapping responsibilities. Together, the branches create a system of checks and balances on one another.

The legislative branch of federal and state government is responsible for writing legislation called *statutes*. Bills passed by both houses of the U.S. Congress (House of Representatives and Senate) or by state legislatures will become law when they are signed by the U.S. president or by a state's governor, respectively. When ordinary citizens think of laws, they are generally thinking of *statutory law*. The major federal statutes addressed in this book are the Individuals With Disabilities Education Act (2004), (hereafter IDEA '04) and Section 504 of the Rehabilitation Act of 1973 (hereafter Section 504), with secondary attention to the Family Educational Rights and Privacy Act (1974), (hereafter FERPA), the Americans With Disabilities Act (1990), (hereafter ADA), and the No Child Left Behind Act of 2001 (hereafter NCLB).

The executive branch of federal and state government is responsible, among other things, for implementing and enforcing statutes. The executive branch is made up of a chief executive officer (such as the President or governor) and the departments, agencies, and staff that report to that person. The executive branch is also known as the administrative branch because it administers the laws of the land. As part of this responsibility, the administrative departments are given the authority by the legislature to write more detailed rules and regulations (hereafter called *regulations*). These regulations attempt to amplify and clarify the statutes so that those who are affected by them know how they are expected to implement the statutes. These regulations have the force of law and must be obeyed. The administrative department that writes a regulation has the responsibility to monitor its implementation, to ensure compliance with the statute and its regulations. For instance, at the federal level, the U.S. Department of Education (hereafter ED) is the agency responsible for writing the regulations to implement IDEA and Section 504 (in education settings), and then for monitoring and enforcing them. At the state level, state boards of education have similar responsibilities for developing special education regulations (sometime called rules, to differentiate them from federal regulations).

The judicial branches of federal and state governments are responsible for interpreting ambiguity in statutes, policies, and regulations; determining whether laws are constitutional; and deciding how the laws apply to factual situations that give rise to legal challenges. This kind of judicial decision making is referred to as *case law*.

At the local level, local school boards exercise legislative functions when they develop policies to guide the operation of their schools.† For instance, they determine personnel policies, school boundaries, and student codes of conduct; they then delegate to the superintendent the responsibility for implementing board policies, as well as federal and state requirements. Typically, an administrative hearing system is established to resolve certain kinds of school disputes—hearing officers function like judges and make *quasi-judicial* decisions. For instance, under IDEA, hearing officers can determine how IDEA applies to individual special education students when parents and the child's school cannot resolve their disagreements. The hearing officer's decision can then be appealed in court. The administrative hearing decision becomes a source of law; it must be obeyed until or unless overturned on appeal to a higher court.

> † Each state determines whether to establish local boards of education. For instance, in Hawaii, there are no local boards of education, and the state itself assumes that role. In some New England states, the town council, rather than a school board, may be responsible for policies governing the local public schools.

Although the three branches of government have different responsibilities, their roles in setting policy overlap, and they influence one another. For instance, although statutes set some limits on the discretion that can be exercised by the other two branches, administrators in the executive branch interpret statutes to clarify their meaning, and so do judges. Legislators sometimes rewrite statutes in response to court decisions that limit the application of, or invalidate, a statute or a part thereof. This happened, for instance, when the Supreme Court ruled that silence in an early version of IDEA meant that Congress did not intend to provide an award of attorneys' fees to prevailing parents (*See Smith v. Robinson*, 1984). In response, Congress added an explicit attorneys' fee provision to the statute. Although special interest groups attempt to influence all three branches, they usually concentrate their efforts on the legislative and executive branches because the judicial branch is structured to be more independent of political pressures.

When readers of this book set out to understand special education law, they need to understand the relevant provisions of the U.S. Constitution and their own state constitutions. Then they need to know the basic requirements of the special education statutes enacted by the U.S. Congress and their state legislatures. Next, they need to know their own school district policies and be familiar with the regulations that have been issued to clarify and implement the statutes and policies at all three levels. Finally, they need to know the relevant court decisions that interpret the statutes and regulations because constitutions, statutes, regulations, and court decisions must all be obeyed, and ignorance of the law is no excuse for violating it. Table 1.1 summarizes the various sources of law with which readers should be familiar.

Table 1.1.

Governmental Sources of Special Education Law in the United States*

Branches of Government	Levels of Government		
	Federal	State	Local
Legislative	**U.S. Congress** (statutes)	**State Legislature** (statutes)	**School Board** (policies)
Executive	**Department of Education** (regulations)	**State Office of Education** (rules or regs.)	**Superintendent** (district rules)
Judicial	**Federal Courts** (court cases)	**State Courts** (court cases)	**Hearing Officers** (quasi-judicial administrative rulings

*The U.S. Constitution overrides these sources of law. No level or branch of government may violate the U.S. Constitution.

An Introduction to Our Federal Court System

Most educators and parents know something about the work of their state and federal legislatures and their local school boards. They also generally have some experience with the role of government bureaucrats in establishing regulations and enforcing the law, but frequently they know very little about the role and structure of the federal courts.

The federal court system has three levels: (a) the United States Supreme Court at the top, (b) the United States Court of Appeals (with thirteen circuits) in the middle, and (c) more than 100 federal district (trial) courts at the bottom. A court case starts at the bottom of this pyramid and works its way up.

At the bottom level—the trial stage—evidence is introduced, and either a judge or a jury determines the facts of the case. The relevant law is then applied to those facts. Trial courts frequently rely on juries to resolve disputed facts although in the case of special education law, as in many other kinds of civil disputes, cases are usually decided solely by a judge. Although each federal district court has a number of judges to handle the workload, each case is presided over by only one judge. Each federal district court serves either an entire state or, in more populated states, a geographic region within the state. Its decisions are binding only within the geographic region of that court.

At the intermediate level, the U.S. Court of Appeals neither hears the evidence again nor conducts a new trial with new evidence. Instead, panels of three appellate judges drawn from a larger pool of appellate judges review the records of trial courts to ensure that the facts were not incorrectly determined at the trial stage. They then weigh the legal arguments to ensure that the correct law was applied to those facts. The U.S. Court of Appeals is divided into eleven multistate circuits, another geographic circuit solely for the District of Columbia, and one national, specialized "federal circuit" for such matters as personnel and veterans' claims, patent and admiralty claims, and government contract claims (Figure 1.1). Decisions from the geographic circuits of the U.S. Court of Appeals are binding only within the geographic jurisdiction of the circuit that issues the ruling. Most decisions become final at this stage, although a losing party in the U.S. Court of Appeals may petition the United States Supreme Court to review the circuit court decision.

At the top of the pyramid sits the U.S. Supreme Court. It denies most petitions from losing parties in the U.S. Court of Appeals, accepting only those it considers most important. The entire court of nine justices, sitting *en banc* (together), reviews the records of the trial and appellate court decisions below, hears legal arguments, and issues a ruling. Its decisions establish the legal standard for the whole country and must be followed everywhere.†

† Cases at all three federal levels are featured in this book. Cases below the level of the Supreme Court are discussed when they have been influential across jurisdictions even though these cases do not establish the law for regions outside the particular court's jurisdiction. State court cases are rarely discussed in this book, and only if the case provides a particularly helpful interpretation of federal law.

Figure 1.1.

The 13 Federal Judicial Circuits
See 28 U.S.C.A. § 41

State Court Systems

As in the federal court system, state court systems are organized into trial courts and appeals courts, although the names selected for these courts vary by state. All states have trial courts to initially try the cases, and most states have an intermediate court of appeals. All have a high court of appeals (usually, but not always, called a supreme court). The decisions of the highest court of a state establish legal standards only for that state. State court jurisdictions do not cross state lines. Although state courts are authorized to interpret applicable federal law (such as IDEA), state courts are more often asked to interpret the law of the state in which the case is brought.

One final point about federalism in this country: Although there are areas in which federal law is silent (such as much of marriage and divorce law) and, therefore, state law governs, federal law is supreme over state law when state law is incompatible with federal law. The supremacy clause of the U.S. Constitution states that the Constitution and other federal laws are "the supreme law of the Land" (U.S. Const. Art. VI, section 2). This principle of federal supremacy does not prevent a state or local government from operating in spheres in which the federal government does not operate, nor from offering more protections to its citizens than are required by the federal government; it does, however, prevent state and local governments from offering fewer protections. The principle of supremacy applies to special education law because the federal government has determined that it has a crucial role in ensuring that the rights of students with disabilities are not neglected or violated. Congress used its authority under the spending clause of the Constitution and section 5 of the Fourteenth Amendment to offer funds to help states pay for the education of students with disabilities, and to establish federal IDEA standards. Because states have accepted federal IDEA funds, they must comply with the federal standards.† Similarly, both federal and state special education laws are supreme over local special education law if the local law is inconsistent with them.

> † Notwithstanding the supremacy principle, readers will notice as they read this book that in many places they are reminded to consult their own state law. This is because state law sometimes goes beyond the federal law and provides additional protection for students with disabilities. Moreover, as will be seen, the U.S. Congress deliberately left several matters to the discretion of the states. Although the federal law provides the framework, major outlines, and numerous details, the states have the ability to fill in remaining details. In an actual lawsuit, legal advice should be obtained from an attorney who is not only familiar with federal law and the precise facts of the situation but with relevant state law as well.

Special Education Acronyms

Special education is full of acronyms, something that confuses individuals new to the field. Familiarity with the acronyms allows easy shorthand references to public agencies, statutes, and principles of special education law. The time to gain familiarity with these acronyms is now—at the beginning of the book. If the meaning of an acronym is forgotten, refer to the List of Common Acronyms on page xxii. Other terms may be used in individual states but are not included in the table because they vary by state. Unless otherwise indicated, the acronyms, such as LEA and SEA are pronounced as a series of letters rather than as words (e.g. "L-E-A" and "S-E-A"). These acronyms will be defined more fully in relevant portions of the chapters to come. The full meaning of some of the less frequently used acronyms is sometimes repeated in chapters where it seems especially helpful to do so.

The Three Parts of This Book

This book is divided into three parts. Part I has this introductory chapter and three other chapters. Each of the following three chapters presents a brief overview of a major federal law affecting students with disabilities: IDEA, Section 504, and the ADA. All three chapters provide context and background information for the other parts of the book.

Part II concentrates on IDEA '04 and provides basic information about its requirements as well as requirements under FERPA. This is the longest section of the book because the statute, regulations, and court cases are more explicit and extensive than those of Section 504, and there is more material to understand. Although special educators have primary responsibility for implementing IDEA, the IDEA chapters concern general education teachers as well because IDEA mandates their involvement at many points. Administrators and general education teachers have become more deeply involved in IDEA than ever before since the alignment of IDEA with NCLB.

Part III is devoted to Section 504. The chapters in this part of the book explain the nondiscrimination requirements that apply to all students with Section 504 disabilities in all schools accepting federal funds, regardless of whether the students receive special education under IDEA. The definition of disability under Section 504 is broader than the definition under IDEA and includes more students; IDEA students are a subset of the larger group. The Section 504 material is placed after the more detailed IDEA material because an understanding of the specific requirements of IDEA will facilitate an understanding of the broader, more general nondiscrimination requirements of Section 504. Section 504 enlarges the context for the shared responsibility of all school personnel in ensuring equal opportunity for all students with disabilities.

Footnotes and Paragraph Insets

Occasionally, notes are added at the bottom of each page to provide more explanation about a source, or to add other court cases that exemplify the textual material. Paragraph insets are used to provide expanded material about a topic being discussed in the text. Such insets appear after the paragraph to which they relate. In general, they refer to more technical issues than does the material in the body of the text. As such, they function as relevant, informative sidebars.

Citations to Federal Court Cases

To fully understand the legal sources used in this text, one must know how to decipher the citations to statutes, regulations, and judicial decisions. Court cases are published in volumes called *reporters*. The citation for a case indicates the volume number of the reporter in which the case appears, the abbreviated name of the specific reporter, and the page number, followed by the specific court (when needed) and decision year in parentheses. Without such a citation, the decision would be difficult to locate. The abbreviations *U.S., S. Ct.,* and *L. Ed* in the citation indicate a Supreme Court decision. In contrast, a citation for a decision from the U.S. Court of Appeals for a given circuit indicates the specific circuit in parentheses (for instance, 9th Cir.). The reference to F.2d or F.3d is a reference to the *Federal Reporter*, Second or Third Series, in which cases at the circuit court level are published.

Citations to federal district court decisions are comparable to citations to the U.S. Court of Appeals. The specific court refers to the federal district court for the geographic region of the state. Current federal district court decisions are found in the *Federal Supplement*, Third Series, abbreviated as F. Supp. 3d. If a less populous state is not subdivided into eastern, western, northern, southern, and sometimes central districts, the court reference will simply refer to the single district of the given state (D. Utah, for instance).

Citations to Federal Statutes and Regulations

After their enactment or issuance, federal statutes and regulations are organized by subject matter and printed in volumes called codes. Federal statutes are printed in the *United States Code* (U.S.C.), *U.S. Code Annotated* (U.S.C.A.), and *U.S. Code Service* (U.S.C.S.). The U.S.C. is the official government version and is printed every six years, with supplements in between. Regulations are printed in the *Code of Federal Regulations* (C.F.R.), which is updated every year. As with case citations, code citations provide the volume number, the abbreviation for the source, and the page number. The date in parentheses indicates the date on the spine of the code volume. Except where otherwise indicated, statutory references to IDEA in this book are to the 2004 version of IDEA (the latest version) that was published in the 2006 edition of the United States Code.

Citations to Administrative Rulings and Documents

When the references in this book are to OSEP, OSERS, or OCR documents (see List of Common Acronyms for full names of these ED offices) and state administrative hearing decisions under IDEA and Section 504, citations are to the *Individuals With Disabilities Education Law Report* (IDELR, formerly the *Education of the Handicapped Law Report*, or EHLR). IDELR is a comprehensive service that, among other documents, reports administrative hearing decisions at the state level and policy guidance at the federal level. It publishes its material in loose-leaf binders that are generally available in state offices of education and in college and university libraries, including law school libraries. An IDELR citation follows the general rule for legal citations: the name of the ruling, the volume number, the abbreviated name of the reporting service, the page number, and the document source and date in parentheses.

Table 1.2 provides examples of these sources of information.

Table 1.2.

Examples of Legal Citations

Federal Court Cases	
Supreme Court	*Brown v. Board of Education*, 347 U.S. 483 (1954)
U.S. Court of Appeals	*Johnson v. Independent Sch. Dist. No. 4*, 921 F.2d 1022 (10th Cir., 1990)
Federal District Court	*Sullivan v. Vallejo City Unified Sch. Dist.*, 731 F. Supp. 947 (E.D. Cal. 1990)

Federal Statutes and Regulations
Individuals with Disabilities Education Act   20 U.S.C. §§ 1400-1482 (2006)
IDEA Regulations for Parts A and B   34 C.F.R. Part 300 (2006)
Section 504 of the Rehabilitation Act of 1973   29 U.S.C. § 794(a) (2006)
Section 504 Regulations   34 C.F.R. Part 104 (2009)

OSEP/OSERS/OCR Documents
OCR Senior Staff Memorandum, 19 IDELR 894 (OCR 1992)
Letter to Gramm, 17 EHLR 216 (OSERS 1990)
Uxbridge (MA) Pub. Sch., 20 IDELR 827 (OCR 1993)

IDEA Administrative Hearing Decisions
Cornwall Central Sch. Dist. Bd. of Educ., 17 EHLR 1023 (SEA NY 1991)
Conecuh County Bd. of Educ., 30 IDELR 215 (SEA AL 1999)

↳Conclusion

An understanding of the levels and branches of American government is necessary to integrate the material that follows. The concept of multiple sources of law should make clear to the reader the need to understand the statutes, regulations, and court cases that make up the body of special education law. With this basic background information, readers can now proceed to the next three chapters and read about the origins and foundations of IDEA, Section 504, and ADA.

↳Review

1. What is special education law? What are the sources of special education law?

   Simply put, special education law is the body of rules that governs the publicly funded education of students with disabilities. The rules emanate from statutes, regulations, and case law at federal, state, and local levels. The constitutions of the United States and individual states establish the basic framework for the writing of these rules.

2. What is the difference between a statute and a regulation?

   A statute is a law written by the legislative branch of the federal or state government. A regulation is a rule written by the executive branch of federal or state government to more fully explain the statute and clarify statutory ambiguity for those who must comply with the statute. A regulation has the force of law. Regulations are also referred to as administrative rules.

3. Describe the three tiers of the federal court system and their relationship to one another.

   The federal court has three levels: an initial trial court (called a U.S. District Court); a set of intermediate appeals courts (called the U.S. Court of Appeals), which is divided into 13 circuits; and a high court of appeals called the U.S. Supreme Court. A decision by the U.S. Supreme Court can be overturned only by a subsequent decision of that same court. An appellate decision by a circuit of the U.S. Court of Appeals must be followed by all lower courts within the jurisdiction of the circuit.

4. To what does the term *federalism* refer?

   It refers to the balance of power between federal and state governments.

⚡References

Americans with Disabilities Act, 42 U.S.C. § 12101 *et seq.*(Supp. III 2009).

Brown v. Board of Education, 347 U.S. 483 (1954).

Family Educational Rights and Privacy Act of 1974, 20 U.S.C. § 1232g (2006).

Individuals with Disabilities Education Improvement Act, 20 U.S.C. § 1400 *et seq.* (2006).

Meyer v. Nebraska, 262 U.S. 390 (1923).

No Child Left Behind Act of 2001, 20 U.S.C. § 6301 *et seq.* (2006).

Pierce v. Society of Sisters, 268 U.S. 510 (1925).

Section 504 of the Rehabilitation Act of 1973, 29 U.S.C. § 794 (2006).

Smith v. Robinson, 468 U.S. 992 (1984).

⇉Selected Supplementary Resources†

Burgdorf, M. P., & Burgdorf, R., Jr. (1975). A history of unequal treatment: The qualifications of handicapped persons as a "suspect class" under the Equal Protection Clause. *Santa Clara Lawyer, 15*, 855–910.

Heise, M. (1994). Goals 2000: Educate America Act: The federalization and legalization of educational policy. *Fordham Law Review, 63*, 345–381.

Kauffman, J. M., & Hallahan, D. P. (2005). *Special education: What it is and why we need it*. Boston, MA: Pearson Education.

Thomas, S. B., & Russo, C. J. (1995). Introduction. In *Special education law: Issues and implications for the 90s*. Topeka, KS: National Organization for Legal Problems in Education (now Dayton, OH: the Education Law Ass'n)

> † At the end of this and each succeeding chapter, a limited number of articles and an occasional book are included for potential use by those who want to learn more about the policy implications of specific topics relevant to the chapter. Some of the selections also address historical background materials or specific disability issues. They are meant for those who want to do further research, and they will lead readers to other relevant materials as well.

Chapter 2

An Overview of the Individuals With Disabilities Education Act

Chapter Outline

A Legislative History of IDEA

Why Did the Federal Government Get Involved in Special Education?

As noted in chapter 1, public education in the United States has traditionally been the responsibility of state and local governments, and the U.S. Constitution does not mention education. Yet in the 1960s, the federal government began to offer help to the states in educating certain groups of school-age children who were believed to be educationally disadvantaged in one way or another. The federal government got involved for several reasons, but primarily because the need for equal educational opportunity for all students became a national civil rights issue. Students who were African American, later followed by students who were female, immigrants, poor, or who had disabilities, sought enforcement in the federal courts of the right to equal educational opportunity under the Fourteenth Amendment to the U.S. Constitution.†

> † Another reason for the federal government's involvement was its interest in an educated citizenry. The survival and economic well-being of our form of government depends on an educated and self-sufficient citizenry that is capable of earning a living and participating in democratic institutions. In a global economy, it is especially important for the American economy to remain competitive. If certain groups within the society are denied access to an equal educational opportunity, they can become a significant burden on the economy.

Court cases alleging civil rights violations helped to spur congressional legislation, much of which belonged to President Lyndon Johnson's "Great Society" initiatives. For instance, Congress passed a series of civil rights statutes barring recipients of federal financial assistance from discriminating on the basis of race, color, and national origin (Civil Rights Act of 1964), sex (Title IX of the Education Amendments of 1972), and disabilities (Section 504 of the Rehabilitation Act of 1973) in areas such as employment, facilities access, and higher education.

In addition, using its constitutional authority under the spending clause of the U.S. Constitution, Congress enacted a variety of education funding statutes reaching various groups of students whose special needs the states were seen as ignoring. These statutes offered financial help to states in return for compliance with federal educational standards. Foremost among them was the passage in 1965 of the Elementary and Secondary Education Act (hereafter ESEA), Title I of which provided direct federal aid to schools with high percentages of children whose families were living in poverty.† This landmark legislation propelled the federal government into the education of millions of school children across the country. At the same time, ESEA included provisions to improve the education of children with disabilities in state schools for children who were deaf, blind, or had intellectual disabilities (referred to as mental retardation in ESEA and IDEA until statutory changes in 2010). ESEA amendments in 1966 and 1968 provided indirect aid in the form of grants to state agencies for pilot projects to develop promising methods of serving children with various kinds of disabilities.

> † Other groups of students who were helped by federal legislation included students for whom English was not their native language (the Bilingual Education Act of 1968), students who were gifted (The Jacob K. Javits Gifted and Talented Students Education Act of 1988), and students in need of vocational education (Vocational Education Act of 1984).

In 1970, the Education of the Handicapped Act (EHA) was enacted. (At that time children with disabilities were referred to as handicapped.) EHA consolidated and expanded the earlier federal grant programs and continued to fund pilot projects at state and local levels. At the same time, money was offered to higher education institutions for the development of special education teacher training programs and to regional resource centers for the delivery of technical assistance to state and local school districts.

The treatment of children with disabilities in the public schools throughout this period was uneven. The education of many of these children had been viewed as a privilege rather than a right. For example, in some states, although services in regular schools were provided to children with mild intellectual disabilities, mild speech impairments, and mild emotional problems, children with more severe mental or physical disabilities (including blindness, deafness, intellectual disabilities, and cerebral palsy) were sent to institutions and special schools or otherwise excluded from regular education settings. Children with learning disabilities went unrecognized and were often thought of as lazy or stupid. Many children whose emotional disabilities were severe were simply expelled from school. In other words, what was happening around the country was not uniform, and many school districts had been using essentially a sink-or-swim approach to learning for many children with disabilities.

Two 1972 federal court cases, *Pennsylvania Association for Retarded Children (PARC) v. Pennsylvania* (hereafter *PARC*) and *Mills v. District of Columbia Board of Education* (hereafter *Mills*) became landmark cases that were influential across the country and with the U.S. Congress in establishing that all children with disabilities had a right to education. Children with mental retardation were the focus of the PARC case, whereas the plaintiffs in *Mills* were children with many different disabilities, most of which included behavioral problems. Both cases resulted in requiring the public school defendants to provide access to a public school education for children with disabilities. Both cases also resulted in the provision of basic procedural rights—notice and hearing—prior to placing the children in programs separate from general education students. In particular, the *Mills* decision invoked a line of legal precedents going back to *Brown* (1954). In *Mills*, the judge reasoned that because placement of children into segregated public schools on the basis of race was unconstitutional, and because using culturally biased measures to place poor children in inferior education tracks in public school was unconstitutional, total exclusion by the District of Columbia of thousands of students with disabilities from any education was therefore unconstitutional as well.

Public Law 94-142

In 1974, influenced by the *PARC* and *Mills* cases, Congress expanded EHA to incorporate the concept of a right to a full educational opportunity for handicapped children (The Education Amendments of 1974). By this time, numerous suits were pending in states across the country, also catalyzed by the *PARC* and *Mills* decisions. The following year, after holding hearings across the country, Congress amended EHA by enacting the Education for All Handicapped Children Act (EAHCA), also known as Part B of EHA and commonly referred to as P.L. 94-142.† This law offered grants to states for direct services to school children with the following enumerated disabilities: specific learning disabilities, speech and language impairments, mental retardation (the term then used), serious emotional disturbance, hearing impairments (including deafness), visual impairments (including blindness), orthopedic impairments, and other health impairments. No longer was EHA just an indirect aid program, but instead offered formula grants to participating states for direct aid to children with these disabilities. The amount of the grants was based on an annual head count of children served by the program. Public Law. 94-142 also elaborated on the educational rights established in the 1974 EHA amendments and expanded the set of procedural safeguards to parents of children with disabilities.

† Public Law 94-142 refers to the 142nd law passed by the 94th Congress. All public laws are numbered in a similar fashion.

The passage of P.L. 94-142 was a milestone in the education of children with disabilities. The Act engaged the federal government as a partner with the states in educating children with the specified disabilities. Funding was authorized to reach 40 percent of the national average per student expenditure (APSE)—the average spent by state and local educational agencies (SEAs and LEAs) on all students in elementary and secondary education in the fifty states and the District of Columbia, based on average daily attendance data. In reality, during the first five or six years of the Act, federal funding reached 12 percent of APSE. In the early 1980s, it sank to approximately 8 percent, where it remained until fiscal year (FY) 1997. In FY 1997 and FY 1998, federal funding rose considerably, but it did not reach its former level of 12 percent. After 1998, funding rose steadily and by FY 2005 was approaching 20 percent, still conceded to be inadequate to meet the expectations of the Act but nonetheless an attempt to move closer to the original authorization target.†

† In February 2009, President Barack Obama signed the American Recovery and Reinvestment Act. Included in it was 12.2 billion dollars for increased IDEA funding--to be awarded over fiscal years 2009 and 2010. This investment dramatically increased the annual funding for special education and moved the percentage of APSE much closer to the goal of 40% (34.2% for FY 2009). The increased appropriations, however, had to be obligated by September 30, 2011. The temporary increases were intended to help stimulate the economy during its serious recessionary cycle. Nonetheless, full funding remains the goal of special education advocates.

The basic rights that P.L. 94-142 gave to children with disabilities included (a) the right to a free appropriate public education (*FAPE*), (b) in a setting that "to the maximum extent appropriate" allowed education with children who did not have disabilities (least restrictive environment, or *LRE*), (c) governed by a written, individualized education program (*IEP*) that was (d) based on a thorough evaluation of the child's needs. FAPE included publicly supervised and publicly funded special education and related services based on an IEP appropriate to the child's individual needs. All eligible children were to be located, identified, and evaluated. Those previously excluded from public school education were to be served first, along with those with the most severe disabilities. No one was to be rejected (*zero-reject*). Children were to be educated in the setting closest to the instructional mainstream in which an appropriate education could be delivered.

All children with disabilities were considered educable, using a broader definition of educability than just the acquisition of academic skills. The landmark *PARC* case had helped to establish that the definition of education included systematic instruction in the skills necessary for independent living, thereby fostering growth toward goals that met individual and societal needs. For instance, if a child needed to develop language skills, social skills, or self-help skills like dressing and feeding, and if systematic instruction could result in the acquisition of such skills, then the public school system was responsible for educating that child.

Along with the basic rights to specialized instruction and related services came procedural safeguards to ensure the involvement of parents at key stages of educational decision making. The procedural safeguards in P.L. 94-142 built on the *PARC* and *Mills* cases, which had both concluded that removal of children with disabilities from the general education setting required due process of law under the Constitution—that is, some kind of advance notice and some kind of hearing. Beyond that, parents were encouraged and expected to participate in developing their child's IEP.

With respect to the notice and hearing rights, P.L. 94-142 required notice to parents of what the school proposed to do or not do for their children. It also required notice to parents of all their legal rights under P.L. 94-142. These included the right to access their child's records. In addition, if parents disagreed with a school's evaluation of their child, they were entitled, under certain conditions, to an independent educational evaluation at public expense. Furthermore, they were entitled to an impartial hearing if they disagreed with the school's actions with respect to the identification, evaluation, placement, or provision of FAPE for their child. If they were dissatisfied with the results of the hearing, they could then seek a review of the hearing decision, first at a state administrative level if the hearing occurred initially at the local level, and then in federal or state court.

Public Law 94-142, Part B of EHA, is permanently authorized. This means that it does not have to be periodically re-enacted by Congress. In contrast, the discretionary grant programs for a variety of research and technical assistance projects must be reauthorized by Congress every three to five years or so, or they lapse. Partly because these portions of the Act must be reviewed periodically, the entire Act has remained in the congressional eye. Therefore, amendments to Part B are typically enacted or considered when the rest of the Act is being reauthorized.

The 1986 EHA Amendments

During the 1980s, various other amendments to EHA were enacted by Congress and the President. The most important were the EHA Amendments of 1986 and the Handicapped Children's Protection Act of 1986, which together accomplished three major purposes:

1. Over a staged, five-year period, they extended the rights and protections of P.L. 94-142 to preschoolers (ages three through five) with disabilities or developmental delay. They also provided funding incentives separate from the funding available for the education of school-age children.

2. They created incentive state grants for early intervention programs to serve infants and toddlers (birth through two) who had a developmental delay or a diagnostic condition likely to result in a developmental delay. At the discretion of the state, services also could be extended to those who were "at risk" of substantial developmental delay if early intervention services were not provided.

3. They provided for an award of attorneys' fees to parents who prevailed in administrative or judicial proceedings under the Act.†

   † The provision that awarded attorneys' fees nullified the Supreme Court's ruling in *Smith v. Robinson*, 468 U.S. 922 (1984), which had interpreted P.L. 94-142 to prohibit attorneys' fees.

The Individuals With Disabilities Education Act (IDEA) of 1990

Four years later, the EHA Amendments of 1990 eliminated all use of the term handicap, substituting instead the term *disability*. Thus, the Act was renamed the Individuals With Disabilities Education Act (IDEA). Advocacy on behalf of persons with disabilities produced the change. Advocates believed that *disability* was a less stigmatizing term than *handicap*. To many, the term *handicap* implied dependence, based partially on the conjecture that the term originated in medieval times when many beggars, with cap in hand, included persons with physical and sensory disabilities. The adjectives handicapped and disabled were eliminated from the Act as well. "People first" language was preferable because it indicated that all individuals, including those with disabilities, were persons first, with a variety of descriptive characteristics, only some of which might include disability. In other words, no person with a disability should be defined in the eyes of others by the disability alone.

In addition to the terminology changes, IDEA added autism and traumatic brain injury to the other separate categories of disability under the Act, bringing the total number of identified disability conditions to ten. From these ten statutory categories, the regulations carved out two more: multiple disabilities and deaf-blindness. The regulations also separated the category of hearing impairment from that of deafness, bringing the total of regulatory disability definitions to thirteen.

IDEA also added a detailed requirement for transition planning by the age of sixteen for all IDEA students. Another provision of the law explicitly provided that states were not immune from lawsuits in federal court for a violation of IDEA, thereby preventing states from arguing that the lawsuits in which they were defendants had to be tried exclusively in their own state courts.† Finally, Congress incorporated requirements concerning assistive technology devices and services into the Act.

> † The provision abolishing state immunity nullified an earlier Supreme Court interpretation of the statute in *Dellmuth v. Muth*, 491 U.S. 223 (1989). This statutory provision has been upheld in the seven circuits in which it has been challenged.

Under IDEA, states are required to ensure that local school districts comply with the requirements of the statute. If a local agency is unwilling or unable to comply, the state in some circumstances can be held directly responsible for the delivery of FAPE.[1] This is true even if the child is placed out of state.†

> † Residency disputes sometimes can obscure agency responsibility. Usually, the school district where the custodial parent (or person with guardianship) resides is the district responsible for FAPE, even when an out-of-district placement is needed to make FAPE available. In residency disputes, it is important for school officials to check state residency statutes and state and federal court decisions applying to their jurisdiction.

The IDEA Amendments of 1997

In mid-1997, President Clinton signed into law the IDEA Amendments of 1997 (IDEA '97).These amendments were numerous and substantive. They represented a significant change in focus in certain respects and raised outcome expectations for children with disabilities. The changes were consonant with broader federal efforts to encourage clearer state standards and increased national assessment of student achievement. In important ways they paralleled the reform goals embodied in the Goals 2000: Educate America Act of 1994 and the Improving America's Schools Act of 1994, both of which amended the ESEA. Among the broader goals reflected in IDEA '97 were those to increase school readiness, improve competency in challenging subject matter, improve the safety of the learning environment, increase literacy, improve the professional skills of the nation's teaching force, increase graduation rates, and promote partnerships with parents.

Revisions to services and procedural safeguards.

In general, the Amendments focused on improving outcomes largely by increasing student access to general education reforms and the general education curriculum. They also increased the involvement of parents in eligibility and placement decisions, attempted to reduce the opportunities for misidentification and mislabeling, and encouraged mediation as a means of dispute resolution.

---

[1] Letter to McAllister, 21 IDELR 81 (OSEP 1994) (stating that the SEA has the ultimate responsibility for ensuring that children who are legal residents of the state, but who are placed out of state, receive FAPE).

They added major new requirements relating to the development of the IEP and encouraging placement in general education settings, generating considerable speculation and concern about increased responsibilities for both general and special educators. They modified requirements for eligibility, evaluation, IEPs, public and private placements, and due process safeguards.

Discipline amendments.

In addition, IDEA '97 specified procedures for more easily changing the placement of students with disabilities who were deemed disruptive or dangerous, procedures that generated a lot of controversy. The amendments included a requirement to determine whether a student's misbehavior was a manifestation of the disability. They also focused on *behavioral intervention plans* (*BIPs*) and *functional behavioral assessment* (*FBA*) for students whose conduct fell below acceptable standards. The relevant disciplinary amendments were a response to national concern about violent behavior in school, whether from students with disabilities or students without disabilities. The disciplinary provisions particularly reflected pressures to (a) allow school officials to discipline students with disabilities more like students without disabilities, and (b) require school officials to do a better job of addressing behavior as an educational issue. Congress viewed the measures as necessary because more and more children with behavioral disabilities were being included in regular schools and classrooms. Others in the advocacy community viewed the measures as a backlash against inclusion and a largely noneducational response to disability-related behavioral manifestations.

Performance indicators.

Additionally, under IDEA '97, the states were obligated to develop performance goals and indicators for children with disabilities. Indicators included dropout rates, suspension and expulsion rates, and graduation rates. Research had shown that dropout rates were higher and graduation rates correspondingly lower for children with disabilities. Thus, the indicators were required so that the tracking of these students in each state could become more systematic.

State and districtwide assessments.

Moreover, children with disabilities, with few exceptions, were to be included in state and districtwide assessments of student achievement, with appropriate test "modifications" (the term then used) when necessary (20 U.S.C. § 1413(a)(5) (Supp. III 1997)). In the past, many districts had excluded some children with disabilities from standardized achievement testing so that their scores would not lower the standing of the district schools. Under the IDEA '97 requirements, all districts had to include all children except those determined by the IEP team to be unable to participate, even with modifications. Those children were to be assessed in another way to be determined by the IEP team.

Funding provisions.

Other new provisions were added that affected the way SEAs and LEAs administered federal IDEA dollars. One applied to public charter schools and specified that children with disabilities must be served and funds provided in the same manner as they would be in noncharter schools. In other words, Part B must be implemented in public charter schools (20 U.S.C. § 1412(a)(5)(b) (Supp. III 1997)).Another provision required states to assure the federal government that if their funding mechanisms were based on the type of setting in which a child was served, the mechanism did not result in placements that violated the principle of LRE ((20 U.S.C. § 1413 (a)(2)(B) (Supp. III 1997)). This provision was added out of a concern that many school districts were making placement decisions based on a child's disability label rather than on the IEP.

Also, IDEA '97 allowed an LEA to spend federal dollars for special education services that incidentally benefitted students who did not have disabilities (20 U.S.C. § 1411(e) (Supp. III 1997)). For example, the special education staff would be permitted to work with a group of such children in a general education classroom while simultaneously working to implement the IEPs of children with disabilities.

All these changes represented a desire to (a) reduce the extent to which children with disabilities continued to be excluded from various aspects of the school program, (b) improve the postschool outcomes for children with disabilities, and (c) forge more extensive links between general education and special education.

The Individuals With Disabilities Education Improvement Act of 2004 (IDEA '04)

Reauthorization of IDEA became a long and contentious process during the 108th Congress. Numerous amendments to IDEA '97 were proposed over the two-year period. Whether to fully fund IDEA at 40 percent of APSE was vigorously debated behind the scenes, but no such provision emerged. In the closing months of the 108th Congress, the U.S. House of Representatives and the U.S. Senate finally agreed on a compromise bill that passed both houses in November 2004. The bill was signed by President George W. Bush in early December 2004.

As with its predecessor, the amendments to Part B were extensive. They retained the major purposes of IDEA '97 but attempted to correct what were seen as increased burdens on LEAs, particularly with respect to IEPs, procedural safeguards, and disciplinary provisions. The amendments also aligned IDEA more closely with the assessment requirements of the No Child Left Behind Act of 2001 (NCLB), which amended ESEA to increase SEA and LEA accountability for the academic proficiency of all students. (See Table 2.1 for a summary of NCLB.) In addition, they reflected a desire to encourage less adversarial resolution of conflicts between parents and schools, a continuing attempt to balance the need to maintain discipline in the classroom with the right to FAPE for eligible children, a focus on teacher quality, and an emphasis on improving academic outcomes for children with disabilities.

New regulations were required to be published within a year of enactment of IDEA '04, but the deadline was not met. The U. S. Department of Education (ED) finally issued the regulations in August 2006. Congress instructed ED to limit the regulations to provisions that would not go beyond those necessary for compliance with the language of the statute. Therefore, various additional explanatory statements that were attached to the 1999 regulations do not appear in the 2006 regulations. To a large extent, the regulations simply repeat the statutory language without embellishment but are sometimes cited hereafter along with or in lieu of the statute. Where they help to clarify the statute, discussion of these regulations is incorporated into the text itself.

Eligibility, evaluation, and IEPs.

In terms of eligibility and evaluation, IDEA '04 provides more discretion to SEAs in determining whom to classify as having a learning disability, and how a learning disability is determined (34 C.F.R. § 300.307 *et seq.* (2006)). It also tightens the eligibility requirements to avoid misclassification of poorly taught underachievers. It releases schools from any obligation to provide FAPE if a parent withholds consent for delivery of special education services (34 C.F.R. § 300.300(b)(4) (2006)).

With respect to IEPs, IDEA '04 increases the focus on student outcomes. It aligns IDEA assessments with achievement measures required under NCLB. It specifies a focus on academic achievement aligned to the general curriculum. It eliminates the need for objectives and benchmarks on most IEPs in an attempt to reduce the paperwork burdens on special education teachers. It allows various members of the IEP team to be excused from attendance at the IEP meeting when the parent and school agree. The statute modifies the transition plan requirements to make clear that transition plans should focus on academic as well as functional outcomes.

"Highly-Qualified" special educators.

IDEA '04 required that all special educators be "highly qualified" by the end of the 2005–2006 school year (34 C.F.R. § 300.156(c) (2006)). It largely aligned the definition of "highly qualified" with that used in NCLB but is less demanding with respect to the academic content knowledge required for secondary teachers who instruct children with the most significant cognitive disabilities (34 C.F.R. § 300.18(c) (2006)).

Highly qualified special education teachers not only must be appropriately and adequately prepared and trained, but more specifically must have the content knowledge and skills to serve children with disabilities. Under the definition, they must have earned a bachelor's degree and be fully licensed either through state-approved preparation programs or through passing a licensing exam (no more waivers on an emergency, temporary, or provisional basis). Both new and veteran special educators who teach core academic subjects must also meet NCLB requirements in the content areas or must pass a "high, objective, uniform state standard of evaluation" (*HOUSSE*). Elementary special education teachers of students with the most significant disabilities (students eligible for *alternate assessment* using *alternate achievement standards*) also must meet elementary education standards for content knowledge. Teachers of these students above the elementary level must have subject matter knowledge appropriate to middle or secondary levels of instruction. These tightened requirements do not, however, create a private right of action to sue on behalf of an individual student for failure of a teacher or other staff person to be highly qualified.

Discipline.

IDEA '04 simplifies the determination of whether misbehavior is a manifestation of the disability. It extends the unilateral removal provisions, allowing school officials (without parental involvement) to remove a student with disabilities from his or her current placement when the student causes serious bodily injury to others. It provides more discretion to school officials (34 C.F.R. § 300.530(a) (2006)).

Procedural safeguards.

IDEA '04 expands the mediation procedures and requires a *resolution session* prior to a due process hearing unless waived by both parties. Procedural safeguard notices no longer need to be given to parents at each IEP meeting. Parental responsibilities are expanded, and a time limit is established beyond which a hearing request may not be initiated. Parents may be required to pay a school district's attorneys' fees under limited circumstances.

SEA and LEA roles and responsibilities.

IDEA '04 allows LEAs to divert IDEA funds for purposes congruent with NCLB, such as prereferral, *early intervening services* (a new term and program in IDEA '04 for at-risk students), development of alternate assessments, and other ESEA activities. Congress hopes that by intervening early with research-based instruction for at-risk children, the number of children identified with disabilities can be reduced. IDEA '04 also authorizes SEAs to create LEA risk pools for children with disabilities who have extensive and expensive needs, and expands the data collection requirements of SEAs. State educational agencies are required to have policies and procedures designed to prevent misidentification of children from minority and ethnic groups as special education students. If an SEA does not implement the law effectively, ED may impose sanctions on the SEA.

The amendments to IDEA '04 will be described in more detail in Part II to update the reader on current requirements. This section merely summarizes key changes and indicates how the federal requirements have evolved since the early days of EHA. The basic acronym for the statute remains IDEA. When references in the book are to changes adopted in the 2004 reauthorization, the term IDEA or IDEA '04 is used. When provisions of IDEA '97 are singled out for notice, that term is used. A chronology of IDEA and its related predecessor statutes can be found in Table 2.1 at the end of this chapter.

ED Enforcement, Monitoring, and Technical Assistance

Congress has delegated to ED the responsibility for monitoring and enforcing the requirements of IDEA. Within ED, the Office of Special Education and Rehabilitative Services (OSERS) has overall responsibility for IDEA enforcement and implementation. In turn, OSERS delegates to one of its subdivisions, the Office of Special Education Programs (OSEP), the responsibility for writing the regulations implementing the statute. OSEP also has primary responsibility for the actual monitoring and enforcement functions. OSEP staff monitor states' plans for compliance with IDEA and conduct program audits of SEAs and LEAs. They provide technical assistance in a variety of ways, chief among which are the issuance of formal policy clarifications and informal interpretive guidance in response to inquiries.† OSEP also manages the process of applying for and receiving funds under the discretionary grant programs. A new Institute of Education Sciences, however, has been given responsibilities under IDEA '04 to award funds for national studies, evaluations, and assessments of various kinds of outcomes under IDEA.

> † In the authors' view, among the more important past contributions of OSEP have been the issuance of (a) detailed regulations spelling out the due process protections provided to parents under IDEA; (b) detailed regulations and an official appendix to the 1999 regulations interpreting the intent and requirements of an IEP; and (c) interpretive guidance on such issues as the discipline of children with disabilities and the obligations of public schools with respect to children placed in private schools by their parents.

IDEA '97 attempted to clarify OSEP's role in interpreting the meaning of IDEA. IDEA '04 echoes IDEA '97 and continues to require the Secretary of Education to follow the Administrative Procedure Act of 1946 (2007), which requires notice and an opportunity for public comment before establishing a formal rule within a policy letter or written statement on issues of national significance. Written responses that offer policy interpretations in answer to questions from the field still constitute informal guidance in the context of the specific facts and are not to be considered legally binding.

In addition, ED's and OSEP's role has been modified under IDEA '04 to require that ED's primary enforcement focus be on improving educational results and functional outcomes.

The Department of Education has the authority to withhold IDEA funds in cases where states do not comply with IDEA requirements. Although most disputes are negotiated, occasionally ED has invoked its authority to withhold funds.†

> † In 1995, the Secretary of Education decided to withhold approximately $60 million in IDEA funds from the State of Virginia unless it revoked its disciplinary policy that allowed total cessation of services to misbehaving children with disabilities when their misbehavior was not related to their disability. But see *Virginia Department of Education v. Riley*, 106 F.3d 559 (4th Cir. 1997) (overturning the Secretary's decision because IDEA at that time did not contain an explicit provision prohibiting the cessation of services to such students). Now it does contain such a provision.

IDEA Topics in This Book

Part II of this book explores in more detail the various rights and procedural safeguards established under Part B of IDEA (the state grant program). Part A of the act is also discussed because it contains the definitions of disability classifications and services that are detailed in Part B. Unless otherwise designated, all subsequent references to IDEA are references to Parts A and B. Parts C (the early intervention program for infants and toddlers) and D (the discretionary grants program) are not a focus of this book. Figure 2.1 diagrams the structural organization of IDEA. IDEA issues are organized around the following eleven topics, listed alphabetically below:

- Discipline of Students
- Due Process Protections
- Eligibility
- Evaluation/Assessment Requirements
- Free Appropriate Public Education (FAPE)
- Individualized Education Programs (IEPs)
- Least Restrictive Environment (LRE)
- Placement of Students in Private Facilities
- Related, Supplementary, and Nonacademic Services
- Remedies
- Student Records and Privacy Issues

Before reading Part II of the book, one should read the overviews of Section 504 (chapter 3) and the ADA (chapter 4) because they overlap with IDEA, and a basic understanding of their scope and purpose will be helpful.

Figure 2.1.

The Structural Organization of IDEA (formerly EHA)

Part A	Part B	Part C	Part D
General Provisions (Purposes, Definitions)	Assistance to States for All Children With Disabilities (Ages 3 through 21) (formerly P.L. 94-142, EAHCA)	Early Intervention (Infants & Toddlers— Birth through 2)	Discretionary Grant Programs

Table 2.1.

A Chronology of Major Federal Statutes Relating to the Education of Children With Disabilities

1965 ESEA (Elementary and Secondary Education Act): P.L. 89-10

- Provided direct federal aid to states for special instruction of general education students who were economically disadvantaged (Title I funds)
- Was the precursor of direct aid for children with handicaps/disabilities

1965 Amendments to Title I of ESEA: P.L. 89-313

- Provided funds for state-operated programs for the handicapped, such as state schools for the deaf, blind, and retarded

1966 ESEA Amendments of 1966: P.L. 89-750

- Created the federal Bureau of Education for the Handicapped, since renamed the Office of Special Education Programs (OSEP)
- Authorized funds to states to expand their handicapped programs (Title VI)

1968 ESEA Amendments of 1968: P.L. 90-247

- Established discretionary grant programs to serve handicapped children

1970 EHA (Education of the Handicapped Act): P.L. 91-230

- Consolidated Title VI of the ESEA and the discretionary grant programs of EHA
- Expanded basic state grant programs for the handicapped
- Provided indirect aid to handicapped children through discretionary grants for higher education teacher training, regional resource centers, and media programs

1973 Section 504 of the Rehabilitation Act of 1973: P.L. 93-112

- Prohibited discrimination against "otherwise qualified" handicapped persons in programs or activities receiving federal financial assistance

1974 Education Amendments of 1974: P.L. 93-380

- Expanded the funding base for EHA basic state grants
- Incorporated the rights established in the *PARC* and *Mills* cases

1974 FERPA (Family Educational Rights and Privacy Act, also known as the Buckley Amendment): Title V, § 513(a) of P.L. 93-380

- Gave parents access to their student's education records in schools receiving funds from ED
- Prohibited access to unauthorized persons without parental permission

1975 DD Act (Developmentally Disabled Assistance and Bill of Rights Act): P.L. 94-103

- Established a right to treatment and appropriate placement for institutionalized handicapped in states accepting DD funds
- Required creation of protection and advocacy systems in all states, to help individuals with developmental disabilities pursue legal, administrative, and other remedies

1975 EAHCA (The Education for All Handicapped Children Act): P.L. 94-142

- Provided for direct federal aid to states for eligible children with one of the specified handicaps
- Elaborated on the right to FAPE in LRE established in P.L. 93-380
- Required an IEP
- Expanded procedural safeguards, such as parental participation, due process hearings, nondiscriminatory assessment, and access to student records (incorporating many FERPA requirements)

1983 EHA Amendments of 1983: P.L. 98-199

- Expanded and extended the discretionary EHA grant programs
- Created a new "transition" program to help handicapped students prepare for employment, independent living, and postsecondary education

1984 Carl D. Perkins Vocational Education Act of 1984: P.L. 98-524

- Required equal access to recruitment, enrollment, and placement in vocational education programs for "special needs" students
- Set aside 10 percent of funds for children with disabilities

1986 Handicapped Children's Protection Act: P.L. 99-372

- Amended EHA Part B to provide an award of attorneys' fees to parents who are the prevailing party in an administrative proceeding or judicial action

1986 EHA Amendments of 1986: P.L. 99-457

- Introduced state grants to address the needs of infants and toddlers with developmental delays (Early Intervention Programs)
- Extended EHA Part B to 3-through-5-year-olds in participating states

1988 Technology-Related Assistance for Individuals With Disabilities Act: P.L. 100-407

- Authorized funding for states to create systems of technological assistance for individuals with disabilities; defined assistive technology devices and services

1990 The Americans With Disabilities Act: P.L. 101-336

- Prohibited discrimination on the basis of disability in public and private employment, public accommodations, state and local government services (including education), transportation, and telecommunications

1990 Carl D. Perkins Vocational and Applied Technology Education Act: P.L. 101-392

- Interwove with EHA to attempt to provide full vocational educational opportunity for youth with disabilities
- Deleted specific disability categories, incorporated children with disabilities into broader category of "special populations"

1990 EHA Amendments of 1990: P.L. 101-476

- Renamed EHA the Individuals With Disabilities Education Act and redesignated "handicapped" children as "children with disabilities"
- Added traumatic brain injury and autism as new categories of disability
- Added IEP requirement for transition planning by at least the age of 16
- Provided that states are not immune under the eleventh Amendment to the Constitution from lawsuits in federal court for violations of IDEA

1994 Goals 2000: Educate America Act: P.L. 103-227, and Improving America's Schools Act: P.L. 103-382 (ESEA Amendments)

- Amended ESEA to provide additional funds to help state and local education agencies implement reforms that would allow achievement of eight national education goals by 2000
- Required states to create and implement education improvement plans that included curriculum standards for all students, including students with disabilities
- Required participation of all students in assessments of achievement relative to the state standards
- Required states to set proficiency standards that would be the same for all students
- Required measures of adequate progress

1997 IDEA Amendments of 1997: P.L. 105-17

- Added major new IEP requirements and discipline procedures
- Modified eligibility and evaluation procedures
- Provided additional avenues for parental participation
- Required states to offer mediation prior to due process hearings
- Established limits on public services required at private schools and on reimbursement for private placements

1998 Carl D. Perkins Vocational and Applied Technology Education Act Amendments of 1998: P.L. 105-332

- Authorized expenditure of funds for vocational/technical services required in IEPs and under Section 504

2002 No Child Left Behind Act of 2001: P.L. 107-110 (ESEA Amendments)

- Reauthorized ESEA to strengthen requirements that all states pursue a standards-based reform agenda
- Required that all students meet state-established proficiency standards in reading, math, and science by 2013–2014
- Imposed increasing sanctions on LEAs failing to meet the state's standards for adequate yearly progress for two consecutive years or more
- Required that all teachers in core academic subjects be highly qualified by the end of the 2005–2006 school year

2004 Individuals With Disabilities Education Improvement Act of 2004: P.L. 108-446

- Aligned student assessment requirements with NCLB
- Simplified disciplinary provisions, while retaining manifestation determination and FAPE requirements for misbehaving students
- Eliminated need for objectives and benchmarks on most IEPs and reduced some paperwork requirements, while increasing SEA data collection requirements
- Added more dispute resolution provisions in an attempt to reduce adversarial due process hearings
- Extended LEA consultative responsibilities when parents unilaterally place their child in private school
- Defined "highly qualified" special educators
- Changed compliance monitoring to focus on outcomes

↪Review

1. Why did the U.S. Congress enact IDEA (EHA)?

   It enacted IDEA (EHA) in response to court cases and pressure from advocacy groups to offer equal educational opportunity to children with disabilities by providing financial aid to states to help with the excess costs of special education.

2. What are the basic elements of IDEA that have been consistent across time?

   IDEA provides eligible children with the right to FAPE governed by an IEP and offered, to the maximum extent appropriate, in environments with children who do not have disabilities. FAPE in the LRE with an IEP is based on a multifaceted evaluation of the child's needs. IDEA provides an extensive set of procedural safeguards for parents to help ensure that their children are given the rights to which they are entitled.

↯References

Administrative Procedure Act of 1946, 5 U.S.C. § 553 (2006).

Brown v. Bd. of Educ., 347 U.S. 483 (1954).

Civil Rights Act of 1964, 42 U.S.C. § 2000d (2006).

Education Amendments of 1972, Title IX, 20 U.S.C. § 1681 *et seq.* (2006).

Education for All Handicapped Children Act of 1975, Pub. L. 94-142, 89 Stat. 773.

Education of the Handicapped Act of 1970, Pub. L. 91-230, 84 Stat. 191.

Education of the Handicapped Act Amendments of 1974, Pub. L. No 93-380, 88 Stat. 580.

Education of the Handicapped Act Amendments of 1986, Pub. L. 99-457, 100 Stat. 1145.

Elementary and Secondary Education Act of 1965, Pub. L. 89-10, 79 Stat. 27.

Elementary and Secondary Education Act Amendments of 1966, Pub.L. 89-750, 79 Stat. 27.

Elementary and Secondary Education Act Amendments of 1968, Pub. L. 90-247, 80 Stat. 1191.

Goals 2000: Educate America Act of 1994, Pub. L. 103-227, 108 Stat. 125

Handicapped Children's Protection Act of 1986, Pub. L. 99-372, 100 Stat. 796.

Improving America's Schools Act of 1994, Pub. L. 103-382, 108 Stat. 3518.

Individuals with Disabilities Education Act of 1990, Pub. L. 101-476, 104 Stat. 1103.

Individuals with Disabilities Education Act Amendments of 1997, Pub. L. 105-17, 111 Stat. 37, 20 U.S.C. § 1400 et seq. (Supp. III 1997).

Individuals with Disabilities Education Improvement Act, 20 U.S.C. § 1400 *et seq.* (2006).

Individuals with Disabilities Education Improvement Act Regulations, 34 C.F. R. § 300.1 *et seq.* (2006).

Mills v. Dist. of Columbia Bd. of Educ., 348 F. Supp. 866 (D.D.C. 1972).

No Child Left Behind Act of 2001, 20 U.S.C. § 6301 *et seq.* (2006).

Pennsylvania Ass'n. for Retarded Children (PARC) v. Pennsylvania, 343 F. Supp. 279 (E.D. Pa. 1972).

Section 504 of the Rehabilitation Act of 1973, 29 U.S.C. § 794 (2006).

⇉Selected Supplementary Resources

Ballard, J., Ramirez, B., &Weintraub, F. (Eds.) (1982). *Special education in America: Its legal and governmental foundations.* Reston, VA: Council for Exceptional Children.

Huefner, D. S. (1997).The legalization and federalization of special education. In J. W. Lloyd, E. J. Kameenui, and D. Chard (Eds.), *Issues in educating students with disabilities* (pp. 343-362). Mahwah, NJ: Erlbaum.

Lippman, L., & Goldberg, I. I. (1973). *Right to education: Anatomy of the Pennsylvania case and its implications for exceptional children.* New York, NY: Teachers College Press.

Chapter 3

An Overview of Section 504 of the Rehabilitation Act of 1973

Chapter Outline

A History of Section 504

Section 504 is a brief but powerful nondiscrimination provision included in the Rehabilitation Act of 1973. Section 504 extends to individuals with disabilities the same kind of protection extended by the U.S. Congress to individuals discriminated against on the basis of race, color, national origin, age, and sex. Section 504 reads:

> No otherwise qualified individual with a disability . . . shall, solely by reason of her or his disability, be excluded from participation in, be denied the benefits of, or be subjected to discrimination under any program or activity receiving Federal financial assistance (29 U.S.C. § 794(a)).[1]

Originally, Section 504 was targeted at employment discrimination, but amendments to the original language extended its reach far beyond employment. Because the implications of Section 504 are so complex and far-reaching, each department within the executive branch of the federal government was required to issue detailed regulations implementing Section 504 for its own recipients of federal funds.

Because virtually every school district in the country accepts federal funds, public education was directly affected by passage of Section 504. After several years of wrangling, regulations by what was then the Department of Health, Education, and Welfare (HEW) were issued in late April 1977 and took effect on June 3, 1977 (42 Fed. Reg. 22676, 1977).

The Section 504 regulations affecting preschool, elementary, and secondary school programs were written in coordination with the first set of special education regulations under Part B of the Education of the Handicapped Act (EHA, since renamed the Individuals With Disabilities Education Act, IDEA).† The EHA special education regulations were issued in August 1977, and each set refers to the other at various points. After a separate Department of Education (ED) was created in 1980 out of HEW's Office of Education, both sets of regulations were reissued by ED.[2] For summarization purposes, Table 3.1 compares Section 504 regulations with IDEA regulations. Readers may want to refer to it again after reading Part II (IDEA) and Part III (Section 504).

> † ED's current Section 504 regulations cover employment practices; program accessibility; preschool, elementary, and secondary education; postsecondary education; and health, welfare, and social services. It is the section on preschool, elementary, and secondary education with which we are concerned in this book.

---

[1] The original language referred to "handicapped person" but was amended to conform with the terminology used in IDEA.
[2] Section 504 regulations are now found at 34 C.F.R. Part 104. IDEA Part A and Part B regulations are found at 34 C.F.R. Part 300.

The Scope of Section 504

The scope of Section 504 is broad and extends protection in many areas besides public school education—for instance, higher education, employment, social services, health care, transportation, and physical facilities. In certain programs, such as health and social services, coverage may extend from birth to death.

A Civil Rights Mandate

In contrast to IDEA, Section 504 is not a funding statute, and Congress did not provide funds expressly to help cover the costs of any program adaptations necessary to ensure nondiscrimination. Section 504 simply prohibits discrimination in programs and activities receiving federal money, from whatever source.

Although it is not itself a funding statute with strings attached, Section 504 must be taken seriously as a civil rights statute with enforcement teeth. Failure to comply can result in loss of federal funds. In the public school setting, its obligations fall on all school districts because they all receive federal funds from many sources, among them ESEA and IDEA. If school districts are found to be discriminating and do not remedy the problem, the ultimate sanction is loss of all federal funds from whatever source. The responsibility not to discriminate applies to all school personnel—district-level and school-level administrators, general and special educators, secretarial and custodial staff, school psychologists and social workers, cafeteria workers, student teachers, and so on.

Table 3.1.

Comparison of IDEA-B and Section 504 Public Education Standards

	IDEA Provisions	**Section 504 Provisions**
Eligibility	Evaluation for specific disability conditions	Evaluation for functional disability (physical or mental impairment that substantially limits a major life activity)
	Child must need special education	— (Note: "—" signifies no comparable provision)
	Child of public school age (3 through 21)	Same as IDEA-B
	LEP & instructional failures in math and reading cannot be primary factors	—
	Parent is on eligibility team	—
	—	Broader coverage (IDEA students plus other students with 504 disabilities)
	Qualified professionals	Trained evaluators
	Multiple measures, including educational measures	Same
	Technically sound, valid & reliable assessment measures	Valid tests
	Assessments of relevant academic, functional, & developmental areas	—
	Assessments that measure what they purport to measure	Tests that measure what they purport to measure
	Assessments in language and form most likely to yield accurate results	—
	Administration and scoring that avoids racial and ethnic bias	—
	Input from parents	—

	IDEA Provisions	Section 504 Provisions
Procedural Safeguards	Written notice of procedural safeguards	Notice (form is unspecified)
	Prior written notice	—
	Informed consent required for initial evaluation & provision of special education	No explicit consent requirement for evaluation, but OCR policy requires consent
	Consent must be sought for re-evaluation	—
	Access to educational records	Access to educational records
	Parental input into eligibility, evaluation, IEP & placement	—
	Independent Educational Evaluation	—
	Surrogate parent	—
	Stay-put procedure	—
	Mediation & Hearing	Hearing
	Resolution Session	—
	Review Process	Review Process
	SEA Complaint Procedure	OCR Complaint Procedure
FAPE	Special education + related services	"Regular or special education" + related aids and services
	Benefit standard	Comparability standard
Placement	Presumption that education will occur in settings with students who do not have disabilities	Education in LRE to maximum extent appropriate to the child's needs
	Explanation required in IEP for removal from regular classroom	—
	Continuum of placement options required	—
	Parent on placement team	—
	—	Re-evaluation before significant placement change
IEP	Required	Section 504 plan (not IEP) recommended for "stand-alone" students

	IDEA Provisions	Section 504 Provisions
Discipline	10-school-day limit on suspension or removal from placement without IDEA protections	Similar 10-day rule (in policy, not regulations)
	More than 10 cumulative days of suspension allowed if no pattern constituting change of placement	More than 10 cumulative days of suspension allowed if no discriminatory pattern
	45-day placement change by LEA for drug & weapon violations or serious bodily injury to others	—
	Manifestation determination (M-D) required for disciplinary placement change	Same (in policy, not regulations)
	No cessation of services; placement change not longer than for students without disabilities if behavior is not a manifestation of disability	Long-term exclusion (cessation of services) allowed if behavior is not a manifestation of disability
	Procedural safeguards for placement changes based on alcohol & illegal drug use	No special protection based on current alcohol & illegal drug use
Funding	Federal IDEA funds toward excess costs of educating children with disabilities	No federal funds under Section 504 itself
ED Administering Agency	OSEP	OCR
Overall Implementation Responsibility within State	SEA Special education	LEAs or covered private schools General education

"Otherwise Qualified" Recipients

Section 504 protects only those individuals with disabilities who are "otherwise qualified" for the program, job, or service in question. In other words, the individual must be qualified in spite of the disability.† In employment situations, this means that if an employee with a disability can fulfill the essential functions of the job, either with or without "reasonable accommodations," he or she is "otherwise qualified." An employer who believes that the requested accommodations are unreasonable, however, may invoke the defense of "undue hardship." These standards apply to public school employees and employers.

> † *In Southeastern Community College v. Davis*, 442 U.S. 397 (1979), the Supreme Court interpreted the "otherwise qualified" language of Section 504 to mean that the person with the disability must be able to meet all the program requirements in spite of the disability. The plaintiff, who had a serious hearing impairment, was denied admission to the nursing program on the grounds that her hearing impairment would not allow her to safely communicate with her patients, either in her clinical training or as a registered nurse. The Court concluded that Section 504 did not require the nursing program to lower its standards or make major modifications to accommodate the applicant.

In general, as applied to public education students, an "otherwise qualified" student with a disability simply means a student of public school age. However, cases where more specific criteria are applied in school settings (such as eligibility of the applicant for a program, similar to the *Davis* case, or eligibility for a competitive athletic team), "otherwise qualified" generally means that the student has demonstrated that he or she meets the skill criteria in spite of the disability.

Parents with disabilities who have school-age students also must not be discriminated against at school—that is, in their enjoyment of the benefits offered to other parents at school. For instance, the U.S. Court of Appeals for the Second Circuit ruled in *Rothschild v. Grottenthaler* (1990) that a school district must provide deaf parents with an interpreter during their parent-teacher meetings. The court reasoned that failure to provide the parents with meaningful communication about academic or disciplinary aspects of their child's educational programming was discriminatory. On the other hand, the court stated that subsidizing parental involvement in voluntary extracurricular activities was not required by Section 504. This judicial decision has been generally accepted across the country as a satisfactory interpretation of the law.

Program Accessibility

Schools must be aware of the architectural requirements under both Section 504 and the Americans With Disabilities Act (ADA). In general, all educational programs must be accessible to those who need them, but not every *room* in a school building must be accessible to all students. In some situations, accessibility may require moving a given program into another facility or making a portion of a building accessible. If a facility is to be structurally altered in a manner that affects its usability, at that time the altered portion must be made physically accessible. Of course, any newly constructed facilities must be readily accessible to and usable by persons with disabilities. If a separate facility is permissible, then it must be comparable in quality to the facilities used by persons without disabilities (see chapter 19).

The Meaning of "Program or Activity"

Early lawsuits attempted to restrict the definition of "program or activity receiving federal financial assistance" to specific programs or activities within an agency. In other words, some recipients of federal money argued that a finding of discrimination in one grant program or activity within the institution should not subject any other of the institution's nonfederally subsidized programs to the nondiscrimination requirements. After the Supreme Court, in *Grove City College v. Bell* (1984), agreed with this interpretation of the same wording in Title IX of the Education Amendments of 1972, the U.S. Congress amended Title IX, Section 504, and other civil rights statutes† by adding language making explicit its view that the definition of a "program or activity" extended to *all* the operations of a recipient of the federal funds (29 U.S.C. § 794(b), 2006). Therefore, if discrimination occurs anywhere within a school district that receives federal funds, all federal funds can be withdrawn, not just those attached to the activity or program in which the discrimination occurs. In other words, Congress did not want to subsidize any institution that was discriminating anywhere within its programs.

> † The amendment to Section 504 was part of the Civil Rights Restoration Act of 1987. It is now located at 29 U.S.C. § 794(b) (2006). It not only clarified the definition of "program or activity" under Section 504 and Title IX (sex discrimination) but also under Title VI of the Civil Rights Act of 1964 (race discrimination), and the Age Discrimination Act of 1975.

The Definition of "Disability" Under Section 504

Under Section 504, the definition of disability with respect to an individual means "a physical or mental impairment that substantially limits one or more major life activities of such individual, (b) a record of such an impairment, or (c) being regarded as having such an impairment." (34 C.F.R. § 104.3(j)(1)(2009). A *physical impairment* includes any physiological disorder or condition, cosmetic disfigurement, or anatomical loss affecting one or more enumerated body systems. A *mental impairment* is defined as "any mental or psychological disorder, such as mental retardation, organic brain syndrome, emotional or mental illness, and specific learning disabilities" (34 C.F.R. § 104.3(j)(2)(i)(2009). If one's "impairment" is not physical or mental but rather a form of cultural or economic disadvantage, then, by definition, it is not a Section 504 disability.

Section 504 regulations describe *major life activities* as functions such as breathing, walking, talking, seeing, hearing, using one's hands, taking care of oneself, working, and learning (34 C.F.R. § 104.3(j)(2)(ii)(2009). Impairments in any one of these life activities can require modifications to a child's school program.

The 2008 Amendments to the ADA added examples of major life activities (42 U.S.C. § 12102) that also apply to Section 504. They include eating, sleeping, standing, lifting, bending, reading, concentrating, thinking, and communicating, as well as major bodily functions such as neurological and respiratory functions. The expanded list is not exhaustive; other activities and functions could also constitute major life activities.

The Department of Education's Office for Civil Rights (OCR) declines to define what is meant by a substantial limitation on a major life activity, leaving it up to school districts and courts to determine on a case-by-case basis. Although the limitation should be more than minor, the term must be interpreted in a manner consistent with the broad, nondiscriminatory purposes of the ADA Amendments of 2008. Several lower courts have ruled that the pool of persons against whom the student's alleged substantial limitation should be measured is "average persons in the general population," that is, other children in the general population, rather than, say, classroom peers.[3]

In the school context, the first prong of the Section 504 definition is usually the relevant one for purposes of ensuring that a nondiscriminatory, free, appropriate public education is provided (*Senior Staff Memorandum*, 1994). Schools discriminate against students with disabilities in multiple ways, such as (a) failing to provide physical access to necessary programs or facilities, (b) imposing double standards for eligibility for extracurricular activities, (c) failing to design regular classroom programs to meet the student's individual needs as adequately as the needs of students without disabilities are met, (d) requiring far longer bus rides to school than the bus rides of children without disabilities, and (e) allowing students to be repeatedly harassed because of their disability.† Moreover, even though a student with a disability may be achieving at or above grade level without extra help, it will still be discriminatory not to provide access to a private, wider toilet stall if the student must use a wheelchair for mobility. Similarly, even if a student with a hearing loss is progressing well in class, it will be discriminatory not to provide suitable access to adapted telephone facilities if telephone facilities are made available to students without disabilities. Other examples of discrimination include the failure to provide interpreter services, guide dogs, or service dogs to Section 504 students who need them to help compensate for their substantial limitations in the major life activities of hearing, seeing, or walking. In these situations and others, Section 504

---

[3] See, e.g., *Costello v. Mitchell Pub. Sch. Dist.* 79, 266 F.3d 916, 923 (8th Circ. 2001), *Ballard v. Kinkaid Sch.* 147 F. Supp. 2d 603, 606 (S.D. Tex. 2000).

is intended to protect students with disabilities from lack of equal opportunities to benefit from educational programs and facilities.

> † School districts have a responsibility not only to provide a nondiscrimination policy but also to have a set of grievance procedures and widespread notification of how to utilize the procedures. The staff should be trained to handle harassment of students with disabilities by other students, and districts can be liable for knowingly ignoring harassment and allowing it to continue. See *Davis v. Monroe County Board of Education*, 526 U.S. 629 (1999) (school districts are liable under Title IX for deliberate indifference to severe, pervasive, and objectively offensive student-on-student sexual harassment; *Gebser v. Lago Vista Independent School District*, 524 U.S. 274 (1998) (school districts are liable for deliberate indifference to sexual harassment of students by school staff if one with authority to correct the situation had actually noticed and acted with deliberate indifference).

Occasionally, the second prong of the definition also applies. For instance, if a school refuses to allow an otherwise qualified student to participate in a sports activity on the basis of a history of leukemia that has since gone into remission, or on the basis of a history of past (but not current) drug abuse, the student would be protected from such discrimination. If the student meets the competitive criteria, then the student must be given an opportunity to participate. Unsubstantiated fears about the health or safety of the student should not bar participation.

The third prong can also apply if a school incorrectly treats a child as disabled and discriminates against the child on that basis when no physical or mental impairment is present, such as when a child with limited English proficiency is misperceived as having a disability. The third prong can also be relevant when a physical or mental impairment substantially limits a major life activity only because of the attitudes of others. Examples might be a student with a cosmetic disfigurement or asymptomatic HIV/AIDS.

Coverage for Students of Public-School Age

As the Section 504 regulatory definition of "otherwise qualified" individuals makes clear, IDEA students automatically qualify as having a Section 504 disability (34 C.F.R. § 104.3(k)(2)(2009).† The Section 504 protection covers all aspects of the IDEA student's curricular and extracurricular life at school. Because the IDEA protections are more specific than those of Section 504, the Section 504 protections usually apply only when an IDEA remedy is not applicable, such as when discrimination occurs in areas of an IDEA student's education outside the IEP.

> † Chapter 5 provides the definition of children with IDEA disabilities.

Because the Section 504 definition of disability is broader than the IDEA definition, it extends to another significant group of students who are not IDEA-eligible, either because their condition does not constitute an IDEA disability or because even if it does, they do not need special education as a result. These students are sometimes referred to as "pure" Section 504 or *stand-alone* Section 504 students. Among the possible candidates could be a student with a visual impairment who does not require special education, but who does need large-print books or additional time to read texts and do assignments in order to succeed in the regular classroom. Others potentially eligible for accommodations or program modifications could be students with attention deficit disorders (ADD/ADHD), epilepsy, HIV/AIDS, allergies (such as asthma), arthritis, chronic fatigue syndrome, heart disease, diabetes, oppositional defiant disorder (ODD), Tourette syndrome, and, under some circumstances, even broken limbs. Of course, all these students must show that their impairment substantially limits a major life activity; the impairment or condition alone is insufficient. Some have even wondered if certain students with mild dyslexia or reading disability might be eligible if, although they do not meet a state's requirements for IDEA eligibility as learning disabled, their impairment nonetheless interferes with their reading and language arts performance in the general classroom, so that they would benefit from program modifications. Arguably, however, if the only major life activity affected by a child's learning disability is learning, and the child does not require special education, it will be difficult to establish that the disability substantially limits learning under the Section 504 definition.

Figure 3.1 shows the relationship among the student populations.

Advocates for students with ADD/ADHD had hoped that ADD/ADHD would be recognized as an IDEA disability in its own right, but Congress declined to extend such recognition and instead funded more research on ADD/ADHD. Also, OSEP, OCR, and ED's Office of Elementary and Secondary Education (OESE) issued a joint policy memorandum explaining that ADD/ADHD students could be eligible for IDEA services only if they qualified under another label, such as "learning disability," "emotional disturbance," or "other health impairment" (Joint Policy Memorandum, 1991). Otherwise, if their impairment was a disability because it substantially limited their learning, they could seek programming modifications or other supplementary aids and services that addressed their needs as Section 504 students.

Figure 3.1.

IDEA Students as a Subset of Section 504 Students, and Section 504 Students as a Subset of All Public School Students

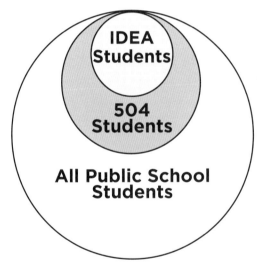

In 1990, the U.S. Congress specified that a current illegal drug user is not considered a person with a disability under Section 504 (29 U.S.C. § 705(20)(c) (2006).[4] On the other hand, a rehabilitated drug user or one undergoing treatment (and not using illegal drugs) is protected by the second prong of the definition and cannot be discriminated against on the basis of the former drug use. Also, although students currently addicted to alcohol may be protected from discrimination, current users of alcohol at school or school functions are not protected from school disciplinary action comparable to that taken against students without disabilities (29 U.S.C. § 705(20(c)(iv) (2006), even if a separate disability would protect them in other ways.

---

[4] The same exception applies under the Americans with Disabilities Act.

Judicial Rulings on Eligibility

Many court cases have ruled that students with HIV/AIDS are eligible for protection under Section 504. A number of the cases involved attempts to exclude the students from school or general classrooms when the child did not present a significant risk of contagion (see chapter 17). Other court cases dealing with other eligibility issues fall into two categories: the school district's failure to evaluate a suspected disability under Section 504, or the inability of the student to demonstrate that he or she met the definition of disability under Section 504.

Administrative Enforcement and Monitoring

The Department of Education's Office for Civil Rights (OCR), not OSEP, enforces Section 504 in educational institutions that receive federal funds. The office has twelve regional offices throughout the country, and is also responsible for enforcing a number of other civil rights statutes in educational institutions. In addition to providing technical assistance, OCR performs two major roles: (a) it sometimes conducts compliance investigations on its own initiative, and (b) it investigates complaints of discrimination from individuals or groups.† Some of its time is spent on *early complaint resolution* (*ECR*), but it will move to an investigation when resolution between the parties proves unlikely. When OCR investigates complaints, it negotiates for compliance but will issue *Letters of Findings* (*LoFs*) to the educational agency investigated and, if necessary, will issue corrective action plans with which it seeks compliance. In extreme circumstances, it can initiate administrative enforcement proceedings to terminate federal funds or can refer a case to the Justice Department for litigation. School districts that have undergone an OCR investigation report that it usually involves tedious data collection, is very time-consuming, and is worth avoiding by resolving discrimination complaints internally whenever possible. A complaint on a narrow issue can become the catalyst for a systemwide investigation of compliance with Section 504.

† Examples of successful changes to school district policies as a result of OCR investigations of noncompliance are (a) implementation of a prereferral intervention process to reduce the disproportionate number of African American students in special education classes, (b) creation of accessible playground facilities for children with mobility impairments, (c) Section 504 services for a student with Asperger syndrome, (d) expungement of a student's disciplinary record because the school district had retaliated against the child and not treated him equitably compared to other misbehaving children, and (e) readmission to a charter school of a child with behavior problems who had been denied services there. <www.ed.gov/about/offices/list/ocr/success-disabilities> [Retrieved 2005; url no longer available]

Source Materials

This book cites IDELR when providing references to OCR policy memoranda and complaint or compliance letters. Otherwise, citations refer to the regular statutory and judicial reporters.

Section 504 Topics in This Book

Part III of this book contains five chapters explaining in more detail the obligations that arise under Section 504. The chapters discuss: (a) evaluation issues, (b) contagious diseases, (c) FAPE and programming issues (instruction and related aids and services), (d) discipline and placement issues, and (e) due process and dispute resolution.

↻Review

1. What is the definition of an individual with a disability under Section 504?

   The individual has a physical or mental impairment that substantially limits one or more major life activities, has a record of such an impairment, or is regarded as having such an impairment.

2. What are the key differences between Section 504 and IDEA in preschool and K–12 educational settings?

   Section 504 is a federal civil rights (nondiscrimination) statute; IDEA is a federal funding statute.

   Section 504 requires the recipients of federal funds to refrain from discriminating against individuals with disabilities who are otherwise qualified for the service or program in question. This may or may not require the expenditure of money, depending on what kinds of program modifications are needed to provide an equal educational opportunity. In contrast, IDEA requires participating states to ensure that students with eligible disabilities receive special education and other kinds of services necessary for students to benefit from their special education. This does require an expenditure of money.

   Section 504 protects more people. It covers more students in the public schools than does IDEA because its definition of disability is broader. It also covers private school students in K-12 and preschools that accept federal money. Unlike IDEA, it also protects employees and parents in public education settings from discrimination on the basis of disability (and protects them in private educational settings too if the private schools receive federal funds).

   Implementation and compliance with Section 504 in public schools is the primary responsibility of each LEA, not the special education staff, and not the state office of education. Both general and special education teachers share the same obligation not to discriminate. In contrast, under IDEA, primary responsibility for implementation and compliance is turned over to the special education section of the state office of education and, in turn, to special education staff within each school district.

3. What public school students are eligible for protection under Section 504?

   IDEA students, other students with a physical or mental impairment that substantially limits a major life activity, and students who have a record of such an impairment, or who are treated as if they have such an impairment are eligible.

⚡References

Americans with Disabilities Act Amendments of 2008, 42 U.S.C. § 12101 *et seq.* (Supp. III 2009).

Grove City College v. Bell, 465 U.S. 555 (1984).

Joint Policy Memorandum, 18 IDELR ¶116 (OSEP, OCR, OESE, 1991).

Rehabilitation Act of 1973, 29 U.S.C. § 705 (2006).

Section 504 ED Regulations, 34 C.F.R. Part 104 (2009).

Section 504 of the Rehabilitation Act of 1973, 29 U.S.C. § 794 (2006).

Rothschild v. Grottenthaler, 907 F.2d 286 (2d Cir. 1990).

Senior Staff Memorandum, 19 IDELR ¶894 (OCR 1994).

⇉Selected Supplementary Resources

Council of Administrators of Special Education. (1999). *Section 504 and the ADA promoting student access: A resource guide for educators* (2nd ed.). Albuquerque, NM: Author.

Frequently asked questions about Section 504 and the education of children with disabilities. Retrieved April 20, 2011 from http://www2.ed.gov/about/offices/list/ocr/504faq.html

Norlin, J. W. (2011). *What do I do when . . . The answer book on Section 504 (4th ed.).* Horsham, PA: LRP.

Russo, C. J., & Osborne, A. G., Jr. (2009). *Section 504 and the ADA.* Thousand Oaks, CA: Corwin.

Zirkel, P. A. (2011). *Section 504, the ADA, and the schools* (3rd ed.). Horsham, PA: LRP.

Chapter 4

An Overview of the Americans With Disabilities Act

Chapter Outline

Provisions of the Statute

The Americans With Disabilities Act (ADA) (42 U.S.C.§ 12101 *et seq.*(Supp. III 2009)), enacted in 1990 and amended in 2008, is the latest in a series of civil rights laws protecting various groups of persons from discrimination by American society. Readers will recall that under Section 504 of the Rehabilitation Act of 1973, recipients of federal funds are prohibited from discriminating against otherwise qualified individuals with disabilities in areas such as employment, public school and higher education, and health and social services. Under ADA, private employers and commercial enterprises serving the public are also among those obligated not to discriminate. In other words, the protections against discrimination are not limited to those served by programs or activities receiving federal funds. In effect, ADA expands the reach of Section 504.

The U.S. Congress used its authority to regulate interstate commerce as the tool for extending ADA to the private sector. Most private businesses engage in interstate commerce, as the term has come to be defined, and therefore Congress may prohibit most private businesses from discriminating against employees or job applicants with disabilities. It may also prohibit private businesses that accommodate the public from discriminating against members of the public who have disabilities.

The ADA and Section 504 definitions of an individual with a disability are the same—that is, an individual with a mental or physical impairment that substantially limits one or more major life activities, one with a record of such an impairment, or one who is regarded as having such an impairment (42 U.S.C. § 12102(1), Supp. III 2009)). Parts 2 and 3 of this definition are particularly applicable to job discrimination situations. For instance, an individual who has been hospitalized for a heart attack will have a record of a physical impairment but may no longer have the impairment itself. The record does not constitute a basis for discrimination. Neither does the employer's perception that anyone who has had a heart attack should be considered unable to do certain kinds of work, regardless of the current state of the employee's physical fitness. The definition reflects the view that evidence of current ability to perform is what matters, not stereotypes or dated information.

On September 25, 2008, President Bush signed into law the ADA Amendments Act of 2008 (ADAAA). The ADAAA overrules four Supreme Court decisions that had narrowed the application of ADA. The Amendments also overruled Equal Employment Opportunity Commission regulations that had interpreted the term "substantially limits" to mean "significantly restricts"--a stricter interpretation than Congress intended.

The ADAAA expands the definition of disability and emphasizes that the definition must be construed broadly. The definition clarifies that an impairment which substantially limits one major life activity does not need to limit other major life activities. The definition further states that mitigating measures other than "ordinary eyeglasses or contact lenses" are not to be considered in determining whether an individual has a disability. Of considerable importance, the ADAAA significantly expands the examples of major life activities to include major bodily functions, and activities of special significance to students, such as reading, concentrating, thinking, communicating, and interacting with others. Another subsection of the expanded definition of disability specifies that impairments that are episodic or in remission are disabilities if they would substantially limit a major life activity when active (asthma or diabetes, for instance) (42 U.S.C. § 12102, 2009).

Interpretation of Section 504 by OCR will now reflect the expansive definition of a person with a disability in the ADAAA because the definition of such a person under Section 504 was changed in 2010 (29 U.S.C.S. § 705(20)(b) (2010)) to conform with the ADAAA.

Title I

ADA contains five separate titles, or major sections. Title I prohibits employment discrimination against individuals with disabilities who are qualified, that is, who can perform the "essential functions" of the job "with or without reasonable accommodations." The prohibition extends to hiring, firing, advancement, compensation, and job training. Only when an accommodation creates an "undue hardship" may employers be excused from providing it. Public employees, such as schoolteachers, are already protected under Section 504 from employment discrimination against persons with disabilities who are qualified for the position in question.

Title II

Title II applies to public services and extends the Section 504 nondiscrimination requirements to all subdivisions of state and local government, including those that do not receive federal financial aid. The nondiscrimination language is slightly different from that of Section 504 and states that "no qualified individual with a disability" shall "by reason of such disability" be subject to discrimination (42 U.S.C. § 12132, Supp. III 2009).[1] The word "solely" (included in Section 504) has been omitted before the phrase "by reason of such disability," which would seem to slightly expand the reach of prohibited discrimination.

Government agencies are expected to make "reasonable modifications" to their rules, policies, and practices so that otherwise eligible persons with disabilities can participate in government services, programs, or activities. A qualified individual is one who meets eligibility requirements, with or without reasonable modifications. What constitutes a "reasonable" modification is subject to judicial interpretation.†

> † An addition to the Title II regulations, effective March 15, 2011, stated that the use of service animals is a reasonable modification. The addition specifies that service animals are limited to dogs, however, and that dogs must be individually trained to do work or tasks that are directly related to the individual's disability. Mere emotional support or comfort given by the dogs is insufficient. See 75 Fed. Reg. 56178, Sept. 15, 2010, and correction, 76 Fed. Reg. 13285, March 11, 2001 (to be codified at 28 C.F.R. §§ 35.104 and 35.136).

Students in public schools are covered under Title II as well as Section 504. The provisions and regulations are similar in most respects. Title II also applies to public transportation.

Title III

Title III pertains to public accommodations. Do not be misled by this term. Public accommodations are commercial facilities and private businesses in commerce serving the public—in other words, private businesses that provide accommodations to the public at large. Title III requires these businesses to make "reasonable modifications" to their policies, practices, and procedures for persons with disabilities. Such persons are to have ready access to commercial businesses such as

---

[1] At least one court has found the difference significant. See *Baird v. Rose*, 192 F.3d 462 (4th Cir. 1999) (ruling that discrimination can be a motivating cause, rather than the sole cause of an adverse actions).

professional offices, clothing stores, beauty and barber shops, food stores, restaurants, day-care centers, places of public lodging, entertainment facilities, recreation facilities, and secular private schools. Educators should take note that private schools are public accommodations unless they are controlled by religious organizations. (Religious entities and private clubs are exempt from Title III requirements for the most part.) Architectural modifications to buildings and grounds are required in order to achieve facilities that are "readily accessible" to persons with disabilities.

Title IV

Title IV governs telecommunications practices and requires common carriers that provide intrastate or interstate telephone service to provide dual-party telephone relay services. The relay services must be "functionally equivalent" to the telephone services available to hearing persons. Title IV also requires television public service announcements to be closed-captioned if they are produced or funded in whole or in part by the federal government.

Title V

Title V contains a series of miscellaneous provisions, including the following:

- ADA shall not be construed to apply lesser standards than those applied under Section 504;
- ADA applies to the U.S. Congress;
- states are not immune under the Eleventh Amendment to the U. S. Constitution from lawsuits in federal court for ADA violations;† and
- a person who is currently an illegal drug user is not considered to be a person with a disability.

The last two provisions are also part of Section 504.

> † The explicit abrogation in ADA of a state's right to be immune from suits for monetary damages has been challenged in court under Title I and Title II of ADA. The Supreme Court struck down the abrogation clause as it applied to suits for monetary damages against states for employment discrimination under Title I (*Board of Trustees of the University of Alabama v. Garrett*, 531 U.S. 356 (2001)). On the other hand, in *Tennessee v. Lane*, 124 S. Ct. 1978 (2004), the Court upheld the legitimacy of the abrogation under Title II as it pertained to access to state courts. The Court found that Congress had ample evidence that states had denied individuals with disabilities meaningful access to judicial services and court proceedings, which violated the due process principle that states must "afford to all individuals a meaningful opportunity to be heard in its courts." Whether the Supreme Court will determine that states can be sued for other kinds of discrimination under Title II remains to be seen. Note, however, that in states where local school districts are deemed not to be arms of the state, LEAs can be sued for monetary damages under ADA.

Administrative Enforcement and Judicial Relief Under Titles II and III

If parents do not wish to sue under Titles II and III, administrative enforcement mechanisms are available to them. Administrative enforcement under Title II is essentially the same as it is under Section 504. This means that when parents allege discrimination in their children's education programs, OCR will investigate and monitor compliance. It can refer unresolved complaints to the Justice Department for litigation, if necessary.

Under Title III, unless a public accommodation is receiving federal funds under Section 504, there will not be a line agency (like ED) responsible for administrative enforcement and monitoring. Instead, the attorney general of the United States will investigate alleged violations of ADA and initiate compliance reviews. The attorney general is authorized to commence a lawsuit in federal court if there is a pattern or practice of resistance to ADA, or if the discrimination raises an issue of general public importance. Otherwise, the aggrieved individual must bring the lawsuit on his or her own behalf (28 C.F.R. §§ 36.501-.505 (2009)).

When an individual believes that a public accommodation, such as a secular private school, is violating ADA, the individual can sue for an injunction to require an auxiliary aid or service; modifications to policies, practices, or procedures; or removal of architectural barriers if "readily achievable." Also, if an individual reasonably believes that a public accommodation is about to remodel a facility without making the alterations or new construction readily accessible to and usable by persons with disabilities, the individual may sue to stop the construction until it is ADA-compliant.

In addition to injunctions, other kinds of relief can be ordered by a court, including monetary damages (in some situations) and civil penalties against the entity violating ADA. The court may also award attorneys' fees to the party (other than the United States) who prevails in the lawsuit. The Supreme Court has ruled, however, that a private individual may not receive punitive damages in a discrimination suit brought under Title II (*Barnes v. Gorman*, 2002).

ADA encourages what are known as "alternative means of dispute resolution" to the extent that they are authorized by law. Among the alternatives are such methods as settlement negotiations, conciliation, facilitation, mediation, fact-finding, mini-trials, and arbitration, each of which is somewhat different from the other.

Judicial Interpretation of Student Rights Under the ADA

Students complaining about alleged discriminatory treatment in public schools can sue under Title II, while private school students can sue under Title III. For students covered under Section 504, the protections of Section 504 are generally coextensive with ADA protections. Nonetheless, if such students believe that they are being discriminated against, they usually sue under both Section 504 and ADA. They "test the waters" to see if ADA provides slightly different protection from that provided by Section 504,† as may occasionally be the case, such as with the more extensive architectural accessibility standards of ADA.

† A case in which the plaintiff was not a student is worthy of note here, because the defendant was a public school district. The school district expelled a student because his mother could not attend mandatory PTA meetings as a result of her need for kidney dialysis. The mother claimed discrimination under Title II and received a $53,500 jury award. The case is Alexander v. School Board of Pinellas County, 97-311-CIV-T-24C (W.D. Fla. 1998).

Cases Under Title II

Federal courts have ruled that if redress is available under IDEA for an ADA (or Section 504) claim of discrimination, the claim is subject to IDEA's requirement for "exhaustion of administrative remedies." This means that aggrieved persons must use the IDEA hearing process before going to court. Several cases have resulted in dismissal of ADA claims for failure to request a hearing. One in particular, *Glen v. Charlotte-Mecklenburg School Board of Education* (1995), held that a special education student who was suspended for bringing a gun clip with live bullets to school could not circumvent IDEA requirements by bringing an ADA discrimination claim.[2]

On the other hand, if relief is not available under IDEA, then the case may be brought directly under Title II of ADA, and exhaustion of administrative remedies is not required. In general, independent ADA claims would go beyond a student's special education programming and placement and would address issues that are not part of a student's IEP. Such a case was *Bechtel v. East Penn School District of Lehigh County* (1994),[3] in which a student with spina bifida sought access to school facilities, including the football stadium. When the school district renovated its facilities, it failed to meet ADA access standards in spite of having been informed of them. The ADA claim was allowed to proceed.

At least two courts have ruled explicitly that ADA does not create broader programming or placement standards than does IDEA. In *Conner v. Branstad* (1993), the court ruled that Title II of ADA creates no mandate for deinstitutionalization of the entire class of mentally and physically disabled individuals in Iowa's intermediate care facilities. The case, a long-standing class action, was continued on other grounds.

The other case was *Urban v. Jefferson County School District R-1* (1994), in which the parents of an IDEA student were unable to convince the court that they had a right under ADA to a neighborhood school placement for their child. The federal district court concluded that ADA was not designed to result in alterations of the pre-existing and more specific framework of IDEA, notwithstanding ADA language encouraging the provision of services in the "most integrated setting appropriate to the student's needs." According to the court, giving parents control over where their child attends school would cause the school district to lose control over the utilization and allocation of its resources, and would go beyond IDEA placement requirements. The decision in *Urban* was affirmed by the U.S. Court of Appeals for the Tenth Circuit in 1996.

Another decision initially seemed to allow the possibility that ADA language could be considered separately from IDEA, even though ultimately IDEA standards prevailed. In *Petersen v. Hastings Public Schools* (1993) a modified Signing Exact English II system (SEE-II) was upheld as a means of implementing the IEPs of three IDEA students with hearing impairments. The parents had sought an unmodified SEE-II system. The federal district court ruled that, under IDEA, the modified system provided FAPE because the students were clearly making progress at school.

---

[2] See also *Hope v. Cortines*, 872 F. Supp. 14 (E.D.N.Y.), *aff'd*, 69 F.3d 687 (2d Cir. 1995).

[3] But see *Pace v. Bogalusa Cnty. Sch. Bd.*, 2005 U.S. App. LEXIS 3926 (5th Cir. 2005), which reached a different conclusion about the independence of architectural inaccessibility claims, given incorporation into IDEA '97 of the ADA new construction guidelines.

Then the same court ruled on whether Title II of ADA required something else. The relevant Title II regulation specifies that the parents' choice of auxiliary aids and services (here stipulated to include a specific signing system) should be honored unless another effective means of communication is available (see 28 C.F.R. § 35.160 (1995) and accompanying comments). The court concluded that the modified SEE-II system was an effective alternative to the parents' choice.† On appeal, the Eighth Circuit upheld the lower court's decision that the school district's choice of signing method met the ADA requirement of providing an effective means of communication. It appears that an "effective" means of communication may be comparable to IDEA's requirement for an "appropriate" means of communication.

> † The lower court in *Petersen* did allow the parents an opportunity to demonstrate that the LEA's choice of the modified SEE-II was not as effective as their own choice, a burden they were unable to meet. The Eighth Circuit upheld this legal approach. The result opens the door to the possibility that another plaintiff might be able to meet the burden, thereby requiring an LEA to select a communication system that is not only effective but as effective as the parent's preference.

Another Title II case concerning the mental health system is included here because some may find it analogous to the needs of some deaf students in the public schools. In *Tugg v. Towey* (1994), the issue was whether the use of sign language interpreters in providing mental health counseling to persons who were deaf or hard of hearing violated ADA and Section 504. Advocates for the deaf argued that the use of sign language interpreters in a therapeutic setting did not produce mental health services equal to those provided to individuals without disabilities because reliance on the interpreters and the inability of the counselors themselves to use sign language created too many miscommunication possibilities. The court issued a preliminary injunction ordering the state Department of Health and Rehabilitation Services to provide counselors who could use American Sign Language (ASL) and who had an understanding of the mental health needs of the deaf community—that is, those who identify themselves as culturally deaf—for whom ASL is the primary language.

Finally, several cases challenging age-eligibility and other eligibility rules imposed by high school athletic associations have been filed under Title II as well as Section 504. One question has been whether athletic associations whose members are dues-paying high schools are public entities or private associations. Another question has been whether the dues they receive make them a recipient of federal financial assistance under Section 504. In *Bingham v. Oregon School Activities Association* (1999), a federal district court ruled that the Oregon School Activities Association was a public entity under Title II (but not a public accommodation under Title III), and not a recipient of federal aid under Section 504. The case relied, among other things, on a 1999 Supreme Court ruling that dues paid to the NCAA by postsecondary recipients of federal aid did not make the NCAA a recipient of federal financial aid under Title IX (*NCAA v. Smith*, 1999). A later case in a federal district court in Pennsylvania reached the same conclusion.† Whether a case is brought under Title II or Section 504 is generally immaterial to the actual outcome. (See also the material in chapter 18 on participation in athletic competitions under Section 504.)

> † The court in the *Bingham* case ordered a waiver of the rule that limited athletic participation to eight semesters. The court concluded that waiver was a reasonable modification for a student with learning disabilities and ADHD. The student was still age-eligible and was retained in 10th grade for academic and not athletic reasons. The evidence indicated that his athletic participation was important in coping with his disability and would not result in a competitive advantage for him or his team Similarly, the court in the Pennsylvania case enjoined enforcement of the age 19 rule against a student with a disability who was over that age. The court found that no undue burden or fundamental alteration in the football and track program would result from allowing the student to play (*Cruz v. Pennsylvania Interscholastic Athletic Association*, 157 F. Supp. 2d 485 (E.D.

Penn. 2001)). The Association subsequently developed a waiver process to allow exceptions to its rule.

Can Enforcement of a "Neutral" Rule Be a Pretext for Discrimination?

A claim of ADA discrimination under Title II that was allegedly based on a student's depression was addressed in a first-of-its-kind case in *Baird v. Rose*, 192 F.3d 462 (4th Cir. 1999). Baird was dismissed from a role in a middle school's show choir performance because of her absence from rehearsals, although the absenteeism policy had been previously unenforced. The instructor refused the mother's requests to allow Baird to demonstrate that she knew the dance routines, ignoring the mother's plea that participation in the show choir was important to her daughter's recovery from a suicide attempt attributed to severe depression.

In the subsequent ADA discrimination suit, both sides acknowledged that Baird's depression was a disability under ADA, and that she was otherwise qualified for the benefit she had been denied (that is, participation as a singer and dancer in the show choir in spite of her depression). Nonetheless, the district court dismissed the discrimination claim. The Fourth Circuit reversed and allowed the claims to go to trial. The Circuit held that the allegations, if proven at trial, were sufficient to support a determination that application of the absentee policy was a pretext for discrimination on the basis of Baird's disability. The court stated: "The post hoc [after-the-fact] application of a neutral rule does not excuse discrimination when the neutral rule would not have been enforced but for the discrimination."

What do we learn from this case? School officials, at least in the Fourth Circuit, are on notice that if they differentially enforce an absenteeism policy, it can be viewed as a pretext for prejudging a student as incapable of performing based on disability. Moreover, the court also ruled that discrimination can be established if it is a "motivating cause" (not necessarily the "sole cause") of adverse action. The court was distinguishing ADA from Section 504 of the Rehabilitation Act, which states that discrimination must be the "sole cause" for the adverse action.

Private School and Day-Care Cases Under Title III

The federal Department of Justice (DOJ) has mediated and settled a number of private child-care cases, some of which can be accessed through the ADA enforcement web site.[4] In addition, several cases have resulted in published court decisions determining the extent of responsibility of secular private schools to provide auxiliary aids and services to students with disabilities in order to assure "full and equal enjoyment of the goods, services, facilities, privileges, advantages, or accommodations"(42 U.S.C. § 12182(a) (Supp. III 2009)) of the private school. Title III excuses the private school from this obligation only when the provision of such goods and services would fundamentally alter the nature of the program or result in an undue burden on the school (42 U.S.C. § 12182(b)(2)(A)(iii) (Supp. III 2009)). The cases involve issues that do not implicate IDEA.

One early case that tested the limits of Title III is *Roberts v. Kindercare Learning Centers* (1996). Kindercare, a public accommodation, denied admission to a four-year-old with multiple disabilities on the basis that it had no legal duty to provide one-to-one care during the times when a personal care attendant (PCA) could not be present. The child's IEP called for a PCA, whose paid services

---

[4] http://www.ada.gov/enforce.htm

were authorized in the day-care center for thirty hours a week under a Medicaid program. The parents, however, wanted the center to provide a one-to-one aide for the remainder of the time at the center, and when the PCA was ill or otherwise unable to accompany the child. A federal appeals court upheld the lower court's ruling that Kindercare's refusal to admit the student did not violate ADA. The appeals court reasoned that the parents were seeking more than a reasonable "accommodation" [i.e., modification] by attempting to force Kindercare to provide far more than its usual group child care. To require one-to-one care would fundamentally alter the nature of its business and create an undue financial burden on the center, the court concluded.

On the other hand, two other interesting cases produced preliminary injunctions in favor of the plaintiffs. The first also involved a Kindercare center. In *Orr v. Kindercare Learning Centers* (1995), a nine-year-old student with severe developmental disabilities who required assistance in eating, walking, toileting, and interacting with others was placed in Kindercare's after-school two-year-old class. Kindercare gave notice of its intent to terminate the boy on the basis that it could not meet his individual needs in a group care setting. The parents wanted to provide an aide to accompany him and also wanted him placed in a school-age class. The court granted a preliminary injunction to the parents, allowing them to keep their son at the facility pending a trial on the merits. The court found no evidence to indicate that a personal aide, paid for with outside funds, would fundamentally alter the nature of the program, and it held that the likelihood of harm weighed in favor of the parents. Whether the aide was a reasonable modification of Kindercare's activities remained an issue, depending on who trained and supervised the aide, among other things. This issue was to go to trial, but the parties reached a settlement agreement, and the court entered a consent decree (DOJ, 1996).

The second case, *Alvarez v. Fountainhead* (1999), involved a preschooler with asthma who was denied entrance to a Montessori preschool because of his need for a hand-held Albuterol inhaler at school. The court granted the parents' motion for a preliminary injunction and ordered the child's entry at the school. The court found that no fundamental alteration in the program would result, because the child did not require continuous monitoring and could use the inhaler by himself with minimal adult supervision. Furthermore, staff training was simple and would not constitute an undue administrative burden.

Two cases bearing on students with behavior problems are also worth noting. In *Burriola v. Greater Toledo YMCA* (2001), a district court granted a preliminary injunction to parents of a preschooler with autism. The court required the YMCA child-care center to readmit the child and make appropriate modifications, such as hand signals and the use of breaks. Because the preschooler did not need one-to-one attention and did not pose a direct threat to others, and because the modifications could be implemented at modest cost, the court found that the proposed modifications would not fundamentally alter the nature of the program.

In contrast, the First Circuit in *Bercovitch v. Baldwin School* (1998) vacated a preliminary injunction, concluding that the lower court had expected the school to go far beyond the reasonable modification requirements of the ADA in attempting to manage an ADHD teenager's repeated disruptive behaviors. Of particular importance to educators and parents is the court's conclusion that the ADA does not require a private regular education school to adopt IDEA-type programming or standards to manage a student's misbehaviors. Furthermore, the court concluded that a private school need not exempt a student from conforming to the school conduct code when the school has tried a variety of reasonable ways to accommodate a student's misbehavior. Ultimately, the appeals court held that an arbitration contract voluntarily entered by the parents and the school was the valid mechanism for deciding whether the teenager could be expelled for his misbehavior.

An Unusual Title III Safety Issue With an HIV-Positive Student

A 1999 case concerning a child who was HIV-positive and who wanted to participate in private group karate lessons may provide useful information to school districts. In *Montalvo v. Radcliffe,* (167 F.3d 873, 4th cir. 1999), the father of a twelve-year-old boy filed a discrimination suit under Title III of ADA against a private karate school that refused to allow the boy to join its group karate classes. The program was a combat-oriented, traditional Japanese martial arts program. Its training methods resulted in many minor abrasions and bloody noses that allowed blood to transfer from one student to another, and the school argued that the boy's blood spillage could present a direct threat to the health and safety of classmates and instructors. It was willing to instruct the boy privately as a reasonable modification of its programming that would not require a fundamental alteration of its training program.

The Fourth Circuit upheld the district court decision in favor of the karate school. It noted that the district court had considered the specific circumstances and made an individualized assessment of the risk presented by the boy's participation in group classes. Because AIDS can be transmitted by blood-to-blood and blood-to-eye contact, and precautions could not be taken to minimize the risk of transmission in the context of the group training methods, the school did not need to change its methods to accommodate the boy. Even the use of "universal precautions" such as eye coverings and gloves could not eliminate or minimize the otherwise significant risk.

Implications

The body of relevant ADA case law affecting students with disabilities who are already covered by IDEA or Section 504 remains quite small. To the extent that IDEA and Section 504 provide more specific rights and standards, they are being used instead of ADA. In a few areas, however, such as discrimination in secular private schools and day-care centers that are not recipients of federal funds, ADA establishes rights for an additional group of students with disabilities not otherwise covered. Case law affecting students under ADA is still developing. Schools may find helpful the child-care guidelines provided by the DOJ (1997).

↪Reminder

A comparison of ADA with Section 504 and IDEA is found on page xxiv.

↳Review

1. What is the primary difference between Section 504 and ADA?

   ADA is broader in scope. It extends to private-sector employment and public accommodations, which include secular private schools and day-care centers that do not receive federal funds. It also extends to state and local government agencies, regardless of whether they receive federal funds. In contrast, Section 504 is limited to recipients of federal funds.

2. What are the primary similarities of Section 504 and ADA?

   Both use the same definition of disability, and both prohibit discrimination against qualified persons with disabilities. The two laws use comparable standards in determining what constitutes unlawful employment discrimination and unlawful discrimination in state and local government programs.

⚡References

Americans with Disabilities Act of 1990, Pub. L. 101-336, 104 Stat. 327 (1991).

Americans with Disabilities Act Amendments of 2008, 42 U.S.C. § 12101 *et seq.* (Supp. III 2009).

Alvarez v. Fountainhead, 55 F. Supp. 2d 1048 (N.D. Cal. 1999).

Barnes v. Gorman, 536 U.S. 181 (2002).

Bechtel v. East Penn Sch. Dist. of Lehigh Cnty.,1994 U.S. Dist. LEXIS 1327 (E.D. Pa. 1999).

Bercovitch v. Baldwin Sch., 133 F. 3d 141 (1st Cir. 1998).

Bingham v. Or. Sch. Activities Assoc., 37 F. Supp. 2d 1189 (D. Or. 1999).

Burriola v. Greater Toledo YMCA, 133 F. Supp. 2d 1034 (N.D. Ohio 2001).

Conner v. Branstad, 839 F. Supp. 1345 (S.D. Iowa 1993).

Department of Justice (DOJ) (1997). Commonly asked questions about child care and the ADA. Retrieved March 11, 2011 from http://www.ada.gov/childq&a.htm

Department of Justice (DOJ) (1996). Retrieved May 4, 2011 from http://www.justice.gov/crt/foia/readingroom/frequent_requests/ada_settlements/ca/ca8.txt

Glen v. Charlotte-Mecklenburg Sch. Bd.of Educ., 903 F. Supp. 918 (W.D.N.C. 1995).

NCAA v. Smith, 119 S. Ct. 924 (1999).

Orr v. Kindercare Learning Ctrs., 23 IDELR ¶181 (E.D. Cal. 1995).

Petersen v. Hastings Pub. Sch., 831 F. Supp. 742 (D. Neb. 1993), *aff'd*, 31 F. 3d 705 (8th Cir. 1994).

Section 504 of the Rehabilitation Act of 1973, 29 U.S.C. § 794 (2006).

Roberts v. Kindercare Learning Centers, 86 F. 3d 844 (8th Cir. 1996).

Tugg v.Towey, 864 F. Supp. 1201 (S.D. Fla. 1994).

Urban v. Jefferson Cnty. Sch. Dist. R-1, 870 F. Supp. 1558 (D. Colo. 1994), *aff'd*, 89 F. 3d 720 (10th Cir. 1996).

⇉Selected Supplementary Resources

ADA Title I Final Rule (Amended Regulations), 29 C.F.R. Part 1630 (effective May 24, 2011).

ADA Title II Final Rule (Amended Regulations), 28 C.F.R. Part 35 (effective March 15, 2011).

ADA Title III Final Rule (Amended Regulations), 28 C.F.R. Part 36 (effective March 15, 2011).

Colker, R. (2005). *The disability pendulum: The first decade of the Americans with Disabilities Act.* New York, NY: NYU Press.

Federation for Children with Special Needs, Peer Project (2008). *Section 504, the Americans with Disabilities Act, and educational reform.* Retrieved February 14, 2011 from http:// www.wrightslaw. com/info/section 504.ada.peer.htm

Marczely, B. (1993). The Americans with Disabilities Act: Confronting the shortcomings of Section 504 in public education. *Education Law Reporter, 78*, 199–207.

Morrissey, P. (1993). *The educator's guide to the Americans With Disabilities Act.* Alexandria, VA: American Vocational Association.

Shipley, T. E. (2002).Child care centers and children with special needs: Rights under the Americans With Disabilities Act and Section 504 of the Rehabilitation Act. *Journal of Law and Education, 31*, 327.

U.S. Department of Justice, Civil Rights Division. (1992). *The ADA Title II technical assistance manual.* Washington, DC: Author.

Wenkart, R. D. (1993). The Americans With Disabilities Act and its impact on public education. *Education Law Reporter, 82*, 291–302.

Part II

The Individuals With Disabilities Education Act

Chapter 5

IDEA Eligibility

Chapter Outline

Disability Categories

The Individuals With Disabilities Education Act, in all its iterations, was and is designed to ensure a full educational opportunity to those students with disabilities who are eligible for services under the Act. In deciding to help school districts serve children with disabilities, the federal government specified both the kinds of disabilities and, initially, the percent of students it would serve as disabled.

The reasons were both financial and philosophical. Financially, the federal government did not want to spread its limited funds too thinly, and until 1997 it capped the number of children for whom it would provide funding at 12 percent of the school population ages three through seventeen. The cap was removed in IDEA '97.† Philosophically, Congress did not want to label children with disabilities as "special education" students if they did not need specially designed instruction. Moreover, it did not wish to expand the disability label to other students at risk of school failure or with just any kind of impairment. For instance, IDEA was never intended to serve students whose sole difficulty is learning at a slower rate than the average student, that is, so-called slow learners. Nor is it meant to serve those who develop temporary behavior problems resulting from a family crisis or who simply miss a lot of school because of family moves.

> † The most recent figures from ED indicate that under IDEA-B, states and the District of Columbia served an average of 9.1 percent of children ages 6 through 21; and 5.8 percent of children ages 3 through 5 (U.S. Department of Education, OSERS, OSEP (2010).*Twenty-Ninth Annual Report to Congress on the Implementation of the Individuals With Disabilities Education Act, 2007*, Vol. 1, pp. xvii–xviii. Washington, DC: Author). The 2007 Report was not issued until December 2010, and the most recent statistics are for either fall 2005 or July 2006.

To be eligible for IDEA services, children over the age of nine must be determined to have one of the following disabilities: specific learning disability; speech or language impairment; mental retardation[1]; serious emotional disturbance (referred to generally as emotional disturbance); other health impairment; orthopedic impairment; hearing impairment, including deafness; visual impairment, including blindness; autism; or traumatic brain injury (20 U.S.C. § 1401(3)(A)(i) (2006). All these conditions are defined in the regulations. Deafness and hearing impairment are defined separately from each other; blindness and visual impairment are defined together. The regulations go beyond the statute to provide additional definitions for deaf-blindness and multiple disabilities, because they represent special combinations of disabilities (34 C.F.R. § 300.8(a)(1)(2006)). This brings the total number of definitions of disability terms to thirteen (see Table 5.1 at the end of this chapter).

For children ages three through nine (or any subgroup of those ages, including preschoolers 3 through 5), the eligibility categories need not be used. Instead of determining whether a child has one of the specified disabilities a state, at its option, may allow eligibility for a child who is experiencing "developmental delays" in one or more of the following areas: physical, cognitive, communicative, adaptive, or social or emotional development. A state may define these kinds of delays for itself, as long as they are measured by "appropriate diagnostic instruments and procedures"(20 U.S.C. § 1401 (3)(B)(i) (2006)). The relaxed criteria reflect the fact that it is often difficult to pinpoint an exact disability during the early developmental years, and it may not be wise to force a premature disability classification on young children.

---

[1] As of Oct. 5, 2010, the term used in the Act is "intellectual disability." We will generally use this term throughout the remainder of this text.

A state may choose to narrow the age ranges to which it will apply the term "developmental delay," and to continue to use the disability categories and the developmental delay category simultaneously—but for different children. If a state chooses not to adopt the classification of developmental delay, neither can the LEA.†A local school district, however, need not adopt the classification even if the state does so.

> † Only four states do not use the developmental delay classification. See U.S. Department of Education, OSERS, OSEP (2010). *Twenty-Ninth Annual Report to Congress on the Implementation of the Individuals with Disabilities Education Act, 2007*. Vol. 2, Appendix A, Table A-3. Washington, DC: Author.

Approximately 6.8 million children ages three through twenty-one were served under IDEA in fall of 2005 (the latest year for which totals have been reported), and the total has continued to rise for three- to five- year-olds but may have stabilized for six through twenty-one year-olds (U.S. Dept. of Education, 2010, Vol. 1, pp. xvii-xviii). Children with a specific learning disability accounted for 45 percent of those served, while children with speech-language impairment, other health impairment (OHI), intellectual disability, and emotional disturbance together accounted for another 45 percent (U.S. Dept of Education, 2010, Vol. I, Figure 1-21). In short, collectively, 90% percent of the children served come from these five disability categories. (Since 2000, the number of children with LD has been decreasing while the number of children with OHI and speech-language impairment has been growing.) The remaining eight disability categories represent low-incidence disabilities.

Other Eligibility Factors

For children evaluated as having an IDEA disability, a determination must be made that the disability necessitates "special education." The existence of the disability alone is insufficient. The general language of the regulations adds that the disability must "adversely affect educational performance" or, in the case of deaf-blindness and multiple disabilities, produce "severe educational problems" that cannot be accommodated in a special education program developed solely for one of the child's disabilities.

Special education is defined as specially designed instruction, at no cost to the parents, to meet the student's unique needs. The statute specifically includes instruction in physical education [(20 U.S.C. § 1401(29)(B)(2006)].† The regulations state that it also includes vocational education, travel training, and speech-language pathology services or other related services if they are considered special education under state law (34 C.F.R. § 300.39(2) (2006)). If the effect of the disability is not to require special education, the student may still be eligible for protection under Section 504 of the Rehabilitation Act of 1973.

> † For an application of the statute, see *Pittsburgh Board of Education v. Commonwealth Department of Education*, 581 A.2d 681 (Pa. Commw. Ct. 1990), in which a state court found that a student's paralysis limited her educational performance in physical education. The court rejected the school district's argument that because the student's academic performance was not adversely affected, she could be declassified.

A student is eligible for IDEA Part B services beginning at age three. Ordinarily, services will cease when the student graduates from high school with a regular diploma or no longer requires special education. A student who has not received a regular diploma and continues to need special education remains eligible through the age of twenty-one unless state law or court order provides otherwise. The statute says that for students ages three through five and eighteen through twenty-one, FAPE need not be available if such application "would be inconsistent with State law or practice, or the order of any court" (20 U.S.C. § 1412(a)(1)(A) & (B)(2006)). In other words, Congress allows state law to override this particular provision of the federal statute. Every state, however, is serving students within these age ranges (U.S. Dept. of Education, 2010).

Because graduation with a regular diploma is a change of placement, advance notice must be given to the parents. Termination of services under these circumstances, however, or when the student is no longer age eligible, does not require a re-evaluation of the student as it does in other circumstances (20 U.S.C. § 1414(c)(5)(B)(i) (2006)).

Eligibility Determination

IDEA requires that a parent of the child be invited to participate with "qualified professionals" in determining the child's eligibility for IDEA services (20 U.S.C. § 1414(b)(4)(A) (2006)). The determination takes place only after a full evaluation of the child's needs (see chapter 6). The eligibility team must determine that the disability is the key factor in the eligibility decision rather than limited English proficiency or lack of "appropriate instruction" in math or reading. If any of these three factors are what produce the need for special help, the child should not be declared IDEA eligible. The elements of appropriate instruction in math are not specified, but the elements of effective reading specified in NCLB (2001) are incorporated in the IDEA regulations and include phonemic awareness, phonics, vocabulary development, fluency, and reading comprehension (20 U.S.C. § 1414(b)(5)(A) (2006)).

IDEA's Early Intervention Program for Infants and Toddlers

Part C of IDEA establishes a separate program of services for infants and toddlers (birth through age two). The eligibility criteria and programming requirements for early intervention services for infants and toddlers are separate from Part B because the services need not be primarily educational in nature and are frequently coordinated by health or social services agencies.

Eligibility is extended to infants and toddlers who need early intervention services because they are experiencing developmental delays or have a diagnosed condition likely to result in developmental delay. At the state's discretion, eligibility can also be extended to those who are "at risk" of experiencing a substantial developmental delay if early intervention services are not provided. A provision under IDEA '04 allows the state to extend Part C services beyond the third birthday, if an education component is present that addresses school readiness and preliteracy, language, and numeracy skills (20 U.S.C. § 1432(5)(B) (2006)). Part C services may continue until these children are eligible to enter kindergarten. If a state chooses to adopt such a policy, the parents must have the choice of whether to continue Part C services or have their child served under Part B (20 U.S.C. § 1435(c) (2006)). If the preschooler remains under Part C, the state is not obligated to provide FAPE under Part B (20 U.S.C. § 1412(a)(1)(C) (2006)).

Part C services are governed by an Individual Family Service Plan (IFSP). The IFSP is similar to an IEP in many ways but is family centered rather than child-centered. It includes a statement of the family's resources, priorities, and concerns and requires written parental consent for its implementation. In addition, a service coordinator must be identified, and transition plans must be included in the IFSP. In particular Part C is concerned with interagency coordination and a smooth transition from Part C to Part B services. Under IDEA '04, at the request of the parent, when the child transitions to Part B, a representative of the Part C system must be invited to the initial IEP meeting (20 U.S.C. § 1414(d)(1)(D) (2006)).

The Part C program requires that services be delivered to the maximum extent appropriate in "natural environments," which include the home and community settings in which children without disabilities participate (20 U.S.C. § 1432(4)(G) (2006). The governor designates the lead agency for implementing and coordinating Part C services, and appoints members of a state interagency coordinating council. Funding is based on the ratio of the number of infants and toddlers in a state to the number of infants and toddlers in all states. Services are at no cost to the family except where federal or state law permits the use of sliding fee scales.

A new provision in IDEA '04 requires states that submit applications for funding to also submit descriptions of policies and procedures mandating the referral to early intervention services of any child under the age of three who has been subject to a substantiated case of child abuse. Policies mandating referral are also required with respect to infants and toddlers "identified as affected by illegal substance abuse, or withdrawal symptoms resulting from prenatal drug exposure" (20 U.S.C. § 1437(a)(6) (2006)).

State participation in the early intervention program is optional, but its purpose is to minimize the need for (or costs of) special education after infants and toddlers reach school age. All states are participating in the program. More than 298,000 infants and toddlers were receiving services in 2005, or 2.4percent of the total number of infants and toddlers in the fifty states and the District of Columbia (U.S. Department of Education, 2010, Vol. 1, p. xvii).

The Part C provisions are found at 20 U.S.C. §§ 1431-1443 (2006).

Another IDEA provision states that "nothing in this Act requires that children be classified by their disability" as long as a student is regarded as IDEA-eligible (20 U.S.C. § 1412(a)(3)(B) (2006)). In other words, after a determination of eligibility has been made and a report sent to the federal government listing eligibility by category, a school district need not attach a specific label to a student in order to provide services to that student. Giving the school district this option is intended to allow avoidance of the stigma that is sometimes attached to disability labels. Some SEAs and LEAs have chosen to utilize this flexibility.

Definitional Issues

Definitions of the disability categories appear in the regulations, not the statute. They have been examined carefully over the years. Several terms have generated continuing political debate in recent years, particularly "specific learning disability" and "emotional disturbance" and, to a lesser extent, "autism," "traumatic brain injury," and "other health impairment." Each is discussed in more detail below.

Specific Learning Disability

In general terms, the IDEA regulations define *specific learning disability* as "a disorder in one or more of the basic psychological processes" involved in understanding or using spoken or written language, including listening, thinking, speaking, reading, writing, spelling, or performing mathematical calculations (34 C.F.R. § 300.8(c)(10) (2006)).

Specific learning disability is generally abbreviated as learning disability (LD) and is an educational, not a medical, term. It is applied to children who have average or above-average intelligence but who show underachievement and idiosyncratic learning patterns that are not attributable to other disabilities, socioeconomic status, poor teaching, or limited English proficiency. To a greater extent than is true of their peers, they are good in some subjects and poor in others, skillful in some areas but not in others. For instance, they may be good in math and struggling in reading, or vice versa. They may be excellent in listening comprehension but extremely poor at decoding words. Because of their fluctuating educational performance, these children can be a real puzzle. Although most of them fall within normal intelligence ranges, some are gifted.

Before the passage of IDEA '04, the IDEA regulations required the eligibility team to find a "severe discrepancy" between a student's intellectual ability and achievement in one or more of the specified language arts and mathematical areas. The regulations, however, did not provide criteria for measuring a "severe discrepancy" but left the measurement criteria to the states. States adopted different standards, and the lack of uniformity in measuring severe discrepancy was the subject of considerable concern, particularly for parents of children with learning disabilities who moved from one state to another and found that their children were no longer eligible for services in their new state.† Moreover, the Learning Disability Association criticized the severe discrepancy requirement because it forced many children to fail academically before they could be served under IDEA. Most young children cannot meet the severe discrepancy requirement until they have been underachieving in school for two to three years. A third criticism emerged from scholars who asserted that the concept of a severe discrepancy could not be validated empirically as a distinguishing characteristic of learning disability, because many other children with reading difficulties exhibited similar discrepancies (Fuchs, Mock, Morgan, & Young, 2003).

† In some places, such as Texas and Louisiana, state statutes prevented a diagnosis of dyslexia (a specific reading disability) from qualifying a student as having a learning disability if the student did not otherwise meet the state LD criteria. In effect, a medical diagnosis of dyslexia did not indicate a learning disability if the student did not demonstrate a significant-enough discrepancy between intellectual ability and academic achievement.

In spite of the arguments that many young children with learning disabilities were being overlooked, the numbers steadily increased until 2000. Since that year, although the number of LD students ages twelve to seventeen has increased, the number of LD students ages six to eleven has been decreasing. In the decade leading up to IDEA '04, the large number of students identified with reading disabilities led Congress to hypothesize that many children with reading difficulties may not have been instructed effectively, and may have been identified incorrectly as having a learning disability.

In IDEA '04, Congress for the first time allows LEAs to use another measurement process in lieu of the severe discrepancy requirement. As part of the evaluation and eligibility process, LEAs may choose procedures that determine "if the child responds to scientific, research-based intervention" (20 U.S.C. § 1414(b)(6) (2006)). Such procedures typically go under the name "responsiveness to intervention" or "response to treatment intervention" (RTI). The RTI model requires academic instruction based on validated interventions that address the needs of at-risk learners. Several models of RTI are being used across the country, all of which require curriculum-based performance data and empirically validated academic interventions. Levels of increasingly intensive instruction —from small-group instruction to one-on-one instruction—are typically offered as a way to determine if at-risk students can be taught effectively by general education teachers or tutors. If the student does not respond well to any of the interventions, then the suspicion of a learning disability is heightened. The models were developed first for elementary school students but are now being extended to secondary school students. The effectiveness of the models for widescale evaluation and eligibility purposes has yet to be established, although early pilot models have been encouraging. The RTI model requires the use of best practices and documentation of interventions before children are referred for more comprehensive LD evaluations.

SEAs and LEAs eagerly awaited the 2006 IDEA regulations for clarification about the actual process to be used if LEAs chose to adopt the RTI approach. One question was whether Congress had considered the practical dilemmas of having different LEAs within a state select different eligibility standards for students with learning disabilities. A second question was whether to view RTI as a screening procedure or as an evaluation procedure that would be subject to the sixty-day evaluation timeline established in IDEA '04.

The Office of Special Education Programs (OSEP) attempted to address both the above questions in the 2006 regulations (34 C.F.R. §§ 300.307-.310) First, the regulations require the SEA to adopt criteria for use by LEAs in determining the existence of a learning disability, and LEAs must use the SEA criteria. The regulations state that the SEA must permit LEAs to use an RTI process and may permit use of "alternative research-based procedures" (34 C.F.R. § 300.307). (No explanation of the difference between scientific, research-based intervention and alternative research-based procedures is provided.) This provision may reduce the possible variability across LEAs if, in effect, it allows an SEA to prohibit the use of severe discrepancy entirely if it cannot be validated by research.

The eligibility team of "qualified professionals" and parents is to determine the existence of LD by first establishing inadequate achievement in one or more of eight academic areas: oral expression, listening comprehension, basic reading skills, reading comprehension, mathematics calculation, mathematics problem solving, written expression, and reading fluency. The underachievement is to be based on the child's age or the state-approved grade-level standards required by NCLB (2001). Reading fluency was added to, and spelling was deleted from, the original academic areas listed in earlier regulations although spelling may still be included under the area of written expression.

The next step in the eligibility team's determination of an LD presents two options: (a) lack of sufficient progress to meet the previously mentioned age or grade-level standards in one or more of the eight designated areas when using an RTI process, or (b) a pattern of strengths and weaknesses in performance, achievement, or both relative to age, state-approved grade-level standards, or intellectual development. The team must determine the relevance of this second option for the child in question One wonders whether this second option, part of which retains a vestige of the concept of severe discrepancy, may be prohibited by SEA criteria, if an SEA so chooses.

Second, addressing the RTI screening question, OSEP clarified in the regulations that screening to determine appropriate instructional strategies is not evaluation (34 C.F.R. § 300.302 (2006)). The regulatory language seems to clearly indicate that the sixty-day evaluation period does not automatically begin at the first RTI stage. If, during the RTI screening stage, however, parents consent to an LD evaluation of their child, the sixty-day timeline will commence at that point. The regulatory Comment and Analysis section adds that "[a]n RTI process does not replace the need for a comprehensive evaluation" (71 Fed. Reg. 46648, Aug. 14, 2006). OSEP emphasized that all other general eligibility criteria, including use of a variety of assessment instruments and classroom observations, must be met. Additionally, the eligibility team must continue to find that the LD determination is not primarily based on a sensory or motor disability, intellectual disability, emotional disturbance, limited English proficiency, or environmental or economic disadvantage (34 C.F.R. § 300.309(a)(3) (2006)).

Emotional Disturbance

What IDEA formerly labeled as "serious emotional disturbance" has been referred to since IDEA '97 as "emotional disturbance." The word serious has been dropped to avoid any unnecessarily negative meaning because this adjective is not applied to any other disability category. The definition itself, however, is the same and has remained controversial over the years. It includes children with schizophrenia and explicitly excludes those with social maladjustment unless they are found to also have an emotional disturbance (34 C.F.R. § 300.8(c)(4)(ii) (2006)). Many SEAs interpret this exclusion to prohibit IDEA-eligibility for students with conduct disorders—that is, antisocial, rule-breaking, aggressive behaviors and disorders.† Others choose to serve these students by classifying them as having an emotional disturbance. In either event, any one of the following five characteristics can qualify a child as having an emotional disturbance, provided that it is exhibited over a long period of time and to a marked degree that adversely affects a child's education performance:

1. Inability to learn that cannot be explained by intellectual, sensory, or health factors;

2. Inability to build or maintain satisfactory interpersonal relationships with peers and teachers;

3. Inappropriate types of behavior or feelings under normal circumstances;

4. General pervasive mood of unhappiness or depression;

5. Tendency to develop physical symptoms or fears associated with personal or school problems. (34 C.F.R. § 300.8(c)(4)(i) (2006))

† The American Academy of Child and Adolescent Psychiatry describes "conduct disorder" (CD) as a complicated group of symptoms characterized by "great difficulty following rules and behaving in a socially acceptable way." Continuing, the Academy states that children or adolescents with CD may be aggressive toward people or animals, destructive of property, deceitful, and rule violators. Often adults view them as delinquent rather than having a mental illness. Without early treatment, these problems are often irresolvable. Retrieved March 15, 2011 from http://www.aacap.org/publications/factsfam/conduct.htm

In 1993, ED proposed a more inclusive regulatory definition of emotional disturbance and invited public comment (58 Fed. Reg. 7938, February 10, 1993). The definition seemed to allow the inclusion of students with conduct disorders (CDs) and social maladjustments if their educational performance, broadly defined, was adversely affected so that they required special education. The proposed definition required that the disability be consistently exhibited in two different settings, at least one of which was school-related. In other words, any disorder showing up in only an out-of-school context or in only one school setting (for example, one classroom) would not be considered a genuine emotional disturbance. The proposed definition generated a polarized response from service providers. Some feared expansion of the category, whereas others asserted that many additional students with behavior problems needed special education services and should be included. Because of the inability to garner a working consensus, no change in the regulatory definition emerged.†

† Some states, however, may reflect parts of the defunct proposed definition in their state definitions of emotional disturbance while still maintaining the current federal definition. *See, e.g.,* Ala. Admin. Code r290-8-0-.3 (r)(a)1–5 (cited in *Katherine S. v. Umbach,* 2002 U.S. Dist. LEXIS 2523 (M.D. Ala. 2002).

Courts continue to struggle to differentiate emotional disturbance from social maladjustment and psychiatric syndromes which may or may not produce characteristics that meet the education definition of emotional disturbance.† Half of those who do meet the definition of emotional disturbance drop out before graduation, a worrisome statistic and a higher percentage than any other disability category (U.S. Dept. of Education, 2010,Vol. 2, Table 4-2d). Some commentators have observed that the education system has a difficult time addressing the needs of children with emotional and behavioral disturbances and that it spends far too little time preventing emotional disturbance and addressing the mental health needs of children within the education system.[2]

† See, e.g., *C.J. v. Indian River County School Board,* 39 IDELR 186 (S.D. Fla. 2003), aff'd on appeal, U.S. App. LEXIS 20181 (11th Cir. 2004) (holding that a medical diagnosis of bipolar disorder was insufficient to require a re-evaluation of a student for eligibility under IDEA). See also *Katherine S. v. Umbach,* 2002 U.S. Dist. LEXIS 2523 (M.D. Ala. 2002), in which an adolescent girl who showed multiple signs of emotional disturbance was found ineligible under IDEA because her ADHD, depression, sexual promiscuity, and oppositional defiant disorder traits did not produce serious academic or behavior problems at school.

---

[2] See, e.g., the Dimoff and Kauffman articles listed under Selected Supplementary Resources in this chapter.

Autism

Autism is a disability that was initially viewed as a subset of the category of emotional disturbance, and then as a subset of other health impairment. Due to advances in medical understanding and parent advocacy, autism was recognized in 1990 as a separate disability under IDEA. At that time, Congress acknowledged autism as a discrete developmental disability significantly affecting verbal and nonverbal communication and social interaction. Influential in effecting the change was the fact that, by 1990, theories of biochemical causation had gained scientific dominance over the discredited theory that lack of maternal bonding was the cause of autism. Also, methods of treatment had evolved that were significantly different from those used with children who have an emotional disturbance.

The autism definition in the 1999 regulations acknowledged for the first time that, although the disability is usually evident by the age of three, a child who manifests the necessary characteristics after that age could be diagnosed as having autism. This definition is retained in the 2006 regulations (34 C.F.R. § 300.8(c)(1)(iii) (2006)).

The number of children ages six to twenty-one identified as having autism has grown dramatically over the past fifteen years, from 3,539 in 1991–1992 (U.S. Department of Education, 1994, Table AA22) to 193,637 by fall 2005 (U.S. Department of Education, 2010, Vol. 2, Table 1-3.). More than 30,000 were served in the three to five age group by fall 2005 (U.S. Department of Education, 2010, Vol. 2, Table 1-2). Despite much study and speculation, the reasons for this increase are still uncertain and not well understood. Some attribute the rise to an increase in environmental contaminants. Others attribute it to better diagnosis. Still others point to the fact that the Diagnostic and Statistical Manual of the American Psychiatric Association (DSM IV) (1994) has identified a broad cluster of syndromes under the label of Autism Spectrum Disorders (ASD). The label includes such syndromes as pervasive developmental delay (PDD) and Asperger syndrome, in which some but not all of the symptoms of classical autism are present. Some SEAs and LEAs are choosing to serve all children with ASD under the autism category, while others are excluding them from IDEA because they do not fully meet the IDEA definition of autism.†

> † See *Letter to Coe*, 32 IDELR 204 (June 28, 1999), in which ED provided an informal opinion that a child with PDD might be IDEA-eligible under another disability category, such as OHI, if the child did not meet the definition and diagnostic criteria for autism.

Traumatic Brain Injury

The source of controversy in the definition of traumatic brain injury (TBI) is its limitation to an acquired injury caused by "external" physical force (34 C.F.R. § 300.8(c)(12) (2006)). The definition explicitly excludes injuries that are congenital or degenerative, such as those resulting from strokes or induced by birth trauma. OSEP (*Letter to Harrington*, 1993) has explained that its restriction of the definition to externally imposed injuries is consistent with use of the term TBI in professional practice. This raises the question of whether students with nontraumatic brain injuries will be covered under another category of disability. For instance, some students who have contracted central nervous system infections such as meningitis or encephalitis, or who have suffered a stroke, heart attack, or brain tumor may have lasting neurological impairments that do not produce limitations on their strength, vitality, or alertness such that they would qualify as "other health impaired." They also may not fall within any other category, such as intellectual disability or learning disability. Nonetheless, they may have an erratic profile of cognitive strengths and weaknesses that produces a need for special education, yet fall between the cracks and be ineligible for coverage under IDEA. Because the number of children with nontraumatic brain injury is small, the controversy over their inclusion has not garnered widespread visibility. Anecdotal evidence suggests that, in practice, these children are categorized as having TBI or "other health impairment" regardless of whether they technically fit the definition.

Other Health Impairment

The category of other health impairment (OHI) generated some misunderstanding in past years because ED took the position in a 1991 memorandum that the symptoms of ADD/ADHD might qualify a child as "other health impaired." The OHI definition itself, however, referred to limited strength, vitality, or alertness, and many children with ADD/ADHD appear to have heightened rather than limited alertness. Their heightened alertness, however, can create distractibility and inattentiveness to educational tasks. To clarify ED's position, a 1999 regulatory provision (retained in 2006) interpreted limited alertness to include "heightened alertness to environmental stimuli, that results in limited alertness with respect to the educational environment" (34 C.F.R. § 300.8(c)(9) (2006)). To cement the point, ADD and ADHD are included in the regulatory definition of OHI as examples of conditions that can constitute an OHI. In 2006, Tourette syndrome was also added to the examples.

Largely as a result of the inclusion of ADD/ADHD, the number of children served under OHI has grown to over 9 percent of the special education population (ages six to twenty-one), making it the third largest special education category (U.S. Dept. of Education, 2010, Vol. 1, Figure 1-21).† It may be that the decrease in the LD population over the past several years is partially explained by the increase in the OHI category.

> † OSEP does not require a physician's report as part of the ADD/ADHD eligibility determination, but some states do, so readers should consult their own state law on this point. The medical evaluation alone is insufficient, however, as the student's educational needs must be assessed.

Judicial Interpretations

Although numerous cases have arisen in which parents have claimed that their child is eligible under IDEA when an LEA determined otherwise, they mostly are resolved by careful applications of the eligibility criteria. Two categories of disability, however, have generated more complex eligibility issues: multiple profound disabilities and emotional disturbance. These issues are explored next.

Eligibility of Children With Multiple, Profound Disabilities

The best-known federal case testing the IDEA eligibility criteria is that of *Timothy W. v. Rochester, New Hampshire School District* (1989). In *Timothy W.*, the U.S. Court of Appeals for the First Circuit held that eligibility under the Act did not require determination of a child's ability to benefit from special education. In other words, a child's "need" for special education was distinguished from the ability to benefit from it.

Timothy was a child with multiple disabilities, including cerebral palsy, quadriplegia, cortical blindness, and complex developmental disabilities. The school district argued that Timothy's disabilities were so profound that he lacked the ability to benefit from educational services and, therefore, did not need to be served by the educational system. The court ruled, however, that even children with the most profound disabilities were covered under the Act's long-standing "zero-reject" policy and deserved to be given a chance to make progress, regardless of whether they could, in fact, do so (see chapter 10 for a discussion of what kind of progress is required for an appropriate education). Although the decision is binding only in the First Circuit, it has been influential across the country.

Left unanswered by *Timothy W.* was the question of whether, applying the First Circuit's logic, a school must offer sensory stimulation to a comatose child. The Office of Special Education and Rehabilitation Services (OSERS) has since taken an informal position that special education services can be required on a case-by-case basis even for a comatose student (*Letter to Gramm*, 1990).

A Comatose Student's IEP

In *Wenger v. Canastota Central School District*, 961 F. Supp. 416 (N.D. N.Y., 1997), a student injured in an auto accident suffered traumatic brain injury that left him in a so-called persistent vegetative state. The school chose to serve him, but the parents challenged his IEP. The court determined that his IEP provided FAPE. It was designed to encourage responses to visual, auditory, and multisensory stimuli, and to develop a functional range of motion. He received special education services two hours per day, plus thirty minutes per week of speech therapy. He was to receive physical therapy and occupational therapy once a week for eight weeks and then once a month.

Do you think a school district should be required to provide special education and related services (e.g., occupational and physical therapy) to a comatose student? What are the options for the student? What if insurance does not cover these services?

Eligibility on the Basis of Emotional Disturbance

Several controversial decisions have arisen in the context of determinations of eligibility on the basis of emotional disturbance. For instance, a federal district court in the 1990 case of *Doe v. Board of Education of Connecticut* ruled that a violent, depressed student who performed well in school and demonstrated no academic underachievement was not emotionally disturbed, despite evidence of behavior problems in school settings. However, OSEP has made clear its own position that educational performance covers more than just academic performance (*Letter to Lybarger*, 1989).

More recently, in the 2002 decision in *Venus Independent School District v. Daniel*, a federal district court in Texas ruled that although Daniel's academic performance was clearly above average, his significant levels of misbehavior, refusal to do his work, hyperactivity, anxiety, and social interaction problems were adversely affecting his overall educational performance. The court found him IDEA-eligible as a student with both OHI and emotional disturbance.

In a 1998 case, the Second Circuit ruled that a high school student had an emotional disturbance that had been overlooked by the school district. The result was to make her parents eligible for reimbursement of private school costs. The case, *Muller v. Committee on Special Education of the East Islip Union Free School District*, involved an adopted Thai orphan named Treena who had experienced various speech, language, and reading problems during elementary school. She failed multiple subjects in the seventh and eighth grades and exhibited a series of behavior problems in the ninth grade, including cutting classes, failing to complete assignments, staying out late, disobeying her parents, and attempting suicide. She was hospitalized briefly, subsequently treated in a private psychiatric facility, then placed in day treatment, readmitted to the psychiatric facility, and eventually placed in a longer-term residential treatment center and then a private special education school near her home. In between these placements, she was returned to the public school twice, where her behavior each time disintegrated.

During Treena's residential placement, her public school district evaluated her and concluded that she was not IDEA-eligible, primarily because she had been diagnosed as having a conduct disorder and because school personnel thought that her depression was not severe enough to affect her ability to learn or to require special education. Private evaluators at different times throughout this period had diagnosed her variously as having a conduct disorder, oppositional defiant disorder, posttraumatic stress syndrome, and major depression coupled with learning disabilities.

At an administrative hearing, a local hearing officer gave credence to information suggesting that the source of the emotional problems was primarily within the family.† The hearing officer therefore upheld the school district's determination that Treena did not have an emotional disturbance. The state-level review officer likewise concluded that Treena did not meet the eligibility criteria. A federal district court judge overturned these determinations. On appeal, the Second Circuit also rejected the administrative determinations, stating that the source of the emotional problems was irrelevant if it affected the student's ability to learn in school. Ignoring various medical labels that are not part of the definition of emotional disturbance, the court concluded that the student had met the educational definition. She amply demonstrated an inability to learn that was partly caused by emotional problems, and she clearly manifested a pervasive mood of unhappiness, or depression, and a cluster of behaviors that together were inappropriate under normal circumstances. All of these characteristics had been exhibited to a marked degree and over a long period of time. In other words, she demonstrated not just one but three of the five characteristics for eligibility.

> † Is the source of the emotional disability relevant (or should it be) in considering whether a child is eligible for services? If not, why not?

Two additional cases demonstrate conflicting approaches to distinguishing social maladjustment from emotional disturbance, highlighting the definitional dilemma. The court in *A. E. v. Independent School District No. 25* (1991) ruled that a student with a conduct disorder that included poor impulse control, suicidal tendencies, excessive anxiety, and poor student interactions was socially maladjusted rather than emotionally disturbed for purposes of determining whether her suspension was valid. The court upheld the suspension, finding her misbehavior to be unrelated to her previously diagnosed learning disabilities. Another effect of the decision was to deny services addressing her emotional needs and limit her special education services to academic subjects related to her learning disabilities.†

> † Several years later, a provision in the 1999 IDEA regulations (retained in 2006) specified that all aspects of a child's special education needs must be identified, not just those commonly linked to the particular disability category. The implication is that all identified needs should be addressed in the child's IEP, so the outcome in A.E. would appear to no longer be justifiable. See 34 C.F.R. § 300.532(h) (1999) and 34 C.F.R. 300.304(c)(6) (2006).

The characteristics of social maladjustment identified in *A.E.* (impulsivity, suicidal tendencies, anxiety, social deficits) contrast with those in *Springer v. Fairfax County School Board* (1998), which produced a similar but more defensible rejection of eligibility. In *Springer*, a high school student was determined to be a juvenile delinquent with social maladjustment and conduct disorder rather than emotional disturbance. His misbehavior included truancy, drug abuse, and auto theft. Despite failing grades, he scored in the average-to-superior range of intellectual ability on standardized tests. None of the psychologists who evaluated him argued that he had an emotional disturbance. Even the student acknowledged that his academic success or failure depended on his motivation. The court ruled that the student's educational difficulties resulted from his misbehaviors, not vice versa.

What differentiates a social maladjustment from a conduct disorder and a conduct disorder from emotional disturbance, is still subject to debate among professionals (Clarizio, 1992), so it is not surprising that emotional disturbance should be described in different ways in court cases.

Reminders and Tips

1. Only certain disabilities qualify a child for special education under IDEA.

2. Many students at risk for school failure may not be eligible for IDEA services because they do not have a disability, even though they might benefit from special services. Many students at risk should receive early intervening services, and students suspected of having a learning disability should receive general education interventions (such as appropriate instruction in reading, based on elements of effective reading instruction specified in NCLB) to establish whether they, in fact, can respond to sound instruction and do not need to be referred for an IDEA evaluation.

3. No child is eligible without a full initial evaluation.

4. States are allowed to adopt the term developmental delay for use with children ages three through nine, or a subset of that age range. Local school districts can then decide whether to adopt the term for children within that age range.

5. Qualified professionals and the parents determine the child's eligibility.

6. The eligibility team must ensure that the need for special education is not the result of limited English proficiency, lack of appropriate instruction in math, or lack of appropriate instruction in reading.

7. Although OSEP requires school districts to submit the number of IDEA-eligible students by disability category, the category itself is not needed in order to provide services and in no way dictates the student's placement. Instead, placement emerges from development of the student's IEP (see Chapter 7).

8. Eligibility for special education under IDEA can be based on the need for special physical education rather than solely on the need for specially designed academic or behavioral instruction.

Table 5.1.

Definitions of Disability Classifications in 2006 IDEA Regulations

34 C. F. R. § 300.8(c)(2006). Definitions of disability terms. The terms . . . are defined as follows:

(1) (i) *Autism* means a developmental disability significantly affecting verbal and nonverbal communication and social interaction, generally evident before age 3, that adversely affects a child's educational performance. Other characteristics often associated with autism are engagement in repetitive activities and stereotyped movements, resistance to environmental change or change in daily routines, and unusual responses to sensory experiences.

(ii) Autism does not apply if a child's educational performance is adversely affected primarily because the child has an emotional disturbance, as defined in . . . this section.

(iii) A child who manifests the characteristics of "autism" after age 3 could be diagnosed as having "autism" if the criteria in paragraph (c)(1)(i) . . . are satisfied.

(2) *Deaf-blindness* means concomitant hearing and visual impairments, the combination of which causes such severe communication and other developmental and educational needs that they cannot be accommodated in special education programs solely for children with deafness or children with blindness.

(3) *Deafness* means a hearing impairment that is so severe that the child is impaired in processing linguistic information through hearing, with or without amplification, that adversely affects a child's educational performance.

(4) (i) *Emotional disturbance* means a condition exhibiting one or more of the following characteristics over a long period of time and to a marked degree that adversely affects a child's educational performance:

(A) An inability to learn that cannot be explained by intellectual, sensory, or health factors,

(B) An inability to build or maintain satisfactory interpersonal relationships with peers and teachers,

(C) Inappropriate types of behavior or feelings under normal circumstances,

(D) A general pervasive mood of unhappiness or depression,

(E) A tendency to develop physical symptoms or fears associated with personal or school problems.

(ii) Emotional disturbance includes schizophrenia. The term does not apply to children who are socially maladjusted, unless it is determined that they have an emotional disturbance under [subsection (i) above].

(5) *Hearing impairment* means an impairment in hearing, whether permanent or fluctuating, that adversely affects a child's educational performance but that is not included under the definition of deafness in this section.

(6) *Mental retardation* [intellectual disability] means significantly subaverage general intellectual functioning, existing concurrently with deficits in adaptive behavior and manifested during the developmental period, that adversely affects a child's educational performance.

(7) *Multiple disabilities* means concomitant impairments (such as mental retardation-blindness or mental retardation-orthopedic impairment), the combination of which causes such severe educational needs that they cannot be accommodated in special education programs solely for one of the impairments. Multiple disabilities does not include deaf-blindness.

(8) *Orthopedic impairment* means a severe orthopedic impairment that adversely affects a child's educational performance. The term includes impairments caused by congenital anomaly, impairments caused by disease (e.g., poliomyelitis, bone tuberculosis) and impairments from other causes (e.g., cerebral palsy, amputations, and fractures or burns that cause contractures).

(9) *Other health impairment* means having limited strength, vitality or alertness, including a heightened alertness to environmental stimuli, that results in limited alertness with respect to the educational environment, that

(i) Is due to chronic or acute health problems such as asthma, attention deficit disorder or attention deficit hyperactivity disorder, diabetes, epilepsy, a heart condition, hemophilia, lead poisoning, leukemia, nephritis, rheumatic fever, sickle cell anemia, and Tourette syndrome; and

(ii) Adversely affects a child's educational performance.

(10) *Specific learning disability*—(i) *General.* Specific learning disability means a disorder in one or more of the basic psychological processes involved in understanding or in using language, spoken or written, that may manifest itself in the imperfect ability to listen, think, speak, read, write, spell, or do mathematical calculations, including conditions such as perceptual disabilities, brain injury, minimal brain dysfunction, dyslexia, and developmental aphasia.

(ii) *Disorders not included.* Specific learning disability does not include learning problems that are primarily the result of visual, hearing, or motor disabilities, of mental retardation [intellectual disability], of emotional disturbance, or of environmental, cultural, or economic disadvantage.

(11) *Speech or language impairment* means a communication disorder, such as stuttering, impaired articulation, a language impairment, or a voice impairment, that adversely affects a child's educational performance.

(12) *Traumatic brain injury* means an acquired injury to the brain caused by an external physical force, resulting in total or partial functional disability or psychosocial impairment, or both, that adversely affects a child's educational performance. Traumatic brain injury applies to open or closed head injuries resulting in impairments in one or more areas, such as cognition; language; memory; attention; reasoning; abstract thinking; judgment; problem solving; sensory, perceptual, and motor abilities; psychosocial behavior; physical functions; information processing; and speech. Traumatic brain injury does not apply to brain injuries that are congenital or degenerative, or to brain injuries induced by birth trauma.

(13) *Visual impairment including blindness* means an impairment in vision that, even with correction, adversely affects a child's educational performance. The term includes both partial sight and blindness.

↪Review

1. How is eligibility under IDEA determined?

   The student must (a) be evaluated as qualifying under one of the specified categories of disability (or have a developmental delay, if within the eligible age range), (b) need special education, (c) be age-eligible, and (d) not have limited English proficiency or lack of appropriate instruction in math or reading as the determining factor.

2. Which categories of disability account for more than 90 percent of the children served under IDEA?

   Learning disability, speech or language impairment, other health impairment, intellectual disability, and emotional disturbance account for this percentage.

3. Which two disability definitions continue to generate the most controversy?

   Learning disabilities and emotional disturbance remain the most contentious.

⚡References

A. E. v. Indep. Sch. Dist. No. 25, 936 F. 2d 472 (10th Cir. 1991).

American Psychiatric Association. (1994). *Diagnostic and statistical manual of mental disorders* (4th ed). Washington, DC: Author.

Clarizio, H. F. (1992). Social maladjustment and emotional disturbance: Problems and positions. *Psychology in the Schools, 29,* 131–140.

Doe v. Bd. of Educ. of Conn., 753 F. Supp. 65 (D. Conn. 1990).

Fuchs, D., Mock, D., Morgan, P. L., & Young, C. L. (2003). Responsiveness-to-intervention: Definitions, evidence, and implications for the learning disabilities construct. *Learning Disabilities Research and Practice, 18,* 159–171.

Individuals with Disabilities Education Improvement Act, 20 U.S.C. § 1400 *et seq.*(2006).

Individuals with Disabilities Education Improvement Act Regulations, 34 C.F. R. § 300.1 *et seq.* (2006).

Letter to Gramm, 17 EHLR ¶216 (OSERS 1990).

Letter to Harrington, 20 IDELR ¶623 (OSEP 1993).

Letter to Lybarger, 16 EHLR ¶82 (OSEP 1989).

Muller v. Comm. on Special Educ. of East Islip Union Free Sch. Dist., 145 F. 3d 95 (2d Cir. 1998).

No Child Left Behind Act of 2001, 20 U.S.C. § 6301 et seq. (2006).

Springer v. Fairfax Cnty. Sch. Bd., 134 F. 3d 659 (4th Cir. 1998).

Timothy W. v. Rochester (New Hampshire) Sch. Dist., 875 F. 2d 954 (1st Cir. 1989).

U.S. Department of Education, OSERS, OSEP. (1994). *Sixteenth annual report to Congress on the implementation of the Individuals With Disabilities Education Act.* Washington, DC: Author.

U.S. Department of Education, OSERS, OSEP. (2010). *Twenty-ninth annual report to Congress on the Implementation of the Individuals With Disabilities Education Act, 2007*. Vols. 1 & 2. Washington, DC: Author.

Venus Indep. Sch. Dist. v. Daniel, 2002 U.S. Dist. LEXIS 6247 (N.D. Tex. 2002).

⇉Selected Supplementary Resources

Dimoff, J. C. (2003). Comment: The inadequacy of the IDEA in assessing mental health for adolescents: A call for school-based mental health. *DePaul Journal of Health Care Law, 6*, 319–342.

Forness, S. R., & Kavale, K. A. (1997). Defining emotional or behavioral disorders in school and related services. In J. W. Lloyd, E. J. Kameenui, & D. Chard (Eds.), *Issues in educating students with disabilities* (pp. 42-61). Mahwah, NJ: Erlbaum.

Kauffman, J. M. (1999). How we prevent the prevention of emotional and behavioral disorders. *Exceptional Children, 65*, 448–468.

Landrum, T. J., Tankersley, M., & Kauffman, J. M. (2003). What is special about special education for students with emotional or behavioral disorders? *Journal of Special Education, 37*, 148–156.

Vaughan, S., & Fuchs, L. S. (2003). Redefining learning disabilities as inadequate response to instruction: The promise and potential problems. *Learning Disabilities Research and Practice, 18*, 137–146.

Chapter 6

Assessment and Evaluation Requirements Under IDEA

Chapter Outline

Child Find

IDEA requires a state receiving money under IDEA to establish policies and procedures to ensure that all children with disabilities who reside in the state are "identified, located, and evaluated" (20 U.S.C. § 1412(a)(3)(2006)). This provision is referred to as the child find provision. It applies to all children, regardless of the severity of their disability, including children with disabilities who are attending private schools. In the child find requirements, IDEA '04 included children who are homeless or wards of the state. It did not, however, specifically mention migrant children, although the child find obligation that was specified for them in the 1999 regulations still remains in the 2006 regulations (34 C.F.R. § 300.125(a)(2)(1999) and § 300.111(c)(2) (2006)). The regulations also make the point that children suspected of being IDEA-eligible should be evaluated even if they are advancing from grade to grade. For example, social promotions to keep a child with age-appropriate peers do not prevent the need for evaluation and ultimate eligibility. Failure to identify a child as needing an IDEA assessment can result in school district liability (*Compton Unified School District v. Addison*, 2010).†

> † The LEA has appealed the ruling to the U.S. Supreme Court, arguing that the lower court ruling would expose schools to malpractice claims. Two other decisions have found systemic, districtwide child find failures: *DL v. District of Columbia*, 55 IDELR 6 (D.D.C. 2010) (failure of child find at preschool level); and *Jamie S. v. Milwaukee Public Schools*, 519 F. Supp. 2d 870 (E.D. Wis. 2007). All three cases involve potentially significant financial liability for the districts.

The purpose of the child find requirement is to ensure that no child with a disability lacks an opportunity to receive services under IDEA. The child find evaluation requirement is subject, however, to the parental consent provisions discussed below.

Initial Evaluation

An SEA, other state agency, LEA, or a parent may initiate a request for a special education evaluation (20 U.S.C. § 1414(a)(1)(B) (2006)). Evaluation of a child suspected of having a disability is an important part of IDEA because it is the mechanism not only for establishing eligibility for services under the Act but also for determining the nature of needed educational services (20 U.S.C. § 1414(a)(1)(C) (2006)). No initial provision of special education services may occur without a full, individualized evaluation of the student's educational needs (20 U.S.C. § 1414(a)(1)(A) (2006)).

Procedural Requirements

Prior to conducting an IDEA evaluation for special education eligibility, school officials must seek the informed, written consent of the parent. If consent is not obtained, the school can use the IDEA mediation or due process hearing procedures to override lack of parental consent (unless the procedures conflict with state law governing parental consent) (20 U.S.C. § 1414(a)(1)(D) (2006)). In other words, school officials may not act on their own to initially evaluate a student for IDEA eligibility. In deciding whether or not to consent, parents are entitled to descriptions of each evaluation procedure to be used (20 U.S.C. § 1415(c)(1)(B) (2006)). School district failure to provide explanations can be a serious enough legal error to produce liability.†

† In *Holland v. District of Columbia*, 71 F.3d 417 (D.C. Cir. 1995), the D.C. Circuit returned the case to the lower court for a factual determination of whether the school district responded to a reasonable inquiry from the parents about the specific procedures to be included in a "clinical evaluation" of their troubled teenager; if the district did not provide the requested information, then the parents were within their rights in rejecting the evaluation and were entitled to be reimbursed for private school tuition for their daughter.

Schools are required to solicit parental input into the evaluation process because, among other reasons, parents frequently can provide data about the child's developmental history, prior school history, and medical history. Also, when parents are involved in the data collection, they are more likely to be comfortable with the evaluation process. Readers will recall from the previous chapter that after the evaluation data have been gathered, the determination of eligibility is made by a team of qualified professionals and the parent. Together, the qualified professionals and the parent must ensure that the determination is not based on a child's limited English proficiency or lack of appropriate instruction in reading or math (20 U.S.C. § 1414(b)(4) and (5) (2006)). A copy of the evaluation report and the documentation of eligibility must be given to the parent at no cost. (20 U.S.C. § 1414(b)(4)(B) (2006); 34 C.F.R. § 300.306(a)(2) (2006)). Who writes the report is left to the discretion of the educational agency.

IDEA '04 establishes a sixty-day time frame within which an evaluation for eligibility must be completed after parental consent for the initial evaluation has been obtained (20 U.S.C. § 1414(a)(1)(C)(i) (2006)). The time frame applies only to eligibility determinations, not to completion of the determination of all needed services. Perhaps this is because not until the IEP meeting can the determination of needed services be finalized, although obviously evaluation team input about these needs could facilitate the development of the IEP. The 2006 regulations continue the requirement that an IEP meeting be held within thirty days of an eligibility determination and add that the IEP must be implemented as soon as possible after its development (34 C.F.R. § 300.323(c) (2006)). Some states have adopted their own timelines, and these are allowed to override the federal time frame (20 U.S.C. § 1414(a)(1)(C)(i) (2006)).†

† If states have a longer time frame than sixty days, one might question at what point the time frame becomes unreasonable. Exceptions to the federal time frame are also allowed when a student transfers from one school district to another during the evaluation period, provided that the new LEA is making sufficient progress toward completing the evaluation, and the parents and LEA agree on a new deadline. Assessments of such a student are to be coordinated as expeditiously as possible (20 U.S.C. § 1414(a)(1)(C)(ii) and (b)(3)(D) (2006)). A second, more obvious exception is allowed if the parent repeatedly fails or refuses to produce the child for the evaluation.

Sometimes, a school district may not see a need to honor a particular parental request to evaluate his or her child. Yet the district may be hesitant to refuse to evaluate the child for eligibility lest the refusal itself be seen as a violation of IDEA.† In the early 1990s, OSEP interpreted IDEA as not requiring a school to evaluate every student at parental request. Instead, the school may explain, in writing, the reason for believing that the student does not have a disability and does not need an evaluation, thereby meeting the requirement to notify parents when it refuses to perform a requested evaluation (34 C.F.R. § 300.503 (2006)).[1] If the parent disagrees with the school's refusal, the parent may request a due process hearing to contest the school's decision.

---

[1] *Letter to Anonymous*, 21 IDELR 998 (OSEP 1994); see also *Letter to Williams*, 20 IDELR 1210 (OSEP 1993).

† The Supreme Court's 2009 decision in *Forest Grove School District v. T. A.*, 129 S. Ct. 2484 (2009), drives home the need for an accurate evaluation. In *Forest Grove*, parents challenged the school district's evaluation that found their son ineligible for special education. The parents placed their son in private school and sought tuition reimbursement. Even though their son had not received special education services from the school district, the Court held that the parents were entitled to reimbursement because of a flawed evaluation that resulted in no provision of FAPE.

Substantive Requirements

Of what should the actual evaluation consist? The requirements are multifaceted and collectively are meant to constitute an evaluation of the whole child—strengths, weaknesses, and unique needs. If implemented in good faith, the evaluation measures go a long way toward providing the kind of comprehensive assessment envisioned by IDEA. To the extent that any of the requirements is not met, the possibility of error is magnified.

Throughout the entire IDEA '04 evaluation section, the term assessments has replaced the term tests. This may reflect the fact that many schools are placing more and more emphasis on criterion-referenced, curriculum-based assessments that measure what students know in areas of the general curriculum and what they can do functionally and developmentally. Correspondingly, less reliance is being placed on norm-referenced tests. Such tests remain part of the assessment process, but the broader term is preferred and better reflects effective practices in terms of whole-child assessment.

An IDEA evaluation must use a variety of technically sound tools and strategies that assess the relative contribution of cognitive, behavioral, physical, and developmental factors. No single measure is sufficient.† The data generated must include relevant functional, academic, and developmental information, including information provided by the parent. The assessment tools and strategies must assess the child in all areas of suspected disability and provide relevant information on educational needs (20 U.S.C. § 1414(b)(2)(A)-(C) and (b)(3)(B)-(C) (2006)). When appropriate, the initial evaluation data also should include current classroom-based assessments and observations (20 U.S.C. § 1414(c)(1)(a) (2006)).

> † The court in *Bonadonna v. Cooperman*, 619 F. Supp. 401 (D.N.J. 1985), invalidated an IEP because it was developed from a single assessment—evaluation by a teacher.

Assessment materials must be selected and administered so that they are not discriminatory on a racial or cultural basis. They must be valid and reliable for the purposes for which they are used. They must be administered by trained and knowledgeable personnel, and in accordance with the producer's instructions (20 U.S.C. § 1414(b)(3)(A) (2006)). Finally, they must be administered "in the language and form most likely to yield accurate information on what the child knows and can do academically, developmentally, and functionally, unless it is not feasible [to do so]" (20 U.S.C. § 1414(b)(3)(A)(ii) (2006)).

The 2006 regulations clarify the above quote from the statute by adding that evaluation must be in the "*native* language or *other mode of communication* and in the form most likely to yield accurate information" [italics added] unless it is "clearly" not feasible (34 C.F.R. 300.304(c)(1)(ii) (2006)). In both the statute and regulations, what is new is the phrase "in the form most likely to yield accurate information." Among other things, this phrase seems to allow assessment accommodations if necessary to yield accurate information on what the child knows and can do.

The evaluation must be comprehensive enough to identify all of the child's special education and related service needs, even if they are not commonly linked with the child's disability category (34 C.F.R. § 300.304(c)(6) (2006)). School districts that overlook this requirement do so at their peril.

The regulations also state that tests must be selected and administered so as to measure what they purport to measure rather than the child's impaired sensory, manual, or speaking skills, if the intent of the test is not to measure those skills (34 C.F.R. § 300.304(c)(3) (2006)). This awkward phraseology is meant to ensure that any inferences drawn from the test are accurate, and that the test is valid for the purpose for which it was used. For instance, a child with a visual impairment should not be penalized on a reading comprehension test by being asked to read print that is too small for the child to see, nor should a child with handwriting disabilities (for instance, from cerebral palsy) be penalized by having to write the answers if handwriting is not being evaluated. Analogously, a child with a learning disability who has a visual or an auditory processing deficit should be allowed extra time to complete a test, if performance speed is not part of what is being measured. If school officials do not observe this standard, the performance measures will reflect the disability instead of accurately reflecting what the student knows or can do. Indirectly, this regulation is supporting the use of accommodations when assessing students with disabilities.

Additional Regulations for Learning Disability Evaluation

For a student suspected of having a specific learning disability, the 2006 IDEA regulations continue the earlier requirement of additional procedures, including classroom observations of academic performance by a team member other than the child's regular teacher, as well as a written team report that includes minority reports if consensus is not reached. Also, the team of qualified professionals must include a general educator and at least one person qualified to conduct diagnostic examinations of children (such as a school psychologist, speech-language pathologist, or remedial reading teacher) (34 C. F. R. §§ 300.308 and 300.310). These requirements exist for several reasons: the lack of a clear, operational definition of learning disability; congressional fear that students would be overclassified as learning disabled; and parental fear that determinations would be made without the participation of sufficiently knowledgeable individuals.

Misclassification based on race.

Misclassification on the basis of race is a serious issue of real concern to OCR and OSEP. Overrepresentation of minority groups in specific disability categories can be evidence of discrimination, and can result in restricted access to future educational and employment opportunities, especially if students are given less than full access to the general curriculum. African American students, in particular, appear to be significantly overrepresented in special education programs serving students with intellectual disabilities and emotional disturbance.[2]

IDEA attempts to address the issue of racial misclassifications by specifying that assessments and other evaluation materials must be selected and administered so as not to be racially or culturally discriminatory. Who assesses, and what assessments are used, should be carefully considered. The statute amplifies these points in the following ways, restated here for emphasis:

1. Assessments and evaluation materials must be administered by trained and knowledgeable personnel in accordance with the instructions provided by the producer.

---

[2] 20 U.S.C. § 1400(c)(12) (2006) and U.S. Department of Education, OSERS, OSEP (2009).*Twenty-eighth Annual Report to Congress on the Individuals With Disabilities Education Act, 2006. Vol. 1*, Table 1-7. Washington, DC. 2009. See also *Twenty-ninth Annual Report, Vol. 2*, Tables 1-16c and 1-16d.

2. Assessments and evaluation materials must be used for purposes for which they are valid and reliable.

3. Sole use of a general IQ test is prohibited. Multiple measures must be used, and they must address education needs. Therefore, they cannot be limited to tests of cognition only.

These measures emerged partly as a result of an important early federal district court case alleging racial bias in the evaluation of African American students suspected of mental retardation. *Larry P. v. Riles* (1984) preceded P.L. 94-142 and the initial (1977) IDEA regulations, and the federal court decision influenced their development. *Larry P.* was a class action suit originally filed in the northern district of California in 1971. The class was initially limited to African American students in the San Francisco Unified School District who had been classified as educable mentally retarded (EMR) on the basis of standardized intelligence tests. The class was eventually extended to all such students in the State of California. After passage of P.L. 94-142 and Section 504, the claims of racial discrimination under California law and the U.S. Constitution were amended to include these federal statutes.

In 1984, after thirteen long years of litigation, the U.S. Court of Appeals for the Ninth Circuit upheld the decision of the trial court and held that school district overreliance on IQ tests to place African American students in EMR classes violated both IDEA and Section 504. Such overreliance failed to honor the multiple evaluation requirements of both laws. In particular, the defendants failed to establish that the IQ tests were valid for the purpose for which they were used, that is, to accurately establish the general intelligence of African American students believed to have an intellectual disability.

A moratorium on the use of these IQ tests for placement of African American students in EMR classes, or their substantial equivalent, remains in effect in the Ninth Circuit, although a subsequent, expanded moratorium on their use for any special education placements of African American students was lifted in 1994 in *Crawford v. Honig* (1994).

A second case, *PASE v. Hannon* (1980), involved factual circumstances similar to the *Larry P.* case, but the ruling in *PASE* held that the multifaceted evaluation requirements for students with a suspected intellectual disability were being met. In *PASE*, the plaintiff African American students were overrepresented in Chicago classrooms for the educable mentally handicapped (EMH—the equivalent of EMR), and they too alleged racial bias in the use of standardized intelligence tests as a part of the EMH placement process. The evidence presented in *PASE*, however, unlike that in *Larry P.*, tended to show that by the late 1970s the Chicago school district was complying with the multifaceted, multidisciplinary assessment process established under P.L. 94-142. After examining each question on the commonly used intelligence tests, the court concluded that the test scores were unlikely to produce an inaccurate classification when used in conjunction with the other statutorily mandated evaluation procedures.

What both decisions reveal is the necessity of using multiple measures instead of relying solely on an IQ measure in classifying a racial minority student as having an intellectual disability. As mentioned, these views are reflected in the evaluation procedures written into IDEA. Nonetheless, African American students continue to be overrepresented, so the issue remains. IDEA '04 highlights this in the statutory findings section, noting that studies show that schools with predominantly white students and teachers place disproportionately high numbers of their minority students into special education (20 U.S.C. § 1400(12) (2006). The findings also note that the numbers of minority teachers produced by postsecondary institutions are decreasing, and that more opportunities for full participation by minority individuals and organizations (for example, in grants, contracts, and training opportunities) are essential to greater success in educating minority students (20 U.S.C. § 1400(13) (2006). IDEA '04 requires states to report, among other things, the number and percentage of children with disabilities, by race, gender, and ethnicity, who are receiving early intervening services. It also requires LEAs with significant overrepresentation of minority students to reserve 15 percent of their federal allocation to develop comprehensive, coordinated early intervening services to serve children, particularly these children (20 U.S.C. § 1418(a)(1)(B) and (d) (2006)).

Misclassification based on limited English proficiency.

Assessing students with *limited English proficiency* (LEP, the term used in IDEA) is also a special challenge. (The preferred term among educators is *English Language Learners*.) These students represent the fastest-growing population in the nation (20 U.S.C. § 1400(c)(11) (2006)). A proportional number of LEP students (approximately 10 percent) can be expected to have disabilities, yet evidence suggests that, in various situations, they are both overrepresented and underrepresented in the special education population (McCardle, Mele-McCarthy, Cutting, Leio, & D'Emilio, 2005). On the one hand, too many LEP children are vulnerable to being misidentified as children with intellectual disabilities, emotional disabilities, or speech and language impairments. On the other hand, their underachievement is sometimes ignored because it is presumed to be the result of their language difference when an actual disability may also be present.

The LEP Definition in IDEA and NCLB

IDEA uses the broad definition of LEP that is found in NCLB (20 U.S.C. § 7801(25) (2006). The definition includes students ages 3–21 who (a) were not born in the United States, or whose native language is not English, (b) are Native American, Alaska Natives, or natives resident in the outlying areas [i.e., Guam, American Samoa, the Northern Marianas, and the Virgin Islands] and who come from an environment where a language other than English has had a significant impact on the student's level of English language proficiency, or (c) are migratory, whose native language is not English, and who come from an environment where a language other than English is dominant. The student's difficulties in speaking, reading, writing, or understanding English must put the student at risk of not meeting the state's proficiency levels on NCLB assessments or not succeeding in an English-language classroom.

It is worth noting that the American Indian/Alaska Native population has the largest percentage (14.27%) of any ethnic or racial group served in special education programs (U.S. Department of Education, OSERS, OSEP, 2010, Vol. 2, Table 1-18a). In the view of the authors and other observers, the educational needs of this group of students who also are assessed as having high-incidence disabilities (particularly those with learning disabilities, intellectual disabilities, speech/language impairments, and emotional disturbances) have not been given sufficient attention.

The IDEA evaluation procedures attempt to address the problem of language-based misclassification in several ways. If use of a particular intelligence test is not valid for assessing an LEP student, then, of course, an alternative measurement tool should be selected. It should be obvious, for instance, that it is discriminatory to administer an intelligence test in English if English is not the child's native language. For Spanish-speaking children, for example, a validated Spanish version of a standardized IQ test should be used. If a validated native language version is not available, then school officials should consider using nonverbal tests for measures of cognitive and problem-solving ability. Sometimes interpreters have been employed to facilitate the testing process, but this is not considered good practice because use of interpreters has not been validated, and items in translated form may not have the same level of difficulty as the original items in English. Assessing the child's adaptive behavior at home and when interacting with others who speak the child's language can be an alternative means of obtaining crucial information that helps determine whether a child who has LEP also has an intellectual disability.

Especially critical for students who are LEP is the requirement for evaluators to provide and administer all assessments and other evaluation materials "in the native language or mode of communication and in the form most likely to yield accurate information on what the child knows and can do academically, developmentally, and functionally, unless it is clearly not feasible to so provide or administer" (34 C.F.R. § 300.304(c)(1)(ii) (2006)). This wording, similar to wording in NCLB, provides more discretion to evaluators than did the precursor IDEA '97 provision.† One would presume that assessment in the native language would be needed to properly assess intelligence, aptitudes, and developmental and functional skills of an LEP student, but apparently evaluators are free to determine for themselves whether it is better to assess that student's academic achievement in English, the student's native language, or both.†† The 1999 regulations addressed the validity issue by stating that, in evaluating students who are LEP, materials and procedures must measure the extent of any possible disability rather than measuring English language skills (34 C.F.R. § 300.532(a)(2) (1999)). This provision was omitted from the 2006 regulations without explanation.

> † The new provision seems applicable not just to LEP students but also to students with disabilities who need test accommodations to demonstrate what they know academically. It retains its applicability to students who are deaf, and who may need to be assessed in American Sign Language or in a form of signed English in order to demonstrate what they know and can do.

> †† It is pedagogically useful for evaluators to assess the child's proficiency in the language normally used by the child in the home. If the child is old enough, measures of proficiency should assess not only oral fluency but also the child's ability to read, write, and comprehend in his or her native language. If the performance in the native language is satisfactory for the child's age, it tends to indicate that the student does not have a language-based disability. On the other hand, if the child has significant problems processing written and oral language in his or her native language despite developmentally appropriate opportunities in that language, and the child is significantly below grade level in English despite appropriate instruction in English, then the assessment may indicate that the child has a learning or language disability under IDEA.

The 1999 regulations also contained a provision which stated that if an assessor deviated from standard procedures, such as in the method of administration or the qualifications of the person administering the assessment, details of the deviation must be part of the evaluation report [(34 C.F.R. § 300.532(c)(2) (1999)]. Presumably, this allowed the eligibility team to assess the effects of the deviation on the reliability and validity of the assessment. The provision does not appear in the 2006 regulations. The Department of Education stated in its comment and analysis section that this provision was unnecessary because it is standard practice for assessors to describe deviations from standard assessment procedures.

Supreme Court Case on Educational Services for LEP Students

LEP students were the beneficiaries of an important 1974 Supreme Court ruling in *Lau v. Nichols*, 414 U.S. 563. The Court ruled that the San Francisco School District was violating Title VI of the Civil Rights Act of 1964 by not providing meaningful instruction to many of its Chinese students in a language they could understand. The Court stated that "there is no equality of treatment merely by providing students with the same facilities, textbooks, teachers, and curriculum; for students who do not understand English are effectively foreclosed from any meaningful education" (p. 566). *Lau* and federal regulatory guidelines give discretion to school districts as to the methods they use to rectify the language problem, but rectify it they must.

When an LEP child also qualifies for services under IDEA, teachers must consider English language and communication adaptations so that the instruction is understandable and meaningful. Otherwise, the lack of appropriate special education may result in a violation of Title VI as well as a denial of FAPE under IDEA.

Re-evaluation

In IDEA '97, in response to complaints about unnecessary re-evaluations when the IEP team agreed that a child's eligibility had not changed, Congress simplified the re-evaluation process. IDEA '04 extends the simplification. It specifies that a re-evaluation for eligibility will occur no more often than once a year, and no less often than once every three years, unless in either situation the parent and LEA agree otherwise (20 U.S.C. § 1414(a)(2) (2006)). In between these times, a re-evaluation will be performed at the request of the student's parent or teacher, or at the initiative of the LEA: The possibility of evaluation errors or a significant change in a child's needs or performance may dictate a re-evaluation more often than every three years.

Before conducting a re-evaluation, the LEA must seek parental consent. If the parent fails to respond after multiple attempts by the LEA, the LEA can proceed with the re-evaluation if it can demonstrate that it took reasonable measures to seek consent (20 U.S.C. § 1414(c)(3) (2006)). In the 2006 regulations, reasonable measures mean measures that are consistent with those used to obtain parental attendance at IEP meetings—for instance, a record of telephone calls, correspondence, and home visits (34 C.F.R § 300.300(d)(5) (2006)).

When a re-evaluation is initiated, IEP team members and other qualified professionals review existing evaluation data and determine if additional data are needed. If no more data are needed, no further re-evaluation is required unless the parent requests it.

Re-evaluation is required prior to determining that a student no longer needs special education, unless the student is graduating with a regular diploma or has aged out of eligibility. In these two situations, a new, IDEA '04 provision requires the LEA to provide the student with a summary of his or her academic achievement and functional performance, including recommendations on how to further the student's postsecondary goals (20 U.S.C. § 1414(c)(5)(B) (2006)). Such a summary could prove useful to the student in working with postsecondary institutions and social service agencies.

Who Performs the Evaluation?

IDEA does not designate who should perform various evaluation tasks, as long as those who are administering the assessments are trained and knowledgeable, and as long as the IEP team consists of someone qualified to interpret the instructional implications of the evaluation results. If the student is being referred for initial evaluation after experiencing difficulties in the general education classroom, however, the general educator is expected to provide input and to share observations about the child's performance levels in the general curriculum (20 U.S.C. § 1414(c)(1) (2006)).

The special educator is likely to be a participant any time that measures of the child's strengths and weaknesses involve the administration of educational diagnostic assessments. The school psychologist is likely to be involved if measures of general intelligence and social and emotional functioning are indicated. Depending on the child's needs, speech-language therapists, physical therapists, assistive technology specialists, pediatricians, and others with particular expertise may be involved in the evaluation. The point is to take enough care on the evaluation not only to determine eligibility but also to identify the child's specific needs, so that appropriate teaching goals, strategies, and services may be designed. It is likely to be time well spent in the long run.

Assessment Issues That Do Not Involve Eligibility

Continuing Assessment of Progress

Evaluation and re-evaluation of IDEA students are meant to determine student eligibility and special education needs at specific points in time. Assessing and reporting ongoing special education needs and progress, however, are built into the IEP process. These kinds of regular monitoring are not concerned with eligibility but with the student's progress toward his or her special education goals. For instance, IEPs must be reviewed at least annually. Furthermore, during the year, periodic progress reports must be given to parents. The intent of these requirements is not solely to keep parents informed but to allow the IEP team to make changes in the IEP if the student is not making sufficient progress toward the achievement of annual IEP goals. In other words, continuing assessment of progress or lack thereof is built into the IEP requirements. These forms of continuing assessment are discussed more fully in chapter 7.

Alignment With No Child Left Behind Act

Under the NCLB amendments to Title I of ESEA (2006), all students, including students with disabilities, must be tested annually in grades 3–8 and once between grades 10–12. The great majority of special education students are expected to take grade-level achievement tests in reading and language arts, mathematics, and science, with or without accommodations. Like all other students, they are expected to achieve proficiency in these basic academic subjects by the end of the 2013–2014 school year. Each SEA sets its own proficiency standards and its own standards for what constitutes *adequate yearly progress* (AYP) toward proficiency. Achievement scores must be disaggregated within each school by subgroups, and students with disabilities constitute one of the subgroups, as do students with LEP (20 U.S.C. § 6311(b)(3)C) (2006)). IDEA students with LEP must have their academic proficiency levels reported as part of both subgroups. The state standards within a given state are the same for all subgroups. Failure of any ESEA Title I school to reach AYP in any of its subgroups for two consecutive years results in sanctions on the school. The penalties increase if the school does not meet AYP standards in subsequent years.

No Child Left Behind regulations that took effect in January 2004 (34 C.F.R. §§ 200.1, 200.6, and 200.13 (2009)) allow a small number of students with "the most significant cognitive disabilities" to take alternate assessments using **alternate** achievement standards (such as measures of ability that differ in complexity from grade-level standards or that align with general curriculum standards closer to the student's actual ability level). Each SEA sets the criteria for determining which students qualify to take this kind of assessment, and IEP teams actually determine which students will take the assessment. Generally, the needs of these students are extensive, requiring intensive instruction. Student proficiency (or lack thereof) on this alternate assessment must be reported as part of the AYP of all students. The number of scores of these students that can be reported as meeting AYP is capped at 1 percent of the total number of students in the grades assessed (or approximately 9–10 percent of all students with disabilities). For this reason, the regulation is referred to as the *1 percent rule*. If the number of these alternate assessment scores that are at or above proficiency exceeds the cap, the SEA and LEA must determine which scores not to count. At the same time, however, the LEA must inform parents as to their children's actual academic achievement levels, regardless of whether their child's score was reported as meeting AYP.

Under NCLB regulations, states are also allowed to provide alternate assessments for students with disabilities who do not have the most significant cognitive disabilities, but who nonetheless cannot take the general grade-level AYP paper-and-pencil or computer-based assessments, even with accommodations (34 C.F.R. § 200.1(c) (2009)). A student with severe emotional/behavioral difficulties who cannot concentrate during standardized testing situations might be one example of a student who would qualify. Other examples might include a student with multiple physical disabilities who cannot meet the demands of a prolonged test administration, or a student with significant motor disabilities who requires extended periods of time in which to demonstrate what she knows and can do. For such students, portfolios might be an alternative to standardized tests. Although states have been using alternate assessments from the time that IDEA '97 mandated that special education students participate in state and districtwide assessments, only a few states have implemented this option for AYP academic proficiency measures under NCLB.

In response to requests for still more assessment flexibility, another kind of assessment was introduced in a 2007 NCLB regulation. Students with "persistent academic disabilities" may now take assessments based on **modified** achievement standards.[3] Applying the new regulatory standards, SEAs determine the criteria for which students may qualify, while IEP teams select the eligible students. Scores of up to 2% of all students (or close to 20% of students with disabilities) may be reported as proficient on AYP measures under this relaxed standard. This assessment is designed for students who are receiving instruction at the grade level in which they are enrolled but who are progressing at a slower rate than their peers and are not expected to reach grade level. In other words, although the content standards must remain at grade level, the test items for these students can be simplified. Out-of-level tests, however, are prohibited because, by definition, the content of such tests is not at grade level. This new form of assessment is referred to as the *2 percent rule*. Together, the 1% rule and 2% rule will allow the scores of approximately 27-30% of students with disabilities to be reported as proficient using assessments that differ from the regular assessments used for nondisabled students. Arriving at the 2 % figure was based on research estimates rather than "hard" empirical data.†

---

[3] 72 Fed. Reg. 17747 *et seq.*, April 9, 2007; codified at 34 C.F.R. 200.1(e), 200.6, 200.7, 200.13, 200.20(f) & (g) (2009).

† The 2% rule has proved controversial and uneven in its application. Even though, as of 2009-2010, the federal government must approve a State's assessment using modified standards, policy makers and disability advocates have complained about states that continue to game the system. Congressional lawmakers and Department of Education officials are currently preparing to abolish the 2% rule. See Shah, N. (2011, March 9). Overhaul of ESEA could drop option of alternate exams. *Education Week*, p. 1.

Additional flexibility is provided by another revision in the NCLB regulations that relaxes the 95 percent participation requirement for each subgroup of students who are tested.[4] The revised regulation allows states to average the participation rates of each subgroup over either two or three years to offset such problems as unavoidable testing-day absences.

Another element of flexibility is provided by the provision allowing AYP to be met if the percentage of students in any given subgroup who do not meet the state's AYP standard is reduced by 10 percent from the previous year (20 U.S.C. § 6311(b)(2)(I)(i) (2006)). Also, the scores of transient students who are enrolled for less than a full academic year are excluded from the AYP reporting requirements (20 U.S.C. § 6311(b)(3)(C)(xi) (2006)).

IDEA '04 is aligned with the NCLB requirements; IDEA accommodates all three kinds of alternate assessments (20 U.S.C. § 1412(a)(16)(C)(ii) (2006)). Of considerable importance, however, is the fact that NCLB regulations superseded a previous OSEP interpretation that allowed out-of-level testing as an accommodation under IDEA '97 (68 Fed. Reg. 68700 and 68705, Dec. 9, 2003). Under NCLB, out-of-level assessments instead must be counted as alternate assessments and are possible only for students with the most significant cognitive disabilities who are assessed using alternate achievement standards. The impact of the NCLB requirements is to put pressure on IEP teams to try to ensure that most students with disabilities meet the state's grade-level academic proficiency standards (see chapter 7).†

    † Many aspects of NCLB remain controversial, and various states and advocacy groups continue to urge Congress to amend NCLB, or ED to relax its regulatory interpretation, so that SEAs have more flexibility in determining whether LEAs meet AYP. One evidence of the ongoing federalism tension was the suit filed by the National Education Association and representative LEAs challenging enforcement of the accountability standards, on grounds that NCLB is an unfunded mandate and contains a provision exempting states from being required to use their own money to meet the federal standards. See Keller, B. & Sack, J. L. (2006, April 27). Union, states wage frontal attack on NCLB. *Education Week*, p. 1. See also *School District of Pontiac v. Secretary of the U.S. Dep't of Educ.*, 585 F.3d 253 (6th Cir. 2009) upholding the district court's dismissal of the claim that NCLB was an unfunded mandate. The Supreme Court declined to hear the school district's appeal of this decision and also the State of Connecticut's appeal of a similarly adverse ruling in *Connecticut v. Duncan*, 612 F.3d 107 (2nd Cir. 2010).

    Title I of NCLB has received additional money under President Obama's stimulus package adopted by Congress in February 2009. The temporary extra funding for FYs 2009 and 2010 helped to relieve the funding shortages. NCLB was due for reauthorization in 2009 but is still awaiting reauthorization as of this writing. What changes will be made remain to be seen.

---

[4] *Sec'y Paige Issues New Policy for Calculating Participation Rates Under No Child Left Behind*. March 29, 2004. Retrieved March 2011 from http://www2.ed.gov/news/pressreleases/archive/index.html (under Press Releases for March 2004).

Accommodations in State and Districtwide Assessments of Achievement

Under IDEA, special education students must participate in general state and districtwide assessments of achievement, which, as mentioned, now must include measures of AYP toward state-determined proficiency levels in reading, mathematics, and science under NCLB. The intent is to hold LEAs accountable for the achievement of all students, including special education students. If accommodations are necessary to allow students to demonstrate what they know or can do academically and functionally, "appropriate accommodations" must be specified on the IEP and provided (20 U.S.C. § 1414(d)(1)(A)(VI)(aa) (2006)).

A problem that arises in determining appropriate accommodations is differentiating an *accommodation* from a *modification*. These terms have been clearly distinguished definitionally from one another only over the past ten to fifteen years. It is now generally accepted that an accommodation is a change in administration of an assessment (for instance, in presentation, timing, scheduling, location, response mode) that is necessary for the student to participate and demonstrate what he or she knows while the results remain an accurate measure of what the test is intended to measure. Accommodations do not fundamentally alter or lower the test standards.

In contrast, a modification is a change that fundamentally alters what the test is intending to measure and thereby affects the validity of the test results. Modifications are likely to be inappropriate accommodations (labeled *nonstandard accommodations* in some states) although perhaps an IEP team may wish to allow them in nontesting situations. In IDEA '97, the term *modifications* was used with respect to finding ways to allow students to participate in state and districtwide assessments; in IDEA '04, the term *appropriate accommodations* has replaced it.

Test producers are expected to help SEAs and IEP teams determine whether a proposed accommodation will destroy the validity of the test results, and SEAs are required to develop guidelines for the provision of appropriate accommodations (20 U.S.C. § 1412(a)(16)(B) (2006)). Whether a requested accommodation is really a modification depends very much on the test itself. If a test is not measuring speed of performance, then allowing a student to have extended time may be an appropriate accommodation. If visual acuity is not being measured, generating a large-print version of the test may be acceptable. On the other hand, if reading or decoding skills are being tested, reading the selections aloud to the student will be a modification that destroys the validity of the test results, whereas if only listening comprehension is being assessed, reading the test to the student may be an appropriate accommodation. Depending on the purpose of the assessment, other appropriate accommodations could include such things as a separate room or private carrel, extra breaks, an interpreter for a deaf student, and assistive technology devices.

Under IDEA '04, if the IEP team determines that a special education student has certain impediments accompanying the disability that preclude participation in state and districtwide assessments, even with accommodations, the IEP document must indicate why this is so (20 U.S.C. § 1414(d)(1)(A)(i)(VI) (2006)). The IEP team must also select the appropriate type of alternate assessment and explain why its selection is appropriate for the student. The SEA or LEA must develop guidelines for the participation of these children in these alternate forms of assessment (20 U.S.C. § 1412(a)(16)(C) (2006)). Also, the education agency is expected to use "universal design" principles in developing assessments, so that with or without assistive technology, the assessments are accessible to students across a wide variety of functional abilities (20 U.S.C. § 1412(a)(16)(E) and § 1401(35) (2006)).

Finally, the SEA or LEA must make available to the public the number of IDEA students participating in the general assessments and the number participating in alternate assessments. It must also make performance data available, provided that release of the data would be statistically sound, and would protect the confidentiality of the children involved (20 U.S.C. § 1412 (a)(16)(D) (2006)).

High-Stakes Testing

Many schools conduct a special kind of districtwide achievement testing with the intent to determine whether students meet certain standards for high school diplomas or, less often, for promotion or ability grouping. Often in the past called competency-based testing, minimum competency testing, or outcome-based performance testing, it is increasingly referred to as high-stakes testing; the evaluations produce high-stakes consequences for those being tested. They raise questions as to whether or when they discriminate unfairly against students with disabilities. On the one hand, they may discriminate if students with disabilities are not allowed to take the tests and measure themselves against the same standards as students without disabilities. On the other hand, if accommodations to the test-taking procedures are denied, the tests may measure the disability rather than what the student knows in the subject area being tested.

In the past, courts have upheld high-stakes graduation test requirements for students with disabilities, provided that three basic conditions were met: (a) sufficient advance notice was provided to the students, (b) the students were given an adequate opportunity in school to learn the skills being tested, and (c) appropriate testing accommodations were provided to allow the tests to measure what they purported to measure and not the disability, if the disability was not meant to be measured.†

> † Two of the most important, early competency-based testing cases were *Debra P. v. Turlington*, 564 F. Supp. 177 (M.D. Fla. 1983), aff'd, 730 F.2d 1405 (11th Cir. 1984), which required that the tests have instructional validity for all students, and *Brookhart v. Illinois State Board of Education*, 697 F.2d 179 (7th Cir. 1983), which required test modifications or accommodations, in appropriate circumstances, for students with disabilities.

In recent years, advocacy groups for students with disabilities have challenged the accommodations provided on high-stakes graduation tests in Indiana, Oregon, California, and Alaska. They have also challenged the validity of standardized assessments for some students. In *Rene v. Reed* (2001), the Indiana graduation qualification examination (GQE) withstood a claim that it violated IDEA by not providing certain testing accommodations for students with disabilities. An Indiana appellate court upheld a lower court ruling which concluded that the state did not have to permit all IEP-based accommodations on the test. The state allowed certain accommodations (such as oral or sign language responses, questions in Braille, special lighting or furniture, enlarged answer sheets, individual or small-group testing), and disallowed others (such as reading the questions to a student on a reading comprehension test, allowing unlimited time to complete test sections, allowing responses in other than English, and reducing the complexity of the directions on test questions). The Indiana Supreme Court declined to hear the case on appeal.

In a similar suit, the Oregon Department of Education agreed to settle a class action brought by a disabilities advocacy group on behalf of students with disabilities.[5] A blue-ribbon panel of national testing experts found that Oregon's list of acceptable accommodations did not allow a broad enough range of accommodations for individual students with disabilities to demonstrate what they knew. As a result of the panel's recommendations, the Oregon Department of Education agreed to expand the available options to IEP-based accommodations (such as use of a spell-checker on handwritten essay tests) unless the state could prove that their use invalidated the test results.

A subsequent case in California, *Chapman v. California Department of Education* (2002) resulted in a preliminary injunction that prevented the state from disallowing accommodations specified in the IEPs of students with disabilities. On appeal, the Ninth Circuit affirmed that portion of the injunction but reversed the portion that would have prevented the state from denying a waiver of the graduation requirement. The court concluded that the waiver issue was premature ("not currently ripe for adjudication") because denial of diplomas represented only potential future harm, not yet actual harm. Issues about alternate assessment were also deemed premature (*Smiley v. Caifornia Department of Education*, 2002).

Finally, in 2004, Alaska settled a class action lawsuit similar to the ones filed in Oregon and California (*Noon v. Alaska State Board of Education.*, 2004). The settlement allows high school students with disabilities to use a broader set of accommodations (such as word processors and calculators, dictionaries, and computerized spell-checkers) on the state's mandatory graduation exam although LEAs retain the right to deny a request on a case-by-case basis. Modifications may also be allowed on a graduation exam, subject to SEA approval. A nonstandardized assessment such as a portfolio or a system of individualized assessment is also a possibility for students with severe physical or emotional problems who are working near grade level, but who cannot demonstrate proficiency on a standardized assessment for specific reasons related to the disability.

All these lawsuits demonstrate the desire by parents of students with disabilities that their children be able to earn a high school diploma rather than a certificate of completion. The big issue is determination of which accommodations and modifications level the playing field, and which give an unfair advantage to students with disabilities—an advantage that is not provided to students without disabilities. The issue remains contentious.

↳Reminders and Tips

1. Base the evaluation for eligibility on multiple measures of educational need, and assess both the student's abilities and disabilities.

2. Be familiar with the validity and reliability measures of standardized assessment instruments and use those instruments only for the purposes for which they were intended.

3. Consider the need for testing accommodations to ensure that assessments measure what they are supposed to measure and not the disability. At the same time, be sure that any individual accommodations do not destroy the validity of the test score.

---

[5] *A.S.K. v. Oregon St. Bd of Educ.* (settled 1999). See Fine, L. (2001). Oregon special needs students to get testing assistance. *Education Week, 20*(22), 5.

4. Be sensitive to the possibilities of racial, cultural, and language-based discrimination in all assessments, and select and administer them so that they do not unfairly discriminate on the basis of race, ethnicity, or national origin. Introduce assessments that will distinguish a disability from LEP or racial and cultural difference. Misclassifications based on flawed evaluations can have serious legal consequences under both special education law and civil rights laws.

5. Remember that assessment of student needs is ongoing and not limited to initial evaluation and formal re-evaluation. It is difficult to program effectively for a special education student if good measures of the student's current levels of performance, and the student's strengths and weaknesses, are not available. Making time for accurate and continuing assessment enables good programming to follow. In other words, evaluation should drive the programming.

⟲ Review

1. What is the meaning of the child find requirement?

   Child find requires each state education agency to ensure that all age-eligible children with disabilities who reside within the state are identified, located, and evaluated, whether in public or private school settings.

2. How extensive are the IDEA evaluation requirements? Describe their components.

   The requirements are very extensive. They require that assessments or tests (a) be valid for the purpose used; (b) be administered by trained personnel in accordance with instructions provided by the test producer; (c) measure what they purport to measure and not the child's impaired sensory, manual, or speaking skills (unless those are factors the test purports to measure); and (d) measure specific areas of educational need and not merely a single general intelligence quotient (IQ). In addition, the evaluation requires (e) functional, academic, and developmental information, including information provided by the parent; and (f) assessment in all areas of suspected disability. The evaluation regulations provide ways to avoid racial, cultural, and language-based discrimination; encourage classroom-based assessments and teacher observations; and specify additional requirements for evaluation of a learning disability.

3. What are the re-evaluation requirements?

   A re-evaluation for eligibility must occur no more often than once a year but at least once every three years unless the parent and LEA agree otherwise. Especially if eligibility is not in question, the re-evaluation can be limited to examination of existing data to determine if additional data are needed. If no more data are required, the re-evaluation can conclude unless the parent requests more.

   Re-evaluation is required prior to determining that a student no longer needs special education, unless the student is graduating with a regular diploma or has aged out of eligibility.

4. What are the two principal forms of alternate assessment allowed under NCLB and IDEA?

   They are (a) alternate assessment using alternate achievement standards, and (b) alternate assessment using modified achievement standards. Each must be aligned or linked with the general curriculum, but using alternate achievement standards allows assessment that varies significantly from the actual grade-level content. Assessment using modified achievement standards retains grade-level content but at a simpler, more basic level.

⚡References

Chapman v. Cal. Dep't.of Educ., 220 F. Supp. 2d 981 (N.D. Cal. 2002).

Compton Unified Sch. Dist. v. Addison, 598 F.3d 1181 (9th Cir. 2010).

Crawford v. Honig, 37 F.3d 485 (9th Cir. 1994).

DL v. Dist. of Columbia, 55 IDELR 6 (D.D.C. 2010).

Individuals with Disabilities Education Improvement Act, 20 U.S.C. § 1400 *et seq.* (2006).

Individuals with Disabilities Education Improvement Act Regulations, 34 C.F. R. Part 300 (2006).

Jamie S. v. Milwaukee Pub. Sch, 519 F. Supp. 2d 870 (E.D. Wis. 2007).

Larry P. v. Riles, 793 F.2d 969 (9th Cir. 1984).

Letter to Anonymous, 21 IDELR 998 (OSEP 1994).

Letter to Williams, 20 IDELR 1210 (OSEP 1993).

McCardle, P., Mele-McCarthy, J., Cutting, L., Leos, K., & D'Emilio, T. (2005). Learning disabilities in English language learners: Identifying the issues. *Learning Disabilities Research and Practice, 20(1),* 1–5.

No Child Left Behind Act of 2001, 20 U.S.C. § 6301 *et seq.* (2006).

No Child Left Behind Act, Title I Regulations, 34 C.F.R. Part 200 (2009).

Noon v. Alaska St. Bd. of Educ., Case No. A04-0057 CV (JKS) Settlement Agreement (approved by the court, September 2004).

Pase v. Hannon, 506 F. Supp. 831 (N.D. Ill. 1980).

Rene v. Reed, 751 N.E.2d 736 (Ind. Ct. App. 2001).

Smiley v. Cal. Dep't of Educ., 2002 U.S. App. LEXIS, 18466 (9th Cir. 2002).

U.S. Department of Education, OSERS, OSEP. (2009). *Twenty-eighth annual report to Congress on the Individuals With Disabilities Education Act,* 2006. Washington, DC: Author.

U.S. Department of Education, OSERS, OSEP. (2010). *Twenty-ninth annual report to Congress on the Implementation of the Individuals With Disabilities Education Act,* 2007. Vols. 1 & 2. Washington, DC: Author.

⇥Selected Supplementary Resources

Aitken, A. A. (2004). A high stakes mistake: Ignoring the IEP team's recommendations in implementing California's high school exit exams. *Hastings Race and Poverty Law Journal, 2*, 107.

Artiles, A. J., & Zamora-Duran, G. (1997). *Reducing disproportionate representation of culturally diverse students in special and gifted education.* Reston, VA: Council for Exceptional Children.

Browder, D. M., Spooner, F., Algozzine, R., Ahlgrim-Delzell, L., Flowers, C., & Karvonen, M. (2003). What we know and need to know about alternate assessment. *Exceptional Children, 70,* 45–61.

Hosp, J. L., & Reschly, D. J. (2003). Disproportionate representation of minority students in special education: Academic, demographic, and economic predictors. *Exceptional Children, 70,* 185–199.

Huefner, D. S., & Gardner, A. E. (2007). Alternate assessments for students with disabilities: How much do we know about implementing the NCLB and IDEA rules? In S.A. Meyerowitz & J. Ortman [Eds], *Current developments in K-12 education: Near and longer term trends* (pp.83-107). Washington, DC: Thompson.

MacArdy, A. (2008). Note: *James S. v. Milwaukee Public Schools*: Systemic challenges cause systemic violations of the IDEA. *Marquette Law Review, 92*, 857-888.

Morrison, C. M. (2000). High-stakes tests and students with disabilities. *Boston College Law Review, 41,* 1139–1173.

O'Neill, P. T. (2003). High stakes testing law and litigation. *Brigham Young University Education and Law Journal, 2003*(2), 623–662.

Rowe, J. (2004). High school exit exams meet IDEA: An examination of the history, legal ramifications, and implications for local school administrators and teachers. *Brigham Young University Education and Law Journal, 2004*(1), 75–137.

Thurlow, M. L., Elliott, J. L., & Ysseldyke, J. E. (1998). *Testing students with disabilities.* Thousand Oaks, CA: Corwin Press.

Wagner, R. K., Francis, D. J., & Morris, R. D. (2005). Identifying English language learners with learning disabilities: Key challenges and possible approaches. *Learning Disabilities Research and Practice, 20*(1), 6–15.

Zatta, M. C., & Pullin, D. C. (2004). *Education and alternate assessment for students with significant cognitive disabilities.* Education Policy Analysis Archives, 12(16). Retrieved March 2011 from http://epaa.asu/ojs/issue/archive.

Chapter 7

Individualized Education Programs Under IDEA

Chapter Outline

Purposes of the IEP

An individualized education program (IEP) for each eligible child with a disability is at the heart of IDEA. An IEP serves multiple purposes: It is the primary tool for individualizing services for each eligible child, and it commits resources on behalf of the child. It is also the key mechanism for gaining participation by parents in the development of the child's specially designed instruction and provides an important opportunity for resolving disagreements between home and school. In addition, it provides a means to both monitor the delivery of special education and evaluate its effectiveness.

The IEP Team

Development of the IEP is a team effort, requiring both a meeting and the production of a written document; neither without the other is sufficient. The meeting must be held at least annually, and the IEP document must be in effect for each eligible child by the beginning of each school year (20 U.S.C. § 1414(d)(2) (2006)). Team development of the child's special education, related services, supplementary aids and services, program modifications, and teacher supports helps to ensure effective implementation of the IEP by all those with key roles to play.

Under IDEA, the IEP team consists of at least one special educator (or special education provider, if appropriate)[†] and at least one "regular" education teacher of the child,[††] "if the child is, or may be, participating in the regular education environment."(20 U.S.C. § 1414(d)(1)(B) (2006)). If the child receives instruction in multiple general education classrooms, the LEA may select which of the child's teachers will serve on the IEP team.[†††] The team also includes the parent(s); a representative of the LEA; an individual who can interpret the instructional implications of the evaluation results; the child, when appropriate; and, at the discretion of the parent or agency, others who have knowledge or special expertise regarding the child (20 U.S.C. § 1414(d)(1)(B) (2006)). When a child who was receiving services under IDEA Part C transitions to Part B, the Part C service coordinator or other representative must also be invited to attend the initial IEP meeting, if the parent so requests (20 U.S.C. § 1414(d)(1)(D) (2006)).

> [†] In the Analysis of Comments and Changes following the 2006 regulations, OSEP stated that the special education teacher or provider "should be the person who is, or will be, responsible for implementing the IEP." (42 Fed. Reg. 46670, August 14, 2006). The likeliest situation in which a provider is not a special education teacher is where a speech-language pathologist is the provider of special services, and the child does not receive special instruction from a special education teacher as such.

> [††] IDEA '04 refers to the term "regular educator," but special educators prefer the term "general educator" because the term regular educator can be read to imply that special educators are irregular educators, a conclusion they reject. We use the terms interchangeably.

> [†††] In *Shapiro v. Paradise Valley Unified School District*, 317 F.3d 1072 (9th Cir. 2003), the court held that because of the IDEA '97 requirement that the child's teacher (not a teacher) be present at the IEP meeting, the presence of the child's private school teacher was required at the public school IEP meeting.

In addition, the regulations require that each of the child's teachers or service providers have access to the IEP if he or she has any responsibility for its implementation (34 C.F.R. § 300.323(d) (2006)). This is particularly relevant to secondary school teachers because one general educator on the IEP team can represent all the others, and can obligate them to various program modifications and supplementary aids and services.

The General Educator

A general educator was first added to the IEP team under IDEA '97, reflecting the fact that the overwhelming majority of children with disabilities spend considerable time in the general education classroom. The general educator should be someone responsible for implementing, in part or whole, the portion of the child's IEP that relates to the general classroom. Therefore, she or he is meant to be an important player in helping the child to meet IEP goals and receive effective services in that environment. For instance, general educators are expected to be able to suggest appropriate positive behavioral interventions and supports, supplementary aids and services, program modifications, and necessary supports for school personnel (20 U.S.C. § 1414(d)(3)(C) (2006)).Their understanding of the general curriculum can also be invaluable, as can the data and observations they collect on the child's progress in the general curriculum.

Though admirable in intent, the need to include a general educator on the IEP team has generated considerable concern about increased burdens on general classroom teachers. To address this concern, IDEA '04 added three provisions. First, required school members of the IEP team can be excused from the IEP meeting if the member's area of the curriculum (or related services) will not be under discussion. The parent and LEA, however, must agree in writing to the excusal. If, however, the absent member's area of the curriculum (or related services) is to be discussed, the parent and LEA must consent in writing (not simply agree) to the excusal.† When excused, the team member still must submit written input prior to the meeting (20 U.S.C. § 1414(d)(1)(C) (2006); 34 C.F.R. § 300.321(e) (2006)). Finally, the general educator can be excused or exempted from participation in the review and revision of the IEP under the same conditions (20 U.S.C. § 1414(d) (2006)).

> † Consent requires that the parent be fully informed of the implications of the consent, whereas an agreement is, more simply, an "understanding." (See OSEP Analysis of Comments and Changes, 71 Fed. Reg. 46673, Aug. 14, 2006).

Other Nonparent Team Members

The special educator or special education provider is an indispensable member of the IEP team. Usually, that person is expected to conduct the meeting and facilitate resolution of any issues that arise. The special educator should be prepared to explain and interpret IDEA to those who have questions about it, to obtain parental input, and to be completely conversant with the required contents of an IEP.

The LEA representative must be someone who is knowledgeable not only about the availability of district resources but also about the general curriculum. In addition, the representative must be qualified to either "provide or supervise the provision of" special education (20 U.S.C. § 1414(d)(1)(B) (2006)). This statutory language is more flexible than regulatory language prior to IDEA '97; that is, the LEA representative no longer need be a supervisor of the provision of special education.

In other words, a key administrator like the principal need not participate in the IEP meeting as long as a provider of special education knows the general curriculum and the availability of district resources.†

> † Nonetheless, if the LEA representative is not a key administrator, OSEP has indicated that he or she must have the authority to "commit" district resources and be able to ensure that whatever services are listed in the IEP will be provided (OSEP Analysis of Comments and Changes, 71 Fed. Reg. 46670, August 14, 2006).

The IEP team must also include an individual who can interpret the instructional implications of evaluation results. Prior to 1997, the law required the presence of such an individual only during the initial IEP meeting. Now the individual's attendance is required at each IEP meeting. This individual could be someone already on the team, such as the general or special education teacher, or it could be someone else, such as the school psychologist.

At the discretion of the parent or the school district, the IEP team may also include others who have "knowledge or special expertise" regarding the child. The regulations interpret this to mean that whoever (parent or LEA) invites the person to join the IEP team makes the determination that the person has the requisite knowledge or special expertise (34 C.F.R. § 300.321(c) (2006)). In the case of the LEA, related service providers come immediately to mind. In the case of a parent, an independent evaluator comes to mind, or someone else who has studied the disability or knows the child well.

In IEP meetings with complex educational and support service requirements, staff from mental health, social service, or vocational rehabilitation agencies may need to attend. When transition planning or transition services are involved, representatives of other agencies participating in the planning or helping to pay for services should be invited to attend. According to the 2006 regulations, however, the invitation to participate must have the consent of the parents (or a child who has reached the age of majority) (34 C.F.R. § 300.321(b)(3) (2006)). The stated reason is to honor the confidentiality and privacy requirements of IDEA. By this stage, if not sooner, the student must also be invited to attend to help develop IEP goals and transition services. If the student does not attend, the team nonetheless must consider the student's preferences and interests (34 C.F.R. § 300.321(b)(2) (2006)).

Parent Participation in the IEP Process

The regulations require that one or both parents† be invited to attend each IEP meeting, and the meeting must be held at a mutually convenient time and place for parents and school personnel. Moreover, the parents must be notified in advance as to who will be attending, at least by role. If neither parent can attend, then school officials must use other methods to include them, such as telephone conference calls. Only when multiple documented attempts to involve the parents have failed may the school proceed to develop an IEP on its own (34 C.F.R. § 300.322(d) (2006)).

> † The term parent is defined in IDEA to include any of the following: a biological or adoptive parent, a guardian generally authorized to act as the child's parent or authorized to make educational decisions for the child, an individual acting in the place of a biological or adoptive parent (such as a grandparent, stepparent, or other relative with whom the child lives), an individual who is legally responsible for the child's welfare, a foster parent (unless prohibited under state law or contractual obligations), or an individual assigned to be a surrogate parent when the parents are unknown or cannot be located, or the child is a ward of the state (20 U.S.C. § 1401(23) (2006)). A biological or adoptive parent will be presumed to be the parent unless deprived of legal authority to make educational decisions for the child. If a judicial decree identifies one of

the above persons as the "parent," then a challenge to that person's authority will not succeed. See 34 C.F.R. 300.30(b)(1) and (b)(2) (2006). Presumably, the language about the guardian excludes a guardian ad litem.

Parents must be given a copy of their child's IEP at no cost (34 C.F.R. § 300.322(f) (2006)). Although this is a regulatory addition, a provision in IDEA '04 states that if the IEP is amended, the parent must be given an amended copy upon request (20 U.S.C. § 1414(d)(3)(F) (2006)). (This would be a good practice even without the parent's request.) Additionally, the regulations state that school officials must make sure that parents understand what is happening at the IEP meeting.† This may mean arranging for an interpreter for parents who are deaf or for whom English is not the native language (34 C.F.R. § 300.322(e) (2006)).

† Compare this requirement with the decision in *Rothschild v. Grottenthaler*, 907 F.2d 286 (2d Cir. 1990), in which the court held that failure to provide an interpreter for deaf parents at parent-teacher meetings concerning academic or disciplinary aspects of the child's education violated Section 504.

It's Risky Not to Engage Parents as Partners

In *W. G. v. Target Range School District No. 23*, 960 F. 2d 1479 (9th Cir. 1992), the LEA made a number of mistakes. First, it overlooked the learning disability of the plaintiff's fifth-grade son, attributing the boy's school problems to poor attention, forgetfulness, and behavior problems. It then rejected an independent educational evaluation that identified the learning disability. In response, the parents placed their son in a private school. Ultimately, the LEA agreed to develop an IEP in conjunction with the private school, but when private school representatives could not make the meeting, the LEA proceeded to develop the IEP without the participation of the boy's general education teacher or any other representative of the private school. The court decision indicates that the LEA took a firm position in support of the Scott-Foresman reading program and refused to budge. After the meeting stalled, the LEA did not attempt to convene another meeting for five months.

The U.S. Court of Appeals for the Ninth Circuit was extremely critical of the public school for failing to consider the recommendations of a knowledgeable teacher, other private school representatives, and the parents. Because the IEP had not been developed correctly and was incomplete, the court awarded reimbursement to the parents for the private tutoring they arranged for their son during the 1987–1988 school year. This is the kind of problem that should not and need not develop if a school understands the IEP requirements.

Contents of the IEP

IDEA specifies what is to be included in an IEP (20 U.S.C. § 1414(d)(1)(A)(i) (2006)). The **initial** component is a description of the child's *present levels of academic achievement and functional performance*. The substitution of *academic achievement* for the earlier term *educational performance* reflects the heightened emphasis on academic proficiency in NCLB and IDEA '04. Present levels of achievement and performance should emerge from the multifaceted, nondiscriminatory evaluation of the whole child (see chapter 6).† The child's disability classification alone provides insufficient information, however, and, in fact, IDEA does not require its inclusion on the IEP although some states may choose to include it.

> † If the parents bring an independent educational evaluation (IEE) to the school, the regulations specify that the school must consider that evaluation in decisions affecting the provision of FAPE (34 C.F.R. § 300.502(c)(1) (2006)). If the school rejects the IEE results, it should have a sound basis for doing so, such as superior documentation of its own, or the fact that the IEE conflicts with LEA evaluation and eligibility criteria.

Under IDEA, the statement of the child's present levels of achievement and performance must include how the child's disability affects the child's "involvement and progress in the general education curriculum" (20 U.S.C. § 1414(d)(1)(A)(i) (2006)).† Lawmakers became convinced by the time of IDEA '97 that the expectations for children with disabilities were too low, and IDEA '04 reflects the same conviction. Although the term general education curriculum is not defined in the statute, the regulations explain that it is "the same curriculum as for nondisabled children" (34 C.F.R. § 300.320(a)(1)(i) (2006)). In short, it is what all children study, not some specialized curriculum for special education students.

> † For preschoolers, the IEP can describe how the disability affects the child's participation in "appropriate activities" rather than the general curriculum. An IFSP is permitted to serve as the IEP, if consistent with state policy, if agreed to by the parents and education agency, and if the parent gives written consent (34 C.F.R. 300.323(b) (2006)). The IFSP, however, must have been developed according to IEP procedures and contain an educational component that addresses school readiness and preliteracy, language, and numeracy skills.

After the description of a child's present levels of academic achievement and functional performance, the **second** component of the IEP document is a statement of *measurable annual goals*. The IDEA '97 requirement to include benchmarks (major milestones) or intermediate short-term objectives† has been eliminated except for those children who take alternate assessments aligned to alternate achievement standards (see chapter 6) (20 U.S.C. § 1414(d)(1)(A)(i)(I)(cc) (2006)). This is one way in which Congress intended to reduce the paperwork burdens on LEAs. On the other hand, paperwork may be increased by the requirement that the annual goals must include academic goals to enable the child to progress in the general curriculum, no matter how severe the disability. Focusing on academic goals is congruent with NCLB expectations that all children will reach levels of academic proficiency defined by each state. The goals, however, must also address each of the child's other educational needs arising from the disability. In other words, important needs independent of achievement in the general curriculum must not be forgotten.

† In 1999, OSEP indicated that benchmarks measure the amount of progress a child is expected to make within specified segments of the year, while objectives generally divide skills described in an annual goal into discrete components (34 C.F.R. Part 300, app. A at question 1). Objectives or benchmarks may need to continue as ways to measure progress, even if not included in the IEP. In its Analysis of Comments and Changes accompanying the final 2006 regulations, OSEP stated its belief that a state could continue to require short-term objectives or benchmarks if it so chose (71 Fed. Reg. 46663, August 14, 2006). According to a survey for Project Forum, 12 of 39 reporting states were still requiring such measures of student progress in 2008 (Burdette, 2009). Retrieved May 2011 from http://www.projectforum.org/docs/StateTrackingtoMeasureStudentProgressTowardIEPGoals.pdf

The **third** component of the IEP is a description of *how the child's progress toward meeting the annual goals will be measured and when periodic reports on that progress will be provided*. In the 2006 regulations, OSEP removed the requirement that parents be informed, at least as often as parents of other children, of their child's actual progress (34 C.F.R. § 300.320(a)(3)(ii)). However, the new wording still mentions that districts could provide "quarterly or other periodic reports, *concurrent with the issuance of report cards*" [italics added] to inform parents of their child's progress toward goals.

Under the new requirements, parents may feel that they are less informed or informed less often about the actual extent of progress being made relative to the goals. Of course, if a student's progress is poor, good pedagogy would dictate revisions to IEP goals or services (or teaching methods and materials). IEPs that stay the same from year to year are particularly suspect.

The **fourth** component of the IEP requires a statement of the specific special education and related services, the supplementary aids and services,† and the program modifications or supports for school personnel that are needed to help the child (a) achieve his or her annual goals, (b) make progress in the general curriculum, (c) participate in extracurricular and other nonacademic activities, and (d) participate with children without disabilities, as well as children with disabilities, in all these activities. New language adds that the special education, related services, and supplementary aids and services are to be "based on peer-reviewed research to the extent practicable" (20 U.S.C. § 1414(d)(1)(A)(i)(IV) (2006)). This addition reflects the NCLB (2006) focus on instructional techniques that are based on empirically validated research.

† The regulations list instruction in a resource room as an example of a supplementary service provided in conjunction with regular class placement (34 C.F.R. § 300.115(b)(2) (2006)). This language indicates that a resource room placement that accompanies a regular classroom placement does not constitute a removal from the regular educational environment. See also § 300.114(b)(2) and Chapter 12.

The **fifth** component of *the IEP continues to require an explanation of the extent to which the child will not be participating in the regular class and in extracurricular and nonacademic activities with children who do not have disabilities*. Prior to IDEA '97, the requirement was the reverse: the IEP had to state "the extent that the child will be able to participate in regular educational programs" (20 U.S.C. § 1401(20) (1994)). The change enhanced the legal support for a philosophy of including children with disabilities in general classrooms. It means that when a dispute arises with respect to an IEP or placement, the school district's burden of producing evidence has shifted from one of showing when the child can participate to one of showing when the child cannot participate in general education activities. The shift is legally significant and creates a presumption against pullout programs. The presumption can be rebutted, however, when a separate setting is required for FAPE, or to deliver a related service (such as one-on-one speech therapy in a quiet space, or orientation and mobility training out in the neighborhood).

The **sixth** component of the IEP under IDEA '04 is a statement of *individual appropriate accommodations that are necessary to measure the academic achievement and functional performance of the child on state and districtwide assessments*. IDEA '04 substitutes the term *appropriate accommodations* for the term *modifications* used in IDEA '97, recognizing that accommodations can be provided to allow the student to demonstrate what he or she knows, but that modifications invalidate the results. If the IEP team determines that the child will take an alternate assessment, the IEP must contain a statement explaining *why the child cannot participate in the regular assessment, and why the particular alternate assessment selected is appropriate for the child*. These provisions are consistent with NCLB, which also allows alternate assessments for children who cannot participate in the general assessments, even with accommodations. The intent of these provisions is to ensure that schools are accountable for the achievement levels of all their students,† not solely general education students (see chapter 6).

> † Children with disabilities who are convicted as adults under state law and jailed in adult prisons are not required to participate in the state and districtwide assessments (20 U.S.C. 1414(d)(7) (2006)).

The *anticipated frequency, duration (including projected starting date), and location of the services and modifications* is the **seventh** component of the IEP. IDEA includes location as a requirement, probably as a way to monitor whether related services are being provided in the general education setting. This increases the pressure to provide related services in a location that does not significantly reduce the child's ability to participate in the general classroom and the general curriculum.

The **eighth** and final component of the IEP deals with transition to postsecondary life. By the time the student has reached the age of sixteen, the first IEP then in effect must contain a statement of *appropriate measurable postsecondary goals based upon age-appropriate transition assessments*. The IEP must also contain the *transition services (including courses of study)* needed to help the student reach those goals.† IDEA '04 eliminated the previous requirement for a statement in the IEP of transition service "needs" at the age of fourteen. The difference between transition needs at fourteen and needed transition services at sixteen proved clumsy, but there is no reason why transition planning cannot occur earlier, if appropriate. The student must be invited to attend each IEP meeting where postsecondary goals will be addressed, and if the student is absent, his or her preferences and interests must be ascertained and considered. The IEP still must contain advance notice of the rights that will transfer to the student at the age of majority under state law.

> † Transition goals and services are not required for children who are convicted as adults under state law and confined to adult prisons if they will age out of eligibility before they are eligible for release. This provision is unsatisfactory to some parent groups because, arguably, transition goals and services are particularly important to reduce the risk of re-entry of young adults into the prison population. Other parts of the IEP may be modified too for a demonstrated bona fide security reason (20 U.S.C. § 1414(d)(7)(A) and (B) (2006)).

Postsecondary outcomes, although improving, are still poor for many children with disabilities, and IDEA expects schools to do a better job of preparing these children for further education, employment, and independent living (20 U.S.C. § 1401(d)(1)(A) (2006)). The postsecondary world includes a range of possible pursuits, and transition services are to focus on improving the student's academic and functional achievement to facilitate movement into such postschool activities as postsecondary education, vocational training, integrated employment (including supported employment), continuing and adult education, adult services, independent living, and community participation (20 U.S.C. § 1402(34) (2006)).† As mentioned in an earlier chapter, an IDEA '04 provision specifies that when a student graduates with a regular diploma or exceeds the age eligibility limits for FAPE, the LEA must provide the student with a summary of the student's academic achievement and functional performance. The summary must include recommendations on how the student can be assisted in meeting his or her postsecondary goals (20 U.S.C. § 1414(c)(5) (B) (2006)). This new provision is intended to facilitate transition to postsecondary options.

> † Interagency agreements must be in effect to facilitate the delivery of transition services. If, however, an outside agency fails to provide the transition services to which it committed itself in the IEP, the IEP team must reconvene to identify alternative strategies for providing the needed services (20 U.S.C.. § 1414(d)(6) (2006)). The LEA must implement the IEP but can claim reimbursement from the nonperforming agency. See 34 C.F.R. § 300.154(b)(2) (2006).

Considerations in Developing the IEP

Like its predecessor, IDEA '04 includes a whole section instructing the IEP team what to "consider" when developing the IEP (20 U.S.C. § 1414(d)(3) (2006)). The first four considerations—relevant to the development of all IEPs—are the strengths of the child, the parents' concerns for enhancing their child's education, the results of the most recent evaluation, and the child's academic, developmental, and functional needs. In addition, a separate subsection entitled *Consideration of special factors* (34 C.F.R. § 300.324(a)(2) (2006) requires IEP teams to do the following:

1) The IEP team must consider the use of positive behavioral interventions and supports if the child's behaviors impede the child's learning,

2) The IEP team must consider the language needs of the child if the child has limited English proficiency,

3) If the child is blind or visually impaired, the IEP team must "provide for" instruction in and use of Braille, unless the team determines, after evaluation, that Braille is not appropriate.

4) The IEP team must consider the child's communication needs, and if the child is deaf or hard of hearing, the team must consider the child's opportunities to communicate directly with peers and staff in the child's language and communication mode. The team must also consider opportunities for that child to receive direct instruction in his or her language and communication mode.

5) The IEP team must consider whether a child needs assistive technology devices and services.

These provisions may be a response to criticism that too often a child's IEP goals and objectives have not directly addressed the child's presenting problems. In requiring attention to overlooked problem areas, Congress appears to have modified its position that instructional methods never have to be included in the IEP. For instance, positive behavioral interventions and strategies can be viewed as instructional methods. So, perhaps, can instruction in Braille and instruction in a certain communication mode (such as American Sign Language or cued speech) although they can also be seen as adaptations to facilitate communication. If a particular reading method is necessary to deliver FAPE to a child with a learning disability, then it too could be specified in the IEP.

The Expanded Definition of Special Education

IDEA continues to define special education as "specially designed instruction, at no cost to the parents, to meet the unique needs of a child with a disability, including (A) instruction conducted in the classroom, in the home, in hospitals and institutions, and in other settings, and (B) instruction in physical education" (20 U. S. C. § 1402(25) (2006)). For the first time, the 1999 regulations defined the meaning of "specially designed instruction." The definition includes adapting instructional *methods*. The definition is retained in the 2006 regulations (34 C.F.R. 300.39(b)(3) (2006)). If no specific method is required to enable a child to receive FAPE, the methodology is left in the hands of those who are actually instructing the child. The decision about whether to include methodology rests with the IEP team.

Here is the full definition of specially designed instruction:

> *adapting, as appropriate to the needs of an eligible child under [Part B], the content, methodology, or delivery of instruction (i) [t]o address the unique needs of the child that result from the child's disability; and (ii) [t]o ensure access of the child to the general curriculum, so that he or she can meet the educational standards within the jurisdiction of the public agency that apply to all children.*

Guidance in Appendix A of the 1999 Regulations

Appendix A of the 1999 regulations, dedicated exclusively to interpreting the IEP requirements, addressed numerous questions about the role of parents, the IEP components, and the overall IEP process (34 C.F.R. Part 300, Appendix A (1999)). It was omitted as an appendix to the 2006 regulations, presumably because Congress stated that the regulations should be restricted to only those necessary for compliance with IDEA '04. Nonetheless, the appendix offered useful and widely accepted guidance. The authors believe that the following points retain their viability, emphasizing several important precepts that underlie the IEP process:

1. Parents are to be considered coequal participants in the development of the IEP (34 C.F.R., Part 300, App. A at question 5 (1999)). Agreement is not a matter of majority rule but rather a process of consensus building.

2. The IEP is not to be completed until the meeting itself, although IEP staff members should come prepared with their own ideas, written or oral, of what would be appropriate to include (34 C.F.R., Part 300, App. A at question 32 (1999)).

3. A child's IEP must address involvement in the general curriculum regardless of the severity of the disability and the setting in which the child is educated (34 C.F.R., Part 300, App. A at question 2 (1999)). Children in special schools, as well as those in general classrooms, should be accessing the general curriculum.

4. The IEP need not include annual goals related to parts of the general curriculum in which the child's disability does not affect participation (34 C.F.R., Part 300, App. A at question 4 (1999)). For instance, if the child needs no program modifications, supportive services, or specialized instruction during social studies, then social studies does not have to be mentioned in the IEP.

5. All services specified in the IEP must be provided, either directly through local school district resources, or indirectly by contracting with another agency or making other arrangements. The district may use whatever sources of public and private support are available, but the services must be at no cost to the parent (34 C.F.R., Part 300, App. A at question 28 (1999)).

6. The IEP must precede a placement decision, not follow it (34 C.F.R., Part 300, App. A at question 14 (1999)). Of all the mistakes that OSEP has uncovered while monitoring state compliance with IDEA, premature placement has continued to be one of the most difficult to eradicate. School officials tend to "slot" children by classification into one of the district's existing service delivery options, whereas IDEA requires an individualized assessment of the nature and extent of special services required for each child. The placement decision should be based on how close to the instructional mainstream those services can be appropriately delivered. Until the IEP is developed and services are specified, any placement decision is premature.†

> † The decision in *Spielberg v. Henrico County Public Schools*, 853 F.2d 256 (4th Cir. 1988), is instructive. The court held that FAPE was denied because the public school had proposed a transfer to a private school placement prior to development of a new IEP.

7. At no time should a staff member attend an IEP meeting in the role of a teacher advocate or union representative (34 C.F.R., Part 300, App. A at question 28 (1999)).The meeting should focus on the child's needs; it is meant as a cooperative venture, not an adversarial proceeding. Also, the school should remain aware of the possibility of overwhelming a parent if too many staff members attend the meeting.

Revising the IEP

IDEA '04 adds a new subsection dealing with changes to the IEP after the initial IEP meeting for the year. It specifies that the LEA and parent may agree that another meeting is not necessary, and instead may develop a written document with the changes. The subsection also clarifies that amending the IEP does not require redrafting the entire IEP (U.S.C. § 1414(d)(3)(D) and (F) (2006)).

A separate provision stipulates that a parent and LEA may agree to use alternative means of meeting participation, such as video conferences and conference calls. This provision applies broadly to all meetings between parents and the LEA (U.S.C. § 1414(f) (2006)).

When revising an IEP, the IEP team must address any lack of expected progress toward the annual goals or in the general curriculum, information about the child provided to or by the parents, the anticipated needs of the child, and any re-evaluation results (U.S.C. § 1414(d)(4) (2006)).

Is an Agreed-Upon IEP Binding?

The school district is expected to implement the IEP as written. The statute states that FAPE, among other things, is special education and related services delivered "in conformity with" the IEP (20 U.S.C. § 1401(d)(2006)). Failure to provide the listed services should constitute a denial of FAPE, although several controversial court interpretations have weakened this proposition by focusing on whether the IEP has been implemented in substantial part.[1] If school team members decide during the course of implementation that an IEP should be modified, parents must be notified† and, of course, be invited to participate in amending the IEP. As mentioned, IDEA '04 provides that the parent and LEA may agree to the changes without a new IEP meeting (20 U.S.C. § 1414(d)(3)(D) (2006)). The regulations add that lack of parental consent for one service or activity is not grounds for the school district to refuse any other services that are necessary for FAPE (34 C.F.R. § 300.300(d) (2) & (3) (2006)). If the parent remains opposed to new services for some reason, the parent's recourse is to request a hearing or file a state complaint.

> † Remember that parents include surrogate parents. In *Abney v. District of Columbia*, 849 F.2d 1491 (D.C. Cir. 1988), the court ruled that the IDEA procedural safeguards had been violated because of a failure to notify the child's surrogate parent that the child's special education program had been curtailed for a period of time.

Faithfully implementing the IEP does not require that all IEP goals be realized. If that were the case, the goals would be set lower than otherwise necessary, but the school is expected to make a good-faith effort to enable the child to progress toward the specified goals. When lack of expected progress toward IEP goals occurs, the IEP should be revised (34 C.F.R. § 300.324(b)(ii) (2006)).

Although school districts are supposed to be obligated to implement the services in an agreed-upon IEP, parents are entitled to change their minds about the effectiveness of that IEP. They can request a new meeting to revise the IEP. If the school declines to introduce services that the parent believes have become necessary, the parent may request a hearing, enter mediation, or file a complaint with the state office of education.

Providing IEPs When Public Agencies Place a Child in a Private School

IEPs are not limited to special education students at public schools but are also required for students receiving publicly financed special education and related services at private schools (20 U.S.C. § 1412(a)(10)(B) (2006)). The regulations add that when the private placement is made by a public agency, the IEP must be developed prior to the placement, and participation at the IEP meeting by a representative of the private school is mandatory (34 C.F.R. § 300.325(a) (2006)). The regulations also specify that after the child has begun to attend a private school, meetings to review and revise the IEP may be conducted by the private school, if the public agency is willing. Nonetheless, the LEA must make sure that the parents and the LEA representative are involved in IEP decisions, and that they agree to any proposed changes before such changes are made (34 C.F.R. § 300.325(b) (2006).

---

[1] See, e.g., *Van Duyn v. Baker Sch. Dist. 5J*, 481 F.3d 770 (9th Cir. 2007) (only "material" failures of IEP implementation are IDEA violations); *Neosho R-V Sch. Dist. v. Clark*, 315 F.3d 1022 (8th Cir. 2003) (no FAPE violation unless an "essential" element of the IEP is not provided); *Houston Indep. Sch. Dist. v. Bobby R.*, 200 F.3d 341 (5th Cir. 2000) (no denial of FAPE for failure to implement some portions of the IEP as long as they were not substantial or significant portions). If these and similar lower court cases give LEAs reason to think they can ignore some aspects of the IEP agreed to by the team, including parents, it will be troublesome and problematic.

Judicial Interpretation of IEP Requirements

Curiously, some courts have been slow to utilize the goals and measurement provisions of the IEP as a means of determining whether a student has been receiving benefit, in the sense of making meaningful educational progress. Although many cases have analyzed the nature and extent of special education and related services in the IEP and whether they addressed the student's needs, some have not pressed for evidence of whether IEP goals and objectives were being achieved. The Supreme Court's decision in Board of Education of *Hendrick Hudson Central School District v. Rowley* (1982) is illustrative. The Court used evidence of Amy Rowley's regular classroom achievement rather than progress toward meeting her own IEP goals and objectives in determining whether she was receiving FAPE (see chapter 10). Her IEP goals were not mentioned.

A clear understanding of the need for a fully developed IEP was reflected by the New Jersey Supreme Court in its 1989 decision in *Lascari v. Board of Education* (1989). The *Lascari* court determined that a child was not receiving FAPE because of inadequacies in his IEP, rendering it incapable of review. Specifically, current levels of performance were not indicated in the IEP, and the goals and objectives were "so vague that they were meaningless"(p. 1190). For instance, the first of two contested IEPs specified that the child was to strengthen his reading skills in a phonetic-linguistic program, develop practical math skills and vocational skills, "develop" a language arts program, and build self-esteem. The IEP contained no indication of how progress toward the goals and objectives was to be measured, nor any rationale for the proposed placement. For these reasons, the court ruled that the IEP was inappropriate.[2]

Because of the IDEA requirements, starting with IDEA '97, for *measurable* annual goals, regular progress reports, and focus on improved outcomes, the door is open to increasing opportunities to litigate IEP goals and the extent of a child's progress. Arguably, IDEA '04 opens the door further by specifying the need for measurable academic and functional goals and by linking achievement to NCLB's assessment requirements. When an IEP fails to produce meaningful progress toward

---

[2] See also *Cnty. of San Diego v. Cal. Special Educ. Hearing Office*, 93 F.3d 1458 (9th Cir. 1996).

achievement of the child's IEP goals, parents may have more leverage than they had before. Therefore, one can query whether court decisions may increasingly have to pay more attention to goals and measures of progress on both academic and functional goals (see chapter 10).

Multiyear Pilot IEP Programs

IDEA '04 allows states to submit applications for permission to implement comprehensive, two- or three-year IEPs that are designed to coincide with natural transition points for the child (from preschool to elementary school, elementary to middle or junior high school, and so forth). Such multiyear IEPs must remain optional for the parents, and a parent must provide informed consent prior to development of such an IEP. The IEP team must establish goals coinciding with the upcoming natural transition point for the child. It must also establish annual goals for determining progress, review the IEP annually, and revise the IEP to facilitate achievement of the longer-term goals, as needed (20 U.S.C. § 1414(d)(5)(2006)). Whether such multiyear IEPs will reduce paperwork while achieving the purposes of IEPs, remains to be seen. Beginning in December 2006, the Secretary of Education was to submit an annual report to Congress regarding the effectiveness of this pilot program. OSEP did not announce the grant application process for the program, however, until October 17, 2007 (in the Federal Register), and no applications were received, so obviously, no report from ED could be submitted to Congress.

The concept of multiyear IEPs appears to be on hold for now.

↳Reminders and Tips

1. Because the IEP is at the core of the substantive requirements under IDEA, all teachers must be trained to understand its purpose and function. This includes general education teachers, not just special educators. General educators who are responsible for implementing any portion of a child's IEP must have access at least to that portion and should be informed of their responsibilities.

2. The general educator should see his or her increased role in IEP development as an opportunity to solicit the program supports needed to make the general education classroom appropriate for a child with a disability. "Dumping" a child into a general classroom without the necessary program supports and supplementary services is unacceptable under IDEA, and general educators need to know that they have leverage to see that it does not happen.

3. Teachers will need to work more closely than ever with parents. The requirement to issue periodic progress reports, and to revise IEPs to address lack of progress, encourages more parental involvement on a regular and continuing basis.

4. Special and general education teachers must balance IDEA students' need for achievement in the general curriculum with their need for a specialized curriculum in other areas. Functional curriculum needs should not be sacrificed to the academic curriculum.

5. Finally, school officials should be aware that hearing officers and courts are still permitted to determine that procedural violations of the IEP process constitute a denial of FAPE if (a) they impeded the child's right to FAPE, (b) significantly impeded the parents' opportunity to participate in the FAPE decision-making process, or (c) caused a deprivation of educational benefits (20 U.S.C. § 1415(f)(1)(E)(2) (2006)).[3] If the procedural violations did not produce these substantive violations, they will be considered harmless.†

  † An example is *Doe v. Defendant 1*, 98 F.2d 1186 (6th Cir. 1990), in which the court found no IDEA violation for IEP omissions because both parties knew the missing information, and the spirit of the law was honored.

↷Review

1. What must be included in an IEP?

  An IEP must include the following: (a) the child's present levels of academic achievement and functional performance; (b) measurable annual academic and functional goals that address the child's special education needs related to both the general curriculum and areas independent of the general curriculum; (c) how progress toward the goals will be measured, and when periodic reports of progress toward the goals will be issued; (d) the specific special education and related services, supplementary aids and services, and program modifications or staff supports to be provided; (e) the extent to which the child will not be participating with nondisabled children in the regular class and in extracurricular and nonacademic activities; (f) appropriate accommodations, if any, in the administration of state or districtwide assessments of achievement (or statements about the child's alternate assessments), (g) the anticipated frequency, duration, and location of services and program modifications; and (h) transition goals and services beginning by the time the first IEP is in effect when the child is 16 years old.

2. Who should be on the IEP team?

  IEP team members include the parent(s), at least one special educator (or provider of special education), and, in most instances, a general education teacher of the child. An official representative of the LEA and someone who can interpret the instructional implications of evaluation results must also be on the team, but the special or general educator might be able to serve in these positions. The child and others who have "knowledge or special expertise" regarding the child may also be on the team, as appropriate.

3. What are some of the reasons that development of an IEP is so crucial to the effective implementation of IDEA?

  It is the best means of developing home-school cooperation in the education of a child with a disability, it is the basis for determining the appropriate placement, and it is the primary mechanism for determining whether FAPE is being provided.

---

[3] For examples of serious procedural violations, see *W. G. v. Bd. of Trustees of Target Range Sch. Dist. No. 23*, 960 F.2d 1479 (9th Cir. 1992); *Blackmon v. Springfield R-XII Sch. Dist.*, 29 IDELR 855 (W.D. MO. 1998); *Amanda S. v. Webster Community Sch. Dist.*, 27; IDELR 698 (N.D. Iowa 1998); *Gerstmyer v. Howard Cnty Pub. Sch.*, 850 F. Supp. 361 (D. Md. 1994)

⚡References

Bd of Educ. of Hendrick Hudson Central Sch. Dist. v. Rowley, 458 U.S. 176 (1982).

Individuals with Disabilities Education Improvement Act, 20 U.S.C. § 1400 *et seq.* (2006).

Individuals with Disabilities Education Improvement Act Regulations, 34 C.F. R. § 300.1 *et seq.* (2006).

Lascari v. Bd. of Educ., 560 A.2d 1180 (N.J. 1989).

No Child Left Behind Act of 2001, 20 U.S.C. § 6301 *et seq.* (2006).

⇉Selected Supplementary Resources

Bateman, B., & Linden, M. A. (1998). *Better IEPs* (3rd ed.). Longmont, CO: Sopris West.

Bateman, B. D., & Herr, C. M. (2006). *Writing measurable goals and objectives.* (2nd ed.). Verona, WI: IEP Resources.

Kukik, S., & Schrag, J. (1998). *IEP connections*. Longmont, CO: Sopris West.

Huefner, D. S. (2000).The risks and opportunities of the IEP requirements under IDEA '97. *Journal of Special Education, 33*, 195–204.

Turnbull, A. P., & Turnbull, H. R. (1997). *Families, professionals, and exceptionality: A special partnership* (3rd ed.). Upper Saddle River, NJ: Merrill/Prentice-Hall.

Chapter 8

Due Process Protections Under IDEA

Chapter Outline

Constitutional Due Process
>   Overview
>   Procedural Due Process

Procedural Due Process Under IDEA
>   Background
>   Procedural Safeguards in IDEA
>   Transfer of Parental Rights to Students

Reminders and Tips

Review

References

Selected Supplementary Resources

Constitutional Due Process

Overview

The origin of the due process protections for public school students is the due process clause of the Fifth and Fourteenth Amendments to the U.S. Constitution. Both amendments provide, among other things, that no person shall be deprived of life, liberty, or property, without due process of law. The Fifth Amendment restrains the power of the federal government, while the Fourteenth Amendment restrains the power of individual states.† The federal courts have interpreted the due process clause to contain two kinds of rights: substantive due process and procedural due process. Substantive due process requires that governmental action be reasonable and within the scope of its authority if fundamental rights such as voting rights and privacy rights are at stake. It has not been of primary importance in special education matters; in contrast, procedural due process has been central to the whole body of special education law. Therefore, this chapter focuses on procedural due process.

> † The relevant portion of the Fifth Amendment reads: "No person shall be . . . deprived of life, liberty, or property, without due process of law." The comparable portion of the Fourteenth Amendment reads: "nor shall any state deprive any person of life, liberty, or property, without due process of law."

Procedural Due Process

Procedural due process requires the use of fair procedures in restricting someone's right to life, liberty, or property. An individual's right to life, liberty, and property in the United States is not absolute; restrictions are placed on the exercise of these personal rights so that the rights of the community as a whole may be protected. In restricting these rights, however, federal and state governments are not allowed to operate in a manner unrestrained by law. What this means is that certain procedures are owed to persons protected by the U.S. legal system before those rights can be seriously abridged.

In the 1960s and early 1970s, prior to the passage of EHA/IDEA, advocates for children with disabilities sought to remedy what they perceived as unfair treatment of those children by invoking the due process protections of the Constitution, among other things. For children to be entitled to due process, advocates first had to establish that they were being denied a liberty or property right to which they were entitled under the Constitution. The advocates argued that excluding children with disabilities from general education classrooms and schools was a substantial infringement of their liberty because it restricted their freedom to be educated "like all the other kids," and it was potentially stigmatizing. The advocates also argued that education is a property right—namely, a legal entitlement to an economic interest, because education is important to one's self-sufficiency and income-producing potential, and because states undertake to provide it to all children between certain ages. In short, advocates asserted that because the proposed treatment of children with disabilities at the hands of school authorities threatened their "good name" and their future economic interests, they were entitled to procedural due process to ensure that the proposed treatment was not arbitrary or otherwise unfair.

In the context of public education, procedural due process requires that students receive the process they are due before government (i.e., the school) restricts their property rights or liberty interests. Schools are not proposing to take away student lives, so their right to life is not a due process issue in schools. Just what process is due—namely, proper or fitting? The basic elements of procedural due process, common across varying circumstances, are (a) notice, that is, informing the person of the contemplated governmental action to restrict one's life, liberty, or property and the reason for the proposed action, and (b) a chance to respond, that is, allowing the person to tell his or her side of the story at some kind of hearing, informal or formal. The less serious the contemplated governmental action against the person, the more informal the procedures. When more is at stake, more extensive procedures are required.

Two landmark lower court cases, *PARC v. Pennsylvania* (1992) and *Mills v. District of Columbia Board of Education* (1992), ruled that before being removed from general education classes or otherwise denied access to general education, children with disabilities had a constitutional right to procedural due process. In *PARC* and *Mills*, formal (that is, written) notice and a formal hearing were determined to be necessary.† In *PARC*, thousands of children with mental retardation had been excluded from public school. Many were placed in institutions that did not provide any educational component. In *Mills*, thousands of children with various kinds of disabilities, ranging from mental retardation to serious emotional disturbance, had been denied entrance to or expelled from public schools. In both situations, the parents of those children had not been provided with prior notice of the pending expulsion or exclusion, nor were they given any kind of hearing at which to protest the intended action.

† Both *PARC* and *Mills* also concluded that children with disabilities have a constitutional right to a public school education, and that their exclusion from school violates the principle of equal educational opportunity for all children of school age.

Goss v. Lopez: Students' Liberty and Property Rights

The procedural due process arguments that were advanced in the *PARC* and *Mills* cases anticipated by several years the Supreme Court's 1975 decision in *Goss v. Lopez*, 419 U.S. 565 (1975). The Court in *Goss* held that all students had a property interest in completing their education, and a liberty interest in their good name—that is, their reputation. In *Goss*, a suspension from school, even for only up to ten days, was determined to involve those interests because students might miss an exam, fail a course, or be stigmatized among their peers as a result of the suspension. The *Goss* decision requires that prior to short-term suspensions from school, students must receive at least a minimal amount of procedural due process—oral notice of the alleged violation and an informal opportunity to present their side of the story. This right applies to all students, including those with disabilities.

Procedural Due Process Under IDEA

Background

Legislation sometimes goes beyond constitutionally required minimums and specifies additional procedures—for instance, to assure parents that school decisions affecting a student's property and liberty interests are fair. One example is IDEA. Influenced by the *PARC* and *Mills* decisions, Congress incorporated extensive procedural safeguards into IDEA when identification, evaluation, placement, and provision of FAPE are at stake. It did so under the authority of section five of the Fourteenth Amendment, which gives Congress the power to enact appropriate legislation to implement the protections of the Fourteenth Amendment. The specific due process safeguards enacted in the statute go beyond the basics of some kind of notice and a chance to respond. They detail a set of explicit protections that are enforceable in court. These procedural safeguards are meant to protect children with disabilities from unilateral and possibly ill-advised school decisions, and to allow parental involvement and advocacy for their children. They have been refined and extended over the years. The extent to which IDEA elaborates on and extends the basic due process requirements of the Constitution is explained in the next section.

Procedural Safeguards in IDEA

Procedural safeguards notice.

A full written explanation of the basic due process safeguards of IDEA, which are extended to parents on behalf of their children, must be given to parents at least once each school year, and also upon initial referral or parental request for evaluation. The notice must also be provided upon an initial filing of a complaint, whether invoking a due process hearing or a state complaint process. It must also be provided upon parental request and in compliance with the discipline procedures (see chapter 14) (20 U.S.C. § 1415(d)(1)(2006)).

Although districts are used to giving parents a formal, written statement of their due process safeguards, frequently parents have not understand their importance. Often, the required statement has been lengthy and legalistic, to the dissatisfaction of parents and teachers alike. To address this problem, IDEA '04 requires that the notice be written in "an easily understandable manner" and in the native language of the parents, unless it is clearly not feasible to do so (20 U.S.C. § 1415(d)(2)(2006)). In spite of this requirement, communicating intelligibly in the right form, and at the right time, to parents has remained a challenge. In response to this challenge, IDEA '04 required ED to provide a model procedural safeguards notice for dissemination to SEAs, LEAs, and Parent Training Centers by the date that the final IDEA '04 regulations were published (20 U.S.C. § 1417(e)(2006)).The model notice is forty-four pages long!! (One can question whether this will be easily understandable, given its length.)

The Procedural Safeguards Notice to parents must contain a complete explanation of parental rights and responsibilities, and detailed explanations of the regulations pertaining to them, principally the following rights to:

1. receive prior written notice before an educational agency proposes (or refuses) to initiate or change the child's identification, evaluation, educational placement, or provision of FAPE;

2. give or withhold consent at specific times;

3. access their child's education records;

4. obtain an independent educational evaluation (IEE) of their child;

5. use mediation to resolve disputes;

6. present and resolve complaints through a due process hearing process (including a state-level appeal if the due process hearing is conducted by an LEA rather than the SEA), and to appeal the final administrative ruling to state or federal court;

7. have evaluation results and recommendations disclosed prior to the due process hearing;

8. present and resolve complaints through the state complaint process;

9. receive reasonable attorneys' fees, if the parent is the prevailing party in court or an administrative proceeding (20 U.S.C. § 1415(b)(3) (2006); 34 C.F.R. § 300.504 (2006)).

These nine rights are, in effect, an elaboration of the basic elements of due process—notice and some kind of hearing prior to the intended government action. The provisions give the parent (as defined in the statute) a chance to have input, or to challenge the school's decision making at various points in the process. Even the attorneys' fees provision fits within this concept, for it allows parents with modest financial resources a way to obtain their day in court; without the provision, many parents with good claims could not attract the services of an attorney.

The notice must also contain explanations of additional procedural safeguards:

1. the requirement that the child remain in his or her current placement while administrative or judicial proceedings are pending, unless the parents and the educational agency agree otherwise (known as the *stay-put* provision);

2. the procedures allowing an exception to the stay-put provision for children who are subject to a disciplinary placement in an *interim alternative educational setting;*

3. the requirement that parents provide prior notice to the educational agency if they intend to place their child in private school and seek reimbursement from the agency for the cost of the placement.

These additional three safeguards have purposes that extend beyond the basic elements of due process. They are intended to safeguard the welfare of children with disabilities who might be subject to ill-advised placement changes, and to ensure fair discipline and the safety of other children. They also address parental responsibility to schools (a basic fairness issue from the school's standpoint).

Each of these twelve safeguards will be explained more fully in turn. An additional safeguard—parental right to participate in decision-making meetings—will also be described, as will the surrogate parent provisions.

Prior written notice.

Prior written notice is meant to keep parents informed about the school's action or inaction with respect to their child's identification as a special education student, the child's evaluation, the child's placement, or the provision of FAPE. The prior written notice must contain a description of what the education agency proposes or refuses to do, an explanation of its position, and an explanation of the various options considered and rejected (20 U.S.C. § 1415(c) (2006)). If evaluation is the issue, then each evaluation procedure, assessment, record, or report relied on by the LEA must be described. In other words, parents are to understand the reasons for agency positions. All this information must be provided in the native language of the parent, "unless it is clearly not feasible to do so" (20 U.S.C. § 1415(b)(4)(2006)). This notice must also tell parents how to obtain assistance in understanding its contents and how to obtain a copy of the more general Procedural Safeguards Notice.†

> † The regulations elaborate on this provision by also requiring that information be provided in the parent's mode of communication. If the native language or mode of communication is not a written language (e.g., American Sign Language), the LEA is to ensure that the notice is translated orally or by other means (34 C.F.R. 300.503(c) (2006)).

Informed consent.

IDEA requires school districts to seek informed consent from parents at three points in time: (a) prior to an initial evaluation for eligibility, (b) prior to initial provision of special education and related services, and (c) prior to re-evaluation (20 U.S.C. § 1414(a)(1)(D) and (c)(3) (2006); 34 C.F.R. § 300.300 (2006)). The regulations specify that the consent must be voluntary and in writing (34 C.F.R. § 300.9 (2006)), both of which are customary for formal consent.

If consent for initial evaluation is not forthcoming, the school district has the right to use the due process or mediation procedures to attempt to obtain permission to perform the evaluation unless to do so would be inconsistent with state law. In the case of re-evaluation, consent can be bypassed if the school district can demonstrate that it took reasonable measures to obtain consent and the parent never responded (20 U.S.C. § 1414(c)(3) (2006); 34 C.F.R. § 300.300(c) (2006)). The 2006 regulations, however, add that the school district is under no obligation to pursue the evaluation or re-evaluation when consent is lacking (34 C.F.R. § 300.300(a)(3) and (c) (2006)). Furthermore, if a child is home schooled or placed in private school by parents at their expense, and the parent declines consent for initial evaluation, the public agency is prohibited from using the override procedures and does not have to provide any services to the child (34 C.F.R. § 300.300(d)(4) (2006)).

IDEA '04 has introduced an important change in the consent requirements with respect to the provision of special education and related services. If, after determination of eligibility, parental consent is withheld for special education services, either by refusal or silence, the LEA may no longer use the procedural safeguards (such as hearing procedures) to gain permission to provide the services. Furthermore, the LEA will not be in violation of the FAPE requirement and is not required to develop an IEP for the child (20 U.S.C. § 1414(a)(1)(D)(ii)(II) and (III) (2006)). In other words, the absence of parental consent trumps any further LEA obligations under IDEA. A further regulation, issued in December 2008, interprets this provision to apply not only to absence of consent for initial provision of special education, but also to subsequent withdrawal of consent for all special education services. The withdrawal of consent, however, must be in writing, and the LEA must give the parent prior written notice of the cessation of special education services (34 C.F.R. § 300.300(b) (4) (2008)). In spite of these changes, the FAPE obligation continues when a parent refuses consent to some, but not all, special education services and activities after initial consent has been given.† Finally, withdrawal of consent is not retroactive and does not negate any actions taken before the consent was withdrawn (34 C.F.R. § 300.9(c)(2) (2006)).

> † Under the regulations, a state could choose to require that parental consent be sought at stages other than those mentioned in the statute, provided that a parent's refusal to consent did not result in a failure to provide FAPE to a child who had already been receiving IDEA services (34 C.F.R. § 300.300(d)(2) (2006)). For instance, states often require that parents sign IEPs as an indication of consent to their content. Nonetheless, refusal to sign the IEP may not be used as an excuse by the school district to refuse to provide appropriate services. Although a signed IEP is protection for a school, and may provide evidence that the parent attended an IEP meeting and agreed to the

IEP at a given point in time, it neither obligates the parent to continue to agree with the IEP until the development of the next one nor allows a district to withhold services if the signature is not obtained.

Why is it more important to obtain consent at initial evaluation and initial delivery of services than at other times? The concept of due process provides an explanation. The student's liberty interests are most vulnerable at the stages of initial evaluation and initial provision of special education because these are the stages at which the student is first identified and treated as a student with different, "special" education needs. Misclassification and misplacement at these stages would seriously infringe on a student's liberty interests. The parent should understand the implications of the process at these stages above all. If the parent consents to the initial evaluation and provision of special education services, then, arguably, subsequent changes in the student's individualized services or placement involve the child's property and liberty interests less than designating and serving a child as a "special education" student in the first place.

Access to records.

The IDEA regulations incorporate the parents' right to access their child's education records found in the Family Educational Rights and Privacy Act of 1974 (FERPA). Access to the education records means the right to "inspect and review" them. With the exception of the IEP, evaluation report, and documentation of eligibility determination, which are provided at no cost to the parent, access does not include a right to receive copies of information in the child's file, unless failure to do so would prevent the parent from being able to inspect and review them (34 C.F.R. § 300.613(b)(2) (2006)). This might be the case for someone who was physically unable to come to the record site. The education agency may charge a fee for copying most of the documents requested by the parents, as long as the fee itself does not prevent the parents from inspecting and reviewing the record (34 C.F.R. § 300.617 (2006)). (More detailed information on access rights is provided in chapter 9.)

Independent educational evaluation (IEE).

School districts view the IEE as one of the more problematic due process protections because of the cost implications. The regulations spell out the expectations for IEEs. The regulations state that parents are entitled to an IEE at public expense if they disagree with the education agency's evaluation (34 C.F.R. § 300.502(b) (2006)). In addition, if the parents obtain an IEE at their own expense and use agency criteria, the education agency must consider the independent evaluation in making decisions about the provision of FAPE to the child.

A school district may ask but not require parents to explain why they want an IEE (34 C.F.R. § 300.502(b)(4) (2006)). Additionally, if parents request an IEE,† the school district must provide information about where to obtain one, and must share its evaluation criteria with the parents, "including the location of the evaluation and the qualifications of the examiner" (34 C.F.R. § 300.502(a)(2) and (e) (2006)). This cryptic phrase has been interpreted to mean that the district can set geographic limits, as long as those restrictions do not prevent parents from obtaining an appropriate IEE for their child. Similarly, a district can designate which kinds of examiners are qualified to make an educational diagnosis of disability. In the past, OSEP allowed school districts to establish cost caps, as long as they were reasonable and did not prevent a given student from obtaining an appropriate outside evaluation.[1] The 1999 and 2006 IDEA regulations however, provide that the school district may not impose conditions or timelines other than the criteria it uses in initiating an evaluation of its own (34 C.F.R. § 300.502(e)(2) (2006)), so, arguably, cost caps are more difficult to impose.

---

[1] See *Letter to Anonymous*, 22 IDELR 537 (OSEP 1995); *Letter to Aldine*, 16 EHLR 606 (OSEP 1990).

† If parents want to be reimbursed for the cost of the IEE, they apparently must "request" their IEE through the LEA. Courts are interpreting the request language to require the parents to notify the LEA and not proceed independently. Otherwise, the LEA does not know that the parents disagree with the LEA evaluation, and it does not have an opportunity to provide its evaluation criteria to the parents or seek an explanation for the parents' dissatisfaction. See *K. R. v. Jefferson Township Board of Education*, 2002 U.S. Dist. LEXIS 13267 (D.N.J. 2002) (school also did not have an opportunity to negotiate a lower rate with the independent evaluator) and *Kuszewski v. Chippewa Valley School,* 131 F. Supp. 2d 926 (E.D. Mich. 2001).

To overcome the parents' right to an IEE at public expense, the LEA must assume the responsibility of initiating a due process hearing and prove either that its own evaluation was appropriate or that the parents did not follow the district's criteria (34 C.F.R. § 300.502(b)(2006)). Often, the cost of the hearing is more than the cost of the lEE, so districts sometimes choose not to exercise this option.

Parental participation at meetings.

Though not among the safeguards listed in the Procedural Safeguards Notice, parental participation in meetings at which key decisions are made is an important part of the procedural safeguards section of IDEA and the regulations (20 U.S.C. § 1415(b)(1) (2006); 34 C.F.R. § 300.501(b) and (c) (2006)). Parental input is consistent with the concept of due process and gives the parents a valuable opportunity to be heard at critical stages in the development of their child's special education program. Failure to require explanation of this right in the Procedural Safeguards Notice is a curious omission, but parental participation is addressed separately in the regulations.

At what points are parents given the right to participate? Parents have a right to provide input into the evaluation process, and to participate in meetings at which eligibility is determined, the IEP is developed, and placement is determined (34 C.F.R. § 300.501(b) and (c) (2006)—all key points at which disagreements can arise. Parents are key participants on the IEP team, and their input must be considered in developing the written IEP, which is not to be written in advance of the IEP meeting (34 C.F.R. § 300.320(a) (2006)). Parents are in a particularly good position to contribute to the annual goals, and to articulate their view of the necessary kinds of special education and related services. When their input is solicited and respected, it furthers the IDEA goal of cooperation between home and school. When it is not sought or is ignored, the likelihood of parental distrust at some future time increases. Failure to involve parents in the development of their child's IEP has produced a number of court decisions adverse to school districts.[2] Conversely, parents' refusal to participate in the IEP process may defeat their claim to the right to a procedurally correct IEP process.†

> † For instance, in *Cordrey v. Euckert*, 917 F.2d 1460 (6th Cir. 1990), the court ruled that the parents had forfeited their right to a procedurally correct IEP meeting because they had refused the school district's offer to convene a properly constituted IEP meeting subsequent to an improperly constituted meeting.

[2] See, e.g., *Greer v. Rome City Sch. Dist.*, 950 F.2d 688 (11th Cir. 1991); *Bd. of Educ. of Cnty. of Cabell v. Dienelt*, 843 F.2d 813 (4th Cir. 1988).

Mediation.†

IDEA '97 required that SEAs and LEAs provide a mediation option for disputes involving identification, evaluation, placement, or provision of FAPE. Under IDEA '04, a modification requires an offer of mediation for any matter in dispute, including matters arising prior to the filing of a complaint (20 U.S.C. § 1415(e) (2006). The mediation process remains voluntary and may not be used to deny or delay a parent's right to a hearing. The mediator must be impartial, qualified, and knowledgeable about special education law. The SEA must pay for the mediation. If an agreement is reached, IDEA '04 specifies that it be set forth in a legally binding agreement signed by both parties and enforceable in court (20 U.S.C. § 1415(e)(2)(F) (2006)). Notwithstanding, "discussions" during the mediation process remain confidential and cannot be used in subsequent hearings or civil proceedings. This will protect the parties from having their verbal comments used against them if a court case is brought on a related but independent matter or after failed mediation. The federal regulations do not prohibit attorneys from representing the parties at mediation proceedings, but state regulations may do so. If an attorney is used, costs will escalate.

> † Mediation is a dispute resolution procedure in which a qualified, impartial third party listens to both sides and then recommends but cannot impose a solution. Mediation is less adversarial than a hearing or court case, but it is important that both parties voluntarily agree to mediate their dispute. If both really do not want to settle the dispute, mediation is likely to fail.

Presenting and resolving complaints.

The procedural safeguards thus far mentioned are meant to place parents on something of an equal footing with school districts. If the safeguards fail to satisfy the parents that the school is acting in the child's interests, and if the parents believe that their child's rights are being denied, they have the right to present a complaint with respect to identification, evaluation, placement of their child, and the provision of FAPE. Under IDEA '04, *a statute of limitations* is introduced for the first time; that is, the complaint must allege a violation that occurred "not more than two years before the date the parent or public agency knew or should have known about the alleged action that forms the basis of the complaint" (20 U.S.C. § 1415(b)(6)(B) (2006)). If the state has a different limitation on the time period within which a claim may be brought, the state's timeline will be followed instead. Filing a complaint acts as a check on the school district and allows more thorough consideration of the school's intended actions prior to their implementation.

After receipt of the complaint, the parents have the opportunity for a due process hearing.† IDEA '04 requires the complaining party (or the attorney representing the party) to submit a formal *due process complaint notice* to the other party (with a copy to the SEA) within the two-year time constraints. The notice must contain the following information: (a) the child's name, home address, and school the child is attending, (b) a description of the nature of the presenting problem (including relevant facts), and (c) a proposed resolution, if possible (20 U.S.C. § 1415(b)(7)(2006)).

> † The educational agency may also initiate a hearing when not prohibited from doing so by IDEA. For instance, an LEA may request a hearing to prove that its evaluation was appropriate so that it does not have to reimburse a parent for an IEE. On the other hand, it cannot request a hearing to override refusal of parental consent for special education and related services.

If the child is homeless, then contact information must be provided in lieu of the child's address. In the past, some of this basic information was not always available until close to the hearing date, thereby impeding the ability of the school district to prepare its defense, or pursue mediation or a settlement agreement. Until this complaint notice is submitted, no hearing will be held.† Various timelines are established that allow for procedural maneuvering prior to the hearing (for instance, opportunity for the defending party to reply to the complaint, for the plaintiff to try to amend the complaint, and for the hearing officer to respond to the complaint and set a hearing date).

† The SEA must develop a model form to help parents file a complaint and a due process complaint notice (20 U.S.C. § 1415(b)(8) (2006)).

Resolution process.

IDEA '04 has added a new requirement as part of the procedures to resolve a due process complaint. After a complaint has been filed and prior to a due process hearing, parents and relevant members of the IEP team (those who have knowledge about the facts identified in the complaint) must participate in a resolution session (20 U.S.C. § 1415(f)(1)(B) (2006)). This session is convened by the LEA and must include someone from the LEA with decision-making authority. The LEA may not bring an attorney unless the parent does. This session is to give the LEA an opportunity to resolve the complaint. The session must be convened within fifteen days of receipt of the parents' complaint, and if a resolution satisfactory to the parents is not achieved within thirty days from the receipt of the complaint, the hearing may occur.† If both parties agree, they can waive the resolution session or mediate the dispute, but they must put this agreement in writing. If the resolution session proceeds and a resolution is achieved, that agreement also must be in writing and will be legally binding and enforceable in court, if it is not voided within three business days by either party (20 U.S.C. § 1415(f)(1)(B) (2006)).

† The resolution session timeline delays commencement of the timeline for a due process hearing. So do the timelines established for answering and amending the complaint.

Due process hearing.

Unlike mediation, the due process hearing is a formal hearing, presided over by an impartial hearing officer who is empowered to decide the dispute and impose a solution on the parties. If the parties proceed to the hearing, both parties have the right to examine, cross-examine, and subpoena witnesses; to use the services of an attorney and others with special knowledge or training with respect to the education of children with disabilities; to obtain a verbatim transcript of the hearing; and to obtain a written decision, including findings of fact (20 U.S.C. § 1415(h) (2006)). (The parent also has the right to a record of the hearing and the factual findings and decision at no cost.) In addition, no fewer than five business days before the hearing, each party has the right to know of all completed evaluations, and recommendations based on those evaluations, that the other party will use at the hearing (20 U.S.C. § 1415(f)(2) (2006)). The regulations add that parents have the right to decide whether to open the hearing to the public, and whether to have the child present at the hearing (34 C.F.R. § 300.512(c) (2006)). This provision respects the privacy rights of the family.

The impartial hearing officer must not be an employee of a public agency involved in the education or care of the student, nor have any other personal or professional conflict of interest. The hearing officer also must know and be able to understand the relevant federal and state statutes, regulations, and judicial decisions and be able to conduct the hearing and write decisions in accordance with appropriate, standard legal practice (20 U.S.C. § 1415(f)(3)(A) (2006)).The hearing officer's decision must be made on substantive grounds based on a determination of whether FAPE was "received." If procedural violations are alleged, they can result in denial of FAPE only if they impeded the child's right to FAPE, "significantly impeded" the parent's opportunity to participate in decision making regarding FAPE, or caused a "deprivation of educational benefits"(20 U.S.C. § 1415(f)(3)(E) (2006)).[3] This requirement does not prevent the hearing officer from ordering an education agency to comply with the procedural safeguards. If the decision of the hearing officer is not appealed, it is final (20 U.S.C. § 1415(i)(2006)).†

> † States have the option of establishing a one-tier or two-tier administrative hearing system (20 U.S.C. § 1415(g) (2006)). If a one-tier, state-level due process hearing is established, appeal of the hearing decision is to a court. If a two-tier hearing system is established, then a state-level review of the local hearing decision precedes any appeal to a court. The review of the local hearing must be conducted impartially, and the reviewing officer(s) must make an independent decision after completion of the review.

Litigation (civil action).

At the end of the administrative hearing process, the appealing party has ninety days to appeal the decision to state or federal court, unless the state has established a different timeline. The court receives the records of the administrative proceedings, hears additional evidence at the request of a party, and bases its decision on the preponderance of the evidence, granting "such relief as the court determines is appropriate"(20 U.S.C. § 1415(i)(2)(C) (2006)) (see chapter 15). Preponderance means that the weight of the evidence favors one side more than the other—namely, the evidence on one side is more convincing than the evidence on the other side, even if only slightly.

Technical issues arise at both the hearing stage and in court—issues as to which party has the *burden of proof* and what constitutes the appellate *standard of review*. Because IDEA is silent on these matters, these standards vary across state and federal jurisdictions.[4] In 2005, however, the Supreme Court accepted an appeal from the losing party in a Fourth Circuit case, and in November of that year ruled that, at the administrative hearing stage, the party initiating the hearing to challenge an IEP bears the burden of proof that the IEP will not provide FAPE. In nearly all cases, the party challenging the IEP is the parents. The decision means that when the evidence is equally balanced, the party with the burden of proof will lose. The Court determined that, in close cases (which are actually fairly rare), Congress intended to follow the traditional rule that places the burden of proof on the party complaining about the government action (*Schaffer v. Weast* (2005).†

> † Justice O'Connor's majority opinion reasoned that Congress had provided enough protections to parents to ensure that "the school bears no unique informational advantage" at the hearing (Schaffer v. Weast, 546 U.S. 49, 61 (2005)). The majority also reasoned that Congress wished to reduce litigation under IDEA and encourage parental and school cooperation. Placing the burden of proof on school districts when their IEPs are challenged, the Court concluded, would be an unwarranted addition to their administrative and litigative burdens.

---

[3] The regulations change the word "benefits" to "benefit." 34 C.F.R. § 513.(a)(2)(iii) (2006).
[4] For further background information on these matters, see Mayes, T. A., Zirkel, P. A., & Huefner, D. S., (2005). Allocating the burden of proof in administrative and judicial proceedings under the Individuals With Disabilities Education Act, *West Virginia Law Review, 108*, 30-94; Huefner, D. S., & Zirkel, P. A. (1993). *Burden of proof under the Individuals With Disabilities Education Act* (Special Report No. 9). Horsham, PA: LRP.

Attorneys' fees.

Although attorneys' fees are listed in IDEA as one of the procedural safeguards for parents (20 U.S.C. § 1415(i)(3)(B) (2006)), they are discussed in this book under the topic of remedies (see chapter 15). The reason for this is that school districts, perhaps incorrectly, tend to see attorneys' fees as an additional remedy for a prevailing parent rather than as a means of parental access to the hearing system and the courts.

Techniques of Principled Negotiation

Parents and educators need to communicate often about a child with disabilities. They need to share their perceptions, insights, concerns, and knowledge. If the school's and parents' views of the child's strengths, weaknesses, and educational needs vary considerably, conflicts can easily arise. Some of these conflicts are resolved by one side giving in to the other; others are resolved by flexibility and compromise on both sides. Others may seem more intransigent, yet still can be resolved without the need for mediation, resolution sessions, hearings, and ultimately litigation, if the parties are skilled at using win-win techniques. Development of one of the best known of these kinds of techniques is credited to Roger Fisher (1991) and his colleagues at the Harvard Negotiation Project. Known as "principled negotiation," the techniques can be mastered by those willing to practice them. In a nutshell, the strategies are as follows:

1. *Separate the personal relationships (the "people") from the problem*. Build working relationships before the negotiation begins. Understand the reality of the other side's perceptions, and validate the expression of appropriate emotions without letting them take control of the negotiation. Learn to listen and acknowledge what you have heard. Communicate explicitly and clearly.

2. *Focus on interests, not positions*. Bargaining over set positions usually degenerates into a contest of wills. Do not assume that there are no interests in common just because the positions of the school and parents are different. Any one position reflects multiple interests and human needs. Identify the underlying interests on both sides. Spend energy explaining your interests rather than attacking the other's position.

3. *Create options that will be mutually beneficial*. Learn to brainstorm without making premature judgments about the ideas presented. Broaden the range of acceptable options. Then, prioritize the options, and select the best ideas for follow-up.

4. *Rely on objective criteria for resolving the conflict*. Jointly identify objective standards (for instance, empirical data, recognized research, trusted independent opinions, outside experts, relevant court decisions). Frame each issue as a search for objective criteria acceptable to both sides. If no such criteria can be identified, then agree to use fair procedures, and be open to reason. Do not succumb to pressure tactics.

Fisher and his colleagues believe that principled negotiation can be initiated by one party alone because the approach tends to be contagious. They recognize, however, that high hostility levels, large ego needs, an irrational participant, unequal bargaining power or skill, and similar issues create real barriers to the success of principled negotiation.

Principled negotiation is not suitable for some kinds of disputes, such as win-lose situations involving major civil rights issues in need of legal resolution, or a dispute over which party should pay the cost of a child's private school education. On the other hand, many disputes about identification, evaluation, placement, discipline, and IEP services are hospitable to resolution by principled negotiation techniques.

Stay-put provision.

While administrative or judicial proceedings are pending on an IDEA complaint, IDEA requires that the child remain in the "then-current educational placement," unless the parents and the SEA or LEA agree otherwise (20 U.S.C. § 1415(j) (2006)). Taken literally, this provision ensures that a student is not buffeted back and forth or uprooted, based on who is winning a placement argument after any given stage in the proceedings. Until the issue is resolved, the child is to stay put in the current placement.† Over time, however, the meaning of the stay-put provision has been narrowed in some respects and expanded in others. For instance, a number of court decisions have ruled that a transfer from one precise location to another is not a change in placement if the new environment has not changed the setting (that is, the degree of inclusion with children who do not have disabilities) and replicates the child's educational program as closely as possible.[5] Conversely, disputes about significant changes in the child's program of services have been held to be subject to the stay-put provision,[6] which is an expansion from the literal reading of the provision. Courts do not share a common understanding of the meaning of the stay-put provision.

> † IDEA stipulates that if the child is applying for initial admission to public school, then, with the parent's consent, the child is to be "placed in the public school program" until all the proceedings are completed (20 U.S.C. § 1415(j) (2006)). If a child has turned three and is transitioning from Part C to Part B, the public agency is not required to provide the Part C services, and the child no longer has a "current educational placement" (34 C.F.R. 300.518(c) (2006)) and Analysis of Comments and Changes, 71 Fed. Reg. 46709 (August 14, 2006). Nonetheless, the Part C provisions require that the child receive any IFSP services not in dispute (20 U.S.C. § 1439(b)).

The regulations interpret the stay-put provision to mean that a state-level hearing decision in support of a parent's preferred placement is an agreement between the parents and the SEA (34 C.F.R. § 300.518(d) (2006)). Therefore, what was once the stay-put (current) placement may no longer be the stay-put placement. One result is to allow the parents to keep their child in a private school throughout any LEA appeal of the parents' unilateral placement. Under these circumstances, a court may order reimbursement for a unilateral private school placement from the time of the favorable state-level hearing decision until the time of a court decision reversing the state hearing decision (*MacKey v. Board of Education for the Arlington Central School District*, 2004). In some situations, a school district may decide not to appeal an adverse state hearing decision because the costs of pursuing the litigation may be more than the cost of reimbursing the parents for the private placement. If the school district appeals, however, the parents will still bear the risk of having their request for reimbursement denied by a higher court.†

> † In any event, the stay-put provision binds school districts but not parents. The Supreme Court so ruled in *Burlington School Committee v. Massachusetts Department of Education* (471 U.S. 359, 1985)). Parents can remove their child from public school and place the child in a private school because parents cannot be at the mercy of a school district thought to be violating IDEA. If, however, they seek reimbursement, the private placement continues at their own financial risk because whether they will be reimbursed will depend on the final outcome of the litigation.

---

[5] See, e.g., *AW v. Fairfax Cnty. Sch. Bd.*, 372 F.3d 674 (4th Cir. 2004) (transfer of student to a different school was not a change of placement because the settings were materially identical). Cf. *Ms. S. v. Vashon Island Sch. Dist.*, 337 F.3d 1115 (9th Cir. 2003) (when a student transfers to a different school district, the new district need not provide a placement identical to the former placement; approximating the last-agreed-upon IEP as closely as possible under the circumstances met the stay-put requirement).

[6] See, e.g., *Susquenita Sch. Dist. v. Raelee S.*, 96 F.3d 78 (3d Cir. 1996) (purpose of stay-put provision is to prevent school districts from unilaterally changing a child's educational program); *Sherri A. D. v. Kirby*, 975 F.2d 193 (5th Cir. 1992) (educational placement is not a place, but a program of services).

Special disciplinary stay-put provisions.

In response to safety considerations, IDEA '04 allows LEA removal of a child to an alternative stay-put setting if the child carries or possesses a weapon in school, at school functions, or on school premises. Similarly, an alternative setting is permitted for a child who knowingly possesses or uses illegal drugs, sells or solicits the sale of a controlled substance, or has inflicted serious bodily injury upon another person at school, school functions, or on school premises (20 U.S.C. § 1415 (k)(1)(G) (2006)). Placement changes are also allowed for other violations of the code of student conduct. All of these unilateral LEA placement changes are subject to various additional procedural protections. These provisions are discussed in chapter 14.

Notice by parents seeking reimbursement for unilateral private school placement.

Most of the IDEA procedural safeguards are meant as protections for parents and their children with disabilities. This one, however, is a safeguard for the school. It obligates parents to notify the public school when they plan to remove their child from the school and then seek reimbursement for a private school placement. If they do not do so, any reimbursement for which they might become eligible can be reduced. This provision is explained in more detail in chapter 13.

State complaint procedures.

Since its inception, IDEA has had state complaint procedures that could be used by an organization or individual willing to submit a signed written complaint to the SEA alleging a violation of IDEA. For many years, the procedures were lost from view because they were moved to the ED General Administrative Regulations. Since 1992, the procedures have been back in the IDEA regulations. They have been strengthened and formalized over the years. OSEP believes that the State Complaint Procedures (also called Complaint Resolution Procedures) are an increasingly important component of an SEA's role in monitoring compliance with IDEA. As a result, the procedures were given increased visibility in the 1999 regulations (34 C.F.R. § 300.660-.662 (1999)) as an alternative to mediation and due process hearings. It is not surprising that these regulations remain in the 2006 regulations because, among other reasons, IDEA '04 specifically mentions that the impartial hearing requirements do not affect the right of a parent to file a complaint with the SEA (20 U.S.C. § 1415(f) (3)(F) (2006); 34 C.F.R. 300.151-153 (2006)).

The regulations specify that an SEA complaint must include facts supporting an alleged violation of IDEA. It can be about systemwide noncompliance or any individual matter that could be subject to a due process hearing. Generally speaking, the complaint must allege a violation that is no more than a year old. The SEA must investigate the complaint and issue a written decision within sixty days of its receipt, except under exceptional circumstances; it can permit time extensions, if agreed to by the parties. The SEA, if it chooses, can require that the complaint be initiated with the LEA, subject to SEA review. It can also encourage mediation, if appropriate.

If the SEA determines that there has been a failure to provide appropriate services, the SEA must determine how to remedy the failure, including taking corrective action to address the needs of the child. Corrective action can include compensatory services and monetary reimbursement. It also must address the appropriate future provision of services for all children with disabilities. In other words, it must take corrective action with regard to both individual and systemic denials of FAPE.

If a written complaint is submitted that contains one or more issues that are or have been subject to a due process hearing, the state must defer to the hearing decision. Any issues that are not part of the hearing, however, must proceed within the 60-day time limit. If an issue has already been decided in a hearing, the hearing decision is binding. Finally, if the complaint alleges an agency's failure to implement a due process hearing decision, the SEA must resolve the complaint.

The state's procedures must be widely disseminated to parents and various advocacy groups within the state. For this reason, the regulations require a reference to the state complaint procedures in the Procedural Safeguards Notice (34 C.F.R. § 300.504(5) (2006)).

The person or group filing a complaint need not have been directly affected by the school district's actions or inactions; therefore, a bystander or a teacher's association can be among those filing the complaint. Complaints can also come from outside the state.

One of the major advantages of filing an SEA complaint instead of seeking a due process hearing is that an attorney is not necessary. The cost savings can be significant for the individual or group bringing the complaint. In addition, the procedures allow an investigation rather than an adversarial hearing with its quasi-judicial procedures. A 1995 survey of how state complaint managers rated the comparative effectiveness of hearings, mediation, and complaint procedures found that mediation was the preferred option, with complaint procedures next. Due process hearings were seen as the least desirable alternative for dispute resolution, in terms of either parent or LEA satisfaction, and in terms of cost effectiveness and effective results for the children involved (Suchey & Huefner, 1998).

Surrogate parent.

When the parents of a child with an IDEA disability are not known (cannot be identified) or cannot be located after reasonable efforts, or when the child is a ward of the state, IDEA requires protective procedures, including the appointment of a surrogate for the parents (20 U.S.C. § 1415(b)(2) (2006)). The statutory definition of parent is broad, however, so appointments of surrogate parents are infrequent. In addition to biological or adoptive parents, the definition of parent includes a guardian or an individual acting in place of the biological or adoptive parent with whom the child lives (such as a grandparent, stepparent, or other relative). It also includes an individual who is legally responsible for the child's welfare and can include a foster parent, unless state law prohibits a foster parent serving as a parent (20 U.S.C. § 1402(23) (2006)).

The statute specifies that the surrogate not be an employee of a public agency that is involved in the education or care of the student. The regulations add that the educational agency is permitted to select a surrogate in any way permitted by state law, as long as the surrogate also has no interests that conflict with the student's interest and has sufficient knowledge and skills to adequately represent the student (34 C.F.R. § 300.519(d) (2006)).† The expectation is that the surrogate will be appointed within thirty days of the decision that the child needs a surrogate. Whether the education agency pays the surrogate to represent the student is a matter of state law.

> † If a child is a ward of the state, a surrogate who meets the requirements may be appointed by the judge overseeing the child's case (34 C.F.R. § 300.519(c) (2006)).The LEA appoints the surrogate for an unaccompanied homeless youth (20 U.S.C. § 1415(b)(2)(A) (2006)). A temporary surrogate from appropriate staff (e.g., emergency shelter staff) may be appointed until one who meets the requirements can be appointed (34 C.F.R. § 300.519(f) (2006)).

The surrogate is to ensure that the student's rights are protected and to represent the child in matters of identification, evaluation, placement, and the provision of FAPE—in short, the same matters that are the subject of a due process hearing. Issues of surrogacy, though rare, occasionally have been litigated in federal court. Failure to appoint a surrogate parent, for instance, has resulted in the denial of a motion to dismiss a case (*Ramon H. v. Illinois State Board of Education*, 1992).

Explanation of the surrogate provision is not required in the Procedural Safeguards Notice. Presumably, this is because a surrogate will be appointed if necessary, and the notice will be given to the surrogate instead of the parent.

Tips for Parents

In working with your child's school, it may help to remember the following:

1. Ask for what you think your child needs. Share your expectations for your child. Put your hopes and requests in writing, if necessary.

2. Be courteous and civil. Educators are people like everyone else; they appreciate being treated with respect. Assertiveness, combined with a cooperative attitude, is more persuasive than aggressiveness or hostility.

3. Know your rights and responsibilities. If you do not have information on your rights and responsibilities under federal and state law when you need it, ask the school district for the information and study it.

4. Ask for explanations of what you do not understand. You should not feel that you are in the dark. For instance, you should understand your child's evaluation data, current levels of academic achievement and functional performance, and progress under the IEP.

5. Be willing to share information about your child with the school. Keep important medical records, past school records, and so on.

6. Understand the school's challenges and burdens. Realize that sometimes your request may not be realistic. In general, educators in many states are overworked and underpaid. They get tired, as parents do. Funds are limited. IDEA does not require schools to fulfill a child's potential but rather to meet the child's special needs in a way that provides meaningful progress toward IEP goals.

7. Be willing to participate in meetings that determine your child's eligibility, IEP, and placement under IDEA. Also be willing to help your child at home and in school, if appropriate. Never forget that you are an important teacher of your child.

8. Be willing to brainstorm various options to meet your child's needs. There is more than one way to solve a problem.

9. Work for "win-win" solutions to problems. Education is not like competitive athletics. No one should have to lose.

10. Know where to turn for help. Resources include your child's teacher and principal, school district special education director, school district Section 504 coordinator, state office of special education complaint officer, state parent training and information center, parent advocacy groups, state protection and advocacy center, public library, and multiple Web sites (see appendix D at the end of this book).

Transfer of Parental Rights to Students

Students with IDEA disabilities who have not graduated from high school with a regular diploma, or who have not otherwise exited the public school system, are eligible for services up to the age of twenty-two, unless state law establishes a younger age ceiling. At the age of majority established by state law (usually eighteen), IDEA allows states to transfer parental rights to the student with the disability unless he or she has been judged incompetent under state law (20 U.S.C. § 1415(m) (2006)). If a state exercises this option, it must still provide parents with all the notices that it would provide to students, but other IDEA rights will shift to the student. The regulations allow the SEA to provide for transfer of the rights to students who are incarcerated in a state or local correctional institution, whether an adult or juvenile facility (34 C.F.R. § 300.520(a)(2) (2006)). IDEA requires that notice of any transfer rights be given to the student one year before the student reaches the age of majority (20 U.S.C. § 1414(d)(1)(A)(VIII)(cc) (2006)).

If, under state law, a student has not been declared incompetent but is determined nonetheless not to have the ability to give informed consent about his or her educational program, then the state must establish procedures to allow the parent to continue to represent the educational interests of the student. If the parent is not available, then another appropriate individual must be selected (20 U.S.C. § 1415(m)(2)(2006)).

↳Reminders and Tips

1. Due process of law is a constitutional right with additional statutory protection under IDEA. Therefore, it deserves utmost respect by school personnel.

2. If school personnel extend basic courtesy and fairness to parents, they honor the concept of due process. If they keep the parents informed and encourage their input, they are providing notice and a chance to be heard. Keeping parents in the dark has led to many court cases.

3. Sharing information with parents helps create a cooperative learning environment and also helps parents assume their responsibilities to their children with disabilities.

4. Learning to use the techniques of principled negotiation can help to resolve many disputes.

↺Review

1. What are the two basic requirements of procedural due process under the Constitution of the United States?

   They are (a) notice of the intended government abridgment of life, liberty, or property interests and (b) a chance for the recipient of the proposed action to respond.

2. Name two major and separate kinds of notice provisions in IDEA.

   A. One is written notice by an LEA prior to taking action or refusing to act in a matter concerning the child's identification, evaluation, placement, or provision of FAPE. This notice will contain information specific to the individual child.

   B. Another is written notice to parents of all the procedural safeguards available under IDEA. This notice will be the same notice to all parents.

3. Name the ways in which parents can be heard on behalf of their child.

They can give or withhold consent at key stages. They can obtain an IEE if they disagree with the school district's evaluation. They can have access to their child's education records and can place information in the record under certain conditions. They can participate in the evaluation process and in eligibility, IEP, and placement decisions. They can utilize a number of informal and formal mechanisms, including mediation, resolution sessions, hearings, and litigation to resolve disputes. They can receive attorneys' fees under certain conditions. They can use the State Complaint Procedures when they believe IDEA is being violated. Finally, a surrogate can be appointed to speak in lieu of a parent under certain conditions.

⚡References

Family Educational Rights and Privacy Act (FERPA), 20 U.S.C. § 1232g.(2006).

Fisher, R., Ury, W., & Patton, B. (1991). *Getting to yes: Negotiating agreement without giving in* (2nd ed.). New York, NY: Penguin Books.

Individuals with Disabilities Education Improvement Act, 20 U.S.C. § 1400 *et seq.* (2006).

Individuals with Disabilities Education Improvement Act Regulations, 34 C.F. R. § 300.1 *et seq.* (2006).

MacKey v. Bd. of Educ. for the Arlington Cent. Sch. Dist., 386 F.3d 158, 164 (2d Cir. 2004).

Mills v. Dist. of Columbia Bd. of Educ., 348 F. Supp. 866 (D.D.C. 1972).

PARC v. Pennsylvania, 343 F. Supp. 279 (E.D. Pa. 1972).

Ramon H. v. Ill. St. Bd. of Educ., 1992 U.S. Dist. LEXIS 11798 (N.D. Ill. 1992).

Schaffer v. Weast, 546 U.S. 49 (2005).

Suchey, N., & Huefner, D. S. (1998). The state complaint procedure under the Individuals With Disabilities Education Act. *Exceptional Children, 64,* 529–542.

⇉Selected Supplementary Resources

D'Alo, G. E. (2003). Accountability in special education mediation: Many a slip 'twixt vision and practice? *Harvard Negotiation Law Review, 8,* 201–269.

Edmister, P., & Ekstrand, R. E. (1987, Spring). Lessening the trauma of due process. *Teaching Exceptional Children,* 213–217.

Etscheidt, S. (2003). Ascertaining the adequacy, scope, and utility of district evaluations. *Exceptional Children, 69,* 227–247.

Goldberg, S. S., & Huefner, D. S. (1995). Dispute resolution in special education: An introduction to litigation alternatives. *Education Law Reporter, 99,* 703–711.

Herr, C. M., & Bateman, B. D. (2006). *Better IEP meetings: Everyone wins.* Verona, WI: IEP Resources.

Huefner, D. S. (1999). A model for explaining the procedural safeguards of the Individuals With Disabilities Education Act (IDEA '97). *Education Law Reporter, 134,* 445–451.

Kuriloff, P. J., & Goldberg, S. S. (1997). Is mediation a fair way to resolve special education disputes?: First empirical findings. *Harvard Negotiation Law Review, 2,* 35–66.

Marchese, S. (2001). Putting square pegs into round holes: Mediation and the rights of children with disabilities under the IDEA. *Rutgers Law Review, 53,* 333–364.

Zirkel, P. A. (2005). The over-legalization of special education. *Education Law Reporter, 195,* 35–40.

Zirkel, P. A. (1994). Overdue process revisions for the Individuals With Disabilities Education Act. *Montana Law Review, 55,* 403–414.

Chapter 9

Student Records and Privacy Issues Under FERPA and IDEA

Chapter Outline

Background

The Family Educational Rights and Privacy Act (FERPA)

    What Is an Education Record?

    Access Rights

    Privacy Rights

    Controversies

    Remedies for FERPA Violations

Incorporation of and Additions to FERPA in IDEA

Destruction of Records Under FERPA and IDEA

Miscellaneous Privacy Rights

    Protection of Pupil Rights Act

Reminders and Tips

Review

References

Selected Supplementary Resources

Background

Since the 1970s, federal and state governments alike have developed heightened awareness of the need for public access to many kinds of government documents, as a way of checking on their accuracy and also discouraging government officials from acting in secrecy when secrecy is not justified. Simultaneously, personal privacy issues have grown in importance as the potential for the unwarranted dissemination of personal information has increased, due to the rapid proliferation of computerized data banks. The issues of access to information and privacy of information are reflected in laws that apply to students in general and to special education students in particular.†

> † In effect, access and privacy rights provide additional kinds of procedural protections for parents of students with disabilities, although these rights emerged from a concern for the rights of parents and families more generally. As you read the material in this chapter, note how access and privacy rights correlate with the procedural due process rights of notice and chance to be heard.

Two federal statutes have particular importance for the access and privacy rights of students with disabilities and their parents. The first is the Family Educational Rights and Privacy Act (FERPA) (2006).[1] The second is IDEA, which incorporates and expands many FERPA rights specifically for students with disabilities. Of course, state laws and regulations—such as health codes and state freedom of information acts—may extend beyond the federal protections and become additional sources of privacy or access rights. This chapter, however, is limited to the major federal protections and access rights for students and their parents.

The Family Educational Rights and Privacy Act (FERPA)

FERPA applies to all educational agencies or institutions that receive federal education funds; failure to comply risks loss of the federal funds. FERPA was enacted at a time when parents had been routinely denied access to their children's school records, usually on grounds that the records were written by and for professionals, and would not be understood by parents. In a climate encouraging greater access to public documents, advocates argued successfully that the school should be willing to share information with parents about their child's performance and needs, especially information that might adversely affect their child.

FERPA provides two basic kinds of rights to parents of public school students (and also to parents of private school students if the school receives any federal education dollars): (a) the right to inspect and review their child's education records, and (b) the right to prevent unauthorized persons from seeing that same information. Every year parents must be notified† of these rights (34 C.F.R. § 99.7 (2009)). The rights transfer to students when students reach eighteen years of age or attend an institution of postsecondary education (20 U.S.C. § 1232g(d) (2006)).

> † Any form of notice to parents that is reasonable under the circumstances may be selected, such as mailed notices, published notices, or distribution of the notice in the student handbook. Education agencies must notify parents or adult students with disabilities "effectively" (34 C.F.R. § 99.7 (2009)).

---

[1] FERPA was enacted in 1974 as Title V § 513(a) of P.L. 93-380, 88 Stat. 571—the Education Amendments of 1974. FERPA is also sometimes referred to as the "Buckley Amendment," a reference to former New York Senator James Buckley, sponsor of the FERPA provisions. FERPA is codified at 20 U.S.C. § 1232g (2006).

What Is an Education Record?

To understand the scope of FERPA's access and privacy rights, one must understand what information is considered to be a part of a student's "education record." The Act defines education records as "those records, files, documents, and other materials which (i) contain information directly related to a student; and (ii) are maintained by an educational agency or institution, or by a person acting for such agency or institution"(20 U.S.C. § 1232g(a)(4)(A) (2006)).

Materials that are likely to be education records include reports of attendance, academic performance, and behavior at school; results of standardized tests and psychological examinations; disability classifications, evaluations, and program and placement decisions; teacher and counselor observations; and health information.† The information may be recorded in a variety of ways, "including, but not limited to, handwriting, print, computer media, video or audio tape, film, microfilm, and microfiche" (34 C.F.R. § 99.3 (2009)). One must consider the likelihood that in this age of electronic transmissions, teacher-to-teacher e-mails about individual students may also be part of the student's education record if the emails are stored (maintained) by the LEA or agent of the LEA.

> † If LEAs create and manage intranet chat rooms for instructional purposes and then store or maintain the information, they must remember that these too may be education records that require FERPA protection. If other individuals, such as parents, have access to the students' communications, the LEA may need to seek consent from each parent for their child's involvement in the chat room.

In 2002, in *Owasso Independent School District v. Falvo*, the Supreme Court ruled that student-corrected tests, papers, and homework assignments were not education records under FERPA. The Court ruled that grades are not "maintained" until they become part of the institution's record-keeping system. Assuming (but not deciding) that teachers' grade books were education records, the Court concluded that peer-grading is not "maintaining" the grades. Furthermore, the Court determined that students are not acting as agents of the school when grading each other's papers but are participating in a long-standing, effective pedagogical process that should remain under control of the states. The Court's holding has been incorporated into the 2008 amendments to the FERPA regulations (34 C.F.R. § 99.3(b)(6) (2009)).

Also excluded from the definition of education records are anecdotal notes and memoranda of instructional, supervisory, and administrative personnel that are in the sole possession of the maker and not accessible to or revealed to anyone else except a substitute (20 U.S.C. § 1232g(a)(4)(B)(i) (2006)). The FERPA regulations add that the notes are "used only as a personal memory aid" (34 C.F.R. § 99.3 (2009)).To allow such private notes to be accessible would not only be seen as an invasion of privacy but might inhibit certain necessary professional activities (such as a teacher's notes in a grade book, or a psychologist's notes of a counseling session with a student). Of course, even these records could be discoverable if subpoenaed by a court.

The definition of education records also excludes law enforcement records on a student that are maintained by the law enforcement unit of the school district, if they were created for law enforcement purposes (20 U.S.C. § 1232g(a)(4)(B)(ii) (2006)). If information from these police files becomes part of a student's educational file, however, it becomes an education record. Conversely, a record maintained by the law enforcement unit for a non-law-enforcement purpose (such as disciplinary records) is not a law enforcement record (34 C.F.R. § 99.8(b)(2) (2009)).

Additionally, employee records are excluded from the definition unless the employee is also a student at the institution and is employed because of his or her student status (20 U.S.C. § 1232g(a)(4)(B)(iii) (2006)). Finally, medical treatment records of students eighteen years of age and older are not education records if they are not shared with anyone other than those who are providing the treatment (20 U.S.C. § 1232g(a)(4)(B)(iv) (2006)). This means that the student cannot access these records, although they can be reviewed by a physician or other appropriate professional of the student's choice. These exclusions will usually not apply to public school-age students with disabilities, but they could if, for instance, a student with disabilities is employed by the school district or is receiving services until the age of twenty-one.

When Are Juvenile Court Records Education Records?

Daniel Belanger (*Belanger v. Nashua New Hampshire School District*, 856 F. Supp. 40 (D.N.H. 1994))was an adolescent who was placed in a residential school pursuant to a court order under the New Hampshire juvenile delinquency statute. He was also a child with a disability under IDEA. His mother wanted access to all his education records to help her contest his residential placement. She also was seeking reimbursement for the sums she had to pay for that placement.

The attorney who worked for the school district kept files on Daniel separate from the cumulative educational file. She was a member of the team evaluating Daniel's IEP and placement. Because her records related to the juvenile court action, the LEA refused to give the mother access to them, arguing that they were not education records but juvenile records.

The court determined that the attorney's files on Daniel met the definition of an education record because they contained information directly related to Daniel and were used by the LEA in making decisions that affected Daniel's life. The clincher was that the records were being maintained by an educational agency rather than a law enforcement agency. The source of the records was immaterial.

Access Rights

When parents request information from their child's education record, school districts must produce that information for review and inspection within a reasonable time, and in any event within forty-five days of the request (20 U.S.C. § 1232g(a)(1)(A) (2006)). Either parent, even one who is not living with the student, may inspect the records unless the agency has been informed that, under state law, parental rights have been terminated (34 C.F.R. § 99.4 (2009)). (A court order denying access to the education record will also have the same effect.) Making the child's education record available to parents serves several purposes: (a) it allows parents to catch errors in their child's record, (b) it recognizes the role of parents as partners with the school in addressing a child's school-related issues, and (c) it discourages undocumented, stigmatizing, and possibly defamatory remarks about a child in the record.

If a parent believes that information in the education record is inaccurate, misleading, or a violation of the child's privacy rights, the parent may request its removal or amendment (20 U.S.C. 1232g(a)(2) (2006)). If the request is denied, the parent may request a hearing to challenge the information. If the hearing officer determines that the information should remain in the record, then the parent is entitled to place a statement in the record commenting on the retained information.

If a hearing is held, the FERPA regulations specify that (a) it must occur within a reasonable period of time after the institution has received the request, (b) parents must be afforded an opportunity to present all relevant evidence, and to use an attorney of their choice, at their cost; and (c) the agency must render a written decision within a reasonable period of time (34 C.F.R. § 99.22 (2009)). This hearing is different from an IDEA due process hearing in two key respects: first, it can be an in-house hearing conducted by an official of the educational agency, as long as the official has no direct interest in the outcome; and second, it lacks many of the formal procedures established for IDEA due process hearings.

Privacy Rights

Of equal importance with the access provisions in FERPA are the provisions prohibiting dissemination of student record information to unauthorized third parties. Only "directory information" may be released to unauthorized persons without the prior written consent of parents (or eligible students) (20 U.S.C. § 1232g(b)(1) (A) (2006)). Directory information is information in an education record that is not generally considered harmful or an invasion of privacy to disclose.

Directory Information

Directory information can include the student's name, address, phone number, date and place of birth, grade level, major field of study, participation in school activities and sports, dates of attendance at school, honors, awards, and other similar information (20 U.S.C. § 1232g(a)(5)(A) (2006)). Photographs and email addresses are increasingly included in directory information and have been added to the regulatory examples of directory information. Social security numbers are excluded (34 C.F.R. § 99.3 (2009)). Schools must notify parents of what constitutes directory information and provide an opportunity for a parent to request that all or part of such information be withheld (20 U.S.C. § 1232g(a)(5)(B) (2006)). Unless the school district complies with procedures for the release of directory information, FERPA does not allow public access to the information. For instance, in *Brent v. Paquette*, 567 A. 2d 976 (N.H. 1989), the court permitted no access to student directory information connected to a "Special Education Plan" because the parents were neither given proper notice nor provided a sufficient comment period. To avoid administrative headaches, some public schools choose not to publish directory information.

In general, those who are authorized to see the education records include school officials with a "legitimate educational interest" in the information, and they must be designated as such by their respective school districts (20 U.S.C. § 1232g(b)(1)(A) (2006)). Typically, teachers, building administrators, other school professionals, and even student teachers and parents who assist teachers in the classroom can be authorized to see those portions of a student's record in which they have a legitimate educational interest. Under the 2008 amendments to the FERPA regulations, parties such as contractors, consultants, or even volunteers can be considered school officials if they are performing work that school employees would otherwise do (34 C.F.R. § 99.31(a)(1)(i)(B) (2009)). Especially with the advent of computerized or electronic records, it is important to limit access to those with a legitimate need to know the information. School personnel must also realize that they are not entitled to redisclose any information from the child's record without parental consent

(34 C.F.R. § 99.33 (2009)). If a student moves to a new district, the new district is also permitted to receive the child's education records, as long as notice is provided to the parents (20 U.S.C. § 1232g(b)(1)(B) (2006)).

Others authorized to see a child's education records under limited circumstances include the following:

(a) certain federal and state officials, for the purpose of evaluating or auditing an education program receiving federal support;

(b) organizations or persons conducting certain types of educational research for, or on behalf of, educational agencies, as long as no personally identifiable information is released with the research results;

(c) official accrediting organizations in conjunction with the accreditation process;

(d) "appropriate parties" who need information to protect students or others in health or safety emergencies;

(e) court officials pursuant to judicial order or subpoena, and without a court order or subpoena if the parent or LEA initiates legal action against the other; and

(f) state and local officials, if the disclosure is allowed by a state statute and concerns the juvenile justice system's ability to serve the student effectively prior to adjudication, as long as redisclosure will not occur without parental consent 20 U.S.C. § 1232g(b)(1)(C)-(J) (2006)).[2]

Certain other exceptions apply primarily to postsecondary institutions.

The above exceptions to the general prohibition of release of student information to third parties are narrow and specific. If the request for student information does not fall within one of these exceptions, written consent from the parent must be obtained.† For instance, if an employer, a physician, or a social worker from outside the educational agency seeks information from a student's record, written parental consent is necessary. To be effective, the consent must be specific, designating the information to be released and to whom the information is to be given (20 U.S.C. § 1232g(b)(2)(A) (2006)). Furthermore, persons receiving the information may not redisclose it to others without parental consent. The school district must also keep a record of which persons or institutions have requested information on the student if such requests come from outside the school system (20 U.S.C. § 1232g(b)(4)(A) (2006)). This list is available only to parents, school officials with custodial responsibilities for the records, and auditors of the system.

† Written consent can now include electronic signatures (34 C.F.R. § 99.30(d) (2009)).

---

[2] Two omitted exceptions pertain to the higher education context. See 20 U.S.C. § 1232g(b)(1)(D) and (H) (2006). See also 34 C.F.R. § 99.31 (2009).

Controversies

Some of the more troublesome privacy issues under FERPA have concerned the disclosure of psychological records, health records, and law enforcement records kept at school. Sometimes, reports of alleged child abuse enter a student's records, in which case school officials usually should protect the anonymity of the reporter by keeping that person's name out of the records. Health records could fall under the definition of an education record, yet a school nurse might wish to keep certain sensitive information out of the child's file, lest it be seen by other school personnel when disclosure could be harmful to the student. The health or medical record of a student with AIDS is one example of information that should be available to only a few people. How to protect the confidentiality of health records may depend on state law but may also depend on the record-keeping procedures of a given school district. Moreover, records of many health care professionals involved in special education may be subject to internal sharing restrictions not only by state law but also by federal requirements under the Health Insurance and Portability Accountability Act of 1996 (HIPAA).

Another problematic situation may arise if the police are called to a school to quell a disturbance. Some school officials in past years have declined to provide specific information about the involved students lest the disclosure violate FERPA rights. In some situations, this would seem to be an overabundance of caution because FERPA allows disclosure to noneducation officials in emergencies, when necessary to protect the health or safety of the student or others. Moreover, FERPA allows release of records to state or local officials, if disclosure is required by state law and concerns the ability of the juvenile justice system to effectively serve a student prior to adjudication (20 U.S.C. § 1232g(b)(1)(E) (2006)). For example, information that the student is a special education student with certain kinds of behaviors and special needs might be valuable to a juvenile detention center in determining how to manage an unruly student.

A 1994 FERPA amendment specified that an educational agency is not prohibited from placing appropriate information in the student's file about disciplinary actions for misconduct that posed "a significant risk to the safety or well-being" of the student or other members of the school community (20 U.S.C. § 1232g(h)(1) (2006)). Nor did FERPA prohibit the disclosure of that information to school personnel with legitimate educational interests in the behavior of the student (20 U.S.C. § 1232g(h)(2) (2006)). That these clarifications were even necessary indicates just how uncertain some school officials had become about what would violate a student's privacy rights.†

> † In the wake of the 33 deaths at Virginia Tech in 2007 at the hands of a disturbed student, a new FERPA regulation was added in 2008. It makes explicit that an educational agency or institution, in connection with an emergency, may disclose personally identifiable information to any person, including the parents of a postsecondary student (or a student over the age of majority), if their knowledge of the information is needed to protect the health or safety of the student or other individuals. The agency may take into account the "totality of the circumstances," and if the determination to disclose has a rational basis, the Family Policy Compliance Office (the enforcement arm of FERPA) will not second-guess the decision (34 C.F.R. § 99.36(a) & (c) (2009)).

What Can LEAs Tell Parents about the Disciplinary Action Taken Against a Child Who Harms Their Child?

In *Jensen v. Reeves*, 3 Fed. Appx. 905 (10th Cir. 2001) [unpublished and therefore not precedent-setting], a boy was disciplined several times, among other reasons for punching a girl in the nose and giving her a nose bleed. Without the consent of the boy's parents, the principal sent a letter to the girl's parents describing the punishment that had been meted out (that is, loss of lunch/cafeteria privileges for a week). This disclosure seems to be a FERPA privacy violation (assuming that a record of the disciplinary action was maintained by the school district), but the Tenth Circuit held that the letter to the parents was not a release of the misbehaving student's education record. To rule otherwise, said the court, "would place educators in an untenable position" because "they could not adequately convey to the parents of affected students that adequate steps were being undertaken to assure the safety of the student" (p. 910). Do you think FERPA allows or should allow disclosure of specific disciplinary action without parental consent?

Consider the following related information: IDEA requires that disciplinary records of suspension and expulsion be kept by the LEA and reported to the state (20 U.S.C. § 1412(a)(22) (2006)). At the postsecondary level, FERPA provisions allow postsecondary institutions to disclose final results (name, violation, sanction imposed) of certain kinds of disciplinary proceedings to alleged victims of any crime of violence or a nonforcible sex offense (20 U.S.C. § 1232g (b)(6)(A) and (C) (2006)). Those institutions are also allowed to disclose final results to the public if a violation of the institution's rules or policies is established with respect to crimes of violence or nonforcible sexual offenses (20 U.S.C. § 1232g(b)(6)(B)). By implication, lesser offenses by postsecondary students are still subject to the confidentiality obligations.

Remedies for FERPA Violations

The remedy specified in the statute for an educational agency policy or practice that violates FERPA is termination of federal funds. Therefore, the question arose whether an individual harmed by a violation lacked a judicial remedy. This question generated a split of judicial opinion that was resolved by the Supreme Court in 2002. In *Gonzaga v. Doe*, the Court found no basis for a civil rights, monetary damage remedy to vindicate FERPA rights. In other words, there is no private right of action in court by an aggrieved parent or student (20 U.S.C. § 1232g(h)(2) (2006)). This means that complaints must be directed to the Family Policy Compliance Office (FPCO), a small administrative office within ED that functions as ED's enforcement arm for FERPA. FPCO, however, is unlikely to recommend termination of federal funds for isolated instances of FERPA violations. Instead, after investigating a complaint, it issues factual findings, and will ask a violating educational agency to comply with certain FERPA conditions within a specified, reasonable period of time. Individual violations, however, are difficult to remedy after the fact, and FPCO's decisions will usually be prospective in nature. (Be aware, however, that LEAs are not prohibited from disciplining employees for a FERPA violation.†) If the FPCO cannot obtain voluntary compliance from an LEA, the Secretary of Education is authorized to withhold further payments to the educational agency, compel compliance through a cease-and-desist order, or terminate eligibility for federal funding under any applicable program (34 C.F.R. § 99.67 (2009)). Such a punishment would be a rare event.

† Violation of privacy also can sometimes be a violation of the due process clause of the Fourteenth Amendment. See, e.g., *L.S. v. Mt. Olive Board of Education*, No 09-3052, 2011 WL 677490

(D.N.J. February 25, 2011) (holding that two instructors had violated a Section 504 student's right to privacy by releasing portions of his psychiatric evaluation as a model for students to use in assessing the mental health of the student protagonist in Salinger's famous novel, *Catcher in the Rye*. Although the boy's name was redacted, the information made the boy identifiable.)

Incorporation of and Additions to FERPA in IDEA

Parental access to a student's education records is especially important to parents of special education students because the risk of stigmatization of these students is great. If the education records contain errors or prejudicial information, a student's instructional program or placement can be affected adversely. In order to stress the importance of the basic FERPA rights for students with disabilities, OSEP incorporated the basic FERPA provisions in IDEA's implementing regulations and added to them in significant ways (34 C.F.R. §§ 300.610-627 (2006)).

Among the elaborations, the IDEA regulations require any agency that maintains or uses personally identifiable information on an IDEA student to give access to that information to the parents. For instance, a private provider of related services with whom the school has contracted must also comply with the FERPA requirements incorporated into IDEA.

The regulations also go beyond FERPA in specifying that "without unnecessary delay and before any meeting regarding an IEP or any [due process] hearing . . . or resolution session," the education agency must comply with parental requests to inspect and review their child's education records (34 C.F.R. § 300.613(a) (2006)).This may result in a foreshortening of the forty-five-day time limit in FERPA for responding to a request. The regulations also require that actual copies of the evaluation report, documentation of eligibility, and IEP be provided to parents at no cost (34 C.F.R. § 306(a)(2) and § 300.322 (f). (2006)), creating an exception to the general rule that inspection is sufficient, and that if copies are needed, a reasonable fee may be charged (20 U.S.C. § 1414(b)(4)(B) (2006)).

Special educators and school psychologists have sometimes worried that a parent will gain access to confidential test protocols and questions, particularly standardized IQ test protocols, in a child's file. When possible (and often it is not), only the answer sheet should be placed in the file, and the protocols and test questions should be retained elsewhere to protect the confidentiality of the questions themselves. Psychologists consider it a breach of their ethical standards to release test questions, yet it seems that test materials in the file can be copied for parents if otherwise they could not access them (34 C.F.R. § 300.613(b)(2) (2006)). An acceptable alternative might be for a representative of the parent to inspect and review the protocols and test questions (34 C.F.R. § 300.613(b)(3). Of course, whenever a parent or parent representative is inspecting the records, nothing prevents a representative of the LEA from being present. In any event, the LEA should be prepared to respond to reasonable requests for explanations and interpretations of standardized test results and other material in the file (34 C.F.R. § 300.613(b)(1)).

Under IDEA, whether the FERPA rights extend to special education students over the age of majority depends on state law. IDEA indicates that a state may transfer parental rights under IDEA to the child at the age of majority if the child has not been deemed incompetent under state law (20 U.S.C. § 1415(m) (2006)). These rights include access to the education record. The parents must be notified of any such transfer of rights. An exception to the transfer can be created, however, if a student is determined not to have the ability to provide informed consent with respect to his or her educational program. The IDEA regulations add that each SEA must determine the extent to which children are given privacy rights similar to those given their parents, "taking into consideration the age of the child and type or severity of disability"(34 C.F.R. § 300.625(a) (2006)).

Under IDEA, parents will be able to see their child's treatment records if they are forwarded to the school by a physician or mental health therapist and placed in the child's education record. This fact has particular relevance in the case of special education students with emotional disturbance. School officials should be alert to the need to return extraneous, sensitive material to the sender, who should be made aware that parents may access all the information in the child's education record. Parental access to their child's treatment records under IDEA is in contrast to FERPA, where "eligible" students (that is, those over the age of majority or enrolled in a postsecondary institution) can be denied access to records "created, maintained, or used only in connection with the provision of treatment" by a physician, psychiatrist, psychologist, or other recognized professional or paraprofessional (20 U.S.C. § 1232g(a)(4)(B)(iv) (2006)).

Finally, IDEA '04 goes beyond FERPA in permitting a state to require a school district to place disciplinary information in a child's education record. If the child subsequently transfers to another school, any records that follow the child to the new school must include the IEP and disciplinary action (20 U.S.C. § 1413(i) (2006)). †If an educational agency reports a crime committed by a child with a disability, it must transmit copies of the education record, including the disciplinary record, for consideration by the authorities to whom it reports the crime (34 C.F.R. § 300.535(b) (2006)). The transmittal, however, is allowed only to the extent consistent with FERPA, which probably means that parental consent is required.

† The No Child Left Behind Act goes one step further and requires states that accept ESEA funds to have a procedure in place to facilitate the transfer of suspension and expulsion records to any public or private school in which a suspended or expelled student intends, seeks, or is instructed to enroll (20 U.S.C. § 7165 (2006)).

Destruction of Records Under FERPA and IDEA

No provision in FERPA stops an educational agency from destroying education records, as long as there is no outstanding request to inspect and review them, and as long as the agency does not single out for destruction a parent's written explanation of challenged information that remains in the file (34 C.F.R. § 99.10(e) (2009)).† Under IDEA, however, if a school district no longer needs a student's education records to provide educational services, it must notify the parents (34 C.F.R. § 300.624(a) (2006)). The parents may then request destruction of the information, and the district must honor the request. At its discretion, however, the school district may permanently retain the following information: name, address, telephone number, grades, attendance record, classes attended, grade level completed, and year completed.

† A 3-year retention is required, however, for certain audit purposes—that is, for records required to document compliance with ED-funded programs. States may have their own retention requirements.

Because the preservation of some kinds of information may prove helpful in establishing eligibility for adult disability benefits, parents should be aware of the possible disadvantages of destroying assessment information in their child's file. (As a matter of good practice, many LEAs give the child's records to parents rather than destroying them.) Moreover, the district should transfer records whenever possible when a student moves out of the district, so that the new school has access to information that is necessary to provide services.

Miscellaneous Privacy Rights

Occasionally, other student privacy rights requiring interpretation or application of FERPA and IDEA to new situations have been litigated. One such case raised the issue of the extent of courtroom privacy for a special education student (*Webster Groves School District. v. Pulitzer Publishing Company,* 1990). IDEA provides that the parent controls whether a due process hearing is open or closed to the public. Both IDEA and FERPA require parental consent prior to disclosure of a student's education record to unauthorized persons. Applying these requirements, the court held that the privacy rights of students under IDEA and FERPA extended to the court setting. The school district in *Webster* was seeking a court injunction to allow expulsion of a student for carrying a loaded handgun to school, and the press wanted to cover the proceedings. The court granted the student's motion for a closed courtroom and sealed records, because it concluded that the privacy rights of the minor outweighed any qualified common law or First Amendment right of courtroom access by the press.

Another case addressed the right of privacy in re-evaluation procedures. In *Andress v. Cleveland Independent School District* (1995), parents asserted a privacy right for their son, who had both a learning disability and a serious emotional disturbance, and who had developed test anxiety and difficulty relating to unfamiliar school personnel. The parents wanted an independent evaluation of their son rather than a school re-evaluation. The U.S. Court of Appeals for the Fifth Circuit held that IDEA provided no exception to the school district's right to re-evaluate a student if the parents wanted publicly funded special education services.

Perhaps partly in response to the Fifth Circuit's ruling, Congress added a requirement in IDEA '97 that parental consent must be sought prior to conducting any re-evaluation.† If the parents actively refuse their consent (rather than not responding), the school district is prohibited from re-evaluating the child for eligibility (20 U.S.C. § 1414(c)(3) (Supp. III 1997). This provision was carried forward in IDEA '04. Because, in general, a re-evaluation is necessary prior to determining that a child is no longer IDEA-eligible (20 U.S.C. § 1414(c)(5) (2006)), a parental denial of consent can be read to mean that an LEA cannot stop serving a child who it believes is no longer eligible. This seems intuitively wrong, and, therefore, the regulations allow the LEA to use the due process hearing procedures to override the parental refusal to consent (34 C.F.R. § 300.300(c) (2006)).

† The regulations clarify that consent is not required for a re-evaluation if all that is needed is a review of existing data. Consent is also not required to administer a test that can be given without parental consent to children without disabilities (34 C.F.R. § 300.300(d) (2006)). Privacy issues do not arise in these contexts.

Protection of Pupil Rights Act

School psychologists, teachers of students with disabilities, and school administrators should also be aware of another law, the Protection of Pupil Rights Act (PPRA) (2006). PPRA establishes privacy protections with respect to surveys, analyses, and evaluations funded in whole or in part by ED. PPRA was amended by a provision in the No Child Left Behind Act and now extends to all elementary and secondary schools receiving ED funds (basically all of them). LEAs must now develop policies in conjunction with parents that allow parental access, upon request, to any third-party survey (that is, a non–ED funded survey) prior to its administration to a student. Upon request, parents must also be allowed to access instructional materials used as part of the educational curriculum. Furthermore, the policies must include the right of parental inspection and student privacy protections for any survey that seeks information on any of the following sensitive topics:

(a) political affiliations or beliefs of the student or student's parent;

(b) mental or psychological problems of the student or student's family;

(c) sex behavior or attitudes;

(d) illegal, antisocial, self-incriminating, or demeaning behavior;

(e) critical appraisals of other individuals with whom the student has close family relationships;

(f) legally recognized privileged or analogous relationships (such as those with lawyers, physicians, ministers);

(g) religious practices, affiliations, or beliefs of the student or the student's parent; and

(h) income (other than legal requirements for eligibility in various programs) (20 U.S.C. §1232h(c) (2006)).

PPRA requires that parents be notified and given an opportunity to opt the student out of participation, not only in the above kind of survey but also in activities that involve (a) "collection, disclosure, and use" of personal information for the purpose of marketing or selling that information to others, or (b) any school-administered, "nonemergency, invasive physical examination" required as a condition of attendance for students generally if the examination is not necessary to protect the immediate health and safety of the student or other students (20 U.S.C. §1232h(c)(2) (2006)). (Such examinations might include various immunizations, but if these immunizations are required under state law, then state law overrides this PPRA provision.)

The FPCO administers the PPRA along with FERPA. The PPRA privacy protections are independent of and do not supersede FERPA. They also do not apply to a survey administered in accordance with IDEA (20 U.S.C. §1232h(c)(5) (2006)). PPRA seems to reflect growing distrust of various kinds of school activities, and it attempts to reinsert the primacy of parental decision making in certain kinds of educational matters affecting their children.

Health Insurance Portability and Accountability Act (HIPAA)

In 2000, the Office for Civil Rights in the Department of Health and Human Services issued its Privacy Rule authorized under the Health Insurance Portability and Accountability Act of 1996 (HIPAA). The HIPAA Privacy Rule restricts health care providers from transferring or disclosing health records to unauthorized persons. Because schools can be health care providers, many school administrators have wondered how HIPAA interfaces with FERPA's rules restricting the transfer or disclosure of education records (which can include health records) to unauthorized persons. Congress and the Department of Health and Human Services have indicated that health information maintained as an education record under FERPA is excluded from the HIPAA Privacy Rule (45 C.F.R. § 160.163, 2003)). FPCO issued a letter reiterating that point and stating that with respect to a student's immunization records, "HIPAA neither authorizes nor permits the disclosure of these records" without patient authorization. *Letter from Leroy S. Rooker*, FPCO Director, to the Alabama Department of Education (February 24, 2004). Retrieved 3/29/11 from http:// www2.ed.gov/ policy/gen/guid/fpco/ferpa/library/index.html. On the other hand, the HIPAA Privacy Rule may make outside health care providers reluctant to share health information that schools need to serve students (such as reports from physicians; immunization records from public health departments). Numerous technical issues arise regarding the interface of HIPAA and FERPA that go beyond the scope of this book. School administrators are advised to keep in touch with guidance offered by the Office for Civil Rights in the Department of Health and Human Services and with their own professional organizations, such as the National School Boards Association.

↳Reminders and Tips

1. School personnel should welcome the interest of parents in their child's education records and respond comfortably and helpfully to requests for information in the child's education record. At the same time, they should know what is considered not to be part of the record.

2. The privacy rights of students have become an important part of our social dialogue about privacy rights in general. School personnel should be conscious of the implications of releasing personally identifiable student information to unauthorized persons, or putting their own interests in disclosure of information ahead of the privacy interests of the child. In this regard, school personnel should remember not to talk too much (gossip) with colleagues or parents.

3. Staff should be trained to prevent leaks of confidential information. In fact, IDEA requires training or instruction regarding both the FERPA and IDEA confidentiality procedures (34 C.F.R. § 300.623(c) (2006)).

4. Staff should be trained about what not to put in a student's file as well as what belongs there. Information and observations with little educational value should be omitted, particularly unsupported characterizations of a student's behavior or performance. Moreover, nurses should carefully consider what information to keep in their own personal records, available only to a substitute nurse.

5. Disciplinary records are part of a child's education record, according to the FERPA regulations. Readers should check with their own states to find out whether their state *requires* that all disciplinary actions be recorded in the student's file.

6. School administrators should establish good procedures to document who accesses each child's education records, with or without parental consent.

↱Review

1. What are the two primary concerns of FERPA?

They are (a) parental access—providing access to the information in their child's education record, and (b) privacy—restricting access so that only authorized persons can see the records.

2. In what ways does IDEA go beyond FERPA in providing for access and privacy?

It requires access to the education record prior to IEP meetings and due process hearings or resolution sessions, which may require a school district to respond more quickly than the forty-five-day maximum allowed under FERPA. It also requires that parents be given, at no cost, an actual copy of their child's IEP, a copy of the child's evaluation report, and documentation of the child's eligibility. It allows states to decide whether to transfer parental rights to the secondary school student at the age of majority, and it allows states to require that disciplinary information be placed in the child's education record.

⚡References

Andress v. Cleveland Indep. Sch. Dist., 64 F.3d 176 (5th Cir. 1995).

Family Educational Rights and Privacy Act (FERPA), 20 U.S.C. § 1232g (2006).

Family Educational Rights and Privacy Act (FERPA) regulations, 34 C.F.R. § 99.1 *et seq.* (2009).

Health Insurance and Portability Accountability Act (HIPAA), Privacy Rule Regulation, 45 C.F.R. Part 160 (2003).

Individuals with Disabilities Education Improvement Act, 20 U.S.C. § 1400 *et seq.* (2006).

Individuals with Disabilities Education Improvement Act Regulations, 34 C.F. R. § 300.1 *et seq.* (2006).

Gonzaga v. Doe, 536 U.S. 273 (2002).

Owasso Indep. Sch. Dist. v. Falvo, 534 U.S. 426 (2002).

Protection of Pupil Rights Act, 20 U.S.C. § 1232h (2006).

Webster Groves Sch. Dist. v. Pulitzer Publishing Co., 898 F.2d 1371 (8th Cir. 1990).

⇉Selected Supplementary Resources

Conn, K. (2003). *Owasso*: A synonym for missed opportunity. *Education Law Reporter, 177*, 765–770.

Daggett, L. M., (2008). Student privacy and the Protection of Pupil Rights Act as amended by No Child Left Behind. *UC Davis Journal of Juvenile Law and Policy, 12*, 1-71.

Daggett, L. M., & Huefner, D. S. (2001). Recognizing schools' legitimate educational interests: Rethinking FERPA's approach to the confidentiality of student discipline and classroom records. *American University Law Review, 51*, 1–48.

Decman, J., & Bauer, C. (2003). Student discipline and the sharing of records: FERPA, IDEA, and the duty to ensure safety. *Education Law Reporter, 171*, 407–414.

Gelfman, M., & Schwab, N. (1991). School health services and educational records: Conflicts in the law. *Education Law Reporter, 64*, 319–338.

Mawdsley, R. D., & Russo, C. J. (2002). Limiting the reach of FERPA into the classroom: *Owasso School District v. Falvo. Eduation Law Reporter, 165*, 1–13.

Schwab, N., & Gelfman, M. H. B. (2002). *Legal issues in school health services*. North Branch, MN: Sunrise River Press.

Chapter 10

Free Appropriate Public Education Under IDEA

Chapter Outline

Statutory Definition of FAPE

The most important right given to students with disabilities under IDEA is the right to a free appropriate public education (FAPE). Under IDEA, FAPE is not just a privilege bestowed at the convenience of school districts but rather a right that must be made available to all eligible students. Therefore, it is particularly important for educators and parents to understand what is meant by FAPE. This is easier said than done because the definition of FAPE in the statute is cryptic. According to IDEA, FAPE is "special education and related services" that (a) are provided at public expense, under public supervision and direction, and without charge, (b) meet standards of the state educational agency, (c) include an appropriate education at the preschool, elementary, and secondary school levels, and (d) are delivered in conformity with the child's IEP (20 U.S.C. § 1401(9) (2006)). Item (a) addresses the "free" and "public" portion of FAPE. Items (b) through (d) address the "appropriate" portion of FAPE.

Because this definition does not establish any particular level of educational quality, its meaning has been subject to dispute. In 1982, the U.S. Supreme Court provided a definitive interpretation of the statutory language. Its decision remains the Court's most important pronouncement on IDEA, and its interpretation has been the binding precedent, so far, for all FAPE cases in all the courts in the country despite significant additions to IDEA since the decision.

The *Rowley* Case

The case providing the opportunity for the Supreme Court to interpret the FAPE definition was *Board of Education of Hendrick Hudson Central School District v. Rowley* (1982). Amy Rowley was an academically able first grader with a severe hearing impairment. Amy's school had developed an IEP in consultation with her parents, who themselves were deaf. The Rowleys were satisfied with parts of Amy's IEP but also wanted the services of a qualified sign language interpreter for all of Amy's academic classes. Amy's IEP called for her education in the general education classroom with support services from a tutor for the deaf one hour per day and a speech therapist three hours per week, along with the provision of an FM wireless hearing aid in her classroom. During Amy's kindergarten year, she had received the services of an interpreter for a two-week trial period, services that the interpreter stated Amy did not need or use. Based on that assessment and Amy's academic and social achievement without the interpreter, the school declined to provide an interpreter during Amy's first-grade year.

The primary argument in favor of an interpreter was that although Amy was an excellent lip reader, she was nonetheless able to decode only approximately 60 percent of the oral language available to her classmates. Her parents argued, and the lower courts agreed, that this denied Amy an opportunity to learn equivalent to that provided to her classmates. As the federal district court put it, Amy was denied an opportunity to achieve her full potential at a level "commensurate with the opportunity provided to other children" (*Rowley*, 1982, p. 186).

The "commensurate opportunity" standard was borrowed from the public education regulations for Section 504 of the Rehabilitation Act (1973). The Section 504 regulations define an "appropriate" public education as regular or special education and related aids and services designed to meet the student's individual needs "as adequately as the needs of the nonhandicapped" are met (34 C.F.R. § 104.33 (1995 and current version, 2009)). Presumably, because Amy's classmates had the opportunity to access 100 percent of what was being said, Amy should have commensurate or equivalent access.

The Supreme Court declined to apply the Section 504 definition, concluding that IDEA had its own operative definition of FAPE and there was no need to borrow one. After studying both the statute and the legislative history leading to its passage, the Court held that Congress intended the necessary "special education and related services" to be personalized (through the IEP) and of "some educational benefit" (*Rowley*, 1982, pp. 200-201) to the student. In determining that more was not required, the Court drew on landmark federal court cases leading up to IDEA, which had established the constitutional principle that all students with disabilities must be given access to a public education that addressed their needs.[1] Accordingly, the Court concluded that meaningful access, rather than any particular substantive level of educational benefit, was the primary purpose of FAPE. Applying that legal standard to Amy's factual situation, the Court concluded that Amy was receiving FAPE and did not require a sign language interpreter.

In so ruling, the Court addressed the argument that Congress intended FAPE to provide "full educational opportunity" to implement the equal protection clause of the Fourteenth Amendment.† The Court interpreted the concept of equal or full educational opportunity to require meaningful access rather than the same or commensurate services that are provided to students without disabilities. On the one hand, it said, to provide special instruction and related services that would maximize one's potential in a manner commensurate with the opportunity provided to general education students would entail difficult measurements that would be entirely unworkable. On the other hand, providing exactly the same services, it said, would be insufficient in some situations and too much in others, and would not meet the individualization requirement.

The Court, in an important footnote, also rejected the view that self-sufficiency was the substantive standard of the statute. The Court stated that "[b]ecause many mildly handicapped children will achieve self-sufficiency without state assistance while personal independence for the severely handicapped may be an unreachable goal, 'self-sufficiency' as a substantive standard is at once an inadequate protection and an overly demanding requirement" (*Rowley*, 1982, p. 202, n. 23).

> † The "full educational opportunity" language appears in IDEA at 20 U.S.C. § 1412(a)(2) (2006) and has been present since the original EAHCA in 1975.

The Court's translation of "meaningful access" into personalized instruction designed to provide "some educational benefit" came directly from the IDEA definitions of special education and related services. Special education is defined as "specially designed instruction…to meet the unique needs of a child with a disability" (20 U.S.C. § 1401(16) (1980), now 20 U.S.C. § 1401(29) (2006)). Related services are defined as various types of supportive services necessary "to assist a child with a disability to benefit from special education" (20 U.S.C. § 1401(17) (1980), now 20 U.S.C. § 1401(26)). In other words, the Court deduced that if the purpose of related services is to help the child benefit from special education, then, logically, benefit must be the purpose of the specially designed instruction as well. Therefore, according to the Court, if (a) the four items on the statutory FAPE checklist definition are met, (b) the IEP is properly designed to address the student's unique (individual) needs, and (c) the IEP is "reasonably calculated" to produce educational benefit, then that is all the statute requires for FAPE.

What the Court did not decide was how much benefit would be enough for any student other than Amy. Instead, it simply said that the benefit must be "meaningful." In Amy's case, the Court determined that because she was receiving "substantial specialized instruction" and related services,

---

[1] See the discussion in *Rowley* (1982 at pp. 192-194) of *Mills v. Dist. of Columbia Bd. of Educ.*, 348 F. Supp. 866 (D. D.C. 1972) and *PARC v. Pennsylvania*, 343 F. Supp. 279 (E.D. Pa. 1972).

and was at the same time making academic progress in her regular classroom and advancing from grade to grade, she was receiving FAPE.

It is important to understand what the *Rowley* decision does, and does not, stand for. First of all, although the FAPE standards of "some educational benefit" and "meaningful access" are modest, they are real. FAPE is a legitimate legal right with accompanying obligations for educators. By interpreting the meaning of FAPE under IDEA, the Supreme Court established the legal standard for subsequent FAPE cases in the courts. This is not to say, however, that some child other than Amy might not need a sign language interpreter in order to receive some educational benefit from her or his IEP. The facts of each individual situation must be weighed on their own terms. In some situations, some educational benefit or meaningful access might require an interpreter (or some other service or program), and in other situations it might not.

The *Rowley* decision does not stand for the proposition that every child who is advancing from grade to grade is receiving FAPE. The Court was not addressing what are referred to as "social promotions." At the time of the decision, the Court did not anticipate that many children with severe disabilities would be included in the general education classroom with supplementary aids and services. Many of these children receive social promotions so that they remain with their age-appropriate peer group. Commenting on this reality, the 2006 regulations, echoing the 1999 regulations, stipulate that FAPE must be available to any child with a disability who needs special education and related services, "even though the child is advancing from grade to grade" (34 C.F.R. § 300.101(c) (2006).

The *Rowley* standard was criticized by the three dissenting justices, who asserted that it failed to go far enough to provide an equal and full educational opportunity. They worried that in Amy's case a teacher with a loud voice might be deemed of some benefit and thereby meet the FAPE standard. It is difficult to imagine, however, that Amy's instruction would be viewed as specially designed, and her IEP as properly developed, if it did not provide individualized services that went beyond a teacher with a loud voice. In any event, subsequent cases have elaborated on the meaning of "some educational benefit."

Rowley Progeny

Subsequent Interpretations of the *Rowley* Benefit Standard

The Third Circuit case of *Polk v. Central Susquehanna Intermediate Unit 16* (1988) is one of the most frequently cited post-*Rowley* FAPE cases. In applying *Rowley*, the Third Circuit in *Polk* decided that it needed to interpret the meaning of "some educational benefit." It concluded that the Supreme Court's FAPE standard required more than trivial benefit—namely, meaningful progress towards the achievement of IEP goals.

Similar interpretations of the meaning of "some educational benefit" as *educational progress* have been adopted in a majority of circuits of the United States Court of Appeals.[2] In *Burlington School Committee v. Massachusetts Department of Education* (1984/1985), the First Circuit's language is that Congress indubitably desired "effective results" and "demonstrable improvement" for the act's

---

[2] See, e.g., *Deal v. Hamilton Cnty. Bd. of Educ.*, 392 F.3d 840 (6th Cir. 2004) (IEP must confer a meaningful educational benefit "gauged in relation to the potential of the child at issue"); *Walczak v. Fla. Union Free Sch. Dist.*, 142 F.3d 119 (2d Cir. 1997) (meaningful academic and social progress as the FAPE measure); *Cnty. of San Diego v. Cal. Special Educ. Hearing Office*, 93 F.3d 1458 (9th Cir. 1996); *JSK v. Hendry Cnty. Sch. Bd.*, 941 F.2d 1563 (11th Cir. 1991) (appropriate education means "making measurable and adequate gains in the classroom," not necessarily meaningful gains across settings; *Abrahamson v. Hershman*, 701 F.2d 223 (1st Cir. 1983).

beneficiaries (p. 788).† The Third Circuit stated that some educational benefit should result in "significant learning" (*Ridgewood Board of Education v. N E.*, 1996). More recently, the Third and Sixth Circuits have asserted that a student's potential should be a consideration in determining how much benefit is enough (*Deal v. Hamilton County Board of Education*, 2004); *T.R. ex rel. N.R. v. Kingwood Township Board of Education*, 2000)).

> † The Fifth Circuit has established four factors to guide its determinations of whether an IEP is reasonably calculated to provide meaningful educational benefit. They are whether (a) the program is individualized on the basis of the student's evaluation and performance, (b) the program is administered in the LRE, (c) the services are provided in a coordinated and collaborative manner by the key "stakeholders"; and (d) positive academic and nonacademic benefits are demonstrated. See *Cypress-Fairbanks Independent School District v. Michael F.*, 118 F.3d 245 (5th Cir. 1997). These factors merge FAPE and LRE considerations and have been cited in a number of other FAPE cases within and sometimes outside the Fifth Circuit.

While interpreting the *Rowley* (1982) standard to require more than trivial benefit, courts remain clear that it does not require an ideal education or the best that money can buy, nor does it guarantee the achievement of the goals and objectives specified in the IEP. Rather courts have required a school district to implement the IEP, and, in effect, make a good-faith attempt to enable the student to make good progress toward the goals therein. The 1999 IDEA regulations embodied this standard and required that services be delivered "in accordance with the IEP" (34 C.F.R. § 300.350 (1999)). This language was deleted (without explanation) in the 2006 regulations, perhaps as a result of judicial interpretations over the past decade that have weakened the assumption that all services must be implemented as specified in the IEP. Decisions in the Fifth, Eighth, and Ninth Circuits, echoed by several lower court decisions in other circuits, have determined that only "material" or "substantial" failures, as opposed to de minimis failures, to implement the IEP constitute a denial of FAPE.[3]

On the other hand, failure to implement important portions of a child's IEP has resulted in a denial of FAPE in several recent cases. Examples of IEP deficiencies include continuation of the same inadequate IEP for two years in a row, failure to document progress, failure to implement a reading program specified in the IEP, and failure to deliver needed discrete trial training.[4] The Second Circuit rejected the view that substantial compliance with an IEP is sufficient. In *D. D. v. New York City Board of Education* (2006), the court held that the term "substantial compliance" referred only to the portion of IDEA that concerns ED's authority to withhold funds from an SEA when less than substantial compliance with the Act is found. In contrast, with respect to the FAPE obligation, the court stated that "IDEA does not simply require substantial compliance. . . ; it requires compliance (D. D., 2006, p. 512).

Extended School-Year Services

The first case to apply the Supreme Court's interpretation of FAPE to an extended school-year (ESY) context was *Battle v. Pennsylvania* (1980).[5] In *Battle*, the Third Circuit decided that Pennsylvania's statutory 180-day school year would have to yield when IDEA students could demonstrate that failure to provide summer services meant failure to individualize an education to meet their unique needs. Otherwise, the state limit on school days would conflict with the FAPE requirement of IDEA. The case generated the now well-known concept of "regression-recoupment" analysis—that is,

---

[3] *Van Duyn v. Baker Sch. Dist. 5J*, 481 F.3d 770 (9th Cir. 2007); *Neosho R-V Sch. Dist. v. Clark*, 315 F.3d 1022 (8th Cir. 2003); *Houston Indep. Sch. Dist. v. Bobby R.*, 200 F.3d 341 (5th Cir. 2000).

[4] See *Miller v. Bd. of Educ. of Albuquerque Pub.Sch.*, 455 F. Supp. 2d 1286 (D.N.M. 2006), *aff'd* on other grounds, 565 F.3d 1232 (10th Cir. 2009); *S. A. v. Riverside Delanco Sch. Dist. Bd. of Educ.*, 2006 U.S. Dist. LEXIS 22302 (D.N.J. 2006).

[5] See also *GARC v. McDaniel*, 716 F.2d 1565 (11th Cir. 1983); *Crawford v. Pittman*, 708 F.2d 1028 (5th Cir. 1983).

analysis of whether failure to provide certain summer school services would produce such substantial regression in educational benefits that a student could not recoup the loss, either at all or within any reasonable time period.

Two important cases refined the contours of the *Battle* decision and have been generally viewed as providing appropriate standards for ESY. In *Alamo Heights Independent School District v. State Board of Education* (1986), the Fifth Circuit rejected an argument that a student would have to suffer severe regression from the absence of summer programming in order to be eligible for it. Instead, the court concluded that if the benefits that accrued during the regular school year would be "significantly jeopardized," then the district must provide an ESY program. In *Johnson v. Independent School District No. 4* (1990),[6] the Tenth Circuit applied the *Alamo Heights* standard and made the specific point that a decision on ESY cannot be based solely on past evidence of regression-recoupment, but also must consider various factors that address the likelihood of future regression.

Johnson was applied in the case of *Reusch v. Fountain* (1999), in which Maryland's Montgomery County Schools' ESY policies were found to be full of IDEA violations. The court ruled that the school district was using an illegal substantive standard for eligibility because the standard was limited to a regression-recoupment analysis. Additionally, procedural defects included inadequate notice to parents, delayed or untimely decisions, and failure to annually assess the need for ESY. The court ordered an extensive set of affirmative remedies, including distribution of a summer school brochure about ESY to parents before IEP reviews, plus an ESY timeline plan, and staff training.

In general, the ESY court decisions have stood for the proposition that school districts may not establish policies that eliminate any given disability or level of disability from potential eligibility for ESY services: All decisions must be individualized. On the other hand, school officials need not offer ESY services merely to advance or enrich educational progress over the summer, or simply to thwart the normal summer regression of students in their educational performance. Instead, refusal to provide an ESY program must result in the denial of FAPE.

The judicial mandate for ESY services was incorporated into the 1999 IDEA regulations and retained in the 2006 regulations, along with the requirement that the decision to provide ESY services must be made by the IEP team (34 C.F.R. § 300.309 (1999)), now 34 C.F.R. § 300.106 (2006)). The exact standards to determine ESY eligibility are left to each SEA, but eligibility cannot be limited to specific categories of disability. In addition, the type, number, and duration of services cannot be limited unilaterally by a school district. If a court rather than the SEA has already set specific standards in a particular jurisdiction, school officials in that jurisdiction will need to follow those standards unless they conflict with the regulations.

Methodological Disputes

The *Rowley* (1982) decision has been helpful to lower courts in situations where parents have argued that a certain teaching method was superior to the one being used in school with their child. The Supreme Court in *Rowley* cautioned that methodological disputes are best left to educational authorities because such disputes exceed the expertise of judicial officials (*Rowley* at pp. 206-207). This view is consistent with the fact that, generally speaking, instructional methods are not included in the IEP but are left to the determination of professional educators. Unless parents can demonstrate that the method being used by a school resulted in the denial of FAPE, courts generally do not intervene to solve methodological disputes.†

---

[6] See also *MM v. Sch. Dist. of Greenville Cnty.*, 303 F.3d 523 (4th Cir. 2002); *Cordrey v. Euckert*, 917 F.2d 1460 (6th Cir. 1990).

† A number of methodological disputes have concerned requests for such specific methodologies as the Lindamood-Bell and Orton-Gillingham reading programs for students with learning disabilities, or oral communication programs for students with hearing impairments. In the past, these requests have been consistently rejected when the district's program was reasonably calculated to produce or was resulting in student progress. See, e.g., *E. S. v. Independent School District No. 196*, 135 F.3d 566 (8th Cir. 1996); *Watson v. Kingston City School District*, 325 F. Supp. 2d 141 (N.D.N.Y. 2004); *M. B. v. Arlington Central School District*, 2002 U.S. Dist. LEXIS 4015 (S.D.N.Y. 2002); *Logue v. Shawnee Mission Public School Unified School District*, 959 F. Supp. 1338 (D. Kan. 1997).

One of the leading cases making this point was *Lachman v. Illinois State Board of Education* (1988).[7] In *Lachman*, a student with a profound hearing impairment sought the services of a cued-speech instructor in his neighborhood high school. The school district proposed to provide a total communication approach in another school. The dispute was judged to be a methodological dispute rather than the LRE dispute claimed by the parents, and the court deferred to the judgment of school officials.

On the other hand, when courts have found that the methods selected by given school districts failed to produce any meaningful progress, they have ruled that the LEA denied FAPE. One of the first such post-*Rowley* cases was *Adams v. Hansen* (1985),[8] in which the parent of a student with a learning disability was dissatisfied with her son's progress and placed him in a private school. In determining that the public school program had denied FAPE to the boy, the court highlighted his minimal four-month progress in reading achievement and eight-month progress in math achievement after two years of instruction, along with his inability to achieve passing marks and advance from grade to grade.

The Autism Methodology Disputes

Over the past fifteen years, a growing number of parents have brought suit claiming that FAPE for their young child with autism required the Lovaas teaching method (an intensive, applied behavioral analysis [ABA] approach using discrete trial training). Many of the initial due process hearings sided with the parents, but often because the LEA had committed serious procedural errors. (See Yell, M. L. & Drasgow, E. (2000). Litigating a free appropriate public education: The *Lovaas* hearings and cases. *Journal of Special Education, 33*, 205–214.) More recently, the cases have tended to favor LEAs, provided the LEA has not made significant procedural errors and can demonstrate that its choice of method is producing, or is reasonably calculated to produce, progress. See, e.g., *T.B. v. Warwick School Committee*, 361 F.3d 80 (1st Cir. 2004); *Burilovich v. Board of Education of Lincoln Consolidated Schools*, 208 F.3d 560 (6th Cir. 2000); *Tyler v. Northwest Independent School District*, 202 F. Supp. 2d 557 (N.D. Tex. 2002); *J.P. v. West Clark Community Schools*, 230 F. Supp. 2d 910 (S.D. Ind. 2002). In *J.P.*, the court articulated a standard that required evidence from educational experts and LEA justification for its rationale or the benefits of the approach it had chosen.

In IDEA '97, Congress seemed to shift its interpretation with respect to the incorporation of instructional methods in the IEP. Language in IDEA '97, retained in IDEA '04, arguably requires consideration of certain methods and, in some cases, their inclusion in an IEP. One example is

---

[7] See also *Bonnie Ann F. v. Calallen Indep. Sch. Dist.*, 835 F. Supp 340 (S.D. Tex. 1993); *Brougham v. Town of Yarmouth*, 823 F. Supp. 9 (D. Me. 1993).

[8] See also *Nein v. Greater Clark City Sch. Corp.*, 95 F. Supp. 2d 961 (S.D. Ind. 2000) (teaching method produced notable lack of progress in reading).

the mandate, in developing the IEP, to consider "the use of positive behavioral interventions and supports, and other strategies" for a child whose behavior impedes his or her learning or that of others (20 U.S.C. § 1414(d)(3)(B)(i)(2006)).† The 1999 regulations and accompanying analysis clarified that when such behavior has occurred or is likely to occur, a statement of the required intervention or a behavioral intervention plan (BIP), must be included in the IEP (34 C.F.R. § 300.346(c) and analysis at 64 Fed. Reg. 12589 (March 12, 1999)). It would seem that these kinds of interventions or management "strategies" are really instructional methods of reducing misbehaviors and teaching new, substitute behaviors.

> † One case examining the educational benefit provided by a child's IEP determined that FAPE was denied because the IEP did not contain (and the LEA did not implement) an appropriate behavioral management plan for the child. The child's IEP stated that a behavior plan was attached to address the inappropriate behaviors that seriously interfered with his learning, but the administrative hearings, upheld by the court, found that only short-term goals and objectives were attached, without any cohesive behavior management plan. Methods attempted by the boy's teacher and paraprofessional had not been analyzed or approved by the IEP team, and the boy's behavior had deteriorated sharply over time (*Neosho R-V School District v. Clark*, 315 F.3d 1022 (8th Cir. 2003)).

In addition to the BIP clarification, the 1999 regulations defined special education for the first time and included "adapting the content, *methodology*, or delivery of instruction" (emphasis added) (34 C.F.R. § 300.26). Furthermore, the analysis accompanying the regulations included support for the selection of particular teaching methods and approaches when needed to produce educational benefit.[9] It stated that although day-to-day adjustments and lesson plans normally did not require IEP team consideration, overall approaches to instruction might. For instance, cued speech was singled out as an example of a "mode of instruction" that might need to be reflected in a child's IEP. Similarly, for a student with learning disabilities who has not learned to read using traditional reading methods, the analysis stated that a particular instructional strategy might need to be selected and would be integral to a child's IEP.[10] Of interest is the omission of this material in the analysis accompanying the 2006 regulations, but the definition of special education remains.

In any event, educators need to be careful to select teaching methods that match a child's unique instructional needs. Although the referenced statutory and regulatory changes have not often been interpreted in court cases to date, and although most courts remain steadfast in their reluctance to judge the relative merits of various methodologies, nonetheless courts are increasingly asking LEAs to demonstrate the sufficiency of their goals and services.

Courts resolutely cite *Rowley* (1982) in rejecting parental arguments that the LEA's choice of method should be equal or superior to the parents' choice. Yet, at the same time, if LEAs cannot justify their choice of methods as empirically validated or accepted practice, and cannot demonstrate that progress is being made using that method, they are increasingly vulnerable.†

> † The Seventh Circuit issued a curious ruling that casts some doubt on the FAPE standard in that circuit. In *School District of Wisconsin Dells v. Z. S. ex rel. Littlegeorge*, 295 F.3d 671 (7th Cir. 2002), the Circuit seemed to rule that whether an IEP was reasonably calculated to produce educational benefit required only that the LEA's preferred placement be "reasonable." Commentators have worried that the decision would be read by lower courts within the Circuit to allow no analysis of the progress toward IEP goals being made in the current placement. It is not necessary to read the case this way, however, because it really concerned an LRE dispute rather than FAPE per se.

---

[9] See analysis accompanying 34 C.F.R. § 300.347 at 64 Fed. Reg. 12595 (March 12, 1999).
[10] See analysis accompanying 34 C.F.R. § 300.26 at 64 Fed. Reg. 12552 (March 12, 1999).

Another Look at Self-Sufficiency as a FAPE Standard

Three post-IDEA '04 cases have revisited the question whether self-sufficiency should be considered part of the FAPE definition. In a controversial 2004 case (*Deal v. Hamilton County Board of Education*, 2004), the Sixth Circuit appeared to raise the *Rowley* FAPE standard by defining meaningful educational benefit in terms of the need to maximize the child's chances for achieving self-sufficiency. The court instructed the district court, on remand, to use the heightened standard to re-examine the evidence and determine whether FAPE had been provided by the LEA's eclectic methods, methods that the Sixth Circuit viewed as less likely to produce self-sufficiency than the parents' private placement and in-home ABA program. On remand, the district court determined that the child's chances for achieving self-sufficiency were speculative (but not encouraging) and, of more importance, that the Supreme Court had made clear in the Rowley case that self-sufficiency was not the standard for FAPE under IDEA. The district court held (*Deal v. Hamilton County Dep't of Education*, 2006) that the school's IEPs were reasonably calculated to provide educational benefit and were substantially appropriate, citing other Sixth Circuit cases for what constituted the established FAPE standard in the Circuit, thereby diminishing the impact of the 6th Circuit's decision in *Deal* (2004). On appeal, the Sixth Circuit this time affirmed the lower court decision (*Deal*, 2008).

Since the 2006 lower court decision in *Deal*, two appeals courts have considered the self-sufficiency standard. In 2010, the Ninth Circuit ruled that the definition of transition services and the goals outlined in IDEA '97 (emphasizing equality of opportunity, full participation, independent living, and economic self-sufficiency) did not supersede the FAPE standard articulated in the *Rowley* case (*J.L., M.L., & K.L. v. Mercer Island School District*, 2010). A similar decision in the Tenth Circuit rejected self-sufficiency and the need for educational progress to generalize to out-of-school settings as the FAPE standard (*Thompson R2-J School District v. Luke P.*, 2008).

Procedural Errors as a Denial of FAPE

The Supreme Court in *Rowley* (1982) not only interpreted the meaning of FAPE but also considered the role of state and federal courts in reviewing administrative hearing decisions. The Court concluded that if a state complied with IDEA's procedural safeguards, and the IEP was reasonably calculated to enable the child to receive educational benefits, the state had met its obligations and courts "can require no more" (pp. 206-207).

This emphasis on procedural compliance generated a multitude of legal claims that procedural violations produced a denial of FAPE. Over the past twenty-five years, courts have examined in detail whether certain procedural violations were, in fact, significant enough to result in a denial of FAPE, or instead were merely harmless error. Although some courts were more fastidious than others in insisting on procedural compliance, the majority view was that only major errors resulted in denial of FAPE. Such errors have included egregious failures to meet timelines for evaluation and IEPs, IEP meetings that failed to consider the parents' requests, absence of key personnel (like parents) at IEP meetings, IEPs that were completed prior to the IEP meeting, evaluation without involvement of persons knowledgeable about the particular disability, and delivery of services by untrained personnel.

To eliminate the opportunity for any court to elevate minor procedural errors into a denial of FAPE, IDEA '04 now explicitly limits the procedural grounds for finding a denial of FAPE. "In matters alleging a procedural violation," hearing officers can find a denial of FAPE on procedural grounds "only if the procedural inadequacies (I) impeded the child's right to [FAPE], (II) significantly impeded the parents' opportunity to participate in the decision[-]making process regarding the provision of [FAPE] to the parents' child, or (III) caused a deprivation of educational benefits" (20 U.S.C. § 1415(f)(3)(E) (2006); "benefits" was changed to "benefit" in the regulations at 34 C.F.R. 300 513 (a)(2)(iii) (2006)).The phrase referring to allegations of procedural violations may prevent hearing officers from basing a FAPE ruling on procedural violations that have not been raised by the parties. Notwithstanding this provision, the hearing officer can order the LEA to comply with the procedural requirements (20 U.S.C. § 1415(f)(3)(E) (2006)).

Can Severe Harassment Constitute a Denial of FAPE?

In perhaps the first decision of its kind, the Third Circuit upheld an administrative hearing officer's determination that an LEA's failure to protect a ninth-grade New Jersey student from severe and prolonged verbal and physical harassment by fellow students constituted a denial of FAPE. The student had been teased and bullied repeatedly by classmates throughout elementary and middle school based on his lack of athleticism, his physique, and his perceived effeminacy. The boy became socially isolated and depressed, and his grades slipped significantly. Despite repeated complaints from the boy's parents, the school administration did not remedy the situation. After the boy's attempted suicide in eighth grade, he was classified under IDEA as having an emotional disturbance. For the following year, his parents placed him in a neighboring high school to avoid continuing contact with the children who had emotionally and physically abused him in his previous schools. The high school he would have attended refused to pay the out-of-district tuition, and the parents first sought mediation, then a hearing, which they won. The school appealed the hearing decision, and the lower court ruled that FAPE could have been provided at the high school because of its discipline program to deal with bullies. The Third Circuit reversed and faulted the district court for failing to defer to the clear weight of the evidence that the school would be unable to meet the boy's emotional needs or provide adequate protection for him, no matter what discipline program it implemented, given the long-term nature of the harassment and the inability to completely separate the boy from his tormentors.

This is a disturbing case because it suggests that the child developed an emotional disability as a result of the ferocious harassment he experienced because of his perceived effeminacy. The school district's inability or failure to stop the harassment when it first began should also be troubling to educators. The case is *Shore Regional High School Board of Education v. P.S.*, 381 F.3d 194 (3d. Cir. 2004).

State FAPE Standards

One of the four items in the statutory FAPE definition is the delivery of special education and related services that "meet the standards of the state educational agency." This item has had particular significance in states that have FAPE definitions that provide a higher standard than the federal government's, because then the state standard will override the federal standard.† In FAPE cases, it is important to know whether the state in which the case arises has a higher standard than the "some educational benefit" standard established by the Supreme Court in the *Rowley* case.

> † The question arises as to whether a student's failure to meet a state's adequate yearly progress (AYP) standards for proficiency in reading, math, and science can be used to assert a denial of FAPE. Thus far, this argument has not been successful in court.

Michigan, Tennessee, California, North Carolina, Maryland, and Arizona have FAPE standards that on their face appear higher than the federal standard established under *Rowley*.[11] Arkansas, Iowa, Massachusetts, Missouri, and New Jersey formerly had language suggesting a higher standard, but each state changed its statute or regulations to conform to the federal standard.[12] Comparably, a federal court interpreted Tennessee's statutory language ("maximize the capabilities") to establish a FAPE standard no higher than the federal standard.[13]

In contrast, North Carolina and California cases have ruled that the commensurate opportunity (Section 504) standard is their state's FAPE standard under IDEA.[14] Moreover, a federal court case in Michigan has ruled that the FAPE standard in that state ("maximum potential") is higher than the IDEA FAPE standard.[15] Although the higher standard may not result in a mandate for more services than are being provided, it is possible that in some situations, services must be more intensive or extensive than those required under the federal standard alone. Readers will want to keep up to date on their state's current FAPE standard.

What are Charter School Responsibilities for FAPE?

Public charter schools, whether considered to be an independent LEA or part of another LEA, must comply with IDEA. A charter school that is an independent LEA may have particular challenges in terms of resources and service options for children with disabilities. Nonetheless, such a school must make FAPE available. In *Seashore Learning Center Charter School*, 32 IDELR 224 (SEA TX 1999), a hearing officer ruled that limited resources were no excuse for the failure to properly assess a student's disabilities and implement his IEP. In response to the resource challenge, some states require public charter schools to be part of a larger LEA; other states allow charter schools to be part of an LEA for special education services; while yet other states accept varying levels of joint responsibility for the provision of FAPE by charter schools that are independent LEAs. *See* O'Neill, P. T., Wenning, R. J., & Giovannetti, E. (2002). Serving students with disabilities in charter schools: Legal obligations and policy options. *Education Law Reporter, 169*, 1–21.

Provision of FAPE in the Correctional System

In general, IDEA requires states to make FAPE available to all children with disabilities ages three through twenty-one. An exception, however, is possible with respect to students ages eighteen through twenty-one if state law does not require special education for those who, prior to their incarceration in an adult correctional facility, were not identified as IDEA eligible or † did not have an IEP (20 U.S.C. § 1412(a)(1)(B)(ii) (2006)). If an incarcerated student with a disability, eighteen through twenty-one, was mistakenly never identified as having an IDEA disability, that student cannot claim eligibility for services in jail or prison, even if the student has not graduated from high school.††

---

[11] See *In re Conklin*, 946 F.2d 306 (4th Cir. 1991) for a thorough discussion of state standards at that time.

[12] See *In re Conklin*, 946 F.2d 306 (4th Cir. 1991); *Reese v. Bd. of Educ. of Bismarck R-V Sch. Dist.*, 225 F. Supp. 2d 1149 (E.D. Mo. 2002); *Lascari v. Bd. of Educ.*, 560 A.2d 1180, 1189 (N.J. 1989); Mass. Gen'l Laws, Ch. 71B § 1 (effective Jan. 1, 2002).

[13] *Doe v. Bd. of Educ. of Tullahoma City Sch.*, 9 F.3d 455 (6th Cir. 1993). (This case is well known for its statement that FAPE requires the equivalent of a serviceable Chevrolet, but not a Cadillac.) But see *Krichinsky v. Knox County Schs.*, 17 EHLR 725 (E.D. Tenn. 1991).

[14] See *In re Conklin*, 946 F.2d 306 (4th Cir. 1991); *Burke Cnty. Bd. of Educ. v. Denton*, 895 F.2d 973, 983 (4th Cir. 1990); *Pink v. Mt. Diablo Unified Sch. Dist.*, 738 F. Supp. 345, 347 (N.D. Cal. 1990).

[15] *Barwacz v. Mich.Dep't of Educ.*, 681 F. Supp. 427 (W.D. Mich. 1988).

† The 2006 regulations, like the 1997 regulations, change the "or" to "and." See 34 C.F.R. § 300.102 (a)(2)(i) (2006). The difference may be an attempt to clarify that a student is not eligible for services simply by virtue of having something called an IEP under Section 504. At the same time, however, 34 C.F.R. § 300.102(a)(2)(ii) adds that an identified IDEA student has a right to special education in a correctional facility if the IEP has not yet been developed or has lapsed because the student left school.

†† Be aware that inmates with a disability can bring a claim of discrimination under Title II of the ADA if they believe that educational services (or other services) in prison discriminate against them on the basis of their disability. In *Pennsylvania Department of Corrections v. Yeskey*, 524 U.S. 206 (1998), the Supreme Court held that the nondiscrimination requirements of Title II of the ADA apply to state prisons. An earlier case in federal district court concluded that Section 504 applied to educational services for inmates in North Carolina state prison because the Department of Corrections was an LEA and, therefore, covered under Section 504. *Anthony v. Freeman*, 24 IDELR 929 (E.D.N.C. 1996).

The governor of a state, if permitted to do so under state law, may assign to an agency other than the SEA the responsibility for meeting IDEA requirements for students who are convicted as adults under state law and incarcerated in adult prisons (20 U.S.C. § 1412(a)(11)(C) (2006)). This assignment would relieve the LEA or SEA from managing, delivering, and paying for the educational services at the prison but would not relieve the outside agency from implementing Part B of IDEA. Note that this gubernatorial discretion does not extend to convictions under federal law because states have no obligation to individuals assigned to federal correctional facilities for a federal offense.

If an IDEA student is convicted as an adult under state law and placed in an adult prison, the basic FAPE requirement continues—namely, meaningful access to special education and related services designed to provide some educational benefit. The student, however, no longer must participate in state or districtwide assessments of achievement under IDEA or NCLB (2006). In addition, if the student will "age out" of IDEA eligibility before he or she is released from prison, then the transition planning and transition service portions of the IEP no longer are required. Finally, the IEP team may modify the student's IEP or placement "if the State has demonstrated a bona fide security or compelling penological interest that cannot otherwise be accommodated" (20 U.S.C. § 1414(d)(7) (2006)). In other words, safety concerns and other overriding prison interests take precedence over assessment requirements, IDEA placement preferences, and some of the IEP content requirements.

FAPE for Suspended or Expelled Students

Beginning with IDEA '97, IDEA made explicit that all children with disabilities who are suspended or expelled from school must continue to receive FAPE. See 20 U.S.C. § 1412(a)(1)(A) (2006). This provision prevents school districts from totally excluding a disruptive or dangerous child with a disability from educational services addressing his or her needs. Although placements can be changed for the safety and welfare of the child and other children, services cannot cease. If they could, we would be back to the pre-1975 days when some school districts excluded children from school whom they did not want or did not know how to serve. (More information about the nature and extent of required services for students who violate rules of student conduct is provided in Chapter 14.

Implications of IDEA '04 for Future Court Interpretations of FAPE

Given the increased focus on outcomes since IDEA '97, educators and academics have speculated that lower court interpretations of *Rowley* requiring meaningful progress toward IEP goals would become the uniformly accepted judicial standard. That speculation seems more potent in the wake of the IDEA '04 amendments that align IDEA with NCLB (2006). Under NCLB, students with disabilities are expected to reach proficiency in math, reading and language arts, and science by the 2013–2014 school year. Students may demonstrate their proficiency levels by taking the regular grade-level state or districtwide assessments, with or without accommodations. Alternatively, they may be given an alternate assessment that is based on alternate achievement standards (or modified achievement standards, but these may not be retained when NCLB is reauthorized). The IEP team selects the appropriate assessment. Of course, the IEP team must also set whatever other academic and functional goals are appropriate for the student.

Under IDEA '04 the IEP must contain a description of when periodic reports of progress toward IEP goals will be provided (20 U.S.C. § 1414(d)(1)(A)(i)(III) (2006)), and IEP revisions are required to address any lack of expected progress "where appropriate" (20 U.S.C. § 1414(d)(4)(A)(ii) (2006)). Furthermore, the selection of special education services, related services, and supplementary aids and services must be based on peer-reviewed research "to the extent practicable" (20 U.S.C. § 1414(d)(1)(A)(iv) (2006)). This phraseology suggests that the IEP team should be aware of the research base and be able to defend its selection of services.

Given the IDEA '04 focus on academic achievement, measurable progress in the general curriculum, and LEA use of empirically validated practices, courts may feel more obligated than in the past to evaluate FAPE in the context of measurable progress toward annual goals. Instead of limiting their analysis to whether a student is receiving special education services and achieving passing grades, or whether IEPs are "reasonably calculated" to produce progress (that is, look good on paper), courts may be more inclined to carefully scrutinize implemented IEPs to evaluate the extent of the student's actual progress toward specified IEP goals. For members of IEP teams, this means that if progress is not occurring at the expected rates, the team should revise the IEP or be prepared to defend and explain the gap.†

> † A possible development to watch closely is whether courts might view proficient scores on AYP (adequate yearly progress) measures as indications of FAPE—in other words as evidence of sufficient academic progress. Of course, this assumes that AYP proficiency correlates quite explicitly with IEP goals, which may or may not be the case. A few cases have considered AYP scores as measures of progress. For instance, an appeals court in *Bradley v. Arkansas Department of Education*, 443 F.3d 965 (8th Cir. 2006) based its decision that FAPE had been provided partly on the student's standardized test scores that indicated consistent academic progress. Comparably, in *Nack v. Orange City School District*, 454 F.3d 604 (6th Cir. 2006), the Sixth Circuit held that FAPE had been delivered because the student reached proficiency or above on NCLB assessments of AYP. This decision was in spite of IEP omissions—omissions that the court considered harmless. At the same time, the court ordered a new IEP and ruled that the FAPE standard had not been altered by NCLB. These decisions suggest the need for care in the use of AYP scores. To the authors' knowledge, no one has suggested that failure to make AYP should be considered evidence of denial of FAPE. What the IEP specifies as academic goals remains of paramount importance.

↳Reminders and Tips

1. Educators are expected to make a positive difference in the life of a child with a disability. Setting realistic goals and measuring progress toward those goals is a legitimate way of determining whether school personnel are making a difference.

2. FAPE does not require an ideal education, a potential-maximizing set of services, or the best education that money can buy. It does require appropriate, individualized services that meet the child's educational needs that arise from the disability.

3. Misbehaving students retain their right to FAPE. They may be disciplined, but schools cannot give up on these students and withdraw the students' entitlement to FAPE (see chapter 14).

4. Selection of appropriate interventions is increasingly important. Congress expects educators to select interventions that are based on peer-reviewed research and proven to be effective. Inability to justify the selection of interventions may make an LEA vulnerable in court.

5. Meaningful, measurable progress toward IEP goals is likely to become increasingly important as the primary measure of FAPE.

↳Review

1. What was the Supreme Court's interpretation of FAPE in the *Rowley* case?

   The Court specified that the child's special education must be individualized to provide, or be calculated to provide, meaningful access, measured in terms of "some educational benefit." Readers should also remember that FAPE requires publicly supervised special education and related services that are at no cost to the parents, meet state standards, are appropriate for preschool through high school age students, and conform to the IEP.

2. How has the Court's interpretation of FAPE been refined and expanded by a number of circuits of the U.S. Court of Appeals?

   Most circuits have interpreted "meaningful access" and "some educational benefit" to mean meaningful, good, or satisfactory progress toward IEP goals.

3. What aspects of IDEA's IEP requirements support the judicial interpretation of FAPE as requiring meaningful progress toward IEP goals? (Readers may want to review the IEP chapter.)

The IEP must describe how the child's disability affects *progress* in the general curriculum. The goals must relate to meeting the child's educational needs resulting from the disability, to enable the child to *make progress* in the general education curriculum, among other things. The IEP also must include a statement of special education and related services, supplementary aids and services, program modifications, and supports for school personnel to allow the child to advance appropriately toward the annual goals and to *make progress* in the general education curriculum. The IEP must contain a description of how the child's *progress* will be measured and when periodic *progress reports* will be provided. With all these references to progress, it seems difficult to avoid the conclusion that meaningful progress toward IEP goals is expected for FAPE.

⚡References

Adams v. Hansen, 632 F. Supp. 858 (N.D. Cal. 1985).

Alamo Heights Indep. Sch. Dist. v. St. Bd. of Educ., 790 F.2d 1153 (5th Cir. 1986).

Battle v. Pennsylvania, 629 F.2d 269 (3d Cir. 1980).

Bd. of Educ. of Hendrick Hudson Central Sch. Dist. v. Rowley, 458 U.S. 176 (1982).

Burlington Sch. Comm. v. Mass. Dep't of Educ., 736 F.2d 773 (1st Cir. 1984) (Burlington II), *aff'd*, 471 U.S. 359 (1985).

D. D. v. New York City Board of Education, 465 F.3d 503 (2d Cir. 2006).

Deal v. Hamilton Cnty. Bd. of Educ., 392 F.3d 840 (6th Cir. 2004), *on remand* 2006 U.S. Dist. LEXIS 27570 (E.D. Tenn), *aff'd* 258 Fed. Appx. 863 (6th Cir. 2008).

Individuals with Disabilities Education Improvement Act, 20 U.S.C. § 1400 *et seq.* (2006).

Individuals with Disabilities Education Improvement Act Regulations, 34 C.F. R. § 300.1 *et seq.* (2006).

J. L., M. L., & K. L. v. Mercer Island Sch. Dist., 575 F. 3d 1025 (9th Cir. 2010).

Johnson v. Indep. Sch. Dist. No. 4, 921 F.2d 1022 (10th Cir. 1990).

Lachman v. Ill. St. Bd. of Educ., 852 F.2d 290 (7th Cir. 1988).

No Child Left Behind Act of 2001, 20 U.S.C. § 6301 *et seq.* (2006).

Polk v. Central Susquehanna Intermediate Unit 16, 853 F.2d 171 (3d Cir. 1988).

Reusch v. Fountain, 872 F. Supp. 1421 (D. Md. 1994).

Ridgewood Bd. of Educ. v. N. E., 172 F.3d 238 (1996).

Section 504 of the Vocational Rehabilitation Act of 1973, 29 U.S.C. § 794 (2006).

Section 504 ED regulations, 34 C.F.R. § 104 *et seq.*(2009).

T. R. ex rel. N. R. v. Kingwood Township Bd. of Educ., 205 F.3d 572 (3d Cir. 2000).

Thompson R2-J Sch. Dist. v. Luke P., 540 F.3d 1143 (10th Cir. 2008).

⇥Selected Supplementary Resources

Bhat, P., Rapport, M. J., & Griffin, C. C. (2000). A legal perspective on the use of specific reading methods for students with learning disabilities. *Learning Disability Quarterly, 23,* 283–297.

Daniel, P. T. K. (2009). "Some Benefit" or "Maximum Benefit": Does the No Child Left Behind Act render greater educational entitlement to students with disabilities? *Journal of Law and Education, 37,* 347-365.

Eyer, T. L. (1998). Greater expectations: How the 1997 IDEA amendments raise the basic floor of opportunity for children with disabilities. *Education Law Reporter, 126,* 1–19.

Huefner, D. S. (2009). Updating the FAPE standard under IDEA. *Journal of Law and Education, 37,* 367-379.

Huefner, D. S. (1991). Judicial review of the special educational program requirements under the Education for All Handicapped Children Act: Where have we been and where should we be going? *Harvard Journal of Law & Public Policy, 14,* 483–516.

Johnson, S. F. (2003). Reexamining *Rowley:* A new focus in special education law. *Brigham Young University Education and Law Journal, 2003,* 561–585.

Knight, J. A. (2010). Comments: When close enough doesn't cut it: Why courts should want to steer clear of determining what is—and what is not—material in a child's individual [sic] education program. *Univ. of Toledo Law Review, 41*(2), 375-409.

Mead, J. F. (2002). Determining charter schools' responsibilities: A guide through the legal labyrinth. *Journal of Law and Education, 31,* 305–326.

Nelson, C. & Huefner, D. S. (2003). Young children with autism: Judicial response to the Lovaas and Discrete Trial Training Debates. *Journal of Early Intervention, 26,* 1–19.

O'Neill, P. T., Wenning, R. J., & Giovannetti, E. (2002). Serving students with disabilities in charter schools: Legal obligations and policy options. *Education Law Reporter, 169,* 1–21.

Osborne, A. G., Jr. (2004). To what extent can procedural violations of the IDEA render an IEP invalid? *Education Law Reporter, 185,* 15–29.

Zirkel, P. A. (2008). Have the amendments to the Individuals with Disabilities Act razed *Rowley* and raised the substantive standard for "Free Appropriate Public Education"? *Journal of the National Ass'n of Administrative Law Judiciary, 28,* 396-418.

Chapter 11

Related Services, Supplementary Services, and Nonacademic Services Under IDEA

Chapter Outline

Related Services

    Definition and Examples

    Assistive Technology Devices (ATDs) and Services

    Controversial Related Services

    Cost Issues

Supplementary Aids and Services

Nonacademic Services

Reminders and Tips

Review

References

Selected Supplementary Resources

Related Services

Definition and Examples

Under IDEA, education agencies are to make both special education and related services available to eligible students. The definition of related services is "transportation and such developmental, corrective, and other supportive services . . . as are required to assist a child with a disability to benefit from special education"(20 U.S.C. § (1402)(26) (2006)). In other words, if the child does not need special education, then a service that the child might otherwise need cannot be a related service under IDEA (34 C.F.R. § 300.8 (a)(2) (2006)). For instance, if a child with a disability would benefit from an audiology test or counseling services but does not need special education, then the child is not IDEA-eligible, and the service is not a related service under IDEA.† Similarly, a service basically for enrichment purposes that is not needed to assist the child to benefit from special education, and thus need not be part of a student's IEP, will not qualify. Therefore, the federal government will not contribute IDEA funds toward the cost of such a service. The service might be a related aid or service under Section 504, however.

> † In *A.A. v. Cooperman*, 526 A.2d 1103 (N.J. Super. Ct. App. Div. 1987), a student with an orthopedic impairment who was voluntarily enrolled in private school without special education was determined to be ineligible for transportation because it could not be needed to assist the student to benefit from special education if the student was not a special education student. Compare the decision in *Maurits v. Board of Education of Harford County*, 1983-84 EHLR DEC. 555:364 (D. Md. 1983), in which a student with hemophilia was denied physical therapy as a related service because he did not need it to benefit from physical education or academic instruction.

A service admittedly required or needed for some purpose, but not for the student to benefit from special education, is also not a related service. For instance, a substance abuse program was judged not to be a related service for a special education student placed by a public school district into a private school and later expelled from the private school until he underwent drug rehabilitation (*Field v. Haddonfield Board of Education*, 1991). The particular drug rehabilitation program treated drug dependency as a disease, and the court viewed the treatment as separate from the student's special education needs even though it was obviously needed by and beneficial to the student.

Many kinds of services can be related services. In addition to transportation, the list of examples in IDEA includes the following:

- Audiology services
- Early identification and assessment of disabilities in children
- Counseling services, including rehabilitation counseling
- Interpreting services
- Medical services for diagnostic and evaluation purposes only
- Orientation and mobility services
- Occupational therapy
- Psychological services
- Physical therapy
- Recreation, including therapeutic recreation

- School nurse services designed to enable the child to receive FAPE as described in the IEP (the regulations include school health services as well)

- Social work services

- Speech-language pathology services (20 U.S.C. § 1401(26) (2006))

Notice that, in general, these are the kinds of services provided by professionally trained personnel who are not special educators. This list has grown over the years. The examples new to IDEA '04 are interpreter services and school nurse services. At the same time, IDEA '04 excluded from related services a medical device that is surgically implanted (such as a cochlear implant for a student who is deaf) or the replacement of such a device (20 U.S.C. § 1401(26)(B) (2006)). The 2006 regulations go further and exclude optimization of the device's functioning (e.g., cochlear mapping), and maintenance or replacement of the device.†

† This regulation, no doubt, was in reaction to a court case holding that mapping a cochlear implant was a related service. See *Stratham School District v. Beth and David P.*, 2003 U.S. Dist. LEXIS 1683 (D.N.H. 2003). Nonetheless, the 2006 regulation goes on to state that the exclusion of surgically implanted medical devices does not prevent "the routine checking of an external component of a surgically implanted device to make sure it is functioning properly" (34 C.F.R. § 300.34 (b)(2)(iii) (2006)).

The regulations define all these services. (See Table 11.1.) In addition, they add and then define parent counseling and training.† They limit social work services to "social work services in schools"(34 C.F.R. § 300.34(c)(14)(2006)). They define medical services as "services provided by a licensed physician to determine a child's medically related disability that results in the child's need for special education and related services" 34 C.F.R. § 300.34(b)(5)(2006)). In other words, medical services, at least "those to determine a medically related disability," are those provided by a licensed physician rather than by another kind of health care provider.

† Note that parent counseling and training is the only listed related service that is provided to someone other than the eligible special education student. Parent counseling and training has not been the subject of much litigation, but at least a dozen federal court cases have mentioned that parent training or counseling was being provided in the student's IEP. See, e.g., *Chris D. v. Montgomery County Board of Education*, 753 F. Supp. 922 (M.D. Ala. 1990); *Hawaii Department of Education v. Katherine D.*, 727 F.2d 809 (9th Cir. 1983). In *Stacey G. v. Pasadena*, 547 F. Supp. 61 (S.D. Tex. 1982), the court actually ordered parent training as a means to avoid the need for a residential placement.

The regulations define school nurse services as services needed for FAPE that are provided by a qualified school nurse or other qualified person, paralleling the descriptions of occupational and physical therapists.† They also add school *health* services to school nurse services because not all school health services are administered by school nurses, and OSEP determined that the term "school health" had been inadvertently omitted from the statute. The regulations define interpreter services for children who are deaf or hard of hearing to include oral transliteration services, cued language transliteration services, and sign language transliteration and interpreting services, as well as transcription services. Interpreter services also include special interpreting services for children who are deaf-blind.

† The definitions of OT and PT have not prevented the use of certified occupational and physical therapist aides in the schools, so the same should hold true for the use of trained school health aides.

The examples provided and defined may not exhaust the possibilities.[1] For example, under some circumstances, art, music, and dance therapy might be related services. Also, the room and board costs of a residential placement can be considered a related service needed to assist some students to benefit from special education. Transition services can be considered either related services, special education, or supplementary aids and services, depending on the situation. Extracurricular activities and participation in competitive sports may occasionally be related services but, as is true of other services, only if deemed necessary for the student to benefit from special education.†

> † It is worth remembering that the definition of special education is "specially designed instruction to meet the unique needs of a child with a disability" (34 C.F.R. § 300.39 (2006)). Special education is not limited to education delivered by a special educator. Physical education instruction is included within the definition of special education. The definition also includes instructional services provided by a speech pathologist or other related service provider, if the services are considered special education under state standards. Vocational education and travel training to help a student move around effectively and safely in the school and community also can be considered special education if they otherwise meet the definition.

If the parents procure a related service for their child because the education agency refused to provide it, a hearing officer can order that the parents be reimbursed (*Hurry v. Jones*, 1984). The reasoning is analogous to the situation in which a parent enrolls a child in private school and receives reimbursement because the school district failed to provide FAPE in the public setting (see chapter 13).

Prohibition on Mandatory Medication

IDEA '04 includes a new provision that requires SEAs to prohibit state and local educational agency personnel from requiring a child to obtain a prescription for a controlled substance (as defined by the Controlled Substances Act) in order to attend school, receive an IDEA evaluation, or receive Part B services (20 U.S.C. § 1412(a)(26) (2006)). This provision apparently was in response to a few reported situations where a teacher tried to coerce parents into giving their child ritalin or a similar medication for the child's attention deficits. The statutory provision, however, does not prevent school personnel from consulting with or sharing teacher observations with parents regarding the child's performance or behavior, or regarding the child's need for evaluation. Rather, it seems intended to ensure that educators do not assume medical roles, for which they are unqualified, and that decisions about medications are retained by the parents and the child's physician.

---

[1] See 34 C.F.R..§ 300.34(a) (2006). In the past, at least, the list of included examples has been seen as non-exclusive. See 34 C.F.R. Part 300, App. A at question 34 (1999).

Table 11.1.

Definitions of Related Services in the 2006 IDEA Regulations

Audiology includes:

(i) Identification of children with hearing loss;

(ii) Determination of the range, nature, and degree of hearing loss, including referral for medical or other professional attention for the habilitation of hearing;

(iii) Provision of habilitative activities, such as language habilitation, auditory training, speech reading (lip-reading), hearing evaluation, and speech conservation;

(iv) Creation and administration of programs for prevention of hearing loss;

(v) Counseling and guidance of children, parents, and teachers regarding hearing loss;

(vi) Determination of children's needs for group and individual amplification, selecting and fitting an appropriate aid, and evaluating the effectiveness of amplification.

Counseling services means services provided by qualified social workers, psychologists, guidance counselors, or other qualified personnel.

Early identification and assessment of disabilities in children means

the implementation of a formal plan for identifying a disability as early as possible in a child's life.

Interpreting services includes

(i) the following, when used with respect to children who are deaf or hard of hearing: Oral transliteration services, cued language transliteration services, sign language transliteration and interpreting services, and transcription services, such as communication access real-time translation (CART), C-Print, and TypeWell; and

(ii) Special interpreting services for children who are deaf-blind.

Medical services means services provided by a licensed physician to determine a child's medically related disability that results in the child's need for special education and related services.

Occupational therapy means

(i) Services provided by a qualified occupational therapist; and

(ii) Includes (A) improving, developing, or restoring functions impaired or lost through illness, injury, or deprivation; (B) Improving ability to perform tasks for independent functioning if functions are impaired or lost; and (C) Preventing, through early intervention, initial or further impairment or loss of function.

Orientation and mobility services means

(i) Services provided to blind or visually impaired students by qualified personnel to enable those students to attain systematic orientation to, and safe movement within, their environments in school, home, and community; and

(ii) Includes teaching students the following, as appropriate: (A) Spatial and environmental concepts and use of information received by the senses (e.g., as sound, temperature, and vibrations) to establish, maintain, or regain orientation and line of travel (such as using sound at a traffic light to cross a street); (B) To use a long cane to supplement visual travel skills or as a tool for safely negotiating the environment for students with no available travel vision; (C) To understand and use remaining vision and distance low vision-aids; (D) Other concepts, techniques, and tools.

Parent counseling and training means

(i) Assisting parents in understanding the special needs of their child;

(ii) Providing parents with information about child development;

(iii) Helping parents to acquire the necessary skills that will allow them to support the implementation of their child's IEP or IFSP [Individual Family Service Plan].

Physical therapy means services provided by a qualified physical therapist.

Psychological services includes

(i) Administering psychological and educational tests, and other assessment procedures;

(ii) Interpreting assessment results;

(iii) Obtaining, integrating, and interpreting information about child behavior and conditions relating to learning;

(iv) Consulting with other staff members in planning school programs to meet the special needs of children as indicated by psychological tests, interviews, and behavioral evaluations;

(v) Planning and managing a program of psychological services, including psychological counseling for children and parents;

(vi) Assisting in developing positive behavioral intervention strategies.

Recreation includes

(i) Assessment of leisure function;

(ii) Therapeutic recreation services;

(iii) Recreation programs in schools and community agencies;

(iv) Leisure education.

Rehabilitation counseling services means services provided by qualified personnel in individual or group sessions that focus specifically on career development, employment preparation, achieving independence, and integration in the workplace and community of a student with a disability. The term also includes vocational rehabilitation services provided to a student with disabilities by vocational rehabilitation programs funded under the Rehabilitation Act of 1973, as amended, 29 U.S.C. 701 *et seq.*

School health services and school nurse services means health services that are designed to enable a child with a disability to receive FAPE as described in the child's IEP. School nurse services are services provided by a qualified school nurse. School health services are services that may be provided by either a qualified school nurse or other qualified person.

Social work services in schools includes

(i) Preparing a social or developmental history on a child with a disability;

(ii) Group and individual counseling with the child and family;

(iii) Working in partnership with parents and others on those problems in a child's living situation (home, school, and community) that affect the child's adjustment in school;

(iv) Mobilizing school and community resources to enable the child to learn as effectively as possible in his or her educational program;

(v) Assisting in developing positive behavioral intervention strategies.

Speech-language pathology services includes

(i) Identification of children with speech or language impairments;

(ii) Diagnosis and appraisal of specific speech or language impairments;

(iii) Referral for medical or other professional attention necessary for the habilitation of speech or language impairments;

(iv) Provision of speech and language services for the habilitation or prevention of communicative impairments;

(v) Counseling and guidance of parents, children, and teachers regarding speech and language impairments.

Transportation includes

(i) Travel to and from school and between schools;

(ii) Travel in and around school buildings;

(iii) Specialized equipment (such as special or adapted buses, lifts, and ramps), if required to provide special transportation for a child with a disability.

Source: 34 C.F.R. § 300.34 (2006).

Assistive Technology Devices (ATDs) and Services

ATDs and services will sometimes be related services; alternatively, the regulations specify that they can be considered special education or supplementary aids and services, as warranted (34 C.F.R. § 300.105(b) (2006)). Regardless, IEP teams must consider a child's need for assistive technology devices and services when developing an IEP and must provide these devices and services if they are required for FAPE in the least restrictive environment (LRE). ATDs encompass specialized personal needs (such as for a speech synthesizer, Braille materials, computer screen magnifier) as well as access to technology used by all students.† Medication is not an ATD, nor is a surgically implanted medical device (20 U.S.C.§ 1401(1)(B) (2006)). Table 11.2 defines and illustrates ATDs and services.

> † In IDEA '04, new emphasis is placed on providing ATDs to students who are blind or have print disabilities. IDEA '04 requires SEAs to adopt, in a timely manner, the National Instructional Materials Accessibility Standard (NIMAS) promulgated by a new center entitled the National Instructional Materials Access Center (20 U.S.C. § 1412(23) and 1474(e) (2006)). See also 34 C.F.R. § 300.172 (2006) and Appendix C. The U.S. Department of Education established and will support this Center through the American Printing House for the Blind. NIMAS will be used to guide the preparation of electronic files that can be converted into specialized formats for persons who are blind or have print disabilities. Among other items, textbooks in accessible media are

to be provided without cost to IDEA-eligible elementary and secondary school students. In implementing the NIMAS, the SEA is expected to collaborate with the state agency responsible for assistive technology programs.

Increasingly, ATDs and services should be part of IEP team planning when teams consider how to facilitate inclusion across all general education settings. ATDs and services should also become more prominent considerations when IEP teams consider how to improve postsecondary employment and educational opportunities as part of a child's transition plan. In both situations, ATDs may be important for success. ATDs or services can be provided in the home if necessary for FAPE (34 C.F.R. § 300.105(b) (2006)).

Assistive technology issues have surfaced in hearings and court decisions in recent years. Several decisions highlight the importance of an individualized AT evaluation conducted by a qualified AT specialist.[2] Others have required specific AT devices that were determined necessary for meaningful educational benefit. Decisions have also ordered compensatory education for failure to provide ATDs or reimbursement for parents' associated AT costs.[3] On the other hand, hearing officers have denied requests for specific devices in many situations where the student was making progress under the current IEP without additional or different AT devices. The case law is expected to continue to develop in this area.

---

[2] See, e.g., *Williams Bay Sch. Dist.*, 29 IDELR 1141 (SEA WI 1999); *In re Student with a Disability*, 29 IDELR 809 (SEA DE 1998); *Upper Darby Sch. Dist.*, 26 IDELR 1183 (SEA PA 1997).

[3] See, e.g., *Kevin T. v. Elmhurst Community Sch. Dist. No. 205*, 2002 U.S. Dist. LEXIS 4645 (N.D. Ill. 2002); *Bd. of Educ. of Harford Cnty. v. Bauer*, 33 IDELR ¶ 267 (D. Md. 2000); *East Penn Sch. Dist. v. Scott B.*, 1999 U.S. Dist. LEXIS 2683 (E.D. Pa. 1999).

Table 11.2.

Definition and Examples of Assistive Technology Devices and Services

Assistive Technology Device

Any item, piece of equipment, or product system, whether acquired commercially off the shelf, modified, or customized, that is used to increase, maintain, or improve functional capabilities of a child with a disability. 20 U.S.C. §1401(1) (2006).

Examples

Computer Assisted Instruction & Computer Access

Educational software	Talking word processors
Wrist rests	Head pointers
Interactive video discs	Adapted keyboards
Mouse alternatives	Voice recognition software
PDAs (e.g., iPods, iPads)	Laptop computers

Augmentative Communication Devices

Looptapes	
Voice output communication aids (e.g., DynaVox, Speak Easy, Delta Talker, Superhawk)	
Communication boards (e.g., with pictures, words, objects)	
Text-to-speech devices (e.g., Link, Speaking Language Master)	

Visual Aids or Substitutes

Magnifying devices and screen magnification software	Large-screen TV or computer monitors
Large-font Xeroxed or word-processed materials	Audiotapes
Large-print books	
Braille materials	
Reading machines and reading software	

Listening Aids

Hearing aids	Personal FM units
TDD (talking text) and TTY (teletype-writer) devices	Computer/word processor
Closed captioning devices on TV	
Vibrating beepers and other signaling devices	

Mobility and Positioning Aids

Stand-up desks	Wheelchairs, scooters, walkers, canes
Chair inserts, cushions	Arm supports
Adaptive driving controls	

Definition and Examples of
Assistive Technology Devices and Services

Physical Education and Recreation Aids

Beeping balls and goalposts	Computer games
Stencils, adapted pencils, and drawing software	
Game instructions in Braille or on audiotape	
Adapted toys (e.g., with Velcro, magnets, switches)	

Self-Care Aids/Environmental Control

Air-filtering and air-conditioning	Adapted on/off switches
Adapted utensils	Pointer sticks, head pointers
Electric feeders	Remote control switches

Assistive Technology Service:

Any service that directly assists a child with a disability in the selection, acquisition, or use of an assistive technology device (20 U.S.C.§ 1401(2)(2006)).

Examples

Evaluating a child's need for an ATD
Purchasing, leasing, or otherwise providing for the acquisition of an ATD by a child with disability
Coordinating and using other therapies, interventions, and services with ATDs
Providing training or technical assistance for children with disabilities, their families (if appropriate), and the professionals who work with them
Selecting, designing, fitting, customizing adapting, applying, maintaining, repairing, or replacing an ATD

Controversial Related Services

Although any desired auxiliary service can become controversial if the education agency and parents disagree over whether it constitutes a related service, some kinds of supportive services have generated more disputes than others. Among the more controversial have been transportation services, psychotherapy, extensive health services of an arguably medical nature, and services (including room and board services) in a residential setting.

Transportation.

School districts across the country already have transportation policies covering a host of situations, such as when a child lives too far from school to walk, when busing is used to transport children to a setting other than their neighborhood school (such as for racial desegregation purposes), or when dangerous traffic or other environmental hazards necessitate special transportation. The transportation needs of some special education students must also be accommodated within the district's overall transportation policy and services. The determination of whether transportation (beyond that available to children without disabilities) is a related service is made by the IEP team as part of the development of the IEP.

According to the regulations, transportation includes both travel to and from school and between schools as well as travel in and around school buildings. It also incorporates specialized equipment such as ramps and bus lifts, if necessary to provide special transportation for a student with a disability (34 C.F.R. § 300.34(c)(16) (2006)).

The basic question in determining the need for transportation is whether the student requires it to access special education or related services. The decision is made on a case-by-case basis. The provision of transportation as a related service is not limited to those who cannot walk. It can also be required when, because of a child's disability, the child is unable to get to school safely and independently. For instance--in addition to a mobility impairment--intellectual, emotional, sensory, or health disabilities can produce such a need. Vulnerability based on age alone can also necessitate transportation in order for a child to access special education, as is made clear by the transportation needs of preschoolers eligible for coverage under IDEA. Finally, if a school district makes a placement at a distant school in order to provide FAPE, it has obligated itself to pay the transportation costs. If the placement is at a distant residential school, transportation may be required only at the beginning and end of the school year and at holiday times, unless the student needs to be able to return home more often.†

> † The case of *Cohen v. School Board of Dade County*, 450 So.2d 1238 (Fla. Dist. Ct. App. 1984) is illustrative. Notwithstanding the IEP goal to improve interpersonal relationships with the family, the school was not obligated to reimburse family members for costs of additional visits to their child's residential school. See also *Fick v. Sioux Falls School District 49-5*, 337 F.3d 968 (8th Cir. 2003), where no IEP violation was found from the district's refusal to transport a student with epilepsy to an after-school day care center that was located outside the district's cluster boundaries. The district's policy did provide transportation for the plaintiff to and from public schools that were within the cluster boundaries.

After the IEP team has decided to provide transportation, other decisions can arise: how to discipline the student on the bus, how to load and unload the student, whether to provide door-to-door transportation, and when to provide an aide or special equipment on the bus to protect the safety of the student or others. All of these issues have been subject to both IDEA hearing decisions and Section 504 rulings from OCR. Each decision is made on a case-by-case basis.

In general, a district must remember that, under the logic of the Supreme Court's decision in *Honig v. Doe* (1988) (see chapter 14), suspensions from transportation for more than ten school days can constitute a change of placement just as readily as can suspension from a classroom, if transportation has been designated a related service in the child's IEP.[4] Under some circumstances, a day of bus suspension would count as a day of school suspension if the school does not provide the child with access to the setting in which IEP services are delivered. With respect to door-to-door transportation, physician documentation can be helpful in determining whether such assistance is required (*Duchesne County (UT) School District*, 1989). Furthermore, training schoolbus drivers and/or aides to manage the behavior of special education students with behavior problems is a wise measure to prevent injuries on the bus that might open the district to liability. Finally, those who transport children with disabilities should be knowledgeable about specific conditions so that they are in a position to determine what might constitute a medical emergency.

Door-to-Door Transportation

In *Hurry v. Jones*, 734 F.2d 879 (1st Cir. 1984), the court ordered that parents be reimbursed for their cost of transporting their son with severe disabilities to his special education program after the school declined to continue door-to-door transportation service. A state regulation seemed to call only for public assistance to and from the street level of a dwelling, and the school was concerned about the safety of carrying the overweight boy to and from his front door, which was twelve steep steps above street level. The parties eventually reached an agreement, but not before the parents had incurred $5,750 in reimbursable transportation expenses.

School health services.

Two Supreme Court cases address the need for health services as a related service. The first is *Irving Independent School District v. Tatro* (1984). The second is *Cedar Rapids Community School District v. Garret F.* (1999). The cases are 15 years apart, and the Supreme Court's ruling in *Garret F.* was necessary to resolve conflicting applications of *Tatro* in the lower courts.

Amber Tatro, a young student with spina bifida and a neurogenic bladder, required clean intermittent catheterization (CIC) in order to attend a regular class that had been determined to be her LRE. The school subsequently declined to pay for the CIC that she needed during the school day. The Supreme Court held that CIC met the definition of related services and, like transportation, was needed to enable access to FAPE in what was Amber's LRE. Then, it held that CIC was not excluded as medical treatment but rather was a school health service, primarily because it did not need to be performed by a licensed physician, and also because the nature and extent of the service was consistent with the type of service provided by school nurses. The Court opined that the IDEA regulations limited medical services to diagnostic and evaluation purposes in order to contain costs, thereby arguably introducing a cost factor into the determination of what constituted a related service.

---

[4] See *Greenbrier Cnty. (WV) Sch. Dist.*, 16 EHLR 616 (OCR 1990). An interpretive comment accompanying the 1999 regulations also took the position stated in the text. See 64 Fed. Reg. 12619 (March 12, 1999).

Subsequent to *Tatro*, determinations in the lower courts of what constituted a related health service became more complicated as increasing numbers of medically fragile students entered the school system. One judicial view held that the key question was not whether a service was provided by a physician, but rather whether the nature and extent of the required care resembled medical care more than it resembled school health services, even if the care was provided by a nurse rather than a doctor. Applying this view, a number of courts determined that continuous, one-to-one nursing care was not required as a related service.[5]

In contrast, another series of decisions held that *Tatro* established a bright-line test—namely, that if the service was not provided by a licensed physician, it was not a medical service, no matter how extensive the health care.[6] Because of the split of opinion in the circuit courts and the cost implications of the issue, the Supreme Court accepted the petition to review the Eighth Circuit's decision in the *Garret F.* case and resolved the issue during its 1998–1999 term.

The *Garret F.* case concerned a boy whose spinal cord was severed in a motorcycle accident at the age of four, leaving him paralyzed from the neck down and dependent on a ventilator to breathe. Garret's thinking abilities were unimpaired, and he performed successfully in his general education classrooms with the assistance of a personal care attendant throughout his school day. The attendant performed such duties as urinary catheterization, monitoring his ventilator and blood pressure, suctioning his tracheotomy tube, positioning him in his wheelchair, helping with eating and drinking, and other tasks.

Private insurance and a settlement from the motorcycle company provided for the in-school services of a licensed practical nurse until Garret was in the fifth grade. His mother then asked the school district to pay for the continuous, one-to-one care that Garret needed. It refused, arguing that the extent and costly nature of the care qualified the service as medical care rather than school health services.

In a straightforward and succinct decision, the Supreme Court held that the definition of related services under IDEA required the school district to provide Garret with the continuous, one-to-one health care services he needed to remain in regular classes. According to the Court, Garret's nursing services did not fall within the medical services exemption. The Court interpreted its earlier decision in *Tatro* as establishing a bright-line test for distinguishing between medical and school health services: A nurse is not a physician. The Court concluded that although cost may be relevant in construing IDEA, it cannot be the determining factor when a related service is needed to integrate a student like Garret into the public schools.

The impact of the ruling was significant. Lower court cases that conflicted with the Supreme Court decision were no longer good law. The cost implications were worrisome although no accurate estimates were available to indicate how many students would require services like Garret's. Some students in separate special education schools already had access to both a nurse and a doctor on staff. The financial impact was greatest in school districts with medically fragile students in general education classrooms, especially in small school districts. In large school districts, it was possible to cluster some of these children in the same school for economies of scale and still include them in classes and activities with their peers without disabilities. Garret's situation, however, revealed the complexity and difficulty of some of the cost issues raised under IDEA.

---

[5] See, e.g., *Fulginiti v. Roxbury Township Pub. Sch.*, 116 F.3d 468 (3d Cir. 1997) (*affirming, without opinion*, the lower court decision); *Neely v. Rutherford Cnty. Sch.*, 68 F.3d 965 (6th Cir. 1995); *Detsel v. Bd. of Educ. of Auburn*, 820 F.2d 587 (2d Cir. 1987); *Granite Sch. Dist. v. Shannon M.*, 787 F. Supp. 1020 (D. Utah 1992); *Bevin H. v. Wright*, 666 F. Supp. 71 (W.D. Pa. 1987).

[6] See, e.g., *Cedar Rapids Community Sch. Dist. v. Garret F.*, 106 F.3d 822 (8th Cir. 1997); *Skelly v. Brookfield La Grange Park Sch. Dist.*, 968 F. Supp. 385 (N.D. Ill. 1997).

In response to *Garret F.*, LEAs across the country pressed Congress for full funding of IDEA to help offset the expense of providing costly nursing services to medically fragile students. Funding, in fact, has gone up significantly since the *Garret F.* decision, and school nurse services have been added to the list of related services in the statute. SEAs are authorized under IDEA '04 to set aside a small percentage of their IDEA funds to establish risk pools to help LEAs (including charter school LEAs) pay for the steep costs of educating children with high needs (20 U.S.C. § 1411(e)(3) (2006)). If an SEA establishes such a risk pool, it must define a high-need child in consultation with LEAs and must ensure that the cost for such a child is greater than three times the average per student expenditure in that state (20 U.S.C. § 1411(e)(3)(C) (2006)).

Nursing Practice Acts

School officials should be careful not to ask teachers, paraprofessionals, and health aides to perform services that, under their state's nursing practices act, can be performed only by a registered nurse (RN) or a licensed practical nurse (LPN). Nursing practice acts usually differentiate the services that can be performed by RNs, LPNs, and health aides, based on the level of training and risk attached. In addition, guidelines often limit teachers and nonhealth care staff to routine and common health and safety procedures. Of course, teachers and other nonhealth care staff do not wish to perform health procedures for which they are untrained and that carry liability risks, but sometimes school officials ask them to. In *Stamps v. Jefferson County Board of Education*, 642 So.2d 941 (Ala. 1994), special education teachers sued the school board for allegedly requiring them to practice nursing without a license. The Alabama Supreme Court dismissed the case for failure to involve the state nursing association as a party in the suit. If professional nursing associations monitor school district practices and conclude that school districts are requiring school employees to practice nursing without a license, lawsuits from the nursing associations could follow. This happened in *American Nurses Ass'n v. O'Connell*, 110 Cal. Rptr.3d 305 (Cal. Ct. App. 2010). In that case, the California Court of Appeal held that the state's Nursing Practice Act prohibited the administration of insulin injections to students with diabetes by school employees who lacked the proper licensure. There is a move to amend the Act because there is a shortage of school nurses, and others need to be trained.

Psychotherapy.

The term *psychotherapy* does not appear among the examples of related services specified in IDEA or the regulations. Nonetheless, counseling services, psychological services, and social work services in schools are among the listed examples, and each arguably incorporates the concept of mental health therapy for an individual student or group of students. Additionally, even the complete absence of any terms incorporating the concept of psychotherapy would not exclude it from falling within the definition of related services because the list of examples has not been considered inclusive.

Two problems arise with respect to psychotherapy: its general unavailability in schools, and who can be reimbursed for providing it. If provided by someone such as a clinical social worker, licensed family therapist, or clinical or counseling psychologist, it need not be excluded as medical treatment. On the other hand, if provided by a psychiatrist or psychoanalyst (that is, physicians), then under the Supreme Court's ruling in *Garret F.*, it would fall within the medical services exclusion, resolving what was a judicial split in the lower courts.

The issue has cooled down as the health care issue has heated up. Inclusion of behavioral intervention plans (BIPs) and positive behavioral strategies in the IEP may or may not relieve the pressure for more mental health services to individual students.

Residential placement.

Residential placement, including room and board costs, can be viewed as a supportive service necessary to assist a student to benefit from special education. When the placement is made by the public agency, no issue arises over the need to pay for the room and board costs. What does arouse controversy is when the parents make the placement and then seek reimbursement from the LEA (see chapter 13).

Psychotherapy in Hospital and Private Settings

In *Clovis Unified School District v. California Office of Administrative Hearings*, 903 F.2d 635 (9th Cir. 1990), although both parties agreed that Michelle Shorey needed a residential placement, the school district asserted that the need was primarily medical. The Ninth Circuit agreed that Michelle's psychiatric hospitalization was not for educational reasons and that, therefore, her extended psychotherapy, even though provided by nonphysicians, was not a related service. Rather, it was part of the attempt to treat her mental illness, which had reached a crisis stage.

In contrast, when a placement is made for special education reasons, then services such as psychotherapy, if delivered by nonphysicians, can be viewed as related services. See, for example, *Babb v. Knox County School System*, 965 F.2d 104 (6th Cir. 1992). The court concluded in Babb that psychological and counseling services at a psychiatric hospital were related services because hospitalization was necessary to provide FAPE. Similarly, *T. G. v. Board of Education of Piscataway*, 576 F. Supp. 420 (D.N.J. 1983), held that psychotherapy by a social worker at a private day school was a related service.

Cost Issues

Lurking behind virtually all related services disputes is the issue of cost. Although the cost of providing special education instruction is more expensive than general education, it is the cost of related services that is particularly troublesome to many school districts. The burden of the costs of related services falls heavily on education agencies. Under fiscal stress, many LEAs have reduced the availability of auxiliary service providers used by both general and special education students—personnel such as school psychologists, school social workers, and school nurses. Even more difficult to fund (and find) are services provided by qualified occupational therapists, physical therapists, and interpreters for the deaf.

The IDEA regulations demonstrate sensitivity to cost issues by stating that funds to pay for some related services may come from third-party sources, both public and private, and that insurers are not relieved of otherwise valid obligations to provide or pay for services for a child with a disability (34 C.F.R. § 300.154(h) (2006)). Interagency agreements are encouraged, but turf battles often arise when social service and mental health agencies are invited to help pay for the cost of various related services, such as room and board at private residential placements and mental health services. Among the problems are differences in funding mechanisms and regulations, such as the requirement under IDEA that all related services be at no cost to the parent, while state social service and health agencies typically can use a sliding scale and charge for services based on the ability to pay.

Private insurance may be available in some cases to pay for related services, as was the case for *Garret F.* prior to his parents' court action. Using the parents' private insurance requires their written, informed consent, and parental refusal of consent does not relieve the LEA of its obligation to provide the required services at no cost to the parent.† To encourage use of the private insurance, the school district can use IDEA-Part B funds for the cost of any deductibles and co-pays. Nonetheless, if private insurance payouts become too large, or if the insurance company realizes that government agencies can be obligated to pay the full cost of the same service, the insurance company can amend or cancel future coverage.††

> † In *Seals v. Loftis*, 614 F. Supp. 302 (E.D. Tenn. 1985), the court ruled that parents were not required to use their insurance for their child's psychological evaluation because of the lifetime cap on the extent of insurance benefits available for that purpose.

> †† In *Chester County Intermediate Unit v. Pennsylvania Blue Shield*, 896 F.2d 808 (3d Cir. 1990), the court upheld an insurance company's "exclusionary clause," which excluded from coverage services to which the insured was entitled under federal or state law.

Since an EHA amendment in 1988, public insurance, namely Medicaid, has been available to pay for some kinds of related services, if the family meets the poverty requirements for Medicaid eligibility (20 U.S.C. § 1412(e) (Supp. III 1997); 42 U.S.C. § 1396b(c) (2006)). Covered services vary by state, however, as do the reimbursement rates. Related services such as occupational and physical therapy, speech therapy, audiology, and psychological services may or may not be Medicaid-covered services within a given state.

Effectively tapping Medicaid reimbursement sources requires considerable bureaucratic expertise and coordination. Not all school districts go to the time and trouble to seek the reimbursement, and it is bureaucratically cumbersome and confusing to acquire substantial reimbursement monies in this way. Like private insurance, the IDEA regulations specify that written, informed consent from the parents is needed, and parents cannot be required to spend their deductibles or make co-payments. The LEA, however, may pay those costs for the parents. In addition, the LEA may not tap the public insurance if it results in a reduction in lifetime coverage, an increase in premiums, or a loss of eligibility for the parents (34 C.F.R. § 300.154(d) (2006)). As is the case with private insurance, the parents must be informed that their refusal of consent does not relieve the LEA of its obligation to provide the required services at no cost to the parent

In several ways over the years, Medicaid administrators have tried to reduce the extent of the Medicaid obligation to reimburse LEAs. In 1990, a federal appeals court held that the secretary of Health and Human Services (HHS) was interpreting HHS regulations in an obsolete fashion by paying for private-duty nursing only if it was provided at home or in a hospital rather than in an educational setting (*Detsel v. Sullivan*, 1990). As a result, HHS reinterpreted its regulations to allow private duty nurses in school settings.

More recently, the Medicaid-administering agency (now entitled the Centers for Medicare and Medicaid Services [CMS]) within HHS issued complex new guidelines that restricted LEA reimbursements in ways that were alarming to school districts, and that affected several billion dollars of Medicaid reimbursements across most of the states. For instance, administrative costs that accompanied delivery of any services not listed on a student's IEP (such as referral, follow-up, and coordination activities) were eliminated, as were transportation costs to and from home and school. The CMS asserted that some school districts had submitted fraudulent claims for administrative and transportation reimbursements, and concluded that administration activities and transportation from home to school were educational rather than medical functions. A final rule to this effect was issued in December 2007. In response to political pressure from child advocates, Congress issued successive moratoria on enforcement of the new rule until July 2009. In June 2009, CMS rescinded the rule, commenting that it was not fully aware of the magnitude of its potential adverse consequences (74 Fed. Reg. 31184, 31185, 31195, June 30, 2009).

Supplementary Aids and Services

Under IDEA '97, a category of service entitled "supplementary aids and services" was given enhanced visibility. Such services were defined for the first time in the statute as "aids, services, and other supports that are provided in regular education classes or other education-related settings to enable children with disabilities to be educated with nondisabled children to the maximum extent appropriate" (20 U.S.C. § 1401(33) (2006)). Supplementary aids and services are to be included in a student's IEP. They are different from related services because they are not linked to enabling the child to benefit from special education. Instead, they are linked to enabling the child to participate in educational activities with children who do not have disabilities. IDEA '04 added that they are also to be included in an IEP if needed for access to extracurricular and nonacademic activities (20 U.S.C. § 1414(d)(1)(A)(i)(IV)(bb) (2006)). Presumably, these types of aids and services will prove less costly than related services, although the only examples of supplementary services provided in the regulations are resource rooms and itinerant instruction in conjunction with regular class placement (34 C.F.R. § 300.551(b)(2) (1999) and 34 C.F.R. § 300.115(b)(2) (2006)). Educators have presumed that supplementary aids and services in the regular classroom refer not so much to auxiliary personnel as to things like seating arrangements, assistive technology devices, instructional aids, and peer supports that facilitate the inclusion of children with disabilities.

Nonacademic Services

IDEA regulations require that students with disabilities be provided an equal opportunity to participate in nonacademic services and extracurricular activities (34 C.F.R. § 300.107 (2006)). Such an opportunity encourages interaction between children with disabilities and children without disabilities and ensures that children with disabilities are not denied access to various services extended regularly to other students. The list of nonacademic services and extracurricular activities included in the regulations are counseling services, athletics, transportation, health services, recreational activities, special interest groups or clubs sponsored by the school district, referrals to appropriate outside agencies, and student employment opportunities. The regulation basically parallels a similar provision under Section 504 (34 C.F.R. § 104.37 (2009)).

One can see that the above services could become related services under IDEA if written into a student's IEP as necessary to assist the student to benefit from special education. The basic requirement, however, is not that students with disabilities be provided all these services in an IEP or at school but simply that they be given the opportunity to participate on an equal basis with general education students in all aspects of school life.

↳Reminders and Tips

1. School districts constrained by limited budgets sometimes must find innovative ways to provide related services. Training of paraprofessionals is one way and is being systematized and improved in many districts. The use of video technology is another means and may be tapped in creative ways, for instance, (a) by use of videotapes or digital recordings of physical therapy and speech therapy instruction for careful follow-through by special educators, and (b) by interactive diagnostic and instructional sessions from centralized sites.

2. For students with multiple and severe disabilities, sometimes an extended school day combined with parent counseling, or possibly respite care or group home placement, can provide FAPE at less cost than a residential placement with its expensive room and board costs. In general, education agencies should brainstorm nontraditional ways to deliver related services effectively.

3. The need for nurses and nurses' aides in schools is growing. Many school districts have cut back on the number of school nurses in recent decades as the seriousness of infectious disease outbreaks in schools has declined. Now, with the advent of more children who are medically fragile and more children with noncontagious but serious health conditions, such as asthma, diabetes, orthopedic impairments, neurological impairments, and respiratory impairments, the need for health care in schools is rising sharply. Serving the needs of these children will require increased health care services in school. Education agencies and parent advocacy groups should be prepared to make the case to state legislatures to expand school nurse services.

4. School districts also need to gear up to properly evaluate the need of some students with disabilities for assistive technology devices and services. ATD issues are reaching the courts, and school districts must respond appropriately to the growing number of requests for evaluation and provision of augmentative communication devices and computer hardware and software, more sophisticated equipment for children with visual or hearing impairments, and adapted equipment for those with mobility impairments and self-care needs.

5. If a school is to meet the needs of the whole child, as is increasingly expected under IDEA, better links with other state agencies must be established. Interagency agreements are frequently nothing more than statements of good intentions, without the resources to facilitate interagency cooperation and collaborative service delivery. Collaborative interagency models, developed in some states to serve the educational, social service, and health needs of a child by also addressing the family's needs, deserve serious consideration in all states.

↺Review

1. What is the definition of a related service under IDEA?

    It is transportation as well as developmental, corrective, or other supportive services that are required to assist a child to benefit from special education. Without special education, there can be no related service obligation under IDEA.

2. What is the difference between a related service and a supplementary aid or service?

    A related service is one that is required to assist the student to benefit from special education. Without it, some of the child's unique educational goals cannot be met. A supplementary aid or service, on the other hand, helps the child to be included in regular classroom instruction and in extracurricular and other nonacademic activities.

⚡References

Cedar Rapids Community Sch. Dist. v. Garret F., 526 U.S. 66 (1999).

Detsel v. Sullivan, 895 F.2d 58 (2d Cir. 1990).

Duchesne County (UT) Sch. Dist., 16 EHLR 112 (OCR 1989).

Field v. Haddonfield Bd. of Educ., 769 F. Supp. 1313 (D.N.J. 1991).

Honig v. Doe, 484 U.S. 305 (1988).

Hurry v. Jones, 734 F.2d 879 (1st Cir. 1984).

Individuals with Disabilities Education Improvement Act, 20 U.S.C. § 1400 *et seq.* (2006).

Individuals with Disabilities Education Improvement Act Regulations, 34 C.F. R. § 300.1 *et seq.* (2006).

Irving Indep. Sch. Dist. v. Tatro, 468 U.S. 883 (1984).

⇉Selected Supplementary Resources

American Federation of Teachers, AFL-CIO. (1997). *The medically fragile child in the school setting.* Washington, DC: Author.

Bartlett, L. (2000). Medical services: The disputed related service. *Journal of Special Education, 33,* 215–223.

Chambers, A. C. (1997). *Has technology been considered? A guide for IEP teams.* Reston, VA: Council of Administrators of Special Education and the Technology and Media Division of the Council for Exceptional Children.

Council for Exceptional Children. (1992). *Guidelines for the delineation of roles and responsibilities for the safe delivery of specialized health care in the educational setting.* Reston, VA: Author.

Day, J. N., & Huefner, D. S. (2003). Assistive technology: Legal issues for students with disabilities and their schools. *Journal of Special Education Technology, 182*(2), 23–34.

Etscheidt, S. K., & Bartlett, L. (1999). The IDEA amendments: A four-step approach for determining supplementary aids and services. *Exceptional Children, 65,* 163–174.

Golden, D. (1998). *Assistive technology in special education: Policy and practice.* Reston, VA: Council of Administrators of Special Education and the Technology and Media Division of the Council for Exceptional Children.

Heller, K. W., Fredrick, L. D., Best, S., Dykes, M. K., & Cohen, E. T. (2000). Specialized health care procedures in the schools: Training and service delivery. *Exceptional Children, 66,* 173–186.

Herz, E. J. (2009). *Medicaid and Schools.* Congressional Research Service. Retrieved May 14, 2009 from http://assets.opencrs.com/rpts/RS22397_20090217.pdf

Julnes, R. E., & Brown, S. E. (1993). The legal mandate to provide assistive technology in special education programming. *Education Law Reporter, 82,* 737–748.

Pitasky, V. M. (2007). What do I do when: The answer book on transportation for students with disabilities. LRP: Horsham, PA.

Rebore, D., & Zirkel, P. A. (1999). The Supreme Court's latest special education ruling: A costly decision? *Education Law Reporter, 135*, 331–341.

Spaller, K. D., & Thomas, S. B. (1994). A timely idea: Third party billing for related services. *Education Law Reporter, 86*, 581–592.

Thomas, S. B., & Hawke, C. (1999). Health-care services for children with disabilities: Emerging standards and implications. *Journal of Special Education, 32*, 226–237.

Chapter 12

Least Restrictive Environment Under IDEA

Chapter Outline

Background and Definitions

The issue of educational placement of students with disabilities has been controversial over the years. Prior to the 1975 enactment of Public Law 94-142, many school districts denied public school admission to many children with disabilities, especially those with intellectual disabilities, physical disabilities, and behavioral disorders. Other school districts expelled students indefinitely when the district did not know how to manage or teach them, sometimes placing students on waiting lists for nonforthcoming tuition grants to private schools. Public Law 94-142 was designed to help school districts pay for the excess costs of providing to all children with disabilities—including difficult children—an appropriate public education at no cost to their parents. Excluding any child with disabilities from public school education was unacceptable.

Several years before passage of P.L. 94-142, cases such as *PARC v. Pennsylvania* (1972) and *Mills v. District of Columbia Board of Education* (1972) had established the principle that exclusion of children with disabilities from the public school system was a denial of equal protection of the laws under the Fourteenth Amendment to the U.S. Constitution. Both court cases also had declared a legal preference for the education of children with disabilities alongside children without disabilities, to the extent that it could be accomplished appropriately. This preference was labeled the least restrictive placement alternative, or least restrictive environment (LRE), borrowing these terms from cases involving the deinstitutionalization of persons with mental illness.

Over the years, the term LRE has been joined by the terms *mainstreaming* and *inclusion*, all of which are used, sometimes indiscriminately, with respect to placement preferences. Treating these three terms as synonyms represents a misunderstanding of the legal meaning of LRE. No reference to "mainstreaming" or "inclusion" appears in IDEA or the IDEA regulations. Prior to 1997, the term LRE appeared only as a subheading in the IDEA regulations (34 C.F.R. § 300.550 (1995)). In 1997, it was introduced as a subheading in the statute itself and was retained as a subheading in IDEA '04 (20 U.S.C. § 1412(a)(5) (Supp. III 1997) and (2006)). All three terms need more explanation. To avoid misunderstanding, it is also important to ask each user what these terms mean to him or her.

Mainstreaming

Mainstreaming generally refers to an educational placement that allows students with disabilities and students without disabilities to be integrated for some or all of the school day. The term *physical mainstreaming* is sometimes used to refer to integration in the same school building but not in the same classrooms. *Social mainstreaming* refers to integration in the same school settings during times when social interaction is possible—for instance, during lunch and recess. *Instructional mainstreaming* refers to integration in the same general education classroom during academic instructional time.

When the term *mainstreaming* is used generically, it typically refers to instructional mainstreaming. The assumption, at least in the past, has been that a student so mainstreamed should be able to handle the general education curriculum, with or without modifications. The distinction between types of mainstreaming has been important in certain federal court cases, some of which have dealt with physical and social mainstreaming issues, while others have addressed instructional mainstreaming issues.

Inclusion

Since the late 1980s, the concepts of inclusion, full inclusion, partial inclusion, and supported inclusion have gained visibility. In general, inclusion refers to placement of students with disabilities in general education classrooms and schools. Broadly speaking, inclusion means integration of children with disabilities and children without disabilities in the same settings. The term integration, however, at least in the school context, is linked with race, whereas inclusion is linked with placement issues affecting students with disabilities.

Usually, *full inclusion* means that all special education services are delivered in general education classrooms in the school the child would attend if not disabled (hereafter, the "neighborhood school"). Services are brought to the child rather than vice versa. *Partial inclusion*, in contrast, usually indicates some pullout services, with the general education classroom remaining as the child's home base. *Supported inclusion* emphasizes the need for support services in general education settings in order for either partial or full inclusion to be successful.

The term *inclusion* has replaced *mainstreaming* for most purposes related to public schooling. Inclusion reflects the view that society is improved by the interaction of schoolchildren who have disabilities and those who do not. Arguably, children with disabilities learn better what is expected of them in the neighborhood and in society when they have an opportunity to observe and interact with children without disabilities. Conversely, children without disabilities learn better how to understand and accept children with disabilities when both groups learn and play together.

Least Restrictive Environment

The legal term for special education placement preferences is *least restrictive environment* (LRE). Basically, LRE refers to the educational setting closest to the general classroom in which FAPE can be delivered to a special education student. LRE captures the balance between the statutory mandate to provide FAPE and the statutory preference for education of students with disabilities alongside general education students to the maximum extent appropriate. The LRE is not necessarily the general education classroom; the LRE must be determined individually for each child. Although for most students it is the general education classroom with supplementary aids and services, including part-time resource room placements, for some students it is a self-contained placement in the regular school, For others, it is a separate school or even a residential setting.

What Does IDEA Require?

When P.L. 94-142 was enacted in 1975, it adopted the general classroom preference found in the *PARC* and *Mills* cases. The original provision required states to establish procedures assuring that,

> to the maximum extent appropriate, children with disabilities, including children in public or private institutions or other care facilities, are educated with children who are not disabled, and special classes, separate schooling, or other removal of children with disabilities from the regular educational environment occurs only when the nature or severity of the disability of a child is such that education in regular classes with the use of supplementary aids and services cannot be achieved satisfactorily (20 U.S.C. § 1412(5)(B) (1994), now at 20 U.S.C. § 1412(a)(5)(A) (2006)).

Although this provision remains intact in IDEA '04, the statutory section dealing with IEPs has added stronger language. Since IDEA '97, the IEP section has included a requirement of "an explanation of the extent, if any, to which the child will *not* participate with nondisabled children in the regular class and in [extracurricular and nonacademic] activities"(emphasis added) (20 U.S.C. § 1414(d)(1)(A)(iv) (2006)). Prior to IDEA '97, the IDEA regulations had required a description in the IEP of the extent to which the child would be able to participate in regular education programs. In other words, IDEA '97 reversed the expectation: The IEP team now must explain any nonparticipation in the regular education setting rather than describing the extent of services delivered within it. The effect of the reversal has been to buttress the legal underpinnings of inclusion and create a presumption in favor of regular classroom placement.

The revised IEP language in IDEA '97 also emphasized that special education and related services were to be accompanied by supplementary aids and services, program modifications, and supports for school personnel so that students with disabilities could be educated successfully with other children, both those with disabilities and those without disabilities (20 U.S.C. § 1414(d)(1)(A)(iii) (2006)). Moreover, the IEP language also stressed that these same kinds of services were intended to allow children with disabilities to participate in extracurricular and other nonacademic activities, both with children who have disabilities and those who do not (20 U.S.C. § 1414(d)(1)(A)(iii) (2006)). The result of these changes, retained in IDEA '04, has been to focus on the desirability of finding ways to allow children with disabilities to succeed in general education classrooms and schools. Nonetheless, the child's individual needs must come first; not all children can be successfully educated in general education settings.

In an attempt to more fully involve parents at all stages of decision making and perhaps to reduce the number of placement disputes, IDEA '97 and IDEA '04 require that parents be included as members of any group that makes placement decisions (20 U.S.C. § 1414(f) (Supp. III 1997) and (2006)).†

> † The regulations allow the placement decision to proceed if parental participation is unobtainable (34 CFR § 300.501(c)(4) (2006)).

What Do the IDEA Regulations Add to the Statutory Language?

The IDEA implementing regulations flesh out the statutory LRE provisions. The LRE regulations reinforce the requirement that each public agency ensure the availability of a continuum of placement options and supplementary services in conjunction with regular class placement. Placement options include regular classes, special classes, special schools, home instruction, and instruction in hospitals and institutions. Resource rooms and itinerant instruction are viewed as supplementary services provided in conjunction with regular class placement (34 C.F.R. § 300.115(b) (2)(2006)). A separate provision establishes that a public or private residential program, if necessary to provide special education and related services to a child with a disability, must be at no cost to the parents (34 C.F.R. § 300.104 (2006). With all these placement options, it should be clear that special education is not a place, but a set of services that can be delivered in a variety of places, depending on the child's needs.

In detailing various placement considerations, the regulations emphasize the following:

1. Placement decisions are to be made by a group, including the parents, and other persons knowledgeable about the child, the meaning of the evaluation data, and the placement options.

2. Placement decisions are to be made on an individualized basis.

3. Each placement is to be "determined annually."

4. Each placement must be "based on the child's IEP."

5. Each placement is to be "as close as possible to the child's home."†

6. Each placement is to be in the school the child would attend if not disabled, unless the IEP "requires some other arrangement." (34 C.F.R. § 300.116(a), (b), and (c) (2006).

7. In addition, in selecting the LRE, consideration must be given to "any potential harmful effect on the child or on the quality of services that he or she needs" (34 C.F.R. § 300.116(d)(2006)), a potentially important provision that has been frequently overlooked in the past.

> † OSEP recognizes the parent's right to select a charter school, magnet school, or other specialized school without violating the LRE "as long as the child is educated with his or her peers without disabilities to the maximum extent appropriate" (71 Federal Register 46588 (August 14, 2006)).

The regulations contain another provision that a child with a disability is not to be removed from education in "age-appropriate" regular classrooms solely because of necessary modifications in the general curriculum (34 C.F.R. § 300.116(e) (2006)). This statement was added in 1999 in response to concerns that some children with intellectual disabilities might be removed from regular classrooms in an attempt to avoid accountability for their educational performance. Inability to function at grade level without modifications is not viewed in and of itself as a legitimate reason for removing special education students from age-appropriate regular classrooms. Instead, modifications to the general curriculum should accommodate the child's needs in this regard. This provision may seem to conflict with the national momentum to end "social promotions," but the term "age-appropriate regular classrooms" does not preclude classrooms with multi-age groupings and may prove to be a more flexible concept than strict chronological age alone. Of course, if students with disabilities are kept in age-appropriate classrooms, their grades should not mask their true performance and progress.

Discipline and Law Enforcement Provisions

Because school violence has become an issue in recent years, school officials have sought the authority to suspend or expel all students, regardless of disability, who bring a dangerous weapon to school, use or possess illegal drugs, sell controlled substances, or are otherwise likely to injure themselves or others. This concern has resulted in a set of disciplinary provisions under IDEA '97 and IDEA '04 that allow removal to an interim placement without the same stay-put safeguard extended with respect to other changes of placement. The placement changes that occur in the context of disciplinary actions are discussed in fuller detail in chapter 14.

IDEA makes clear that an education agency may report a crime to appropriate authorities, and that IDEA allows state law enforcement agencies to carry out their responsibilities under federal and state criminal law (20 U.S.C. § 1415(k)(9)(A) (Supp. III 1997) and § 1415(k) (6)(A)(2006)). Nonetheless, when the agency reports the crime, it must also ensure that copies of the child's special education and disciplinary records are transmitted for consideration by the authorities to whom it reports the crime, although parental consent may be required in order to do so in many situations (20 U.S.C. § 1415(k)(6)(B) (2006).† One would think that parents would usually want to give consent because knowledge of the disability and the child's unique needs may be relevant to the actions and dispositions taken by law enforcement authorities.

† The regulations require that transmission of copies of the child's education and disciplinary records comply with FERPA (34 C.F.R. § 300.535(b)(2) (2006)). Presumably, this means that, without written parental consent, the child's record can be shared only (a) pursuant to a state law that allows disclosure if it concerns the juvenile justice system's ability to serve the student effectively prior to adjudication, (b) pursuant to a court order or subpoena for law enforcement purposes, or (c) pursuant to legitimate safety or health emergencies (see chapter 9).

If the law enforcement authorities decide to take jurisdiction, presumably no violation of IDEA has occurred if a placement change (such as incarceration or detention) results. The provision does not excuse the school, however, from honoring the procedural safeguards if law enforcement authorities do not remove the child from school and file charges. Furthermore, the substantive right to FAPE does not end when a child is placed in detention or jail. School officials should be aware that there may be a difference between reporting a crime and filing a juvenile court petition or a criminal complaint (that is, pressing charges), so school officials may want to be careful to allow the judicial or law enforcement authorities to actually file the complaint.†[1]

† See, e.g., *Wisconsin v. Trent N.*, 569 N.W.2d 719 (Wis. Ct. App. 1997), in which juvenile court proceedings were allowed to proceed independently of IDEA proceedings because, among other reasons, only the district attorney could file delinquency proceedings. The court also indicated that IDEA procedural requirements are parallel to juvenile court proceedings and do not override them. Also of interest is *Joseph M. v. Southeast Delco School District*, 2001 U.S. Dist. LEXIS 2994 (E.D. Pa. 2001), in which a federal district court upheld an administrative ruling that an LEA can report criminal conduct to juvenile authorities without providing IDEA rights, such as a manifestation determination, that would have been required had not the student's conduct been reported and charges filed by a law enforcement official.

How Do Courts Determine Whether Regular Classroom Placements Are the LRE?

Many school districts and parents alike have been disenchanted with placements for particular children with disabilities because the settings were viewed either as not able to provide FAPE or as not constituting the LRE. Many parents have sought to have their children placed in private schools, including residential treatment centers, at public expense, not trusting the ability of the public schools to educate their children appropriately. This has been true particularly for students with severe learning disabilities, serious emotional disturbance, autism, and multiple disabilities. Other parents have preferred separate but state-operated programs, such as schools for the deaf and blind. At the same time, still other parents of children with disabilities have tried to close separate schools and institutions, especially separate facilities for students with intellectual and physical disabilities, and to return their children to general public school settings. Controversies surrounding the placement of students in private facilities are discussed in the next chapter. Controversies about the placement of students in public school general education classrooms or neighborhood schools are covered in this chapter.

[1] In the analysis accompanying the 1999 regulations, OSERS observed that "the Act does not address whether school officials may press charges against a child with disabilities when they have reported a crime by that student" (64 Fed. Reg. 12537, 12631 (March 12, 1999)).

Prior to IDEA '97, three different circuits of the U.S. Court of Appeals had established the dominant standards or tests for judging whether a general education setting constituted the LRE for a given student. As a result of the presumption in favor of general education placements under IDEA '97, many commentators expected courts to scrutinize disputes over inclusive classroom placements even more closely than in the past. Nonetheless, nothing in IDEA '97 or IDEA '04 contradicts the approaches taken in these earlier cases, and they retain their vitality. As of 2011, the U.S. Supreme Court had not agreed to hear a case involving a general education placement dispute, so it will be useful for readers to understand the specific standard in the circuit in which their school district is located.

Circuits Without a Judicial Standard

The First, Seventh,[2] and District of Columbia Circuits have not adopted a clear, explicit judicial standard for LRE issues involving general education classroom placements. Readers who live within these circuits should ask a school attorney whether there is a federal district court case that establishes the general classroom placement LRE standard for their particular school district. A school attorney should also be able to inform readers when new circuit decisions interpret the LRE provisions of IDEA.

The *Roncker* Standard

In the 1983 case of *Roncker v. Walter* (1983), Neill Roncker's parents wanted him placed in a regular school instead of the special school for children with intellectual disabilities in which the school district proposed to place him. It is important to realize, however, that Neill's parents were not seeking his placement in a general education classroom. The standard adopted by the Sixth Circuit required the lower court to re-examine the facts and determine whether Neill's educational, physical, or emotional needs required a service that could feasibly be provided in a special education class in a regular education school. Frequently referred to as the *Roncker* "portability" or "feasibility" test, the standard also required a determination of whether the mainstreaming benefits to the child would be far outweighed by the benefits of the separate setting, whether the child would be a disruptive force in the regular setting, or whether the cost of the shift would take away too many funds from other children with disabilities. If the answer to any of these questions was yes, the *Roncker* decision indicated that the placement change would not be feasible.

The standard developed by the Sixth Circuit in *Roncker* has been followed in the Fourth and Eighth Circuits. Cases applying the *Roncker* standard have largely upheld services in other than the child's neighborhood school. Several court decisions have supported the cost savings and other efficiencies achieved by centralized services or facilities in nonneighborhood schools, as long as appropriate levels of mainstreaming were provided.[3] Other court decisions applying *Roncker* have upheld pullout placements as the LRE for given students (*McWhirt v. Williamson County Schools*, 1994; *Kari H. v. Franklin Special School District*, 1995).

---

[2] See *Beth B. v. VanClay*, 211 F. Supp. 2d 1020 (N.D. Ill. 2001), *aff'd* 282 F.3d 493 (7th Cir. 2002) in which the Seventh Circuit reviewed other circuit standards without adopting a standard of its own. The court upheld the district court's ruling that the plaintiff could not remain in a regular education classroom because the curriculum had to be modified beyond recognition and because the plaintiff received virtually no nonacademic benefits (she and her aide were, in effect, segregated from the class most of the day).

[3] See *Hudson v. Bloomfield Hills Pub. Sch.*, 108 F.3d 112 (6th Cir. 1997) (adopting district court opinion at 910 F. Supp 1291 (E.D. Mich. 1995)); *Schuldt v. Mankato Indep.Sch. Dist.*, 937 F.2d 1357 (8th Cir. 1991); *Barnett v. Fairfax Cnty. Sch. Bd.*, 927 F.2d 146 (4th Cir. 1991); *DeVries v. Fairfax Cnty.Sch. Bd.*, 882 F.2d 876 (4th Cir. 1989).

The *Daniel R. R.* Standard

In *Daniel R. R. v. State Board of Education* (1989), the parents of a young boy with Down syndrome sought court support for their son's placement in a regular education, half-day prekindergarten class. School officials had placed Daniel there at the parents' request but believed that the placement was failing Daniel. The Fifth Circuit ruled that the class was not Daniel's LRE. The class was found to be too stressful in spite of curriculum modifications and extra attention from Daniel's teacher. Evidence suggested that Daniel was falling asleep and developing a stutter.

Despite the outcome, the two-pronged test established in *Daniel R. R.* has become the basic standard for regular classroom placement in the Second, Third, Fifth, Tenth, and Eleventh Circuits.[4] The standard asks two major questions when a child with a disability has been placed in a regular classroom.

1. Has the school attempted to accommodate the student by providing sufficient supplementary aids and services and sufficient program modifications in the regular education setting?

   If the answer is no, IDEA is violated. (This test can be thought of as the "sufficiency" test.) If the answer is yes, the court then asks whether the student is benefitting, both academically and nonacademically, from the accommodations. In considering the question of benefit, the court also considers the student's effect on the regular education teacher and the other students.

   In Daniel's situation, the court noted that to meet Daniel's developmental level would have required alterations in 90 to 100 percent of the curriculum. The court concluded that, in spite of the supplementary aids and services, Daniel was not benefitting from the placement, and that the effort to help him was draining the teacher's time and attention away from the other students. Although the parents argued that the opportunity for interaction with students who did not have disabilities was a sufficient ground for mainstreaming him, the court concluded that the opportunity for interaction alone was insufficient when balanced against the benefits of a special education placement.

2. If the student cannot be accommodated in the regular education setting (that is, is not benefiting despite sufficient efforts), has the public agency mainstreamed the student to the maximum extent appropriate?

This question, in effect, is addressing the extent of social and physical mainstreaming in cases where instructional mainstreaming is inappropriate. In Daniel's case, the court concluded that mainstreaming Daniel for lunch and recess met the test. It is interesting that in subsequent years, Daniel was able to be successfully mainstreamed into regular classrooms (R. Martin, Daniel's attorney, personal communication, August 1991).

The Eleventh Circuit adopted the *Daniel R. R.* standard in *Greer v. Rome City School District* (1991). It applied the standard to a situation in which parents sought regular classroom placement for their daughter Christy, an elementary school student with Down syndrome. The placement had been rejected by the school. The court ordered regular class placement for Christy on the basis that her school district had not given proper consideration to whether regular classroom placement with supplementary aids and services could be accomplished. The school had considered only two limited options: a self-contained classroom with speech therapy as a related service, and a regular

---

[4] In addition to the *Daniel R. R. case*, which is a Fifth Circuit case, see also *P. v. Newington Bd. of Educ.*, 546 F.3d 111 (2d Cir. 2008); *L.B. v. Nebo Sch. Dist.*, 379 F.3d 966 (10th Cir. 2004); *Oberti v. Bd. of Educ.*, 995 F.2d 1204 (3d Cir. 1993); *Greer v. Rome City Sch. Dist.*, 967 F.2d 470 (11th Cir. 1991).

classroom with speech therapy. No consideration had been given to the range of supplementary services that Christy would need in the regular classroom, such as resource room services, itinerant instruction by a special educator within her classroom, or curriculum adjustments. In effect, the school flunked the first part of the *Daniel R. R.* test. (The school made another major error: It proposed an IEP and placement to the parents at the IEP meeting without having solicited parental input for the IEP.)

The court in *Greer* elaborated on the factors required to ascertain benefit under the *Daniel R. R.* standard. It mentioned that, in weighing the academic and nonacademic benefits of special versus regular class placements, the school board may consider whether regular class placement might cause a child to fall substantially behind peers with disabilities who are being educated in self-contained placements. It also added a cost factor to the *Daniel R. R.* two-pronged test. It specified that if the cost of regular classroom placement for the student with a disability would significantly reduce the money available for the education of other students (presumably including children without disabilities), then the mainstream placement would not be appropriate. Courts following the *Daniel R. R.* two-pronged standard frequently refer to it as the *Daniel R. R./Greer* test.

The *Rachel H.* Standard

The Ninth Circuit used its own test in deciding *Sacramento City Unified School District v. Rachel H.* (1994). It upheld regular second-grade classroom placement for Rachel Holland, a young girl with an intellectual disability and significant speech and language deficits. Rachel had made academic, social, and behavioral progress in a private school classroom with children who did not have disabilities. Her parents sought the same opportunities for her in a public school classroom. The court ruled that Rachel's IEP goals could be implemented satisfactorily in a regular classroom with curriculum modifications and the help of a part-time aide.

The Ninth Circuit said it was adopting the four-factor balancing test employed by the district court, but it paraphrased those factors as follows (district court language is in parentheses):

1. What are the educational benefits of full-time placement in a regular classroom? (How do the educational benefits of full-time placement in a regular classroom with supplementary aids and services compare with special education placement?)

2. What are the nonacademic benefits of such a placement?

3. What effect does the student with disabilities have on the regular classroom teacher and children?

4. What are the costs of mainstreaming the student? (Do the costs significantly impact the education of other students?)

A Comparison of *Roncker*, *Daniel R. R./Greer*, and *Rachel H.*

Similarities

1. All three standards consider the potential disruptive effect of a student with disabilities in the regular classroom.

2. All introduce cost factors.

3. All consider the benefits of regular classroom placement and weigh them against the benefits of special class placement.

4. All employ multifactored analyses. None of them conclude that all children with disabilities should be placed in regular education classrooms and allowed or forced to fail there before they can be placed elsewhere.

Differences

1. The standard in *Roncker* measures the costs of serving a student with disabilities against the needs of similar students, while the standards in *Rachel H.* and *Daniel R. R./Greer* assess the impact of the costs on "other" students, presumably including those without disabilities.

2. Only the *Daniel R. R./Greer* test includes the need to assess the extent of backup interactions with students who do not have disabilities, if instruction in the regular classroom is not appropriate.

3. Only the *Daniel R. R./Greer* standard requires the school district to prove the sufficiency of its past or proposed efforts to serve a special education student with supplementary aids and services in the regular education classroom.

4. Only the *Daniel R. R./Greer* and *Rachel H.* standards include assessment of the nonacademic as well as academic benefits of regular class placement. Issues in #3 and #4 did not arise in *Roncker* because the plaintiff was not seeking regular class placement.

Applying Judicial Standards to Different Factual Situations

The test or standard adopted by a circuit to determine whether a student should be educated in a regular classroom must be applied to a specific set of facts. The standard alone does not dictate the outcome for a given student. A different set of facts can produce a different outcome, as can be seen by reviewing the outcome for Daniel R. R. and Christy Greer.†

> † Often, a student with a severe disability is assigned an aide to assist the student to succeed in a regular education setting. In *Frederick County Independent School District v I.S.*, 325 F. Supp. 2d 565 (D. Md. 2005), the court held that a regular education placement with a one-to-one aide denied a child FAPE in the LRE because of her lack of meaningful progress on IEP goals and because of the child's overreliance on the aide, which was reducing her independence. In *School District of Wisconsin Dells v. Z.S. ex rel. Littlegeorge*, 295 F.3d 671 (7th Cir. 2002), the appellate court upheld a restrictive placement for a highly disruptive child with autism, stating that an aide in a regular classroom would be functioning as a "living straitjacket." The question for consideration in LRE disputes is: When does an aide facilitate inclusion, and when does an aide hinder inclusion?

Incorporation Into IDEA of Aspects of the *Daniel R. R./Greer* Standard

Under the *Daniel R. R./Greer* standard, if a school district has actually placed a student in a general education classroom, then the district must make available a sufficient or reasonable array of support services rather than dumping the student.† Also, before refusing to serve a student in a general education classroom, the school district must consider whether it could serve the student effectively there if it provided a reasonably full set of support services. In effect, these aspects of the *Daniel R. R./Greer* standard were incorporated into IDEA '97 and retained in IDEA '04 through the IEP content additions that require specification of supplementary aids and services, program modifications, and supports for school staff, and consideration of the need for positive behavioral interventions and supports.

> † IDEA '04 removed the IDEA '97 provision requiring hearing officers, before ordering a placement change for safety reasons, to consider whether an LEA had used mitigating measures to reduce the risk of harm from the student's behavior. The IDEA '97 provision had reflected the Eighth Circuit's decision in *Light v. Parkway C-2 School District*, 41 F.3d 1223 (8th Cir. 1994).

IDEA makes no mention of cost factors in determining the LRE. It makes no explicit reference to weighing the benefits of special placement versus regular class placement. At the same time, however, the regulatory provision that requires consideration of any harmful effect of a placement on the child or the quality of services needed creates an inference that some weighing of placement benefits may be acceptable. IDEA also does not refer to weighing academic and nonacademic benefits but instead relies on individual goal setting in the IEP to guide LRE decisions. (The IEP requirements, however, presume that each student will need both academic and functional goals.) Of interest is the statement in the regulatory analysis accompanying the 1999 regulations, explaining that students are not required to fail in regular classrooms before being placed in other settings (See analysis accompanying 34 C.F.R. § 300.551 at 64 Fed. Reg. 12638 (March 12, 1999)).†

> † The statement presumably is not repeated in the analysis section accompanying the '04 regulations because the analysis section responds only to questions or comments raised by commenters.

Applying *Rachel H.* to Different Facts

The case of *Clyde K. v. Puyallup School District*, 35 F.3d 1396 (9th Cir. 1994), illustrates how the Ninth Circuit applied its *Rachel H.* standard to a student with an emotional disability. Ryan K., the son of Clyde K., had been diagnosed with ADHD and Tourette syndrome. Moreover, he demonstrated severe behavior problems in both his regular and resource classrooms in his high school. In addition to receiving some of his academic instruction in a resource room, he was receiving services from the school's behavioral specialist. He had permission to leave class whenever he needed time to relieve the "tics" that were a manifestation of his Tourette syndrome.

For his most recent school year, his academic test results showed that his achievement had actually declined. The court decision reports that Ryan taunted other students with name-calling and profanity, insulted his teachers with vulgar comments, directed sexually explicit comments at female students, refused to follow directions, and kicked and hit classroom furniture. He had been suspended briefly on two occasions—the first for punching another student in the face, and the second for pushing another student's head into a door. Teachers and students reported that Ryan's behavior had a negative effect on them and was disrupting the learning process; he was socially ostracized and had few friends.

After Ryan assaulted a teacher, the school sought a court injunction allowing his removal to a self-contained placement called STARS (Students Temporarily Away from Regular School). His IEP could be implemented there, and the school district asserted that Ryan would be in a more structured environment and receive more individual attention at STARS. Ryan's parents argued that he should remain at his junior high school but should have a personal aide.

Applying the *Rachel H.* four-factor test to the facts, the court decided that Ryan could be kept in his STARS placement over the objection of his parents. The court concluded that Ryan was experiencing few academic and nonacademic benefits from his general education placement, and his behaviors were highly disruptive to his teachers and the other students. Cost was not a factor in the decision.

The Neighborhood School Cases

Many parents of children with severe disabilities have sought placement for their children in their neighborhood schools. Court decisions, however, recognize that although IDEA expresses a strong preference for (and arguably a presumption in favor of) placement in regular classrooms, it does not mandate placement in the neighborhood school. In other words, although children with disabilities are to be educated to the maximum extent appropriate with children who do not have disabilities, the law does not require that the children live in the same neighborhood.

Readers will recall that the regulations specify that children should be educated in the schools they would attend if they were not disabled, but this preference is qualified by "unless the IEP . . . requires some other arrangement" (34 C.F.R. § 300.116(c) (2006)). In several cases that apply the *Roncker* standard, financial considerations were important in determining that the appropriate placement for given students was in schools other than their neighborhood schools. Although the courts in those cases were not asked to rule on whether a child has an absolute right to a neighborhood placement under IDEA, the decisions assume that no such right exists.[5]

---

[5] See, e.g., *Schuldt v. Mankato Indep. Sch. Dist. No. 77*, 937 F.2d 1357 (8th Cir. 1991); *Barnett v. Fairfax Cnty. Sch. Bd.*, 927 F.2d 146 (4th Cir. 1991); *Wilson v. Marana Unified Sch. Dist. of Pima Cnty.*, 735 F.2d 1178 (9th Cir. 1984).

Several cases over the past fifteen years have addressed the neighborhood school issue explicitly. For instance, in *Murray v. Montrose County School District RE-IJ* (1995), the Tenth Circuit ruled that IDEA's LRE mandate neither created a right to placement in the neighborhood school nor a presumption in favor of such a placement. Instead, according to the court, although IDEA "commands schools to include or mainstream disabled children as much as possible, it says nothing about where, within a school district, that inclusion shall take place" (pp. 928-929). At most, the court concluded, IDEA creates a preference for education in the neighborhood school. Other appellate cases, in the First, Fifth, and Sixth Circuits, have reached similar conclusions.[6] A subsequent Tenth Circuit decision in *Urban v. Jefferson County School District R-1* (1996) followed the ruling in *Murray* and also held that no greater right to neighborhood placement exists under Section 504 and ADA than exists under IDEA.

Advocates of full inclusion see these appellate decisions as setbacks because they do not require a child to be educated with his or her neighborhood friends. Nonetheless, the decisions are complying with IDEA because they honor the requirement that children with disabilities be educated in regular classrooms with children who do not have disabilities when such settings can provide FAPE.

The Politics of Inclusion

The movement to fully include all students with disabilities in general education classrooms and schools found support in the initial IDEA preference for regular class placement. Inclusionists moved beyond the initial IDEA legal framework, however, by envisioning the elimination of the IDEA continuum of placement options. Although the continuum has been maintained in IDEA, the effects of the inclusion movement are reflected in what is now, arguably, a presumption, although a rebuttable one, that all children with disabilities will be placed in regular classrooms with support services and that the IEP team will describe the extent to which this will not occur.

IDEA '97 encouraged at least a partial paradigm shift for the delivery of services to IDEA students by emphasizing that special education is a set of services, not a particular place. Not viewing special education as a place, however, implies that a blanket policy of inclusive placements may be as inappropriate as a blanket policy of pullout placements. The law balances the preference for inclusion with the bedrock belief that the education of children with disabilities must be individualized to meet the special needs of each child. Sometimes, that still requires a pullout setting.

For school officials, inclusion continues to create tensions and dilemmas for three primary reasons: (a) parents are split about the value of inclusion for their children with disabilities, (b) special education professionals are also divided, and (c) the regular education community is deeply worried about its ability to meet the needs of students with severe disabilities in regular classrooms without extensive training and support in the classroom. Therefore, whether the IDEA goal of more inclusive education can be successfully implemented is dependent on many factors outside the control of the laws themselves.

Many parents of students with learning disabilities, attention deficit disorders, visual impairments, and hearing impairments support the maintenance of a full continuum of placement options. These parents urge schools to respond to the individual needs of given students, some of whom, in their view, do not or will not benefit either academically or nonacademically from full-time placement

---

[6] See *McLaughlin v. Holt Pub. Sch. Bd.*, 320 F.3d 663 (6th Cir. 2003); *Kevin G. v. Cranston Sch. Comm.*, 130 F.3d 481 (1st Cir. 1997); *Hudson v. Bloomfield Hills Pub. Sch.*, 108 F.3d 112 (6th Cir. 1997), *affirming* 910 F. Supp.1291 (E.D. Mich. 1995); *Flour Bluff Indep. Sch. Dist. v. Katherine M.*, 91 F.3d 689 (5th Cir. 1996). *Cf. White v. Ascension Parish Sch. Bd.*, 343 F.3d 373 (5th Cir. 2003) (LEA has a right to select centralized site rather than neighborhood school for delivery of cued-speech transliterator services; IDEA placement refers to setting (degree of inclusion) rather than location of the site).

in regular classroom settings. Members of the Deaf community (the capital D signifies those who use American Sign Language as their primary language and identify themselves as having a Deaf culture) have been especially vocal in urging retention of separate schools and specialized services in pullout settings for some students who are hard of hearing or deaf. The Deaf community fears that inclusion will erode their culture and fail to meet their highly specialized and separate sign language needs.

On the other hand, many parents of students with intellectual disabilities argue equally forcefully that their children are harmed by removal from the regular education environment and benefit from the social and language modeling that is present in that setting. In particular, parents of children with severe intellectual disabilities advocate full inclusion in the belief that it will produce more acceptance of their children in their neighborhoods and communities, especially as they grow older and prepare for postschool living.

Additionally, the needs of children with severe emotional disturbance and profound multiple disabilities create special dilemmas for both parents and educators. In many instances, the courts have recognized the overwhelming needs of these children and have ordered their placement in residential schools or treatment centers as the only location in which FAPE can be delivered (see chapter 13).

Professionals working with these various groups of children reflect differences in points of view just as parents do. They want good things to happen for children with disabilities, but they differ as to what will produce good outcomes. Then, too, other factors sometimes influence professional outlooks. While some school officials adopt inclusion on the grounds that it enhances the dignity and value of all persons with disabilities, others adopt it because they believe they can save money through a more uniform delivery system. In either event, educators and parents should be aware of two realities. First, in spite of the IDEA preference for inclusion whenever appropriate, the statute does not support blanket policies of service delivery, nor do court interpretations of the statute. Second, if children with disabilities are to succeed in general education classrooms, they must be provided with appropriate supplementary aids and services and program modifications. Dumping such children into general education classrooms without the necessary supports serves no one.

Placement Trends

Although placement disputes have generated more litigation than virtually all other IDEA issues, it is important to keep in perspective the fact that most children with disabilities are educated in general classroom settings for at least part of the day. The heat generated by placement disputes is inversely proportional to the number of children affected.

According to OSEP statistics from July 2006 (the latest figures available), only 4 percent of students with disabilities ages six through twenty-one did not attend regular education schools. Most of these students were in separate day schools; about 1 percent were in residential facilities or homebound/ hospital settings. The disability categories with the highest percentage of children who were not in schools with their nondisabled peers were multiple disabilities (close to 25%) and deaf-blindness (close to 29%) (U.S. Department of Education, 2010, Fig. 1-25 and Table 1-14).

As of July 2006, close to 54 percent of students with disabilities ages six through twenty-one were being removed from general education classrooms for less than 21 percent of the school day, while approximately 26 percent were receiving pull-out services for anywhere from 21–60 percent of the school day. Close to 17 percent were spending more than 60 percent of the school day in separate classes (U.S. Dep't of Education, 2010, Table 1-14). Nonetheless, the percentage of students in inclusive settings varies considerably by age group, disability group, race, and state, raising issues that deserve further examination by researchers and policy makers. Especially deserving more research is the question of what settings are best suited for what children with what kinds of instructional needs. Mounting evidence suggests that the answers are not the same for all students.

↳Reminders and Tips

1. The term *least restrictive environment* does not refer exclusively to the general education environment. (Language in the IEP provisions, however, arguably, creates a presumption in favor of that setting unless FAPE cannot be delivered there.)

2. Placement decisions must be individualized and made annually. Blanket policies of separation or inclusion for all students with disabilities are prohibited by IDEA.

3. Parents must be invited to participate in placement meetings.

4. The generally accepted judicial standards for placing students with disabilities in general education classrooms require the provision of program modifications and supplementary aids and services, plus consideration of any disruptive effect on other students. They also require a weighing of the student's academic and nonacademic benefits from such a placement.

5. There is no entitlement to placement in the neighborhood school under IDEA.

6. Certain kinds of disciplinary placements and referrals to law enforcement agencies are not prohibited by the LRE provisions.

↳Review

1. Explain the legal meaning of LRE.

   LRE refers to the setting closest to the general education classroom in which FAPE can be delivered. It may or may not be the general education classroom.

2. Why does IDEA prefer that children with disabilities be educated with children who do not have disabilities?

   It helps both sets of children learn to work and play together, just as they will need to do as adults after they leave school. The IEP chapter provides other reasons: for instance, it encourages higher expectations and better postschool outcomes than have been achieved to date.

3. Why does IDEA '97 continue to require a continuum of placement options?

   Not all children with disabilities can be appropriately educated in the same type of setting.

4. Why are the courts deciding that all children with disabilities do not have to be educated in their neighborhood schools?

   Although IDEA specifies that children with disabilities and children without disabilities must be educated together to the maximum extent appropriate, it does not require that the children be neighborhood friends. The IDEA regulations, however, go beyond the statute by adding a preference that children be educated in their neighborhood schools unless their IEP dictates otherwise. The preference has not been elevated to a legal right.

5. How does IDEA '97 incorporate aspects of the *Daniel R. R./Greer* standard?

It establishes a presumption in favor of regular classroom placement with a full set of supplementary aids and services, including program modifications and supports for school personnel. It encourages the use of positive behavioral interventions in regular classrooms before deciding that a misbehaving child with a disability is too disruptive to remain there.

⚡References

Daniel R. R. v. St. Bd. of Educ., 874 F.2d 1036 (5th Cir. 1989).

Greer v. Rome City Sch. Dist., 950 F.2d 688 (11th Cir. 1991), *op. withdrawn,* 956 F.2d 1025 (1992), reinstated, 967 F.2d 470 (1992).

Individuals with Disabilities Education Improvement Act, 20 U.S.C. § 1400 *et seq.* (2006).

Individuals with Disabilities Education Improvement Act Regulations, 34 C.F. R. § 300.1 *et seq.* (2006).

Mills v. Dist. of Columbia Bd. of Educ., 348 F. Supp. 866 (D. D. C. 1972).

Murray v. Montrose Cnty. Sch. Dist. RE-IJ, 51 F.3d 921 (10th Cir. 1995).

PARC v. Pennsylvania, 343 F. Supp. 279 (E.D. Pa. 1972).

Roncker v. Walter, 700 F.2d 1058 (6th Cir. 1983).

Sacramento City Unified Sch. Dist. v. Rachel H., 14 F.3d 1398 (9th Cir. 1994).

U.S. Department of Education, OSERS, OSEP.(2010). *Twenty-ninth annual report to Congress on the implementation of IDEA, 2007).* Vol. 1. Washington, DC: Author.

Urban v. Jefferson Cnty. Sch. Dist. R-1, 89 F.3d 720 (10th Cir. 1996).

⇉Selected Supplementary Resources

Bartlett, L. D. (2004). Special education students and the police: Many questions unanswered. *Education Law Reporter, 185,* 1–14.

Bartlett, L. D., & McLeod, S. (1998). Inclusion and the regular class teacher under the IDEA. *Education Law Reporter, 128,* 1–14.

Ferguson, D. L. (1995). The real challenge of inclusion: Confessions of a "rabid inclusionist." *Phi Delta Kappan, 77,* 281–287.

Huefner, D. S. (1994). The mainstreaming cases: Tensions and trends for school administrators. *Education Administration Quarterly, 30,* 27–55.

Kauffman, J. M., &Hallahan, D. (1995). *The illusion of full inclusion.* Austin, TX: Pro-Ed.

Quinn, M. M., Rutherford, R. B., Leone, P. E., Osher, D. M., & Poirier, J. M. (2005). Youth with disabilities in juvenile corrections: A national survey. *Exceptional Children, 71,* 339–345.

Yell, M. L. (1995). Least restrictive environment, inclusion, and students with disabilities: A legal analysis. *Journal of Special Education, 28,* 389–404.

Zigmond, N. (2003). Where should students with disabilities receive special education services? *Journal of Special Education, 37,* 193–199.

Chapter 13

Placement of Students in Private Facilities Under IDEA

Chapter Outline

Overview

IDEA anticipated two basic kinds of private school placements of children with disabilities: (a) placement by a public agency when necessary for FAPE and (b) placement by parents when, for reasons other than FAPE, they prefer a private school for their child. In the first situation, IDEA holds the public agency responsible for ensuring that the placement in the private setting, whether a day school or a residential school or facility, is at no cost to the parents. In the second situation, the parents are responsible for tuition costs, but the education agency retains responsibility for the provision of some special education and related services to some private school students. A third kind of private placement has arisen when parents claim that the LEA has not made FAPE available at the public school, and the parents pull their child out of the public setting, place their child in a private school, and seek reimbursement for the alleged denial of FAPE.

Disputes requiring court resolution have arisen in the latter two kinds of situations. It is helpful for educators and parents to know something about these disputes so that they can understand the implications of parents' removing children with disabilities from public school and placing them in private school. Outcomes of private school disputes can be among the most expensive for school districts and can impact special education budgets heavily.

Placement in Private Facilities for FAPE

Private Placements by School Districts

Sometimes a school district chooses to place a student with disabilities in a private special education day school or residential setting at no cost to the parents. This occurs when, for various reasons, the district can neither provide special education and related services to a particular student, nor contract with another school district or public agency to provide the services. In such situations, school districts must select a private school that meets state standards (the state often maintains such a list), involve the private school in the IEP development, and retain overall responsibility to ensure that the child's rights are honored and that the IEP requirements are met (20 U.S.C. § 1412(a)(10) (B) (2006)). Generally speaking, this kind of private placement has not generated controversy in the courts because the LEA picks up the costs.

Private Placements by Parents When FAPE is the Issue

If a conflict arises as to whether a private setting is necessary for the provision of FAPE, parents may request a due process hearing and appeal an adverse decision to court. Numerous cases have arisen in which dissatisfied parents have pulled their children from the public school system and put them in private schools, and sought reimbursement, first at administrative hearings and then in court. Three Supreme Court cases have established the applicable reimbursement standards in these situations.

In the first Supreme Court case, *Burlington School Committee v. Massachusetts Department of Education* (1985), the Court held that IDEA's stay-put provision applied to education agencies but not to parents. Parents could place their child at a private school but did so at their own financial risk. If the public agency had not made FAPE available to the child and the parental placement was "proper" under IDEA, then parents were entitled to reimbursement for the costs of the private placement. The Court did not elaborate on the factors that would make a parental placement "proper" under IDEA.

In the second case, *Florence County School District Four v. Carter* (1993), the Supreme Court went beyond its *Burlington* decision by holding that reimbursement could be awarded even when a parent selected a private school that did not meet state standards. The LEA had argued that because the private school was not approved by the state for this particular placement, the school district should not have to reimburse the parents. The Court rejected this argument, concluding that a private school selected by the parents was not a public agency to whom the FAPE standards applied. In more concrete terms, because a public agency had not made the private placement, the private school was not obligated to develop an IEP or employ only certified teachers.

As in *Burlington*, the Supreme Court concluded in *Carter* that the "appropriate relief" authorized by IDEA gave a court the discretion to fashion an equitable remedy for a school district's denial of FAPE as long as the private school was otherwise "proper." It then stated that courts could determine what level of reimbursement was reasonable, and that "[t]otal reimbursement will not be appropriate if the court determines that the cost of the private education was unreasonable" (p. 16). School districts took some comfort in this statement, but the underlying lesson of *Carter* and *Burlington* is that school districts must be certain they are offering FAPE to eligible students lest they be held accountable for private school reimbursement costs (see chapter 15).†

> † In a memorandum providing guidance on the *Carter* decision to chief state school officers, OSEP opined that a court might be willing to compare the costs of an unapproved and approved private school in determining the amount of reimbursement (OSEP memorandum 94-14, 20 IDELR 1180 (OSEP 1994)).

The Facts in the *Carter* Case

Shannon Carter was not identified as a child with a learning disability until she was in the ninth grade. Her public school had tested her in seventh grade at her parents' request and had failed to identify what was later found to be a fairly severe learning disability. The school proposed regular ninth-grade classes for most of the day, with two periods per day in the resource room. Her parents rejected this IEP because they did not want Shannon instructed in the resource room with children who had intellectual disabilities and emotional illnesses. In response, the school proposed that Shannon receive individualized instruction from an itinerant special education teacher for three periods each week. The IEP established a goal of four months' progress in reading and math for the entire school year. Her reading was at a fifth-grade level, her math at a sixth-grade level.

Shannon's parents were dissatisfied with this IEP and challenged it at hearings, and then in court. In the meantime, they placed her in a private school for children with learning disabilities where she remained until her high school graduation. The private school evaluated Shannon quarterly and enrolled her in classes with low pupil-teacher ratios. She made significant progress, received passing marks, and increased her reading comprehension by three grade levels in her three years at the school. By the time the case reached the Supreme Court, the public school district had conceded that Shannon's ninth-grade IEP was inappropriate and had set only trivial progress goals. The issue before the Court was whether her parents could select a private school that did not meet state standards for private schools.

In IDEA '97, Congress adopted the underlying rulings of *Burlington* and *Carter* that reimbursement was available to parents when their children were denied FAPE in public settings. It did not, however, speak to the issue of whether the parents' choice of placement must be "proper." Neither does IDEA '04. The IDEA regulations fill the gap by specifying that the private placement must be "appropriate." Presumably, this means that the placement is allowing the student to progress appropriately although the provision does not include a definition of the term. The provision does, however, state that *appropriate* does not mean that the placement must meet state standards (34 C.F.R. § 300.148(c) (2006)).

Congress went further than the *Burlington* and *Carter* decisions in certain other respects. For instance, IDEA '04 states that not only a court but also a hearing officer is authorized to order reimbursement to parents for the cost of private placement when the public agency fails to provide FAPE in a timely manner (20 U.S.C. § 1412(a)(10)(C)(ii) (2006)). The regulations add that an SEA is similarly authorized (34 C.F.R. § 300.151(b)(1) (2006)). These provisions can result in saved court time and costs.

A third issue concerning reimbursement for private school placement arose more recently and was decided by the Supreme Court in June 2009. The issue in *Forest Grove School District v. T.A.* (2009) was whether language in the 1997 IDEA amendments prohibited reimbursement to parents for their private-school costs if they had not first enrolled their child in public school and allowed the district to develop an IEP that could provide FAPE. The Court determined that the IDEA '97 language did not change the remedial purpose of IDEA or supersede the Court's authority to award reimbursement in private school cases. In *Forest Grove*, an Oregon teenager diagnosed privately with ADHD and learning and memory problems was denied special education services by his school district, which concluded that the boy's learning difficulties did not have a sufficiently adverse effect on his educational performance. The parents placed their son in a private school and sought reimbursement. An administrative hearing officer held that the school had not evaluated the student properly and, thereby, had denied FAPE to the student. The school district appealed the hearing officer's decision, which had awarded reimbursement to the student's parents.

After lower court proceedings, The Supreme Court upheld the availability of reimbursement, applying the reasoning of *Burlington* and *Carter* to the *Forest Grove* case. The Court stated: "It would be particularly strange for the Act to provide a remedy . . . when a school district offers a child inadequate special education services but to leave parents without relief . . . [when] the school district unreasonably denies a child access to such services altogether " (p. 2496). Addressing the concern that LEAs would suffer a substantial financial burden as a result of the Court's decision, the Court restated earlier language from *Burlington* and *Carter*, reminding school districts that parents place their children in private schools at their own financial risk, that courts retain discretion to reduce the amount of the reimbursement award when warranted, and that reimbursement is available only when the public placement violated IDEA and the private placement was "proper."†

† The Court remanded the case to the federal district court to weigh the equities under the Court's newly announced standard. The district court declined to order reimbursement, concluding that the parents selected their son's private school primarily to address his drug addiction. The decision was affirmed by the Ninth Circuit (*Forest Grove School District v. T. A.*, 638 F.3d 1234 (9th Cir. 2011)).

IDEA '04 specifies a number of conditions under which the amount of the reimbursement can be limited: (a) if the parents did not inform the IEP team at the most recent meeting they attended that they were rejecting the proposed placement and intended to place their child in private school at public expense, or if the parents did not provide written notice of that intent ten business days prior to removing their child from public school; (b) if the parents did not make their child available for an evaluation by the public agency after proper notification of the agency's desire to do one; or (c) if a court found that the parents had acted unreasonably (20 U.S.C. § 1412(a)(10)(C)(iii) (2006)).

Prior notice from parents is meant to prevent them from surprising school districts, just as prior notice to parents of a school's proposed action or inaction is meant to prevent surprises to the parents. It allows the parties another opportunity to understand the seriousness of each other's positions and concerns to see if an agreement can be reached. Also, when the child stops attending public school, the school will know what has happened.

IDEA '04 specifies that even if parents did not give the required notice, the amount of their reimbursement cannot be reduced if (a) the school district had prevented the parents from providing the required information, (b) the parents had not received notice of the requirement, or (c) compliance would have been likely to result in physical harm to the child. The court can exercise its discretion in determining whether to reduce reimbursement if the parents did not provide notice because they were illiterate or could not write in English, or because providing notice would have risked serious emotional harm to the child (20 U.S.C. § 1412(a)(10)(C)(iv) (2006)). This kind of detail obviously attempts to foresee various circumstances that would make it unfair to limit reimbursement.

Residential Placements

A subset of the private school disputes concerns the need for residential placement, usually for children with multiple and profound physical and intellectual disabilities, severe emotional disturbances, or severe learning disabilities. The IDEA regulations have always contained a provision that when a residential placement (whether public or private) "is necessary to provide special education and related services to a child with a disability, the program, including nonmedical care and room and board, must be at no cost to the parents of the child" (34 C.F.R. § 300.104 (2006)).

A key issue arising in the residential placement cases is whether the placement is necessary for special education reasons (as opposed to medical, custodial, or familial reasons). In general, courts have ordered residential placements when the students' educational, emotional, and behavioral needs are inseparable and/or when the students require continuous and closely supervised special education and related services throughout the day in order to derive educational benefit or make progress toward IEP goals.[1] In these situations, if an LEA does not wish to continue to be obligated for the residential school tuition and room and board, then it should make comparable services available within its own system. Among the possibilities for offering comparable services are the provision of group home and day program combinations, respite care, parent training, after-school services, and perhaps even behavioral aides in the home.[2]

Reimbursement of the program costs, including nonmedical costs and room and board, is not available if the residential placement is not for special education purposes. Some residential placements of children with disabilities may be necessary for familial reasons (for instance, inability of the family to care for the child) or custodial reasons (such as drug addiction).† In these situations, the special education needs themselves are not what drives the placement, and the LEA is not responsible for the costs of the residential placement.

---

[1] Important early cases establishing these principles include *Abrahamson v. Hershman*, 701 F.2d 223 (1st Cir. 1983), and *Kruelle v. New Castle Cnty. Sch. Dist.*, 642 F.2d 687 (3d. Cir. 1981).

[2] See, e.g., *Kerkam v. Superintendent, D.C. Pub. Schs.*, 931 F.2d 84 (D.C. Cir. 1991); *Burke Cnty. Bd. of Educ. v. Denton*, 895 F.2d 973 (4th Cir. 1990); *Abrahamson v. Hershman*, 701 F.2d 223 (1st Cir. 1983).

† A recent example is the case of *Ashland School District v. R .J.*, 558 F.3d 1004, (9th Cir. 2009). In that case, the court determined that R.J.'s out-of-school behavior was the reason for her residential placement. Her performance in school was good when she decided to do the work, and the Ninth Circuit determined that her residential placement was not needed for FAPE but to bring her sexual behavior and other rebellious behaviors under control.

The Fifth Circuit's Approach to Private Residential Placements

In *Richardson Independent School District v. Michael Z.*, 580 F.3d 286 (5th Cir. 2009), the Fifth Circuit announced its own two-part test for determining whether a private residential placement was proper under IDEA '97 (the version of IDEA that was applicable to the chronology of the case). The court first reiterated the basic view that the residential placement must be "essential" (in other words, necessary) for "meaningful educational benefit" (in other words, for FAPE). The second part of its test was a determination whether the services provided were "primarily oriented toward enabling the child to receive an education." The court remanded the case to the district court to decide whether parental reimbursement should be awarded, based on the lower court's factual analysis of the actual services being delivered. In effect, what the court was ordering was a determination of whether the services were nonrelated services being delivered for primarily noneducational reasons (e.g., medical, social, familial). If the services were not related services, presumably reimbursement would be denied. In announcing this second part of the test, the court stated that it was rejecting the view of those courts which took the position that if all the services were inextricably intertwined, then the placement was needed for FAPE. The Fifth Circuit noted that it was borrowing its position from language in the Seventh Circuit's decision in *Dale M. v. Board of Education of Bradley Bourbonnais High School District No. 307*, 237 F.3d 813 (7th Cir. 2001).

One cannot help but wonder if language distinctions among the circuits are essentially semantic. Implicitly or explicitly, courts are trying to distinguish true related services (needed to enable educational benefit) from those needed primarily to serve noneducational goals. The factual analysis remains paramount, and different courts may judge the facts differently and apply broad or narrow constructions of what is considered "educational" in nature.

In limited situations, school districts may need to provide or pay for the appropriate special education and related services in an institutional setting such as a hospital. Most courts, for instance, while viewing hospital placements as medical placements, have held school districts responsible for any special education instruction and related services delivered there.[3] Other courts have occasionally upheld a hospital placement as a special education placement but have attempted to separate the medical from the nonmedical costs by examining the hospital bills closely.[4] (See also the box in chapter 11 on Psychotherapy in Hospital and Private Settings.) Defining nonmedical care by the hospital is not an easy task, however.

The Supreme Court has not heard a residential placement case, but the same judicial standards regarding FAPE that were established in the *Burlington* and *Carter* cases (both private day-school cases) have been applied by the lower courts to residential placements. In other words, if FAPE

---

[3] See, e.g., *Butler v. Evans*, 225 F.3d 887 (7th Cir. 2000); *Tice v. Botetourt Cnty. Sch. Bd.*, 908 F.2d 1200 (4th Cir. 1990); *Clovis Unified Sch. Dist. v. Cal. Office of Admin. Hearings*, 903 F.2d 635 (9th Cir. 1990); *McKenzie v. Jefferson*, 566 F. Supp. 404 (D.D.C. 1983).
[4] See *Vander Malle v. Ambach*, 667 F. Supp 1015 (S.D.N.Y. 1987). Cf. *Babb v. Knox Cnty. Sch. System*, 965 F.2d 104 (6th Cir. 1992) (upholding a hospital placement as necessary for FAPE).

has been unavailable (usually because the IEP developed for the student by the public agency has been inappropriate), and if the private residential placement has been otherwise proper, reimbursement has been awarded. Numerous lower courts have awarded reimbursement to parents under this reasoning.† Now, these courts have an explicit statutory basis for their reasoning because, since IDEA '97, reimbursement provisions apply to all private placements (20 U.S.C. § 1412(a)(10)(C) (ii) (2006)). Other lower courts have addressed residential (and day-school) placement disputes in terms of the balance between FAPE and LRE, to be discussed next.

> † It is interesting to compare *Drew P. v. Clarke County School District*, 877 F.2d 927 (11th Cir.1989), with *Matta v. Board of Education*, 731 F. Supp. 253 (S.D. Ohio 1990). In Drew P., the court concluded that a residential placement in Tokyo and Boston Higashi schools was proper under the Burlington standard. A year later, another court ruled, in Matta, that parents did not prove that the Tokyo and Boston Higashi schools were proper because the parents failed to investigate a recommended residential placement within the state.

The Interaction of FAPE and LRE

Private day-school placements.

The Supreme Court did not factor IDEA's preference for the regular education environment into its decisions in *Burlington* and *Carter*, but the statutory preference has been addressed in lower court, private day-school FAPE cases. Most such cases in the U.S. Court of Appeals have recognized or held that parents are not bound by the same LRE or mainstreaming preferences as education agencies. When FAPE is unavailable in the public school, parents have some latitude in selecting an appropriate or proper private day-school placement.[5]

Private residential placements.

Because residential placements do not easily mesh with IDEA's preference for educating children with disabilities together with children without disabilities, the outcome of residential placement disputes in the lower courts has usually turned on a determination of whether only a residential placement can provide FAPE.[6] The usual priority for resolving a FAPE dispute in the residential placement cases is first to determine the availability of FAPE in the public day school. If it is available, then that setting will facilitate more interaction than a residential school or a treatment center, and will be the LRE for the student. If, however, FAPE is unavailable in a day school, even with extensive support services, then the need for FAPE will override the preference for more inclusive settings. In other words, FAPE has been the first consideration, and the preference for education in general education environments has been second. If FAPE has been available in both or all the alternatives under dispute, however, the setting closest to the regular education environment has been selected (see chapter 12).

---

[5] See, e.g., *C.B. v. Special Sch. Dist. No. 1*, Case No. 09-3104 (8th Cir. Apr. 21, 2011); *M.S. v. Yonkers Bd. of Educ.*, 231 F.3d 96, 105 (2d Cir. 2000) (recognizing that parents may not be bound by the same mainstreaming requirements as the LEA although mainstreaming is a consideration); *Warren G. v. Cumberland Cnty. Sch. Dist.*, 190 F.3d 80, 84 (3d Cir. 1999) (holding that the parental placement must be "appropriate, not perfect" and need not meet the same LRE standards as the LEA); *Cleveland Heights-Univ. Heights City Sch. Dist. v. Boss*, 144 F.3d 391, 399–400 (6th Cir. 1998); *Bd. of Educ. v. Ill. St. Bd. of Educ.*, 41 F.3d 1162, 1168 (7th Cir. 1994). But see *Rafferty v. Cranston Pub. Sch. Comm.*, 315 F.3d 21 (1st Cir. 2002) (holding that mainstreaming requirements cannot be ignored in a private placement); *Roland M. v. Concord Sch. Comm.*, 910 F.2d 983 (1st Cir. 1990) (concluding that analyzing the appropriateness of a student's IEP in a public high school compared to a private school required balancing FAPE against the availability of interaction with general education students and suggesting that FAPE and LRE deserved co-equal legal status).

[6] See, e.g., *Matthews v. Davis*, 742 F.2d 825 (4th Cir. 1984) (viewing round-the-clock training as necessary for any educational progress); *Abrahamson v. Hershman*, 701 F.2d 223 (1st Cir. 1983) (same). See also *Cremeans v. Fairland Local Sch. Dist. Bd. of Educ.*, 633 N.E.2d 570 (Ohio Ct. App. 1993) (holding that residential placement was the only program that could provide FAPE for a student with autism and severely aggressive and disruptive behaviors).

Unilateral Parental Placements of Children in Private Facilities for Non-FAPE Purposes

Many parents choose to enroll their children with disabilities in private school because of preferences for religious education, lower pupil-teacher ratios, a particular curriculum or instructional method, and other reasons. When parents make a private placement for reasons other than public failure to provide FAPE, IDEA requires that parents accept responsibility for the tuition costs.

Notwithstanding the public agency's lack of obligation to pay for private education in the above circumstances, IDEA requires LEAs to identify, locate, and evaluate all students with suspected disabilities in elementary and secondary schools, whether public or private (including religious). The need to identify and evaluate all potential IDEA students is important for two reasons: (a) the child-find provisions are designed to ensure "equitable participation" of these children in special education and related services, and (b) an accurate count is needed to generate the proportion of federal funds that must be spent on private school students with disabilities (20 U.S.C. § 1412(a)(10) (A)(ii) (2006)).

From its inception IDEA has obligated each SEA to ensure that

> [t]o the extent consistent with the number and location of children with disabilities in the State who are enrolled by their parents in private elementary and secondary schools [in the school district served by a local educational agency], provision is made for the participation of those children in the program assisted or carried out under [Part B] by providing for such children special education and related services (20 U.S.C. § 1412(a)(10)(A)(i) (Supp. III 1997)).

IDEA '04 added the long phrase above that appears in brackets. According to the Senate report, this addition was intended to spare LEAs from having to work with private schools located outside the school district boundaries (Sen. Rep. No. 185, 108th Cong., pp. 15–16 (2003)). Under IDEA '04, special education and related services are to be provided in accordance with certain requirements. Chief among them is that the amounts spent by an LEA on these private school students must be equal to (but need not exceed) the proportionate share of federal funds under Part B that these children generate (20 U.S.C. § 1412(a)(10)(A)(i)(I) (2006)). For instance, if 10 percent of the students eligible for FAPE in an LEA are unilaterally enrolled in private schools in that LEA by their parents, then 10 percent of the LEA's IDEA allocation under Part B (assistance to states) must be spent to address the needs for special education and related services of these private school students. The child-find costs are not included in the proportionate amount to be spent on these private school students (20 U.S.C. § 1412(a)(10)(A)(ii) (2006)). Services to these students may be provided on the site of private schools, to the extent consistent with law, and may consist of services provided either by the public agency itself or by individuals or agencies under contract to the public agency (20 U.S.C. § 1412(a)(10)(A)(i) and (vi) (2006)).

The proportionate expenditure provision, first introduced in IDEA '97, resolved long-standing disagreement by clearly indicating that only federal IDEA funds must be spent on parentally placed private school children with disabilities. SEAs and LEAs do not have to spend their own funds, although IDEA does not prohibit it. IDEA '04 adds that all of the proportionate share of federal funds must be spent on these children and can include funds for direct services to the children themselves (20 U.S.C. § 1412(a)(10)(a)(i) (2006)). The Senate report indicated that this addition was intended to encourage school districts to place greater emphasis on such services "rather than devoting funds solely to indirect services such as professional development for private school personnel" (Sen. Rep. No. 185, 108th Cong., pp. 15–16 (2003)).

On the other hand, another aspect of the meaning of proportionate expenditures remained ambiguous under IDEA '97 because it did not clarify whether each student was to get his or her proportionate share of the federal funds, or whether the total was to be allocated collectively for whichever private school students with disabilities an LEA chose to serve. The 1999 regulations adopted the latter view, reiterating OSEP's earlier position that an educational agency may elect not to serve every child unilaterally placed by his or her parents at a private school[7] and that such children are not entitled to receive the same special education services or the same amount of services they would have received in the public schools (34 C.F.R. § 300.455 (1999)). IDEA '04 now also reflects the OSEP position in stating that the LEA must determine the "types of services" and "how such services will be apportioned if funds are insufficient to serve all children" (20 U.S.C. § 1412(a)(10)(A)(iii)(IV) (2006)). The LEA must also determine "how, where, and by whom" these services will be provided (20 U.S.C. § 1412(a)(10)(A)(iii)(IV) (2006)).

What this statutory language means is that when parents opt not to take advantage of FAPE for their children in the public setting, FAPE is not an entitlement for those children attending private school, and special education services become more like a privilege offered by the public agency. Nonetheless, IDEA '04 requires that LEA decisions about services be made in consultation with parents and private schools that represent the children eligible for publicly funded special education services. (How these representatives are to be selected is not specified in the statute or regulations.) Ultimately, the LEA can select which private school students to serve and with what services,† but private school officials can complain in writing to the SEA if they believe that the consultation was not timely or meaningful, and that their views were not given due consideration.[8] Under the regulations, a "services plan" must be developed in lieu of an IEP for the children being served, and the particular services must comply with the IEP requirements only to the extent appropriate (34 C.F.R. § 300.132(b) (2006)).††

　　† In an attempt to avoid service disputes and to cooperate with parents of private school children with disabilities, many school districts have created "dual enrollment" arrangements. Dual enrollment allows the private school student to attend private school for most classes but attend public school for special education and related services. This model usually requires transportation arrangements, but it has worked for many children.

　　†† The 2006 regulations add a new definition of "services plan" (34 C.F.R. § 300.37). The definition includes a description of the special education and related services to be provided to the private school student designated to receive those services. Among other items, it must also include the location of the services and any necessary transportation.

The regulations state that due process hearings do not apply to complaints about the availability and delivery of special services to unilaterally enrolled private school students with disabilities. Instead, complaints must be directed to the SEA, which will use its complaint procedures to investigate compliance (34 C.F.R. § 300.140 (2006)). According to the regulations, the due process hearing procedures apply only to claims that the LEA failed to evaluate a private school student for eligibility under IDEA or failed to accord parents their procedural safeguards in the identification and evaluation process. This makes sense because the child-find activities must be comparable to

---

[7] 34 C.F.R. § 300.454 (1999). See also *Letter to Schmidt*, 20 IDELR 1224 (OSEP 1993); *Letter to Peters*, 19 IDELR 974 (OSEP 1993); *Letter to Mentink*, 18 IDELR 276 (OSERS 1991); *Letter to Livingston*, 17 EHLR 523 (OSERS 1991).

[8] (20 U.S.C. § 1412 (a)(10)(A)(iii) (2006)). Private school officials can appeal the decision of the SEA to the Secretary of ED.

those for public school children.[9] This means that parents of these private school children are entitled to be asked for their consent to the initial evaluation, to participate in the evaluation and eligibility process, to be provided with a copy of the evaluation report, and ultimately to use the due process hearing procedures if they think the child-find process did not comply with IDEA.

Prior to IDEA '97, the court cases that attempted to interpret the meaning of the private school provisions produced conflicting decisions about the extent of LEA obligations to private school students with disabilities. These conflicting rulings were resolved by IDEA '97 and IDEA '04. At this point, to the authors' knowledge, parents of children who have been excluded from special education services at private schools have not challenged the private school provisions as inconsistent with the zero-reject provision of the statute.

Special Education Services on the Site of Religious Schools

From 1985, when the Supreme Court decided *Aguilar v. Felton* (1985), until 1997, when the Court revisited the case, most school officials assumed that no special education services could be delivered on the site of religious schools without running counter to the establishment clause of the First Amendment to the U.S. Constitution. This assumption proved incorrect.

The establishment clause honors the separation of church and state by prohibiting the U.S. Congress from making any law "respecting the establishment of religion." This clause has generally been interpreted to require governmental agencies to remain neutral toward religion, neither favoring it by sponsoring any form of religious worship nor showing hostility toward it.

Aguilar was a case in which the provision of publicly funded remedial instruction to "educationally deprived" students on the site of religious schools was held to violate the establishment clause. The Supreme Court concluded that the instruction unduly entangled the school district in religious matters by requiring excessive monitoring of the remedial teachers and by requiring administrative cooperation with the religious schools. The Supreme Court, however, approached the separation issue differently in a 1993 special education case. In *Zobrest v. Catalina* Foothills School District (1993), the Court ruled that the use of a publicly paid sign language interpreter at a religious school was not a violation of the establishment clause. In the Court's view, such a service to a hearing-impaired student at a Catholic high school did not have the effect of directly benefiting the religious school or of inculcating religious beliefs. The interpreter was viewed as a neutral conduit for the messages but not as the one who actually generated the instructional messages.

Although the Court in *Zobrest* ruled that the Constitution did not prohibit interpreter services, the case did not address whether IDEA requires the provision of special education or related services on the site of religious schools. IDEA '97 addressed this issue by stating that IDEA services may be provided on the premises of religious schools "to the extent consistent with law"; this provision is retained in IDEA '04 (20 U.S.C. § 1412(a)(10)(A)(i)(III) (2006)). In other words, the statute itself creates neither a mandate for the delivery of such on-site services nor a blanket prohibition of them.†[10]

---

[9] See 20 U.S.C. § 1412(a)(10)(A)(ii) (2006) (educational agencies shall undertake child find activities similar to those undertaken for public school children and complete them in a comparable time period).

[10] See a similar position taken earlier in *Letter to Orschel*, 16 EHLR 1369 (OSERS 1990).

† In Letter to Moore, 20 IDELR 1213 (OSEP 1993), OSEP advised that IDEA funds could be used to purchase a personal computer for use at a parochial school if required to mitigate the effects of the student's disability and not for religious instruction.

In 1997, after unusual procedural moves in the lower courts, the Supreme Court agreed to re-examine its decision in *Aguilar v. Felton*. It concluded that, under its evolving standards, *Aguilar* was no longer good law and that on-site remedial services to educationally deprived (Title I) students did not violate the establishment clause (*Agostini v. Felton*, 1997). The clear inference is that the Constitution does not prevent LEAs from delivering special education instruction on the site of a religious school. Whether the law of a state would prevent this is another matter. IDEA '04 specified that special education and related services must be secular, neutral, and nonideological (20 U.S.C. § 1412(a)(10)(A)(vi) (2006)).

Of course, one should recall that any necessarily on-site related services like sign language interpretation and clean intermittent catheterization would not be IDEA services in the absence of a need for special education itself. Under IDEA, related services are linked to the delivery of special education.†† Therefore, if the religious school student declines or is ineligible for special education at the public school or a neutral site, then no related services have to be delivered under IDEA at the religious school.

†† OSEP indicated in Letter to Teague, 20 IDELR 1462 (OSEP 1994), that states could decide on a case-by-case basis whether instructional modifications such as large-print books and interpreter services could be considered specially designed instruction (that is, special education) for a particular student. The IDEA regulations also indicate that the determination of whether a specific related service could be considered special education is up to each state (34 C.F.R. § 300.39(a)(2)(i) (2006)).

Religious Schools, Special Education, and the Free Exercise Clause of the First Amendment

Is a student at a religious school denied the free exercise of his religious beliefs because, as a result of choosing to attend religious school, his special education services were not funded at the same level as they would have been in a public school? The First Circuit said no, concluding that the Constitution does not require federal, state, and local governments to fund private and public schools at the same level. The court observed that the Supreme Court had "consistently refused to invalidate laws which condition a parent's ability to obtain educational benefit on the parent's relinquishment of her right to send her child to private school." See *Gary S. v. Manchester School District*, 374 F.3d 15, 19 (1st Cir. 2004).

↳Reminders and Tips

1. If public school officials understand and meet their FAPE obligations to all IDEA students, they will not be held accountable for the private school costs of students who have been removed from public school by their parents and enrolled in private school.

2. Public school officials can determine when it is necessary to place a student at public expense in a private setting. If they want to avoid costly residential programs, however, they should be prepared to offer a full range of extended services (extended day and extended year) for children with severe disabilities whose needs cannot be met by a regular-length day program.

3. Parents should remember that they must give prior notice to school districts when they intend to remove their children with disabilities from public school on the grounds that FAPE is being denied.

4. Given the preference or presumption established in IDEA in favor of regular classroom settings, school districts and parents should consider the importance of interaction with general education students for a student in a private special education school and whether there are ways to accomplish that interaction while at the private school. At the same time, they should also consider whether a child's interaction with other children with the same disabilities may also be equally or more important.

5. In determining which unilaterally enrolled private school students to serve and in what locations, public school officials will need to develop good procedures for engaging in substantive consultations with appropriate parental and private school representatives of the children.

6. Public school officials need to know whether their state law prohibits the delivery of any publicly funded services to children with disabilities unilaterally enrolled by their parents in private schools or private religious schools. If this is the case, IDEA has established a bypass arrangement whereby the Secretary of Education can arrange for the services and pay for them with a proportionate amount of federal funds under Part B of IDEA.

7. School officials and parents need to know if children who are being homeschooled are considered to be private school children under the law of their state. If they are, then the provisions about child-find and special education services to unilaterally enrolled private school students apply to these children.

8. School officials should not forget that the school district could be liable for residential placement costs on the basis of serious procedural failures, such as failure to (a) review a current placement at parental request, (b) develop an IEP in a timely fashion, or (c) review a child's needs and continuing eligibility at least every three years (*Wirta v. District of Columbia*, 1994)

↱Review

1. Who pays when a child with a disability is placed in a private day school or a residential school?

   It depends on who makes the placement and on whether FAPE was available in the public setting. If the public agency makes the placement, then it will pay for it. If the parents made the placement because FAPE was not available in the public school, then parents may receive reimbursement for the reasonable nonmedical costs, including tuition and room and board, provided that the parents' choice of the private school was proper or appropriate in the eyes of the court, hearing officer, or SEA.

2. When have residential placements been upheld by the courts?

   Generally, this has occurred when such a placement was the only setting in which FAPE could be delivered. Usually, the student's educational, emotional, and behavioral needs were intertwined, and/or the student needed continuous and closely supervised special education and related services throughout his or her waking hours.

3. What kind of services can parents expect for their children with disabilities when they place those children in a private school when FAPE is available in the public school?

   It depends on the state, the school district, and the consultative process with parents and private school officials. Children may receive a number of special educational services, a few services, or no services in some cases. Sometimes, the services may be provided at the public school; at other times, they may be made available on the site of the private school or at a neutral site. Parents have no guarantee that their children will receive the same services they would have received in the public school.

↯References

Agostini v. Felton, 521 U.S. 203 (1997).

Aguilar v. Felton, 473 U.S. 402 (1985).

Burlington Sch. Comm. v. Mass. Dept. of Educ., 471 U.S. 359 (1985).

Florence Cnty. Sch. Dist. Four v. Carter, 510 U.S. 7 (1993).

Forest Grove Sch. Dist. v. T. A., 129 S. Ct. 2484 (2009).

Forest Grove Sch. Dist. v. T. A., Case No. 10-35022, (9th Cir. Apr. 27th, 2011).

Individuals with Disabilities Education Improvement Act, 20 U.S.C. § 1400 *et seq.* (2006).

Individuals with Disabilities Education Improvement Act Regulations, 34 C.F. R. § 300.1 *et seq.* (2006).

Wirta v. District of Columbia, 859 F. Supp. 1 (D.D.C. 1994).

Zobrest v. Catalina Foothills Sch. Dist., 509 U.S. 1 (1993).

⇉Selected Supplementary Resources

Huefner, D. S. (1989). Special education residential placements under the Education for All Handicapped Children Act. *Journal of Law and Education, 18*, 411–440.

Huefner, D. S. (1994). *Zobrest v. Catalina Foothills School District*: A foothill in establishment clause jurisprudence? *Education Law Reporter, 87*, 15–29.

Lambert, S. A. (2001). Note: Finding the way back home: Funding for home school children under the Individuals With Disabilities Education Act. *Columbia Law Review, 101*, 1709–1729.

Osborne, A. G., Jr., Russo, C. J., & DiMattia, P. (1999). IDEA '97: Providing special education services to students voluntarily enrolled in private schools. *Exceptional Children, 33*, 224–231.

Chapter 14

Discipline of Students Under IDEA

Chapter Outline

Background

    The Stay-Put Provision and Its Judicial Interpretations

    The Gun-Free Schools Act of 1994

    The Jeffords Amendment

IDEA '97 Discipline Provisions

IDEA '04 Discipline Provisions

    Short-Term Removals and Suspensions

    Longer-Term Removals and Placement Changes

    Case-by-Case Discretion

    Expedited Appeals

More About Functional Behavioral Assessments and Behavioral Intervention Plans

Protections for Children Not Yet Eligible Under IDEA

Seclusion and Physical Restraints

Reminders and Tips

Review

References

Selected Supplementary Resources

Background

All children, including students with disabilities, are subject to discipline at school. Yet because of the need to protect children with disabilities from being punished for misbehavior over which they have little control, certain safeguards have surrounded the use of some common disciplinary procedures, primarily long-term suspensions and expulsions.

Discipline comes from the same Latin root as *disciple*, meaning a learner (Trumble, Brown, Stevenson, & Siefring, 2002). Discipline as learning is usually more effective in changing behavior over the long term than is discipline as chastisement, punishment, or penance for wrong-doing. In either case, however, the aim of school discipline is to get children to behave in socially acceptable ways. Among the many disciplinary techniques available for use with all school children are the following: detention, loss of privileges, overcorrection, in-school suspension, isolation (such as time-out), corporal punishment (in some states), suspension, and expulsion. In addition, more positive techniques such as positive behavioral supports, stimulating and appropriate instruction, restitution, and community service are also available.

Issues arise as to which kind of discipline is most effective in teaching internalized self-discipline in school, especially from a short-term perspective. Issues also arise when school personnel become so frustrated that they are tempted to give up altogether on some children with exceptionally challenging behaviors and exclude them from access to all schooling. These issues have special poignancy for children with emotional and behavioral disabilities because in the past many of these children were excluded from school on the grounds that they did not belong there or were incorrigible. IDEA was meant to prevent such exclusion. As a zero-reject law, it was intended to ensure that education agencies accepted their responsibility to educate all children and did not give up on any of them.

In recent years, with growing concerns about the use of illegal drugs and dangerous weapons at school, education agencies have felt an urgent need to ensure a safe environment in which misbehaving children do not disrupt or endanger the education of behaving children. Legislators, educators, and citizens have expected schools to adopt zero-tolerance policies for certain kinds of misbehavior and to expel or suspend some children, including children with disabilities, for periods of time up to a year. Sometimes, however, zero-tolerance policies have prevailed over good sense, as in widely circulated news reports of the expulsion of a kindergartner for bringing a five-inch plastic ax to school in his belt as part of his Halloween firefighter's costume.

The alternative to blanket expulsion policies requires an investment of resources (time, money, skills, energy, and research) to improve our ability to teach misbehaving children alternative behaviors to replace the ones that are unacceptable. This chapter explores the legal history and current IDEA provisions for disciplining children with disabilities while still preserving their right to FAPE.

The Stay-Put Provision and Its Judicial Interpretations

Disciplinary measures for children with disabilities were not a focus of IDEA (and its predecessors) until the mid-1990s. Access to public education was the primary focus, with procedural safeguards to facilitate that access. Until passage of the Jeffords Amendment in 1995 (described later in more detail), IDEA made no mention of specific measures that could be used to discipline students with disabilities. The only arguably related provision in IDEA and its predecessors was a requirement that while administrative or judicial proceedings were pending, the student was to "remain in the then current educational placement" unless the parents and state or local education agency agreed otherwise (20 U.S.C. § 1415(e)(3)(A) (1994)). This was and is the stay-put provision (now at 20 U.S.C. § 1415(j) (2006)). Initially, it was a mechanism for ensuring some stability so that a student was not shuffled back and forth in the course of a placement dispute (see chapter 8). Several courts also interpreted the provision to prevent long-term suspension and expulsion of students with disabilities unless an impartial decision so ruled or otherwise determined the appropriate placement for the student.

In the case of dangerous or unduly disruptive students, many school officials over the years objected to the stay-put provision, arguing that it denied necessary flexibility and prevented school officials from protecting the safety of other students at school. Different judicial interpretations of the effect of the stay-put provision on discipline options emerged and were eventually resolved by the United States Supreme Court in its 1988 decision in *Honig v. Doe.*

In *Honig v. Doe*, two adolescent boys with serious emotional disturbances were suspended indefinitely, pending their expulsion from two different public schools in California. Both John Doe and Jack Smith had long records of troublesome behaviors. John Doe was suspended when he choked another student and then kicked out a window while being escorted to the principal's office. Jack Smith was suspended for a number of actions about which he had been warned previously, such as stealing, extorting, and making lewd comments to female classmates. Both students challenged the legality of their suspensions and pending expulsions under IDEA. All parties to the lawsuit acknowledged that the misbehavior of both boys arose from their disabilities.

The Supreme Court ruled that the stay-put provision did not contain a "dangerousness exception." The Court concluded that Congress meant precisely what it said in the stay-put provision, particularly given the history of unwarranted exclusion of students with serious emotional disturbances leading up to the passage of IDEA. In other words, a school district could not unilaterally expel or indefinitely suspend a student with a disability for dangerous or disruptive behavior arising from the disability. Instead, to make a change of placement, even for disciplinary reasons, the procedural safeguards of IDEA had to be honored. Proposed placement changes under IDEA required a placement team to evaluate the student's needs, judge the appropriateness or inappropriateness of the current placement, and determine the relationship of the misbehavior to the disability. If the placement team proposed a placement change and the parents challenged the change by requesting a hearing, then the stay-put provision meant that the current placement would be maintained until the proceedings (including appeals) were completed.

In addition, the Supreme Court in *Honig* (1988) noted that an agency was free to use other disciplinary procedures for dealing with unruly students, including the use of study carrels, time-outs, detention, restriction of privileges, and suspensions of up to ten school days. Suspensions of that length, it held, did not constitute a change of placement and provided time for the placement team to reconvene and determine a future course of action. In all these respects, children with disabilities could be disciplined like children without disabilities.

The Court offered only one way to circumvent the inevitable delay resulting from the hearing process required for a challenged placement change: a court injunction to exclude the offending student from school. Requiring court permission for such an exclusion, the Court observed, would continue to honor the requirement that a school district not act unilaterally, yet it would still provide an opportunity for relief in urgent circumstances. This opportunity, in effect, paralleled the opportunity given to parents to bypass the hearing process and go straight to court when the hearing procedure would be futile or would provide an inadequate remedy for a particular problem.

Honig (1988) indicated that the stay-put provision created a "presumption in favor of the child's current educational placement" (p. 328). *Honig* established that a school seeking an injunction must bear the burden of proving in court the need for injunctive relief.† To obtain an injunction, an LEA must overcome the presumption by proving that the current placement was "substantially likely to result in injury" to the student or others (p. 328).

> † The general four-part test for an injunction requires a school district to show (a) a substantial likelihood that it will prevail on the merits, and (b) a substantial threat that the school and its students will suffer irreparable injury without the injunction. It must then prove that (c) the threatened injury to the school outweighs the threat of harm to the misbehaving student and (d) the injunction would not be adverse to the public interest. See *Texas City Independent School District v. Jorstad*, 752 F. Supp. 231, 233 (S.D. Tex. 1990).

A number of school districts successfully obtained post-*Honig* injunctions.[1] The most important ruling was the 1994 decision in *Light v. Parkway C-2 School District* (1994), which concerned an adolescent girl with severe multiple mental and behavioral disabilities and aggressive behaviors. In *Light*, the Eighth Circuit rejected the parents' argument that a student must be "truly dangerous" and "intend" to cause injury before a court injunction could ensue. Instead, the court reiterated the *Honig* (1988) standard that the behavior simply must be substantially likely to cause injury, which to the court in *Light* (1994) meant an "objective likelihood of injury (p. 1228)."

Especially important was the court's additional requirement, not present in *Honig* (1988), that to obtain an injunction, the school district must show that it had made "reasonable efforts to accommodate the child's disabilities so as to minimize the likelihood" (*Light*, 1994, p. 1228) that the child would injure herself or others. In other words, the school must attempt to mitigate the effect of the misbehavior and the accompanying risk of injury. The court deduced this requirement from IDEA's mandate that removal from the regular educational environment occur "only when the nature or severity of the disability is such that education in regular classes with the use of supplementary aids and services cannot be achieved satisfactorily" (*Light*, 1994, quoting what was then 20 U.S.C. § 1412(5)(B)). In other words, it seemed logical to require the LEA to demonstrate that it had attempted to manage the behavior with appropriate supplementary aids and services.

The school district in *Light* (1994) met its burden by carefully documenting both the rate of the student's kicking, hitting, biting, and other aggressive acts and the extensive steps the district had taken to try to control the student's behaviors. Those steps included a staff-pupil ratio of 2:1 and assistance of behavior management specialists, inclusion facilitators, special education consultants, and crisis prevention trainers.†

> †IDEA '97 adopted the Eighth Circuit's decision in *Light* and required hearing officers, before ordering a placement change for safety reasons, to consider whether an LEA had used mitigating measures to reduce the risk of harm from the student's behavior. IDEA '04 removed this provision.

---

[1] See, e.g., *Roslyn Union Free Sch. Dist. v. Geffrey W.*, 293 A.D. 662 (N.Y. App. Div. 2002); *East Islip Union Free Sch. Dist. v. Andersen ex rel. Chappel*, 615 N.Y.S.2d 852 (N.Y. Sup. Ct. 1994).

The Gun-Free Schools Act of 1994

As the visibility of violent incidents at schools escalated in the mid-1990s, Congress and many state legislatures enacted zero-tolerance laws that provided severe penalties for all schoolchildren who brought guns to school. The Gun-Free Schools Act of 1994 prohibited any state from receiving federal funds under the Improving America's Schools Act of 1994 (extensive amendments to and reauthorization of ESEA), unless the state enacted a law requiring expulsion from the current school setting for at least one year of any student who brought a firearm, including an unloaded gun, onto the school grounds.† The school superintendent was allowed to make exceptions to the expulsion requirement on a case-by-case basis. Although this latter provision was viewed by some as providing the flexibility needed to ensure that Section 504 and IDEA were not violated, Congress also inserted a more explicit provision stating that the Gun-Free Schools Act was to be construed in accord with IDEA (20 U.S.C. § 8921(c) (now at 20 U.S.C. § 7151 (2006)). Congress also required school districts to have a policy requiring referral of a student who brings a firearm to school to the state's criminal justice or juvenile delinquency system.††

> † The definition of firearm incorporated into the Gun-Free Schools Act is "(A) any weapon (including a starter gun) which will or is designed to or may readily be converted to expel a projectile by the action of an explosive; (B) the frame or receiver of any such weapon; (C) any firearm muffler or firearm silencer; or (D) any destructive device. Such term does not include an antique firearm" (18 U.S.C. § 921(a)(3) (2006)).

> †† The Gun-Free Schools Act of 1994 should not be confused with the Gun-Free School Zones Act of 1990. The latter was a federal criminal statute that prohibited possession of weapons on or within 1000 feet of school grounds. It was struck down by the Supreme Court as an unconstitutional exercise of congressional authority to regulate interstate commerce. The Court concluded that weapons possession in a school zone was not an activity having a substantial impact on interstate commerce but was properly a matter for state, not federal, control. *United States v. Lopez*, 514 U.S. 549 (1995). The Gun-Free Schools Act is not subject to such a challenge, because its requirements are simply a condition for receipt of federal funds.

The Jeffords Amendment

A more explicit and carefully tailored means of disciplining IDEA students was incorporated into IDEA in a 1995 amendment called the Jeffords Amendment. The amendment provided that a student with a disability who brought a firearm to school could be placed in an "interim alternative educational setting, in accordance with state law, for not more than 45 days" (20 U.S.C. § 1415(e)(3) (B) (Supp. 2 1994)).This placement was in lieu of being automatically expelled for a year from the current setting. The interim setting was to be determined by the student's IEP team. The 45-day interim placement became the student's stay-put placement for the purpose of any IDEA hearing procedures. This meant that while any administrative and judicial proceedings contesting the placement were ongoing, the student remained in the interim placement rather than being returned to what was the prior current placement.

The Jeffords Amendment obviously strengthened the hand of school districts in dealing with potentially violent students with disabilities while continuing to offer appropriate services (FAPE) to such students. It established a "dangerousness exception" within IDEA that the Supreme Court had declined to establish in *Honig* (1988). That did not satisfy all legislators, however, and for the next 3 years, congressional subcommittees, OSEP staffers, and disability advocacy groups haggled over how to reach consensus about discipline under IDEA. OSEP's position and that of parent advocacy groups was that regardless of disciplinary placements, services to a child with a disability could not cease. Others, including many legislators, insisted that children with disabilities should be treated like children without disabilities and totally excluded from the school system, if warranted. What emerged in IDEA '97 was a fragile compromise, full of procedural ambiguities.

IDEA '97 Discipline Provisions

After the passage of IDEA '97, ED took almost two years to finalize the IDEA regulations. One reason was disagreement over how ambiguous disciplinary provisions of the statute should be interpreted and clarified. Although the statute and the regulations were complex and difficult to understand, two distinct, underlying messages remained clear:

1. School personnel must improve their efforts to manage the misbehavior of disruptive or dangerous students with disabilities.

2. Schools can change the placements of such students quite quickly but must continue to serve them.

   Both messages acknowledged the importance of safe schools and the value of discipline for all students, including those with disabilities. Both messages also recognized the importance of FAPE for all students with disabilities and the reality that exclusion from school would deny that hard-earned right. The compromise produced by the need to honor both sets of values continued to make many educators and legislators uncomfortable.

Part of the problem was that the disruptive and violent behaviors of children with severe emotional or mental disabilities made the news. Yet there was and is no evidence that children with disabilities are likelier to be suspended and expelled than are other children. Based on available data from the states, 1999 estimates were that less than 1 percent of all children with disabilities were involved in serious disciplinary problems, and only about 5 percent of the then close to six million IDEA students were expected to be suspended once or more during a school year.[2] Nonetheless, an unruly child is an unruly child, and teachers know how time-consuming one child can be. If schools can do a better job of managing misbehavior, then the disciplinary procedures will have to be invoked less often.

IDEA '04 Discipline Provisions

The basic purposes of the IDEA '97 discipline requirements remain intact in IDEA '04. More specific elements that are retained include preservation of the right to FAPE and codification of the *Honig* determination that a suspension for no more than ten days is not a change of placement. Also retained is the IDEA '97 expansion of the Jeffords Amendment so that a unilateral placement change into an interim alternative educational setting (IAES) can be made if a student uses or possesses dangerous weapons in addition to firearms, and (b) uses or possesses illegal drugs. IDEA '97's requirement to determine whether the misbehavior was related to the disability is also preserved but in a considerably different form that eliminated the presumption that the misbehavior is a manifestation of the disability.

---

[2] Transcript of OSERS Assistant Secretary Judith Heumann's remarks at the live ED broadcast on the IDEA '97 Regulations, March 18, 1999. These figures have remained consistent in subsequent ED Annual Reports on IDEA implementations.

Generally speaking, the disciplinary provisions in IDEA '04 are clearer, shorter, and simpler than those in IDEA '97. They are less prescriptive and leave more to the discretion of school personnel. They also clarify ambiguities in IDEA '97 and place some of the 1999 regulations into the statute itself. Nonetheless, they remain confusing if not read carefully.

Short-Term Removals and Suspensions

If a child with a disability violates a code of student conduct, an educational agency may use its normal procedures to remove the child from his or her current placement for up to ten consecutive school days.† Short-term removals of this length are not considered placement changes that trigger IDEA protections. Additional removals of up to ten consecutive days are allowed for separate incidents of misconduct if they do not constitute a pattern that indicates a placement change. †† Whenever short-term suspensions, however, cumulate to more than ten days in a given school year, school personnel (in consultation with at least one of the child's teachers) must determine the extent to which services are needed in the removal setting to allow the student to progress toward IEP goals and participate in the general curriculum (34 C.F.R. § 300.530 (d)(4) (2006)). Special parental rights attaching to placement changes are not provided in these removal situations; school personnel determine the services.

> † The regulations define a school day as any day, including a partial day, that children are in attendance at school for instructional purposes. School day has the same meaning for all schoolchildren, including children with disabilities (34 C.F.R. § 300.11(c) (2006)).

> †† Factors to consider in finding a "pattern" include the length of each removal, the total amount of time of the removals, the proximity of the removals to one another, and the similarity of the child's behavior from one incident to another (20 C.F.R. § 300.536(a) 2006)).

Removal options include suspension, removal to an interim alternative educational setting (IAES), or removal to some other setting as long as any removal is only "to the extent that these alternatives are applied to children without disabilities"(20 U.S.C. § 1415(k)(1)(B) (2006)). Readers should remember, however, that even short-term removals require the basic constitutional due process protections of notice and a chance to respond that apply to all students. Law specific to a given state may also impose other requirements on school officials.

In-School Suspension and Bus Suspension

The analysis in the Federal Register accompanying the 2006 regulations indicates that OSEP will not count in-school suspension days, or portions of days as removal days as long as the child retains the opportunity to continue to participate appropriately in the general curriculum, receive his or her specified IEP services, and participate with children who do not have disabilities to the same extent as before the removal. In other words, a student can be removed to another setting within the school as long as the above conditions are satisfied.

The analysis further states that bus suspension will count as a day of suspension if transportation is a part of the child's IEP. This is because unless the school district provides transportation in some other way, lack of transportation would deny the child access to the setting in which other necessary services are delivered (71 Fed. Reg. 46715, August 14, 2006).

Longer-Term Removals and Placement Changes

Two kinds of actual placement changes (that is, long-term removals from the current placement) are allowed under the IDEA '04 discipline provisions: (a) removals for drug or weapon violations or serious bodily injury to another, and (b) removals for other violations of the student code of conduct. Each will be described separately. The parents must be notified immediately of the decision to change the student's placement and informed of all the applicable procedural safeguards (20 U.S.C. § 1415(k)(1)(H) (2006)). Determinations of whether the violations of the student code are manifestations of the disability must be made in both sets of situations.

IAES placements for weapon and drug use and infliction of serious bodily injury.

IDEA '04 allows school personnel to unilaterally remove a student from his or her current placement and place the student in an IAES (a new stay-put placement) for up through forty-five school days for any of the following three reasons:

1. A student carries to or possesses a weapon† at school, on school premises, or to or at a school function;

   † The definition of weapon used in IDEA is the definition of dangerous weapon found in 18 U.S.C. § 930 (2006), which includes a weapon, device, instrument, material, or substance, animate or inanimate, that is used for or readily capable of causing death or serious bodily injury (except for a pocket knife with a blade less than 2.5 inches long). Given the breadth of this definition, a fist or chair could conceivably be a dangerous weapon under some circumstances. A paintball gun (that is, a gun that fires paintballs) was not considered a dangerous weapon, however, by a hearing officer under the specific circumstances described in Independent School District No. 279, Osseo Area Schools, 30 IDELR 645 (SEA MN 1999). The fact-specific context can matter in these determinations.

2. A student knowingly uses or possesses illegal drugs, or sells or solicits the sale of a controlled substance† in any of the above locations; or

   † This provision allows for immediate disciplinary action against a student who attempts to sell or solicit the sale of prescribed drugs such as ritalin and other amphetamines, which can be legally prescribed for use by a student with ADHD but could have a far different effect on another student.

3. A student inflicts serious bodily injury upon another person while at any of the above locations. This provision was added in IDEA '04.

The phrase *serious bodily injury* incorporates by reference the definition in 18 U.S.C. § 1365(h)(3) (2006): "bodily injury which involves (A) a substantial risk of death, (B) extreme bodily pain, (C) protracted and obvious disfigurement; or (D) protracted loss or impairment of the function of a bodily member, organ, or mental faculty." Given this extremely restrictive definition, hitting, biting, kicking, spitting, and similar physical assaults in and of themselves may not result in serious bodily injury.

A student with a disability can be retained in an IAES up through forty-five days for the above reasons regardless of whether the misconduct is a manifestation of the disability. These students, however, must continue to receive FAPE, and the services in the IAES must allow them to continue to participate in the general curriculum and to progress toward meeting their IEP goals.

Nonetheless, OSEP interprets this provision to mean that the services need not be exactly the same as those delivered prior to placement in an IAES (see 71 Fed. Reg. 46716, August 14, 2006).

The IEP team determines the IAES. There is no explicit provision in IDEA for extending the IAES beyond forty-five school days (nine weeks of school) if the misconduct is a manifestation of the disability. Nonetheless, the IEP team (including the parents) can agree that extending the placement would be appropriate, or an LEA can use the expedited appeal procedures. If the conduct is determined not to be a manifestation of the disability, the duration of the IAES can be extended for more than forty-five days if it is for the same length of time applied to children without disabilities.

Change of placement for miscellaneous student code violations.

If an LEA wants to make a placement change for a student code violation other than drug and weapon violations or serious bodily injury to others, the LEA may do so. With all disciplinary placement changes, however, FAPE services must continue, so as to enable the student to participate in the general curriculum and to progress toward achievement of IEP goals. If the code violation is determined to be a manifestation of the child's disability, IDEA '04 states that the child must be returned to the placement from which the child was removed (20 U.S.C. § 1415(k)(1)(F) (2006)). In effect, this limits the placement change to ten school days (enough time to conduct the manifestation determination). An exception to this requirement is if the parents and LEA agree otherwise as part of the modification of the behavioral intervention plan (BIP).

In short, the difference between an IAES placement for a miscellaneous code violation that is a manifestation of the disability and an IAES placement for drug/weapon violations or serious injury is one of duration. Under the former situation, the placement can be imposed for only ten days. Under the latter situation, the IAES placement can be imposed for forty-five days, regardless of the outcome of a manifestation determination.

If the miscellaneous code violation is determined not to be a manifestation of the child's disability, then the disciplinary action must be applied in the same manner and for the same length of time as for a child without a disability (subject still to the FAPE mandate) (20 U.S.C. § 1415(k)(1)(C) (2006)). In other words, a long-term suspension or other placement change could become the stay-put placement for whatever duration would have been imposed on a general education student-code violator.

Manifestation determinations.

No manifestation determination (M-D) is required for disciplinary removals that do not constitute a placement change (such as suspensions of no more than 10 days). When a decision is made to make a disciplinary placement change, however, an M-D must be completed within ten school days of that decision (20 U.S.C. § 1415(k)(1)(E) (2006)). During this time, the placement change is in effect. The M-D team consists of the parents, the LEA, and relevant members of the IEP team (as determined by the LEA and the parent). Who represents the LEA on the team is not specified.

The M-D team members review all relevant information in the student's file, including the IEP; teacher observations, if any; and any relevant information from the parents. The team then determines if the conduct in question "was caused by, or had a direct and substantial relationship to, the child's disability" or, alternatively, if the conduct in question was "the direct result of the [LEA's] failure to implement the IEP."[3] If either of these two conditions exists, then the misconduct

---

[3] An earlier provision requiring consideration of the appropriateness of the then-current placement has been deleted.

is considered a manifestation of the disability. This language suggests that the relationship should not be an attenuated one. How the decision is actually reached is left to M-D team discretion.†
The procedures also are not spelled out.

† In *Fitzgerald v. Fairfax County School Board*, 556 F. Supp. 2d 543 (E.D. Va. 2008), the court stated that parents had neither the right to veto who else would serve on the M-D team nor to veto the decision of the other team members. Instead, if the parents disagreed with the rest of the team, the parents' recourse was to appeal the M-D decision. The court then proceeded to uphold the M-D decision that a boy who, with his peers, shot paintballs at his school building three times in one afternoon was not manifesting his disability in doing so. The court noted that the student planned the incident and repeated the misconduct multiple times over several hours.

If the M-D team finds that the student's misbehavior was a manifestation of the disability, then the IEP team must conduct a functional behavioral assessment (FBA) and implement a behavioral intervention plan (BIP). If a BIP has already been developed, then the IEP team must review it and modify it to address the misbehavior. On the other hand, if the M-D team determines that the student's misbehavior was not a manifestation of the disability, then the student "shall" receive, "as appropriate," a functional behavioral assessment and "behavioral intervention services and modifications" that are designed to keep the student code violation from recurring" (20 U.S.C. §1415(k)(1)(D)(ii) (2006)). In other words, an FBA and BIP are not mandatory.† In addition, the relevant disciplinary procedures applicable to children without disabilities may be applied in the same manner and for the same duration as they would be applied to children without disabilities. For example, for a student committing a drug or weapon violation or inflicting serious bodily injury, the placement change could be for longer than forty-five days, perhaps even for the remainder of the school year if that were the consequence that would be imposed on a student who did not have a disability. Regardless of the duration of the placement change, of course, FAPE must continue.

† But see *Shelton v. Maya Angelou Public Charter School*, 578 F. Supp. 2d 83 (D.D.C. 2008), in which the court concluded that school officials should have performed an FBA even though the M-D team determined that the plaintiff's misbehavior was not a result of the disability. The court upheld the reasoning of the hearing officer that the school district had not presented enough evidence to show that an FBA would have been "inappropriate."

In a nondisciplinary placement dispute, in which an FBA is also not mandated, the 2nd Circuit upheld a hearing officer ruling that the school district did not need to conduct an FBA because the student's IEP adequately addressed his attention problems and need for psychiatric and psychological services (*A. C. and M. C. ex rel M. C. v. Board of Education of the Chappaqua Central School District*, 553 F.3d 165 (2d. Cir. 2009)).

Case-by-Case Discretion

IDEA '04 adds a provision allowing school personnel to consider any unique circumstances on a case-by-case basis when determining whether to order a change of placement for a child with a disability who violates a code of student conduct. Many state Parent Centers (funded under IDEA to support and train parents of children with disabilities) have been concerned about how LEAs will implement this provision. The Centers prefer that school personnel interpret the provision to prohibit an otherwise permitted placement change when it would seem unjust and ineffective under the circumstances of the misbehavior. The regulation paraphrasing the statutory provision states that school personnel should consider on a case-by-case basis whether a placement change is "appropriate," which seems to respond to the Centers' concerns (34 C.F.R. § 300.350(a) (2006)).

Expedited Appeals

As mentioned previously, by the date of a decision to make a disciplinary placement change for a student-code violation, the LEA must notify the parents of the decision and of all procedural safeguards in the discipline section of IDEA. If parents agree to a disciplinary placement change and M-D decision, as they often do, then using the appeals procedure will not be necessary.

If a parent wishes to challenge the basis for a placement change or the M-D, then an expedited hearing is available. The hearing must occur within twenty school days of the date of the request, and a decision must be rendered within ten school days of the hearing (20 U.S.C. §1415(k)(3) (2006)). (This allows six weeks of school to transpire before the "expedited" decision must be made. Whether this is truly expedited may be in the mind of the beholder.) Of great importance to LEAs is the fact that the stay-put placement during the hearing is the IAES, but the hearing officer is authorized to decide that the child should be returned to the placement from which the child was removed.†

> † Under IDEA '97, at an expedited hearing, the misbehavior was presumed to be a manifestation of the disability unless rebutted by an M-D. Hearing decisions had to be based on an evidence standard beyond a preponderance. Both these provisions were deleted under IDEA '04.

An LEA can also ask for an expedited hearing if an M-D or hearing decision allows a child to be maintained in his or her current placement, and the LEA believes that doing so is substantially likely to result in injury to the child or others. When the LEA appeals on this basis, the child must remain in the IAES (34 C.F.R. 300.533 (2006)) pending the outcome of the appeal or expiration of the relevant time period for an IAES (whichever comes first).† The LEA may repeat its appeal as many times a necessary, however, if the likelihood of injury to the child or others is likely to continue if the child is returned to the original placement (34 C.F.R. 500.532(b)(3)(2006)).

> † In *M.M. ex rel. L.R. v. Special School District No. 1*, 512 F.3d 455 (8th Cir. 2008), a hearing officer decided that the LEA violated the stay-put placement for an unmanageable child. The LEA appealed to federal court. After an adverse ruling in district court, the Eighth Circuit reversed and determined that, despite a pattern of multiple suspensions indicating a placement change, the stay-put placement obligation did not attach, and the parent could not prevail in her claim that her daughter had been denied FAPE. The school had offered home placement or a specific separate school placement to avoid more repeated suspensions for the girl's uncontrollable behavior. The parent rejected both options, and no services had been delivered during the excessive suspension

periods. The court cited 34 C.F.R. 300.530(d)(5) for the right of the IEP team to determine appropriate services (in this case undesignated homebound services) and the obligation of the parent to accept whatever services were offered. A careful reading of (d)(5), however, reveals that the services had to enable the child to participate in the general curriculum, even if at home, and to progress toward her IEP goals. Undesignated homebound services may not have fulfilled this requirement. This part of the court's ruling may be an incorrect reading of the statute, demonstrating that even courts can misread the complex disciplinary regulations. Although the Circuit court reversed the rulings of the lower court, faulting the parent for uncooperative behavior, one wonders if a more efficient outcome for both sides could have been achieved sooner if the LEA had not resorted to numerous short-term suspensions but instead had made a placement change unilaterally and then used the expedited appeal process if necessary.

A court injunction or temporary restraining order changing a child's placement under the *Honig* (1988) standard is not mentioned in the statute. Although the new provisions may make resort to a court unnecessary, it remains an option.

Implementing Sound Discipline in Practice

Although school officials need to know the legal standards for disciplining students with disabilities to avoid making mistakes, it is equally important for school personnel to know how to work cooperatively with parents to achieve disciplinary placements that make good sense. It is better to achieve consensus than to have to resort to legal procedures in making placement changes. For instance, students who are not inflicting "serious bodily injury" on others may nonetheless be causing physical harm to others in their current placement, and their misconduct may be caused by their disability. Yet school officials may think it ill advised to keep the child in or return the child to his or her former placement. The need is for IEP teams to be able to effectively explore common interests in the safety and well-being of staff and students, including the student with disabilities. If parents believe that schools can provide good services and teach replacement behaviors in an alternate placement, they are far likelier to agree to a placement change than if they think the placement is being made for the sake of punishment alone.

More About Functional Behavioral Assessments and Behavioral Intervention Plans

In the interest of not overregulating, ED declined to provide a definition of FBA under IDEA '97, leaving its interpretation up to state or local school districts.† No FBA definition appears in the 2006 regulations either. The 1999 regulatory analysis, however, helped to explain the relationship of the BIP to the IEP. It stated that if IEP teams were proactively addressing misbehaviors that impeded a child's learning or that of others, then behavioral strategies, interventions, and supports included in the IEP would constitute the BIP.[4] This statement is missing in the analysis interpreting the 2006 regulations. Instead, the 2006 analysis notes simply that IDEA emphasizes a proactive approach through the use of positive behavioral interventions. OSEP states that the provision addressing BIPs "should ensure that children who need [BIPS] to succeed in school receive them."[5]

> † In Alex R. v. Forrestville Valley Community Unit School District No. 221, 375 F.3d 603 (7th Cir. 2004), the Seventh Circuit addressed a challenge to an updated IEP and a BIP for a very aggressive and disruptive third-grade boy. It determined that the boy's BIP could not be judged substantively insufficient because no criteria for a BIP had been specified in the statute or regulations. The court concluded that the boy's IEP had been reasonably calculated to produce educational benefit. A more recent case highlighted the importance of an FBA when the quality of the student's education was linked to his behavior. The court determined that an FBA was essential to the development of the student's IEP (Harris v. District of Columbia, 561 F. Supp. 2d 63 (D.D.C. 2008)).

Most teachers will assert that sometimes the strategies selected by the IEP team are not effective, that a particular misbehavior was not predictable, and that nothing works at a given period of time with a given child.† IDEA acknowledges these realities by allowing an IAES, subject to various procedural safeguards.

> † Educators know that there is still much to learn about the factors contributing to emotional illness, and about how to improve the behaviors of the most difficult children with emotional disabilities. Educators are trying to ascertain whether the current FBA and BIP methodologies are better suited to shape the behaviors of children with challenging intellectual disabilities than children with significant emotional disorders.

---

[4] See the analysis accompanying 34 C.F.R. § 300.520 at 64 Fed. Reg. 12620 (March 12, 1999).
[5] Analysis accompanying 34 C.F.R. § 300.530(f) at 71 Fed.Reg. 46721 (August. 14, 2006).

One Behavioral Specialist's Approach to Functional Behavioral Assessment

Professor Rob O'Neill, Department of Special Education, University of Utah

What Is Functional Behavioral Assessment?

Functional behavioral assessment (FBA) is a process of gathering information about the things or events that influence a person's problem behaviors. These could either be external events in the person's environment (such as interactions with others, work demands), or internal things (such as illness, fatigue, depression).

Why Do We Do an FBA?

An FBA gathers information that is used to guide the development of a treatment or intervention plan. This plan should focus both on reducing or eliminating the problem behaviors and teaching or supporting appropriate desired behaviors.

How Do We Carry Out an FBA?

There are three major strategies for collecting FBA information.

1. *Indirect informant methods.* These involve collecting information from teachers, parents, or other relevant persons through interviews or the use of checklists, rating scales, or questionnaires.

2. *Systematic observations in typical settings.* These involve conducting structured observations to collect data on the occurrence of the behavior and things that may be related to it. These observations are usually done during the person's typical routine or activities (for instance, during classroom work periods, on the playground).

3. *Experimental manipulations (functional analysis).* These involve setting up situations in which different events are directly manipulated (that is, presented and withdrawn) to assess their effects on the person's problem behaviors. Data on the behavior are systematically collected to allow for comparisons of the effects of different manipulations.

What Should Be the Outcomes of a Good FBA?

1. A thorough description of all of the problem behaviors of concern, including how often they occur, how long, and how intense or potentially damaging they are. Also, it is important to identify behaviors that seem to typically occur together (for instance, the student yells, then throws things).

2. Identification of the general and more specific things and events that seem to "set off" or predict when and where the behaviors are going to occur (for instance, when the student is not getting attention, is asked to do particular activities, is ill, tired, or hungry).

3. Identification of the outcomes or consequences that the behaviors receive that may be reinforcing and maintaining them (such as getting attention, getting help with work, avoiding or escaping work demands or activities).

4. Summarization of this information into statements or hypotheses about the behavior (for instance, "When Janna gets little sleep the night before and is asked to do math problems that are difficult for her, she will put her head down, refuse, and/or throw or destroy her books to escape having to do the task").

5. Some level of systematic observational data that supports the statements or hypotheses you've developed. This could be either the systematic observations or experimental manipulations mentioned above.

The whole purpose of conducting an FBA is to guide the development of a plan. Such a plan should include a comprehensive array of strategies, such as changing curriculum and instruction, teaching new alternative skills, and rewarding appropriate behaviors.

Protections for Children Not Yet Eligible Under IDEA

Under some circumstances, a child subject to disciplinary actions who has not been determined eligible under IDEA can assert the protections of IDEA. IDEA '04 narrows these circumstances. An LEA will be deemed to know of the child's disability and be required to offer IDEA protections if, before the misbehavior subject to discipline, (a) the parents requested an IDEA evaluation or expressed concern, in writing, to supervisory or administrative personnel (or one of the child's teachers) that their child needed special education, or (b) a teacher or other district staff member had expressed specific concerns about a pattern of misbehavior directly to the special education director or other supervisory personnel (20 U.S.C. § 1415(k)(5) (2006)). In other words, the staff member's concern must have been expressed to someone in a supervisory position who could be held responsible for failing to act on that concern.

IDEA '04 specifies that a school district will not be deemed to know that a child has a disability if the parent has not allowed an evaluation or has refused special education services, or if the child has been evaluated and found ineligible for services. If the request for an evaluation is made while the child is being subjected to discipline, the LEA must conduct an expedited evaluation. (No timeline for an expedited hearing is established.) Pending the results, the child remains in the setting selected by school authorities (20 U.S.C. § 1415(k)(5) (2006)).

Seclusion and Physical Restraints

Increasing problems with the use of seclusion and physical restraints on school children, especially IDEA students, have resulted in reports from the Congressional Research Service (CRS), the National Disability Rights Network (NDRN), the Government Accountability Office (GAO), and hearings by the U.S. House of Representatives to consider whether federal rules are needed (see, e.g., GAO, 2009; NDRN, 2010). Reports documenting deaths and injuries from use of these discipline tools have generated considerable passion. According to the GAO, nineteen states have no laws or regulations governing the use of seclusion or restraint in schools, while seven others have some restrictions on the use of restraints but no regulations related to seclusions. Advocates like NDRN are pushing for federal laws on the subject, and federal legislation has been introduced but has generated controversy among legislators. Some advocates would like to see an outright ban on the use of physical restraints (such as handcuffs) and seclusion, or time-out, rooms. Others urge clearer state policies and restrictions on their use. The Council for Children with Behavioral Disorders (CCBD) adopted a policy position in May 2009 that physical restraint or seclusion procedures should occur in schools only in an emergency and not when their purpose is simply to manage student behavior. Among other things, CCBD encourages schools to have a written positive behavior support plan, pre-established emergency procedures, and continuous adult observation of any student during a period of seclusion. Readers should check to see what their state's policies are in this regard and should employ good practices, regardless.

In the past, controversies have arisen over the use of "aversive techniques" (e.g., inflicting physical discomfort or pain, using physical restraints) on students with disabilities as a means to manage situations of out-of-control behavior. A number of states have established conditions or provided guidelines on the use of aversives. In general, except in emergencies, guidelines call for the use of positive behavioral interventions first and documentation of their failure before more aversive techniques can be used. Often, however, these conditions are not enforced because of lack of oversight and monitoring.

A recent case in Pennsylvania exonerated a teacher who had placed her hand over a student's mouth in order to stop his screaming obscenities at his classmates. The student was a six-year-old with autism who exhibited frequent verbal and physical outbursts that were difficult to control. The parent alleged that the teacher's hand had liquid sanitizer on it, which the child allegedly ingested. The parent claimed that her child's right of bodily integrity under the 14th Amendment had been violated. The teacher indicated that she used the sanitizer frequently on her hands and had not attempted to coerce the child to ingest any sanitizer but had been attempting to quiet him and calm him down. The court held that there was pedagogical justification for the use of force, the force was not excessive, it was applied in a good faith effort to restore discipline, and the child was not injured (*JGS by Sterner v. Titusville Area School District,* 2010). The case exemplifies court standards used when a parent claims unconstitutional use of force or aversive discipline.

Reporting Crimes to Appropriate Authorities

The discipline provisions of IDEA '04 do not prohibit an educational agency from reporting a crime to appropriate authorities. Generally, the suspension and expulsion options and state law enforcement responsibilities are on parallel tracks (see chapter 12). Law enforcement agencies can carry out their responsibilities as they see fit. If a student is incarcerated or jailed, then obviously the IEP team cannot simultaneously move a child to an IAES. If the law enforcement agency, however, chooses not to detain or jail an alleged perpetrator of a crime or to prosecute a crime, and the student remains at or is returned to school, then the responsibility will be back on the shoulders of school officials.

School officials are ill advised to involve juvenile court authorities merely in an attempt to circumvent their responsibilities under IDEA. See, e.g., *Morgan v. Chris L., 927 F. Supp.* 267 (E.D. Tenn. 1994), *aff'd,* 106 F.3d 401 (6th Cir. 1997) (school officials' filing of a juvenile court petition seeking to adjudicate an ADHD student as "unruly" or delinquent was done to avoid meeting the school's duty to the student under IDEA). Furthermore, FAPE responsibilities do not end when a student is placed in detention or jail. See chapter 10 for FAPE requirements during incarceration.

↳Reminders and Tips

1. All involved, including general educators, special educators, paraprofessionals, school psychologists, social workers, and administrators, need to receive training and develop skills and strategies to manage the behavior of difficult children with disabilities. All personnel should take very seriously the need to address a student's misbehaviors by teaching replacement behaviors. Avoiding the need for disciplinary placement changes should be a primary goal.

2. IAES options are not as limited as one might assume. The range and kinds of alternative educational settings are not specified in the statute and do not require districts to establish alternative schools. Many options remain open, such as self-contained settings, self-contained placements within resource rooms, separate schools for students with disabilities, alternative schools, in-school suspensions, and even home instruction, if necessary, and if the FAPE requirements can be met there.

3. On the other hand, the service requirements in an IAES are quite formidable, even though ten-day removals and forty-five-day interim placements buy time for school officials to assess the needs of student-code violators. IEP teams must ensure that a student's services, regardless of the disciplinary placement, address participation in the general curriculum and allow the student to progress toward IEP goals.

4. IEP teams must develop skills to conduct manifestation determinations and functional behavioral assessments. It is probably wise to conduct FBAs on all students with disabilities who exhibit significant behavior problems unless a school district can document that an FBA is inappropriate or unnecessary.

5. Remember that only IEP teams can determine in what IAES a student can be placed for more than a short-term removal.

6. School officials can report serious crimes to law enforcement authorities but should retain good communication channels in order to continue to fulfill IDEA responsibilities in whatever setting the student is placed.

↳Review

1. Can students with disabilities be removed from their current placement for up to ten school days without invoking special IDEA placement procedures?

   Yes, if students without disabilities are treated similarly. Such a removal is considered an ordinary disciplinary action that can be applied to all students. (Remember that notice and a chance to defend oneself should be provided prior to the removal, however, as a constitutional due process right of all students.)

2. Does IDEA allow school personnel to change the placement of students with disabilities for disciplinary reasons?

   Yes. Unilateral IAES placements can be made for drug and weapon violations and serious bodily injury to another, regardless of whether the violations are a manifestation of the disability. Unilateral placement changes can also be made for other student-code violations, but the student will be returned to his or her former placement if the violation is determined to be a manifestation of the disability, unless the parents and school agree otherwise. If an expedited appeal to a hearing officer is pending, an IAES will be the placement while everyone awaits the outcome of the appeal.

3. When can a *long-term* suspension or expulsion from the current setting be imposed?

It can be imposed if the code violations are not a manifestation of the student's disability and when such a long-term suspension or expulsion would be imposed for comparable misbehavior on students without disabilities.

4. Can an IDEA student be disciplined by exclusion from all school district services?

No. Cessation of services would be a denial of FAPE. Nonetheless, the student can be removed for varying periods of time from the setting in which the code violation occurred as long as special education services necessary for the student to participate in the general curriculum and make progress toward his or her IEP goals continue.

⚡References

Council for Children with Behavior Disorders (2009). *Physical restraint and seclusion procedures in school settings*. Retrieved April 17, 2011 from http://www.ccbd.net

Government Accounting Office Report (2009). Retrieved April 20, 2011 from http://ccbd.net/category/paper-category/position-paper

Gun-Free Schools Act of 1994, 20 U.S.C. § 8921 (now 20 U.S.C. § 7151 (2006)

Honig v. Doe, 484 U.S. 305 (1988).

Improving America's School Act of 1994, Pub. L. 103-382, 108 Stat. 3518.

Individuals with Disabilities Education Improvement Act, 20 U.S.C. § 1400 *et seq.* (2006).

Individuals with Disabilities Education Improvement Act Regulations, 34 C.F. R. § 300.1 *et seq.* (2006).

Jeffords Amendment, 20 U.S.C. § 1415(e)(3)(B) (Supp. III 1997).

JGS *by Sterner* v. Titusville Area School District, 55 IDELR 39 (W.D. Pa. 2010))

Light v. Parkway C-2 School District, 41 F.3d 1223 (8th Cir. 1994).

National Disability Rights Network (NDRN) (2010). *School Is Not Supposed to Hurt*. Retrieved April 21, 2011 from http://www.ndrn.org/images/Documents/Resources/Publications/Reports/School-is-Not-Supposed-to-Hurt-NDRN.pdf.

Trumble, W. R., Brown, L., Stevenson, A., & Siefring, J. (Eds.). (2002). *The shorter Oxford English dictionary* (5th ed.). New York, NY: Oxford University Press.

⇉Selected Supplementary Resources

Bateman, B. D., & Golly, A. (2003). *Why Johnny doesn't behave: Twenty tips and measurable BIPs*. Verona, WI: IEP Resources.

Dupre, A. P. (2000). A study in double standards, discipline, and the disabled student. *Washington Law Review, 75*, 1–96.

Lohrman-O'Rourke, S., & Zirkel, P. A. (1998).The case law on aversive interventions for students with disabilities. *Exceptional Children, 65*, 101–123.

O'Neill, R. E., Horner, R. H., Albin, R. W., Sprague, J. R., Storey, K., & Newton, J. S. (1997). *Functional assessment and program development for problem behaviors: A practical handbook* (2nd ed.). Pacific Grove, CA: Brooks/Cole.

Rhode, G., Jensen, W. R., & Reavis, H. K. (1997). *The tough kid book*. Longmont, CO: Sopris West.

Skiba, R., & Peterson, R. (2000). School discipline at a crossroads: From zero tolerance to early response. *Exceptional Children, 66*, 335–347.

Smith, C. R. (2000). Behavioral and discipline provisions of IDEA '97: Implicit competencies yet to be determined. *Exceptional Children, 66*, 403–412.

Townsend, B. L. (2000). The disproportionate discipline of African American learners: Reducing school suspensions and expulsions. *Exceptional Children, 66*, 381–391.

Yell, M. L. (1995). *Clyde K. and Sheila K. v. Puyallup School District*: The courts, inclusion, and students with behavioral disorders. *Behavioral Disorders, 20*, 179–189.

Chapter 15

Remedies Under IDEA

Chapter Outline

Judicial Relief Under IDEA

IDEA establishes legal rights and remedies for students with disabilities served under the statute. Because of this, it has spawned much litigation. The statute allows students or other parties still aggrieved after pursuing IDEA administrative hearing procedures to bring a civil action in state or federal court. In addition, a civil action is allowed when exhausting administrative remedies (using the hearing process) would be futile or would provide an inadequate remedy.[1] If a remedy is called for, the court is to "grant such relief as the court determines is appropriate" (20 U.S.C. § 1415(i)(2)(C) (2006)).

Under this broad grant of authority, courts have applied many different remedies for IDEA violations, the most typical of which is declaratory and injunctive relief, that is, a court order to a school district to take a specific action to comply with the law or to stop acting in a way that violates the law. In addition, financial reimbursement and compensatory education have become increasingly prominent as a means to compensate parents for IDEA violations. These kinds of relief fall under the category of *equitable relief*—relief that attempts to right a wrong. On the other hand, monetary damages fall under the category of *legal relief*—providing money to help compensate for harm such as pain and suffering and economic harm that cannot be undone. Monetary damages in IDEA cases have remained essentially off-limits in most jurisdictions. Each major type of relief, and court cases awarding each type, are described below, so that educators and parents can understand the impact on a school district of IDEA violations.

Declaratory and Injunctive Relief

The most common relief under IDEA is declaratory and injunctive relief, where the rights of the parties are declared and illegal actions prohibited. Injunctions can take two forms: an order to do something, and an order to stop doing something. Parents seek declaratory and injunctive relief to keep a school district from continuing an illegal behavior and to force a district to take action, such as changing a placement, providing appropriate services, or otherwise complying with IDEA.†

> † Schools also seek court injunctions, especially to keep disruptive students from remaining in their current school placement. In such cases, the injunction lasts until a due process hearing determines whether to return the student to the placement from which he or she was removed or to place the student in a different setting.

Sometimes, a court orders an extensive set of actions—"affirmative remedies"—in an attempt to prevent past illegalities from continuing. In contrast to a fairly simple order, such as an order to develop an improved IEP, courts may issue detailed prescriptions of what is required when the situation is especially complex, when systemic issues are involved, or when the agency is viewed as especially stubborn and reluctant to change. *Jose P. v. Ambach* (1982)[2] is one of the best examples in special education law.

---

[1] See, e.g., *Honig v. Doe*, 484 U.S. 305, 327 (1988). For examples of alleged injuries where exhaustion was not required because no IDEA remedies were available, see *McCormick v. Waukegan Sch. Dist. No. 60*, 374 F.3d 564 (7th Cir. 2004) (student was seeking redress for permanent kidney and muscle damage caused by physical education teacher's ignoring IEP limitations regarding physical education). *Padilla v. Sch. Dist. No. 1 of Denver*, 233 F.3d 1268 (10th Cir. 2000) (IDEA student who suffered fractured skull when placed in unsupervised windowless closet was seeking redress for physical injuries alone); See also *J. S. v. Attica Central Sch.*, 386 F.3d 107 (2d Cir. 2004) (students were seeking redress for alleged systemic violations, such as failure to notify parents of meetings and failure to prepare and implement IEPs, rather than individual grievances).

[2] The appellate decision contains a description of the lower court's unpublished December 1979 order and judgment.

Jose P. v. Ambach was a class action in which the plaintiffs alleged systemwide violations of IDEA by the New York City schools, which found themselves ill equipped to fully comply with the law. The federal district court agreed with the plaintiffs and ordered an extensive set of actions to enforce compliance by the school district. Among other things, the court ordered the school district to provide timely evaluations, hire additional staff, provide school-based support teams, provide timely placements, prepare a booklet describing parent rights, translate documents into the native language of the parents, develop a plan to make a sufficient number of facilities physically accessible to students with physical disabilities, submit periodic reports, develop more coordinated and uniform data management systems, and enter into contracts with private providers when necessary to meet the evaluation timelines and provide related services. As a result of the decision, New York City agreed to hire 1,200 more special education teachers and clinical staff (Fafard, Hanlon, & Bryson, 1986).

A decade later, a federal court in *Reusch v. Fountain* (1994), in response to a school district's inadequate procedural and substantive standards for extended school year (ESY) services, ordered the following set of remedies: extensive notice to parents at least ten days before review of an IEP, establishment of an ample timeline for decisions and appeals concerning eligibility for ESY services, annual review of ESY decisions, a specific standard for ESY eligibility, individualized programming and placement decisions for each ESY student, staff training, ongoing monitoring, and a yearly progress report filed with the court.

Clearly, if a court determines that it is necessary to give multiple orders to a school district to bring about systemic change, it can do so in great detail. Most school districts, of course, would prefer never to be in the position of having to comply with such an extensive set of judicially imposed requirements. The requirements in the above-cited cases remind one of the detailed requirements issued in desegregation cases, and illustrate what can happen when systemic violations are occurring.

Reimbursement

Readers may recall from Chapter 13 that the Supreme Court ruled in *Burlington School Committee v. Massachusetts Department of Education* (1985) that parents can be reimbursed for the reasonable costs of a unilateral private placement for their child when FAPE is not available in the public setting, and when the parent's placement is "proper." *In Florence County School District v. Carter* (1993), the Court went one step further in holding that a parentally selected private placement did not have to meet the FAPE requirements because FAPE is required only when the placement is made by a public agency. Reflecting these decisions, reimbursement is now authorized by statute as well (20 U.S.C. § 1412(a)(10)(C)(ii) (2006)).

The Supreme Court explained in *Burlington* (1985) that reimbursement is not a monetary damage award but rather a way for a school district to pay for what it should have been providing all along. In short, it is an equitable remedy. In both *Burlington and Carter* (1993), the Court made clear that equitable considerations are relevant in fashioning the amount of monetary reimbursement, and that not all a parent's educational costs are necessarily reimbursable. One illustration of this principle is reflected in *Lascari v. Board of Education* (1989), where the New Jersey Supreme Court determined that the parents were entitled to reimbursement for their child's tuition at an out-of-state residential school but not for room and board expenses.

By extension, the reasonable costs of related services that a school district should have provided are also reimbursable if parents have to obtain them on their own. Such parentally obtained services as transportation,[3] private tutoring,[4] private counseling, occupational therapy (*Rapid City School District. v. Vahle*, 1990), and speech therapy (*Johnson v. Lancaster-Lebanon Intermediate Unit* 13, 1991) have all been reimbursable. Even lost earnings by a parent as a result of time spent protecting the child's rights have been reimbursable (*Board of Education of County of Cabell v. Dienelt*, 1988).

Compensatory Education

Compensatory education allows an extension of a student's entitlement to IDEA services beyond the statutory age limit. ESY services and additional tutoring are also options. These types of relief are a means of compensating for a school district's failure to provide FAPE to a given student during a period of time in which the child was eligible.

The recognition of compensatory education as a legitimate judicial remedy for the failure to provide FAPE accelerated after the Supreme Court's decision in *Burlington*. With the recognition that only affluent parents could afford to place their children in private school and sue for reimbursement came the recognition that an alternative remedy had to be available for less affluent parents. Compensatory education is that alternative. Some have called it the "poor-person's *Burlington*."

Virtually all circuits of the U.S. Court of Appeals have acknowledged the viability of compensatory education in appropriate circumstances but differ in defining what constitutes a serious-enough deprivation of FAPE to justify compensatory education. The amount and duration of compensatory relief also vary widely with the factual circumstances and court. Some courts order equivalent hours for the number of hours of FAPE denied. Others try to determine the amount of educational harm caused by the denial of FAPE and then calculate how much compensatory education is needed to redress the harm. Readers need to ascertain the approach used in their own circuit.†

> † In addition, readers should ascertain whether a state court decision limits the extent of compensatory education available in their jurisdiction. For instance, in *Natrona County School District No. 1 v. McKnight*, 764 P.2d 1039 (Wyo. 1988), the Wyoming Supreme Court held that no compensatory education was possible past a student's 21st birthday. The ruling was based on Wyoming law.

In addition to due process hearing officers, the SEA now has the authority to order compensatory education services if necessary to remediate the denial of FAPE (34 C.F.R. § 300.151 (2006)). Therefore, litigation to achieve this result is not necessary in many instances.

Compensatory education usually should not be available after a student graduates from high school with a regular education diploma.[5] The OSEP position is that because IDEA does not require states to provide postsecondary education, eligibility for IDEA services can end after receipt of a regular education diploma, assuming proper notice of the termination of special education services (34 C.F.R. § 300.102(a)(3) (2006)). This means that a procedurally proper and bona fide graduation should terminate any obligation for educational services, even if a student has been denied FAPE some time during the course of his or her public school education. This is because, notwithstanding a temporary denial of FAPE, the student went on to meet the required standards for graduation from public school. On the other hand, a pretextual "graduation" contrived to exit a student prematurely from the public school system, or graduation with only a certification of completion, could still

---

[3] *Egg Harbor Township Bd. of Educ. v. S. O.*, 19 IDELR 15 (D.N.J. (1992); *Hurry v. Jones*, 560 F. Supp. 500 (D.R.I. 1983), *aff'd in relevant part*, 734 F.2d 879 (1st Cir. 1984); *Northeast Central Sch. Dist. v. Sobol*, 572 N.Y.S.2d 752 (1991), *aff'd as modified*, 595 N.E.2d 339 (N.Y. 1992).

[4] *W. G. v. Target Range Sch. Dist. No. 23*, 960 F.2d 1479 (9th Cir. 1992); *In re Conklin*, 946 F.2d 306 (4th Cir. 1991).

[5] See, e.g., *Bd. of Educ. v. Nathan R.*, 199 F.3d 377 (7th Cir. 2000). But see *Jessie v. Bullitt City Bd. of Educ.*, 2005 U.S. Dist. LEXIS 7270 (W.D. Ky. 2005) (awarding one year of compensatory education to student with regular education diploma).

subject a school district to the possibility of compensatory education after a student graduates.† In the past, the court cases have not always made this distinction explicit, but the IDEA regulations do (34 C.F.R. § 300.102(a)(3)(ii) and (iv) (2006)).

> † If the statute of limitations (a law fixing the time within which parties must bring their lawsuits) has not expired, even a student over the statutory age may be able to bring a lawsuit in some jurisdictions. See, e.g., *Pihl v. Massachusetts Department of Education*, 9 F.3d 184 (1st Cir. 1993), *Lester H. v. Gilhool*, 916 F. 2d 865 (3d Cir. 1990), and *Barnett v. Memphis City Schools*, 113 Fed. Appx. 124 (6th Cir. 2004).

Monetary Damages

As a general rule, monetary damages have not been available for violations of IDEA. Monetary damages are typically of two kinds: compensatory and punitive. Compensatory damages would include payments for pain and suffering resulting from illegal school district policies and practices; they could also include economic harm, such as lost future earnings. Punitive damages are more difficult to obtain and are imposed to deter a liable party from repeating behavior deemed malicious or especially reckless.

The majority view has been that these two types of damages would take money away from school districts that should be spent on educational programs, and that Congress did not intend such a remedy when it enacted IDEA. Instead, injunctive relief has been seen as the appropriate remedy in most circumstances, with reimbursement or compensatory education available when necessary.

A 1992 Supreme Court decision in a Title IX sex discrimination case raised some doubt as to whether the trend against monetary damages would hold. In *Franklin v. Gwinnett County Public Schools* (1992), the Court ruled that monetary damages were available for violation of Title IX's prohibition against sex discrimination in schools. The Court stated that, without clear direction to the contrary from Congress, "we presume the availability of all appropriate remedies" (p. 66). The ruling, however, also indicated that the violation must be intentional. The statutory language of Title IX relief is similar to that of IDEA, leading to speculation that the Court would uphold an award of monetary damages under IDEA in appropriate circumstances if the violation were intentional.

Nine of the regional federal appellate courts (all but the Fifth, Tenth, and the D.C. Circuit), in the years since the *Franklin* (1992) decision have held that compensatory damages are unavailable under IDEA, although the cases have not dealt with the question of intentionality.[6] The trend is clearly away from monetary damages although the issue has not been completely resolved.

Monetary damages under 42 U. S. C. Section 1983 for IDEA violations.

42 U.S.C. Section 1983 is a provision of the Civil Rights Act of 1871, a post–Civil War statute initially intended to provide remedies for civil rights violations against African Americans. It has been revitalized in recent decades and now has far wider application. It provides that "[e]very person who, under color of [law], custom, or usage, of any State," deprives a U.S. citizen of any rights secured by the Constitution and laws "shall be liable to the party injured in an action at law, suit in equity, or other proper proceeding for redress" (42 U.S.C. § 1983 (1994)). In other words, those whose federal civil rights have been violated can sue for monetary damages as well as equitable relief. This

---

[6] See *Chambers v. Sch Dist. of Philadelphia Bd. of Educ.*, 587 F.3d 176 (3d Cir. 2009); *Ortega v. Bibb Cnty. Sch. Dist.*, 297 F.3d 1321 (11th Cir. 2005); *Nieves-Marquez v. Puerto Rico*, 353 F.3d 108 (1st Cir. 2003); *Gean v. Hattaway*, 330 F.3d 758 (6th Cir. 2003); *Polera v. Bd. of Educ.*, 288 F.3d 478 (2d Cir. 2002); *Witte v. Clark Cnty. Sch. Dist.*, 197 F.3d 1271 (9th Cir. 1999); *Sellers v. Sch. Bd. of Manassas*, 141 F.3d 524 (4th Cir. 1998); *Charlie F. v. Bd. of Educ.*, 98 F.3d 989 (7th Cir. 1996); *Heidemann v. Rother*, 84 F.3d 1021 (8th Cir. 1996).

is a significant right for harmed parties because it makes available financial damages that might be unavailable under other statutes. The allegedly violated rights are not named in Section 1983 itself but are found elsewhere in federal law—either in the Constitution or federal statutes. LEAs, along with other local governmental units, are considered "persons" for Section 1983 purposes (*Monell v. Department of Social Services*, 1978).

A provision of IDEA, first passed in 1986 and amended in 1990, seemed to indicate that Section 1983 could be available as a source of monetary damages in cases of IDEA violations. The provision states that:

> Nothing in [IDEA] shall be construed to restrict or limit the rights, procedures, and remedies available under the Constitution, the Americans With Disabilities Act of 1990, title V [Section 504] of the Rehabilitation Act of 1973, or other Federal statutes protecting the rights of children with disabilities, except that before the filing of a civil action under such laws seeking relief that is also available under this part [Part B], [administrative hearing procedures] shall be exhausted to the same extent as would be required had the action been brought under this part.† (20 U.S.C. § 1415(l) (2006))

> † This language indicates, among other things, that if allegations of ADA and Section 504 violations are not independent of alleged IDEA violations, then a plaintiff must use the IDEA hearing procedures before going to court. Most courts have interpreted this to mean that parents cannot skirt the administrative hearing procedures by seeking only monetary damages if an IDEA remedy is available. For example, see *Robb v. Bethel School District*, 308 F.3d 1047 (9th Cir. 2002).

Whether the language in this provision referring to "other Federal statutes protecting the rights of children and youth with disabilities" is meant to include Section 1983 is ambiguous. Since the U.S. Supreme Court's decision interpreting the Telecommunications Act in *Rancho Palos Verdes v. Abrams* (2005), at least three appellate courts have ruled that damages for IDEA violations are unavailable under Section 1983. Applying the standard in *Rancho Palos Verdes*, the First, Third, and Ninth Circuits have held that IDEA establishes a comprehensive scheme of remedies that is incompatible with an alternative remedy under Section 1983.[7] The standard, however, requires a defendant to rebut the presumption that Congress intended both the federal statute and § 1983 to provide alternative remedies, and the Second Circuit has taken a different view of the issue.[8] The argument may seem somewhat abstract, but what is really at stake is the availability of monetary damages under Section 1983 in a jurisdiction where they are unavailable under IDEA.

In any event, court recognition of the viability of a Section 1983 claim for IDEA violations is not the same thing as actually obtaining an award for damages. Few cases have resulted in such awards because proving school district liability under Section 1983 for IDEA violations is difficult. Damages only follow actual provable injury, and only compensatory damages, not punitive damages, are available under Section 1983 against school districts.[9] Also, simple negligence or individual teacher error will not create liability for the school district. Damages can be awarded against school

---

[7] See e.g., *Blanchard v. Morton Sch. Dist.*, 509 F.3d 934 (9th Cir. 2007); *A. W. v. Jersey City Pub. Sch.*, 486 F.3d 791 (3d Cir. 2007) (*en banc*); *Diaz-Fonseca v. Puerto Rico*, 451 F.3d 13 (1st Cir. 2006).

[8] See *D. D. v. New York City Bd. of Educ.*, 465 F.3d 503, 513 (2d Cir. 2006). See also *Smith v. Guilford Bd. of Educ.*, 226 F. Appx 58, 63 (2d Cir. 2007). Older appellate court decisions have also allowed a § 1983 suit to proceed. *Charlie F. v. Bd. of Educ.*, 98 F.3d 989 (7th Cir. 1996); *N. B. v. Alachua City Sch. Bd.*, 84 F.3d 1376 (11th Cir. 1996). *Cf. McCormick v. Waukegan Sch. Dist. No. 60*, 374 F.3d 564 (7th Cir. 2004); *Covington v. Knox County Sch. Sys.*, 205 F.3d 912 (6th Cir. 2000) (both allowing claim to proceed under an exception to administrative exhaustion requirement).

[9] See *City of Newport v. Fact Concerts*, 453 U.S. 247 (1981). But see *Woods v. New Jersey Dep't of Educ.*, 796 F. Supp. 767 (D.N.J. 1992) (stating that punitive damages may be available against the school district for IDEA violations, even though unavailable under § 1983).

districts only if school boards or other policy makers violate the law as a matter of "policy or custom" (*Monell v. Department of Social Services,* 1978). This is difficult to prove although blanket separation or blanket inclusion policies that ignore the individualization requirement of IDEA might create damage liability if plaintiffs could prove their resultant injuries. The same might be said for systemwide failures to identify children with disabilities. Similarly, reckless failure to train teachers in the face of obvious need—for instance, to effectively manage students with emotional/behavioral disturbances—might open a district to liability for injuries flowing from the lack of training.[10]

School personnel have been sued under Section 1983 in their individual as well as their official capacities. If they ignore "clearly established" rights of which a reasonable person would have known, they may find traditional "good faith immunity" unavailable to them and be held personally liable (*Harlow v. Fitzgerald,*1982; *P. C. v. McLaughlin,* 1990)). Because the basic IDEA rights of students with disabilities to FAPE in the LRE with an IEP and appropriate evaluation and procedural safeguards are clearly established, unintentional ("good faith") ignorance of them is likely to be no excuse.

A Case of Individual Teacher Liability

A notable example of individual liability appears in *Doe v. Withers,* 20 IDELR 422 (W. Va. Cir. Ct. 1993), where a state court awarded $15,000 in damages in a Section 1983 suit against a public school history teacher for refusing to implement an IEP of a student with a learning disability. In direct contradiction to the IEP, the teacher declined to allow the student to take his exams orally and untimed, as a result of which the student failed the course. Of the award, $5,000 was in compensatory damages and $10,000 in punitive damages. This decision alerts teachers to their potential vulnerability if they refuse to implement a student's IEP.

Judicial Enforcement Options for Noncompliance With Court Orders

In spite of the split of opinion as to whether Section 1983 provides a source of monetary damages for IDEA violations, courts that have considered the question generally agree that Section 1983 is available in one specific situation: when school districts or school officials have refused to carry out a court order or hearing decision in an IDEA case. In other words, Section 1983 can be a mechanism to enforce a court order or administrative hearing decision under IDEA.[11] Actual noncompliance with judicial or administrative rulings by either a school district or an individual fits the Section 1983 requirements for an award of damages: adoption or implementation of an illegal policy or custom, or an individual's violation of "clearly established" rights.

Other enforcement mechanisms are also available when an education agency refuses to comply with a court order. If damages are not the only fair way to provide a remedy, injunctions to force compliance will be preferred.† Other mechanisms include contempt and the appointment of a

---

[10] See *City of Canton v. Harris,* 489 U.S. 378 (1989). See also *Susavage v. Bucks Cnty. Sch. Intermediate Unit No. 22,* 2002 U.S. Dist. LEXIS 1274 (E.D. Pa. 2002) (refusing to dismiss parents' § 1983, ADA, and § 504 claims alleging that the school district showed deliberate indifference to child's special transportation safety needs that resulted in the child's death).
[11] See, e.g., *Robinson v. Pinderhughes,* 810 F.2d 1270 (4th Cir. 1987); *Reid v. Sch. Dist. of Philadelphia,* 2004 U.S. Dist. LEXIS 17275 (E.D. Pa. 2004); *Joseph M. v. Southeast Delco Sch. Dist.,* 2001 U.S. Dist. LEXIS 2994 (E.D. Pa. 2001); *A. T. and I. T. ex rel. Z. T. v. New York St. Educ. Dep't,* 1998 U.S. Dist. LEXIS 23275 (E.D. N.Y. 1998) (also citing numerous other cases).

special master. Contempt usually involves fining or even jailing a party for failure to comply with a court order.†† A special master is a person with specific expertise who is appointed by the court to oversee and implement court rulings in especially complex cases. A special master can also be appointed to manage parts of the litigation. Such an appointment is authorized pursuant to Rule 53 of the Federal Rules of Civil Procedure. Use of contempt and/or a special master is quite rare in special education cases, yet instances do arise.

† In *Battaglia v. Lexington School Committee*, 762 F. Supp. 416 (D. Mass. 1991), the court granted a preliminary injunction to parents and ordered a student placed immediately in a private school in order to enforce a hearing officer's order for private school placement.

†† Another alternative to a fine or jail sentence for contempt of court was applied in *Murphy v. Timberlane Regional School District*, 855 F. Supp. 498 (D. N.H. 1994). There, because the district failed to comply with the original order, the court ordered additional compensatory education beyond the two years previously ordered.

In *Duane B. v. Chester-Upland School District* (1994) (see also *Blackman v. District of Columbia*, 1999), a Pennsylvania school district and the State Board of Education failed to comply in a timely manner with the court's remedial orders. The court observed that fining defendants in special education cases is not an effective means to coerce compliance or remedy past noncompliance, so instead it appointed a special master to oversee the implementation of the court's earlier orders.

Similarly, the plaintiffs in *Jose P. v. Ambach* (1982) asked the judge to hold the New York City schools in contempt after several years of noncompliance with aspects of the original *Jose P.* order and judgment. The court agreed to do so but referred the noncompliance issues to a special master rather than imposing a fine or jail sentence. The court appointed the special master to help with fact finding and to make recommendations to the judge in the course of the litigation.

SEA Enforcement Options for IDEA Violations

The SEA is charged with responsibility for ensuring that local school districts comply with IDEA (20 U.S.C. § 1412(a)(11) (2006)). In connection with this responsibility, the IDEA regulations require each SEA to adopt written "state complaint procedures" to investigate and resolve written complaints alleging substantive and/or procedural IDEA violations (34 C.F.R. §§ 300.151-.153 (2006)). The procedure is an alternative to the due process hearing and can be essentially cost-free to the complaining party (see Chapter 8).† If a public agency is out of compliance, the SEA may provide technical assistance and impose corrective actions. Ultimately, the state has the authority to withhold IDEA funds from a noncomplying school district. If the complaining party has received, or is in the process of seeking, a hearing decision on any of the same issues, the SEA will not rule on the same issues, and the hearing decision on those issues will be binding.

† In a case that is the first of its kind, the Ninth Circuit ruled that plaintiffs who used the "complaint resolution procedure"—that is, state complaint procedure—to completion without getting the relief they sought had exhausted their administrative remedies and were not required to seek a due process hearing on the same issues prior to litigating (*Christopher S. v. Stanislaus County Office of Education*, 384 F.3d 1205 (9th Cir. 2004)).

The option of requesting the state to investigate noncompliance has been underutilized. It deserves more widespread use and offers a less adversarial means of resolving a dispute than due process hearings and litigation. As mentioned in Chapter 8, anyone may bring a complaint alleging a violation of IDEA, including a teacher or teacher's association. The SEA can be asked to rule on a matter that concerns districtwide policies, or on an individual matter that would otherwise be subject to a due process hearing. No attorney has to be involved.

If the SEA rather than the LEA is out of compliance with IDEA, ED is authorized to enforce compliance by withholding a state's IDEA funds or a part thereof until a state-level violation is remedied (20 U.S.C. § 1416(e) (2006)). ED has asserted its authority in several instances. One was in response to a North Carolina law that denied hearing officers the right to decide parents' reimbursement claims. As a result, North Carolina amended its law in 1990 (*S-1 v. North Carolina State Board. of Education*, 1994). Another was in response to Virginia's insistence that it could terminate all educational services to misbehaving students with disabilities if the misbehavior did not result from the disability.†

> † In *Virginia Department of Education v. Riley*, 104 F.3d 559 (4th Cir. 1997), the Fourth Circuit overturned the decision of the Secretary of Education to withhold IDEA (Part B) funds until Virginia's policy allowing expulsion of students with disabilities conformed to the ED interpretation of the law. The circuit ruled that ED's interpretation went beyond the language of the statute. Subsequent changes to the statute in IDEA '97 mooted the court's ruling.

Attorneys' Fees

With passage of a 1986 amendment to IDEA entitled the Handicapped Children's Protection Act (HCPA), courts were authorized to award attorneys' fees to a parent or guardian who was a "prevailing party" in an "action or proceeding" brought under IDEA (20 U.S.C. § 1415(i)(3)(B-G) (2006)). The attorneys' fee provision in the HCPA is not so much a remedy for a wrong committed as a means of giving parents access to court if they have a viable claim but insufficient financial resources. The attorneys' fee provisions appear in the procedural safeguards section of the statute. Because school districts tend to see attorneys' fees as a financial "remedy" available to parents, however, they are included in this chapter.†

> † The HCPA superseded the Supreme Court's holding in *Smith v. Robinson*, 468 U.S. 992 (1984), that IDEA did not create a right to attorneys' fees by the prevailing party. The general rule in American jurisprudence is that each side pays its own attorneys' fees, and the HCPA is called a fee-shifting statute because it overrides the general rule.

The definition of a "prevailing party" is technical. In general, it does not require parents to win on all issues or even the central issue, but rather to have gained a significant judicially sanctioned benefit or change (a "material alteration of the legal relationship") for their child that would not have resulted but for their action (*Buckhannon Board and Care Home v. West Virginia Department of Health and Human Resources*, 2001).One example of a material alteration is provided by the case of *Weissburg v. Lancaster School District* (2010). As a result of an administrative hearing, the child's classification was changed from intellectual disability to both intellectual disability and autism, resulting in the right to a teacher qualified in both disabilities. Therefore, even though the student had actually received services from such a teacher, the Ninth Circuit ruled that the plaintiffs were entitled to recover attorneys' fees as a prevailing party.

Of course, if a school district loses at the hearing stage and appeals to court, the parents must continue to prevail in court; if ultimately the school district prevails, then the parents are no longer the prevailing party. One can obtain attorneys' fees only at the point that no further appeals are pending.

Rulings in eight circuits of the U.S. Court of Appeals, plus dicta in another, have concluded that when the school district chooses not to appeal an adverse hearing decision, the HCPA permits an independent action in court for attorneys' fees by parents who prevailed at the hearing stage.[12] In other words, the hearing is considered a "proceeding" under IDEA. No circuits have rulings to the contrary. IDEA does not authorize a hearing officer to award attorneys' fees, so the parent must go to court to collect them unless state law provides otherwise. Reimbursable fees will then extend not only to the parent's legal costs at the hearing stage, but also to the legal fees for work in court to gain the fees for the legal work done at the hearing.

In 2001, the Supreme Court made a ruling in *Buckhannon Board and Care Home v. West Virginia Department of Health and Human Resources* that has impacted the availability of attorneys' fees under IDEA for certain kinds of work done outside of an administrative hearing or court. In *Buckhannon*, the Supreme Court ruled that for a prevailing party to obtain attorneys' fees, the party must have a judgment on the merits or a judicially approved settlement. *Buckhannon* was not a special education case, and some commentators believe that it should not apply to IDEA. Nonetheless, it has been generally interpreted to mean that IDEA settlements that fall short of official judicial, or at least quasi-judicial (hearing officer), approval are not eligible for attorneys' fees. Many courts are now denying parental requests for attorneys' fees for private settlements under IDEA.[13] A few courts are distinguishing IDEA cases from the *Buckhannon* standard (*Ostby v. Oxnard Union High*, 2002), but the trend has been to use *Buckhannon* to limit the availability of attorneys' fees.

A judicial split over legal work performed at IEP meetings was resolved by IDEA '97, which specified that attorneys' fees may not be awarded in connection with any IEP meeting unless the meeting is convened as the result of a hearing or court action (20 U.S.C. § 1415(i)(3)(D)(ii) (2006)). Moreover, a provision in IDEA '04 states that for purposes of the attorneys' fee provision, resolution sessions are not considered a hearing or judicial action or a meeting convened as a result of either (20 U.S.C. § 1415(i)(3)(D)(iii) (2006)). This provision seems meant to prevent an award of attorneys' fees for work done at a resolution session. The rationale for both these provisions presumably is that an IEP meeting and a resolution session are not legal proceedings but opportunities for joint problem solving between the LEA and parents and that legal representation (and the incentive of reimbursement) at these meetings runs counter to the intent of the statute.†

> † Although IDEA '04 specified that agreements reached at mediation and resolution sessions must be put in writing and are legally enforceable in court, presumably this does not indicate that they have been approved by either a hearing officer or a court. They remain private settlements even though enforceable in court.

[12] *Neosho R-V Sch. Dist. v. Clark*, 315 F.3d 1022 (8th Cir. 2002); *G. M. v. New Britain Bd. of Educ.*, 173 F.3d 77 (2d Cir. 1999); *Brown v. Griggsville Community Unit Sch. Dist. No. 4*, 12 F.3d 681 (7th Cir. 1993); *Moore v. District of Columbia*, 907 F.2d 165 (D.C. Cir. 1990); *McSomebodies v. Burlingame Elem. Sch. Dist.*, 886 F.2d 1558 (9th Cir. 1989), *as supplemented*, 897 F.2d 974 (1990); *Mitten v. Muscogee Cnty. Sch. Dist.*, 877 F.2d 932 (11th Cir. 1989); *Duane M. v. Orleans Parish Sch. Bd.*, 861 F.2d 115 (5th Cir. 1988); *Eggers v. Bullitt Cnty. Sch. Dist.*, 854 F.2d 892 (6th Cir. 1988); *Arons v. New Jersey St. Bd. of Educ.*, 842 F.2d 58 (dicta) (3d Cir. 1988).

[13] *See, e.g., Smith v. Fitchburg Pub. Sch.*, 401 F.3d 16 (1st Cir. 2005); *Alegria v. Dist. of Columbia*, 391 F.3d 262 (D.C. Cir. 2004); *Doe v. Boston Pub. Sch.*, 358 F.3d 20 (1st Cir. 2004); *John T. v. Delaware County Inter. Unit*, 318 F.3d 545 (3d Cir. 2003); *J. C. v. Regional Sch. Dist. No. 10*, 278 F.3d 119 (2d. Cir. 2002); *Jose Luis R. v. Joliet Township High Sch. Dist. 204*, 2002 WL 54544 (N.D. Ill. 2002); *J. S. & M. S. v. Ramapo Cent. Sch. Dist.*, 165 F. Supp. 2d 570 (S.D.N.Y. 2001). *Cf. T. D. v. LaGrange Sch. Dist. No. 102*, 349 F.3d 469 (7th Cir. 2003) (same, but also holding that the plaintiff was entitled to attorney's fees as prevailing party at hearing prior to settlement).

The actual amount of attorneys' fees is determined by the court based on "rates prevailing in the community" (20 U.S.C. § 1415(i)(3)(C) (2006)). The court will also consider the extent to which the parent prevailed, the efficiency and competence of the legal representation, including the adequacy of documentation of time spent; the complexity of the issues, and similar factors. Ultimately, the amount set is to be "reasonable" under the circumstances of the case.† No fees are to be awarded if a parent rejects a timely settlement offer that turns out to be as favorable as what a court or hearing officer orders in the way of relief (20 U.S.C. § 1415(i)(3)(D)(i) (2006).

> † In *Beard v. Teska*, 31 F.3d 942 (10th Cir. 1994), the court reduced the reimbursable hourly rate from $200 to $125 to reflect what it determined to be the rate prevailing both within the community and the nation as a whole for work done on IDEA matters.

A new provision appears in IDEA '04 that allows a prevailing LEA or SEA to recover attorneys' fees from parents or their attorney under the following limited circumstances:

1. The parent's attorney can be held responsible if he or she files a complaint or subsequent cause of action that is "frivolous, unreasonable, or without foundation," or if the attorney continues to litigate under these circumstances (20 U.S.C. § 1415(i)(3)(B)(i)(II) (2006)); and

2. The parent or the parent's attorney can be held responsible if the complaint or subsequent cause of action was "presented for any improper purpose, such as to harass, to cause unnecessary delay, or to needlessly increase the cost of the litigation" (20 U.S.C. § 1415(i)(3)(B)(i)(III) (2006)).

In May 2007, the Supreme Court decided *Winkelman v. Parma City School District* (2007). The Court ruled that the rights given to children under IDEA are also given to their parents and that parents, therefore, can represent themselves in court without the assistance of an attorney. To sue in court generally, one must be a "party" under the Judiciary Act of 1789 (28 U.S.C. § 1654 (2006)), which allows the parties to "plead and conduct their own cases personally or by counsel." To sue under IDEA specifically, one must be an "aggrieved party." The Court in *Winkelman* concluded that parents are an "aggrieved party" when they are alleging that their child was denied FAPE. The Court stated that, under IDEA, the rights of children and the rights of parents are conjoined, given the role of parents in special education decisions affecting their child, and given the extensive procedural safeguards provided to parents. The bottom line is that parents have independent, enforceable, substantive rights under IDEA, not just procedural and reimbursement-related rights: They can pursue any matter related to their child's FAPE on their own behalf without use of an attorney, which particularly benefits parents who are unable to afford one.

Several courts have ruled that parents who are attorneys cannot receive fees for representing their children in IDEA actions because the purpose of the attorneys' fee provision is to provide access to outside counsel, not to pay parents.[14] With respect to lay advocates, IDEA gives parties to a hearing the right to be "accompanied and advised by" individuals with special knowledge or training about the problems of children with disabilities. (34 C.F.R. § 300.512(a)(1) (2006)). Whether such lay

---

[14] See, e.g., *Woodside v. Sch. Dist. of Philadelphia Bd. of Educ.*, 248 F.3d 129 (3d Cir. 2010); *Ford v. Long Beach Unified Sch. Dist.*, 461 F.3d 1087 (9th Cir. 2006); *Doe v. Bd. of Educ. of Baltimore Cnty.*, 165 F.3d 260 (4th Cir. 1998).

advocates can receive payment for their representation of a child is a different matter, subject to state law. Some courts have ruled that lay advocates cannot "represent" IDEA children in court because it represents the unauthorized practice of law. Others courts have disagreed.[15] Parent attorneys and lay advocates will want to ascertain the law in their own jurisdiction when considering whether to litigate.

In late June 2006, the Supreme Court ruled that expert witness fees are not reimbursable under IDEA because the statute does not contain express language making them reimbursable. *Arlington Central School District Board of Education v. Murphy* (2006). In a congressional conference report issued at the time that IDEA amendments were added to provide for attorneys' fees to prevailing parents, Congress indicated that it intended expert witness fees to also be reimbursable, but no such explicit language was added to IDEA itself. Since the Court's decision, legislation has been introduced in both houses of Congress to amend IDEA to allow parents to recoup their expert witness fees. Such legislation has not yet been enacted. Until such time, the award for expert witness fees and expenses is limited to the amount authorized for ordinary witnesses under a more generic statute.

↳Reminders and Tips

1. Both state and local school officials should be aware of the cost implications of equitable remedies available under IDEA. Reimbursement and compensatory education frequently cost more than FAPE would have, and they are available for substantive violations and serious procedural violations of IDEA that deny FAPE or deprive a student of educational benefit.

2. Overall, monetary damages are seldom available under IDEA, but the law is somewhat unsettled in this regard. If relief short of monetary damages will provide a sufficient remedy, it is likely to be used. Monetary damages, where recognized, are likely to be reserved for situations in which another form of relief is insufficient to redress the grievance. Readers should keep abreast of current case law in their own federal court jurisdiction.

3. Monetary damages under Section 1983 can be invoked in some jurisdictions for IDEA violations when the IDEA remedies prove insufficient to remedy the violations. Monetary damages under Section 1983 require provable injury, however, and are available against a school district only for policies or practices that constitute intentional violations or reckless indifference to a student's IDEA rights.

4. Money damages under Section 1983 are available in some jurisdictions against individual school officials who violate a student's clearly established rights. Ignorance of these rights will not provide an excuse to an individual teacher under Section 1983.

5. If a school district flouts a court order or hearing decision, it establishes intentionality for purposes of damage awards under Section 1983.

6. The best defense against monetary damages, reimbursement, compensatory education, and other costly remedies is to provide FAPE in the first place and to seek parental input in the decision-making process. When disputes arise, negotiation, mediation, resolution sessions, and a complaint to the SEA are tools that can prevent the need for more costly and adversarial hearings and litigation.

---

[15] Cf., e.g., *Collinsgru v. Palmyra Bd. of Educ.*, 161 F.3d 225 (3d Cir. 1998); *Wenger v. Canastota Cent. Sch. Dist.*, 146 F.3d 123 (2d Cir. 1998); *Devine v. Indian River Cnty. Sch. Bd.*, 121 F.3d 576 (11th Cir. 1997) with *Michael M. v. Pemi-Baker Regional Sch. Dist.*, 346 F.3d 247 (1st Cir. 2003). Cf. *In re Arons*, 756 A.2d 867 (Del. 2000) (lay advocate not allowed to represent parent in administrative hearing except in sideline role as adviser) with *Connors v. Mills*, 34 F. Supp. 2d 795 (N.D.N.Y. 1998) (lay advocate allowed to represent the parent). Cf. *Arons v. New Jersey St. Bd. of Educ.*, 842 F.2d 58 (3d Cir. 1988) (lay advocate representation allowed but no recovery for legal fees).

↳Review

1. What are the common forms of remedies that courts order for IDEA violations?

   These are declaratory relief, injunctions, reimbursement of educational costs at private schools, and compensatory education.

2. Under what circumstances are monetary damages most likely to be awarded?

   They are most likely when IDEA violations are intentional, such as when a school district declines to implement a court ruling and institutes a policy or practice that violates IDEA.

3. What remedies can the SEA impose for IDEA violations?

   It can order compensatory education and monetary reimbursement; it is also authorized to take "other corrective action." Ultimately, it can withhold IDEA funds from a noncomplying LEA.

4. When can attorneys' fees be awarded to parents?

   This can happen when the parents are ultimately the prevailing party.

⚡References

Arlington Central Sch. Dist. Bd. of Educ. v. Murphy, 548 U.S. 291 (2006).

Blackman v. Dist. of Columbia, 1999 U.S. Dist. LEXIS 2104 (D.D.C. 1999).

Bd. of Educ. of Cnty. of Cabell v. Dienelt, 843 F.2d 813 (4th Cir. 1988).

Buckhannon Bd. and Care Home v. West Va. Dep't of Health and Human Resources, 532 U.S. 598 (2001).

Burlington Sch. Comm. v. Mass. Dep't of Educ., 471 U.S. 359 (1985).

Duane B. v. Chester-Upland Sch. Dist, 1994 U.S. Dist. LEXIS 18755 (E.D. Pa. 1994).

Fafard, M. B., Hanlon, R. E., & Bryson, E. A. (1986). *Jose P. v. Ambach*: Progress toward compliance, *Exceptional Children, 52*, 313–319.

Florence Cnty. Sch. Dist. v. Carter, 510 U.S. 7 (1993).

Franklin v. Gwinnett Cnty. Pub. Schs., 503 U.S. 60 (1992).

Harlow v. Fitzgerald, 457 U.S. 800 (1982).

Individuals with Disabilities Education Improvement Act, 20 U.S.C. § 1400 *et seq*. (2006).

Individuals with Disabilities Education Improvement Act Regulations, 34 C.F. R. § 300.1 *et seq*. (2006).

Johnson v. Lancaster-Lebanon Inter. Unit 13, 757 F. Supp. 606 (E.D. Pa.1991).

Jose v. Ambach, 669 F.2d 865 (2d Cir. 1982).

Lascari v. Bd. of Educ., 560 A.2d 1180 (N.J. 1989).

Monell v. Dep't of Soc. Serv., 436 U.S. 658 (1978).

Ostby v. Oxnard Union High, 209 F. Supp. 2d 1035 (C.D. Cal. 2002).

P. C. v. McLaughlin, 913 F.2d 1033 (2d Cir. 1990).

Rancho Palos Verdes v. Abrams, 544 U.S. 113 (2005).

Rapid City Sch. Dist. v. Vahle, 922 F.2d 476 (8th Cir. 1990).

Reusch v. Fountain, 872 F. Supp. 1421 (D. Md. 1994).

S-1 v. No. Carolina St. Bd. of Educ. 21 F.3d 49 (4th Cir. 1994).

Straube v. Florida Union Free Sch. Dist., 801 F. Supp. 1164 (S.D.N.Y. 1992).

Weissburg v. Lancaster Sch. Dist, 591 F.3d 1255 (9th Cir. 2010).

Winkelman v. Parma City Sch. Dist., 550 U.S. 516 (2007).

⇉Selected Supplementary Resources

Clark, S. G. (2002). Administrative Remedy under IDEA: Must it be exhausting? *Education Law Reporter, 163,* 1–15.

Dagley, D. L. (1995). Enforcing compliance with IDEA: Dispute resolution and appropriate relief. *Preventing School Failure, 39,* 27–32.

Lin, T. (2003). Recovering attorney's fees under the Individuals With Disabilities [Education] Act. *Education Law Reporter, 180,* 1–24.

Osborne, A. G., Jr. & Russo, C. J. (2006). The Supreme Court rejects parental reimbursement for expert witness fees under IDEA: *Arlington Central School Dist. Bd. of Educ. v. Murphy. Education Law Reporter, 213,* 333-348.

Seven, K. H., & Zirkel, P. A. (2002). *In the Matter of Arons*: Construction of the IDEA's lay advocate provision too narrow? *Georgetown Journal of Poverty Law and Policy, 9,* 193–226.

Wenkart, R. D. (2004). The award of section 1983 damages under the IDEA. *Education Law Reporter, 183,* 313-335.

Zirkel, P. A.(2006). Compensatory education under the IDEA: The Third Circuit's partially misleading position. *Penn State Law Review, 110,* 879-902.

Part III

Chapter 16

Disability Evaluation Under Section 504

Chapter Outline

Overview

School-age children with disabilities, as defined under Section 504, are protected from discrimination in schools that are recipients of federal funds. This includes all public schools and some private schools. It is important for educators to realize that primary responsibility for nondiscrimination rests with general education, not special education. The entire school is responsible for ensuring that all children with disabilities, as defined by Section 504, are provided an equal opportunity to learn.

The definition of disability under Section 504 requires that individuals have a physical or mental impairment that substantially limits a major life activity, have a record of such an impairment, or be regarded as having such an impairment. IDEA students are covered under Section 504, but because the IDEA evaluation requirements for eligibility are more stringent than the Section 504 requirements, those students receive IDEA evaluations. The evaluation requirements in this chapter basically apply to "stand-alone" students with disabilities under Section 504, namely, those who are not suspected of IDEA disabilities. The primary difference between IDEA students and Section 504 stand-alone students is that the former require special education as a result of their disability while the latter tend instead to require only modifications or accommodations to general education or extracurricular activities in order to have an opportunity to learn and participate that is comparable to the opportunity provided to general education students.

Advance Procedures: Notice and Consent

Section 504 regulations require school districts to "take appropriate steps to notify individuals with disabilities and their parents or guardians" of the school district's duty not to discriminate, including the duty to evaluate a student for eligibility under Section 504 (34 C.F.R. § 104.32(b) (2009)). The specific means are left up to each school district. Many school districts post multiple notices within the school building; others also send notices home to all enrolled students or provide notice in the student-parent handbook. It is helpful to include information in the notice about evaluation and grievance procedures, and about whom to contact for further information. The school must give specific, individual notice to the parent of a child whom school personnel want to evaluate under Section 504. Whether to notify the parent verbally or in writing is left to the discretion of each local school district (34 C.F.R. § 104.36 (2009)).

ED's Section 504 regulations do not mention parental consent, in contrast to IDEA evaluation requirements. The Office for Civil Rights (OCR), however, has taken the position that consent is necessary before evaluating a student for eligibility and services under Section 504 (*Letter to Zirkel*, 1995). Because some evaluations can be quite informal and are without implications for a change of status (that is, from a general to a special education student), the need to seek consent is not as serious a due process issue as it is under IDEA. Perhaps that is why consent is not mentioned explicitly in the regulations. Nonetheless, as OCR has determined, obtaining parental consent is always good policy.

A district may refuse a parental request to evaluate a student for eligibility under Section 504, but it should have a reasonable basis for believing that the student will not be eligible. If it does decline to evaluate, it must provide the parent with notice of the parent's right to challenge the refusal (*OCR Memorandum*, 1993).

Evaluation Procedures in the Section 504 Regulations

Section 504 regulations specify that a school district must evaluate any person believed to need special education or related services because of a Section 504 disability "before taking any action with respect to the initial placement of the person in a regular or special education program" (34 C.F.R. § 104.35 (2009)). The use of the word *or* emphasizes that some students with Section 504 disabilities will not need special education; nonetheless, those students must still be evaluated prior to "any action" concerning initial placement in a regular education program. This language is ambiguous; if all that is sought is a related aid or service in a general education setting, one would assume that a Section 504 evaluation could occur simultaneously with, or subsequent to, placement in a general education program. Presumably, all that is meant is that evaluation is required prior to identifying and serving a student as a Section 504 student, regardless of the student's placement.

The regulations are cryptic and leave many details to local school districts. Who should perform the evaluation—a team or an individual—is not specified. The regulations mandate only that the school district establish standards and procedures to ensure that (a) tests are valid for the purpose for which they are used, and are administered by trained personnel in conformity with the test instructions, (b) measures of educational need and not just IQ are obtained, and (c) tests measure what they purport to measure and not an individual's impaired sensory, manual, or speaking skills (unless those skills are intentionally being measured) (34 C.F.R. § 104.35(b) (2009)).

In these respects, the Section 504 requirements and IDEA regulations are comparable (see chapter 6). Unlike IDEA, however, the Section 504 requirements do not require academic, functional, and developmental information; parental input into the evaluation process; or assessment in all areas related to the suspected disability. Perhaps these omissions reflect that, for a student who is believed to need only related aids or services in general education classrooms or activities, a less formal and less comprehensive evaluation of the student's individual needs will suffice to ensure nondiscriminatory programming that is as adequate as that provided to students without disabilities. Of course, as mentioned, if a student is suspected of being IDEA-eligible, then the IDEA evaluation process will supersede that of Section 504. Unlike IDEA, no timeline is established within which a Section 504 evaluation must be completed.†

> † When no timeline is established, the courts and OCR generally require that evaluations be completed within a "reasonable" period of time. See, e.g. *Dade County (FL) School District*, 20 IDELR 267 (OCR 1993) (seven-month delay denied FAPE).

A Section 504 student must be re-evaluated prior to any subsequent "significant change in placement" (34 C.F.R. § 104.35(a) (2009)). This requirement does not appear in the IDEA evaluation provisions, but because IDEA students are covered under Section 504, this requirement applies to them, too. As with IDEA, placement teams must ensure that placements allow education in general education settings to the maximum extent appropriate. Finally, for Section 504 students who receive special education and related services, provision must be made for "periodic" re-evaluation, presumably to determine their continuing need for special education (34 C.F.R. § 104.35(d) (2009)). (IDEA re-evaluation requirements are far more explicit.) Actual placement decisions are to be made by a knowledgeable group of persons and not by a single individual (34 C.F.R. § 104.35(c) (2009)). Because a team must make the decision about placement, most LEAs involve more than one person in the evaluation.

Judicial Rulings and OCR Findings

Litigation with respect to Section 504 evaluations of public school students remains relatively sparse. One federal court decision faults school officials for failing to re-evaluate two students with hearing impairments prior to recommending a significant change in placement from a residential school for the deaf to a public day school setting (*Brimmer v. Traverse City Area Public School*, 1994). Two other public school cases, respectively, have recognized the ability to attend school and the ability to control one's behavior as major life activities that could produce eligibility for Section 504 services.[1]

An alternative to litigation is to file a complaint with OCR, and there are numerous Letters of Findings (LoFs) addressing the failure to evaluate potential Section 504 students. Most of these letters concern students with ADD/ADHD[2], who have sought classroom accommodations under Section 504 after being found ineligible for special education as IDEA students.† Other OCR letters have addressed the need to evaluate students with Tourette syndrome, juvenile diabetes, juvenile rheumatoid arthritis, Crohn's disease, broken limbs, allergies, encopresis (medical disorder resulting in decreased ability to control the bowels), and even obesity when it substantially impairs a major life activity or is perceived by others as doing so.[3]

> † Sometimes, when an evaluation team determines that a student with a physical or mental impairment is not eligible under IDEA, the team automatically writes a Section 504 plan for the student. Instead they should perform a Section 504 evaluation to determine whether the impairment really produces a substantial limitation in a major life activity. For instance, some students with ADD, some kinds of motor impairments, and some health impairments may not need any school accommodations. See, e.g., *Groves County (KY) Schools*, 42 IDELR 237, (OCR 2004), finding that a student with bronchial asthma had a few physical education limitations, but not a Section 504 disability.

Potential Evaluation Trigger Points

The following situations are among those that ought to trigger consideration of a Section 504 evaluation, assuming there is no reason to refer the student for an IDEA evaluation:

- When parents inform school personnel that their child has a physical or mental impairment
- When the school punishes a student for behavior that may be caused by an impairment recognized in the American Psychiatric Association's latest Diagnostic and Statistical Manual but that does not constitute an IDEA disability
- When a child's behavior deteriorates noticeably over time for unknown reasons
- When a student returns to school after a serious illness or injury and needs extra help
- When a student has been evaluated medically as having ADD/ADHD

---

[1] *Weixel v. Bd. of Educ.*, 287 F.3d 138, 147 (2d Cir. 2002); *T. J. W. v. Dothan City Bd. of Educ.*, 26 IDELR 999 (M.D. Ala. 1997) See also *Bartlett v. New York State Bd. of Law Examiners*, 226 F.3d 69 (2d Cir. 2000) (challenging lack of accommodations to the New York State Bar exam; court ruled that reading was a major life activity.).

[2] See, e.g., *Farmington (MI) Pub. Schools*, 17 EHLR 872 (OCR 1991); *Columbia Cnty. (GA) Sch. Dist.*, 17 EHLR 586 (OCR 1991); *Fairfield-Suisin (CA) Unified Sch. Dist.*, 14 EHLR 353:205 (OCR 1989); *Rialto (CA) Unified Sch. Dist.*, 14 EHLR 353:201 (OCR 1989); *Cocke Cnty. (TN) Sch. Dist.*, 14 EHLR 353:169 (OCR 1988); *Knox Cnty. (KY) Sch. Dist.*, 14 EHLR 353:159 (OCR 1988).

[3] See, e.g., *Miller Cnty. (GA) Sch. Dist.*, 56 IDELR 53 (OCR Region VI, 2010) (Tourette syndrome and obsessive compulsive disorder); *Cleburne Cnty. (AL) Sch. Dist.*, 55 IDELR 110 (OCR IV, 2010) (Crohn's disease); *Great Valley (PA) Sch. Dist.*, 16 EHLR 101 (OCR 1989) (encopresis); Bement (IL)

- When a student has been referred or evaluated for an IDEA disability but is found not to qualify under IDEA or the parent does not consent to IDEA services
- When a child has a chronic health condition or sensory impairment that may require accommodations
- When alcohol abuse is suspected and learning is substantially affected
- When school personnel consider a child to be "at risk" of failing, of being held back a grade, or of dropping out, but don't know the reason

At these times, it is wise to review the available information and consider whether an evaluation is needed to determine if a Section 504 disability is present.

A Tourette Syndrome Hypothetical

Tommy was a sixth-grader with undiagnosed Tourette syndrome. The teacher noticed that Tommy had some unusual facial tics and grimaces. She also was bothered by his sudden outbursts of swearing in the classroom. Her ordinary instincts were to discipline Tommy for uncivil language in the classroom, but she knew something about the symptoms of Tourette syndrome and realized that Tommy's actions might be totally involuntary. She referred Tommy for a Section 504 evaluation, which required the expertise of the school district's consulting physician. The evaluation team determined that Tommy had Tourette syndrome and that it was substantially limiting a major life activity—controlling his behavior so as not to disrupt his own learning and that of others, as compared to the ability of average students in his grade to control their behavior. Nonetheless, Tommy's tics and outbursts were not considered intense or frequent enough to qualify him as having an emotional disturbance.

As a result of this determination, Tommy became eligible for modifications to his educational program so that he would not be discriminated against in his general education classroom. He did not need special education. Instead, the team identified possible triggers and determined that he needed to be allowed to leave the classroom when he felt a "spell" coming on. He needed to have his classmates understand and ignore his outbursts. He needed the teacher to make good-faith attempts to calm him when he seemed to be getting anxious about his work.

Without an understanding of Tourette syndrome and Section 504 responsibilities, Tommy's school might have punished him for behavior out of his control, and might also have contributed to a decline of acceptable behavior and a worsening of his interactions with other students.

↳Reminders and Tips

1. Many educators incorrectly believe that disability evaluations pertain only to students who are suspected of needing special education under IDEA. Educators should evaluate students who they suspect may need only related aids and services under the Section 504 definition of disability (34 C.F.R. §§ 104.35(a) and (b) (2009)).

2. Educators have considerable freedom to design their own evaluation procedures for those who are suspected of Section 504 disabilities. Medical records are frequently helpful and can often be used to assess both the impairment and the extent to which it limits a major life activity. Be aware, however, that OCR does not require a medical assessment for ADD/ADHD.† If the school determines that a medical assessment must be performed to determine ADD/ADHD in individual cases, then the assessment must be at no cost to the parents (*Letter to Williams*, 1994; *Letter to Veir* (1993).

    † Medical diagnosis is necessary, however, for the school to have any responsibility to administer prescription drugs to reduce the effects of ADD/ADHD or other health conditions.

3. A medical diagnosis of an impairment does not relieve educators of making an independent determination of whether the impairment substantially limits a major life activity. The medical diagnosis alone does not provide sufficient information to determine the child's educational needs. This is especially true for students with ADD/ADHD, which does not impair major life activities such as walking, talking, breathing, seeing, and hearing, and which may or may not substantially impair learning. In considering whether a disability substantially impairs learning, the student's performance should be compared with the average performance of general education students of the same age or grade.

4. Under the ADA amendments of 2008, corrective devices (excluding eye glasses and contact lenses) or medications to mitigate a disability do not negate the presence of a disability. For example, a student on ritalin or another prescribed drug for ADD/ADHD should be evaluated without consideration of the effect that the medication has on his or her attention span. Also, be aware that although the medication may help focus attention, it may not improve a student's organizational skills. Each of the child's educational needs should be evaluated and addressed.

5. During state or districtwide assessments, school personnel must remember that a student with a Section 504 disability may need testing accommodations in order to demonstrate what he or she knows. For instance, a student may need to type rather than handwrite answers, receive extended testing time, or be given large-print materials. As long as the validity of the test instrument itself is not compromised, needed accommodations must be provided. This is an increasingly important issue for educators and has been discussed more fully in chapter 6.

↳Review

1. Who determines eligibility under Section 504, and who should be evaluated?

   Unspecified school personnel determine eligibility and must evaluate all students suspected of meeting the disability definition.

2. How are the Section 504 evaluation requirements similar to those of IDEA?

   Both require that (a) assessments or tests be valid for the purpose used and be administered by trained personnel in accordance with instructions provided by the test producer; (b) assessments or tests measure what they purport to measure and not the child's impaired sensory, manual, or speaking skills (unless those are factors the test purports to measure); and (c) assessments or tests measure specific areas of educational need and not merely a single general intelligence quotient.

3. In what ways and why are the Section 504 evaluation requirements more limited than those of IDEA?

   Section 504 does not require (a) functional, academic, and developmental information, including information provided by the parent; or (b) assessment in all areas of suspected disability. Also, IDEA (a) provides more detail about the nature of the technically sound assessment tools that must be used; (b) addresses ways to avoid racial, cultural, and language-based discrimination; (c) encourages classroom-based assessments and teacher observations; (d) specifies additional requirements for evaluation of a learning disability, and (e) specifies additional re-evaluation requirements and requirements for termination from eligibility. In short, IDEA requirements are far more extensive.

   Section 504 students whose needs are for nondiscrimination in regular classrooms, appropriate regular classroom accommodations, and equal opportunity to participate and learn in regular education settings generally need less comprehensive evaluations than IDEA students, who also require multiple special education services.

4. What is the role of medical assessments in ADD/ADHD determinations under Section 504?

   Medical assessments can be helpful and, where available, should be reviewed along with the necessary educational data. If unavailable, and the LEA determines such an assessment to be necessary, then it must pay for the assessment.

5. When must Section 504 students be re-evaluated?

   Re-evaluation is required "periodically" for students receiving special education and for all § 504 students before any significant change in placement.

⚡References

Brimmer v. Traverse City Area Pub. Schs., 872 F. Supp. 447 (W.D. Mich. 1994).

Letter to Veir, 20 IDELR 864 (OCR 1993).

Letter to Williams, 21 IDELR 73 (OSEP 1994).

Letter to Zirkel, 22 IDELR 667 (OCR 1995).

OCR Memorandum, 19 IDELR 876 (OCR 1993).

Section 504 of Rehabilitation Act of 1973, 29 U.S.C. § 794 (2006).

Section 504 ED Regulations, 34 C.F.R. Part 104 (2009).

⇉Selected Supplementary Resources

Holler, R., & Zirkel, P. (2008). Section 504 and public schools: A national survey concerning "Section 504-only" students. *NASSP Bulletin, 92*(1), 19-43.

Norlin, J.W. (2008). *What do I do when . . . The answer book on Section 504* (3d ed.). Horsham, PA: LRP.

OSEP, OCR, & OESE (1991). *Memorandum to chief state school officers: Clarification of policy to address the needs of children with attention deficit disorders within general and/or special education.* Washington, DC: U.S. Department of Education.

Zirkel, P. (2003). Conducting legally defensible Section 504/ADA eligibility determinations. *Education Law Reporter*, 176, 1–11.

Chapter 17

Contagious Diseases and Section 504

Chapter Outline

Overview

HIV/AIDS

Hepatitis B

Privacy Rights

Reminders and Tips

Review

References

Selected Supplementary Resource

Overview

Public health problems have been a concern of the public schools for many decades. Flu epidemics and measles outbreaks continue to create attendance problems for many school districts, and cases of head lice are still frequent in some areas. Now, however, such problems are handled routinely by schools and public health authorities. Exclusion of the infected student is only for the brief time during which the condition is contagious, and quarantine of exposed students is nonexistent in most cases,† although students who have received a waiver from a state's immunization law may be asked to leave school during an outbreak of diseases such as measles or whooping cough (pertussis) until they can show evidence of immunization, or until the outbreak is over.

> † During 2009, pandemic flu resulted in quarantines in some geographic regions experiencing a significant outbreak.

On the other hand, when a disease or condition is not only contagious but is perceived as particularly dangerous to the health or even life of the student and others, school districts may become alarmed and attempt to exclude or isolate affected students on a long-term basis. In these cases, the students can usually qualify as a student with a disability under Section 504. Over the past twenty-five years, a number of court cases have arisen concerning the treatment of students with diseases such as AIDS and hepatitis B. As is traditional in matters of health, courts balance the rights of these students with the health and safety needs of others in the school environment. Students with contagious diseases that can potentially threaten their own lives but who are nonetheless well enough to attend school, or who are asymptomatic disease carriers, have the right to be in school as long as other students and staff do not incur significant health risks as a result. Otherwise, they are being discriminated against on the basis of a Section 504 disability.

HIV/AIDS

In the mid-1980s, in the midst of public alarm over HIV, the virus that causes AIDS, a number of important court cases established that medically unsupported fears of HIV transmission via school contacts would not suffice to exclude children carrying or infected with HIV from regular or special education classrooms. Two federal court cases are instructive. The first, *Ray v. Desoto County School District* (1987), involved three general education students with hemophilia who had become HIV-positive (AIDS carriers), presumably from infected blood transfusions. A federal district court enjoined the school district from excluding the three Ray brothers. The medical evidence indicated that the boys posed no significant risk to other students and were thereby entitled to education in a regular classroom. AIDS was determined to be a disabling condition under Section 504,[1] and the boys were protected by Section 504 from discrimination that was based on fear rather than a genuine likelihood of transmission of the AIDS virus.

The second case, *Martinez v. Hillsborough County School Board* (1988/1989), concerned a young student, Eliana Martinez, with an intellectual disability and AIDS, who was not toilet-trained, who sucked her fingers, and who had episodes of thrush (a mouth disease that can produce blood in the saliva). Claims of violation of both Section 504 and IDEA were involved in the case. In *Martinez*, the

---

[1] In addition to judicial rulings that AIDS is a disability, OCR has stated that asymptomatic HIV and HIV-related conditions are physical impairments that can substantially limit a major life activity because of the effect of the condition on others as well as on the individual. See *OCR Staff Memorandum*, 16 IDELR 712 (OCR 1990).

U.S. Court of Appeals for the Eleventh Circuit determined that, under Section 504, Eliana's AIDS constituted a disability because it was a physical impairment that substantially limited a major life activity. Therefore, she was protected from discrimination based solely on her disability as long as she was "otherwise qualified" to be in school, or in a given activity or program within the school. She was also eligible for special education services under IDEA and to placement in the LRE appropriate for her needs.

The Eleventh Circuit determined that Eliana was otherwise qualified, in spite of her AIDS, to receive special education services in a classroom for children with moderate to severe intellectual disabilities (who were then labelled as "trainable"). The court ruled that the lower court had erred in concluding that Eliana's school could isolate her in a glass cubicle within her special education classroom. According to the appeals court, the lower court had incorrectly based its decision on a "remote theoretical possibility" of the risk of AIDS transmission via tears, saliva, or urine. The correct standard should have been whether her presence posed a significant risk of harm to her associates. The appeals court remanded the case for additional findings under the announced standard. Upon remand, the lower court found that the medical evidence suggested no significant risk of transmission and therefore ordered Eliana placed in the special education classroom with her other classmates. Eliana has since died.

At least half a dozen similar cases across the country have invalidated the exclusion of a student who tests positive for HIV, or who has AIDS or AIDS-Related Complex (ARC)† and is otherwise well enough to attend school.[2] Accumulating medical evidence continues to indicate no documented cases of transmission via contact with saliva, tears, or urine. Contact with someone's infected blood is a concern, but only if the blood enters the other person's bloodstream.

† The term ARC has been rarely used since 2000 because of advances in clinical laboratory studies.

Hepatitis B

In contrast, hepatitis B has been found to be a more contagious disease than AIDS, although the risk of fatality is only approximately 1 percent of those affected. Two federal courts have assessed the potential risks somewhat differently from each other. A federal district court in New York ordered a school to stop isolating students with intellectual disabilities who were hepatitis B carriers, finding that the risk of transmission via saliva was remote, and ruling that isolating carriers with intellectual disabilities was discriminatory when the school did not isolate other hepatitis B carriers (*New York State Association for Retarded Children v. Carey*, 1979). On the other hand, the Eighth Circuit concluded that a blind, intellectually disabled, adult carrier of the hepatitis B virus who demonstrated aggressive and maladaptive behaviors created a significant risk of transmission and subsequent harm in his vocational training program (*Kohl v. Woodhaven Learning Center*, 1989). The Circuit ruled that the lower court's mandated inoculation plan was too limited and exposed the uninoculated staff to unreasonable risk. A third decision in a state court ordered a special education placement in school rather than a homebound program for a student with Down syndrome and hepatitis B, based on the school's ability to mitigate the risk of transmission.[3]

[2] See, e.g., *Doe v. Dolton Elem. Sch. Dist. No. 148*, 694 F. Supp. 440 (N.D. Ill. 1988); *Robertson v. Granite City Community Unit Sch. Dist. No. 9*, 684 F. Supp. 1002 (S.D. Ill. 1988); *Parents of Child, Code No. 870901W v. Coker*, 676 F. Supp. 1072 (E.D. Okla. 1987); *Thomas v. Atascadero Unified Sch. Dist.*, 662 F. Supp. 376 (C.D. Cal. 1986); *District 27 Community Sch. Bd. v. Bd. of Educ. of N.Y.*, 502 N.Y.S. 2d 325 (N.Y. Sup. Ct. 1986).
[3] *Community High Sch. Dist. 155 v. Denz*, 463 N.E.2d 998 (Ill. App. Ct. 1984). See also *Jeffrey S. v. Georgia St. Bd. of Educ.*, 896 F. 2d 507 (11th Cir. 1990) (remanding, for a trial on the merits, the question of the potential harm to students of placing a hepatitis B carrier in a school setting compared to the potential harm of placing the student in a homebound program).

Privacy Rights

School personnel should also be aware of the privacy rights of students with diseases. If a parent discloses a student's medical condition to the school and it becomes part of the student's education record, the federal Family Educational Rights and Privacy Act (FERPA) (2006) requires that schools obtain written parental consent before disclosing the student's disease to persons without legitimate educational interest in the information (see chapter 9). Only in the case of imminent health and safety concerns may the confidentiality requirements be breached. Some states may have laws that go beyond FERPA in restricting access by school employees to a student's school medical records, so readers should familiarize themselves with state and local policies on this matter.

Privacy Issue for AIDs Student

The Montgomery County, Maryland, school district was sued for privacy violations under state law because a substitute teacher revealed that a student was infected with the AIDS virus. Apparently ill-informed about how AIDS is transmitted, the teacher revealed the information to students who were sharing lip balm. The student in question, who was absent from class when the information was revealed, transferred to a different school and sought $100,000 in civil damages. See Right to Privacy. (May 22, 1996) *Education Week, 15*, 4.

↳Reminders and Tips

1. School districts should have adopted the recommendations of the Centers for Disease Control and be routinely training staff members to take "universal precautions" when in contact with the blood of any child, with or without a known infectious disease. Careful hygiene and use of disposable gloves should be universal in the school setting. Also, vaccinations should be required for staff members who are likely to come in contact with hepatitis carriers.

2. As a general rule, school officials are advised to adopt a policy that does not expel anyone just for having contracted a contagious disease or having become a carrier. Instead, using standards established by the U.S. Supreme Court in *Nassau County School Board v. Arline* (1987), districts should conduct an individualized examination of the student's health, including such factors as how the particular disease is transmitted, how long the carrier is infectious, what the potential harm is to third parties, and the probability of transmission and of various degrees of harm. Only when it is determined that the specific student creates a significant health risk (to self or others) that cannot be reduced by individual accommodations should the student be placed on homebound instruction or in another restrictive alternative.†

   † After investigation of a parent's complaint, OCR found no discrimination in the Fairfax County Public Schools' policy that allowed for limited, temporary exclusions of students with HIV or HIV-related conditions. The exclusion was limited to a maximum of 10 days, and the policy recognized the LRE mandate of Section 504 (*Fairfax County (VA) Pub. Schs.*, 19 IDELR 649 (OCR 1992)).

3. School officials should not automatically determine that a student who has a contagious disease is a special education student under IDEA. If the student's health condition does not adversely affect educational performance to the extent that special education is required, the student will not qualify under IDEA as "other health impaired" (*Doe v. Belleville Public School District*, 1987). Instead, the student should be evaluated for a Section 504 stand-alone disability.

4. The same rights of students with contagious diseases apply to school employees. Both ADA and Section 504 require that an employee not be discriminated against on the basis of an illness that constitutes a disability, provided the employee is otherwise qualified. This means that the employee is able to perform the essential functions of the job with or without reasonable accommodations and poses no significant risk of harm to others.†

> † The Ninth Circuit enjoined the administrative reassignment of a classroom teacher with AIDS because there was no evidence that he could not perform the essential functions of his teaching assignment, or that he presented any significant risk of transmission of AIDS to his students (*Chalk v. United States District Court, Central District California*, 840 F.2d 701 (9th Cir. 1988)). This decision was consistent with the Supreme Court's decision in the Arline case that a teacher with inactive tuberculosis (TB) had been discriminated against on the basis of her TB when she was relieved of her teaching duties without evidence that her TB affected her ability to perform or created a significant risk of harm to her students.

⌐Review

1. What legal standard should be used in determining whether a student or employee with a contagious disease who qualifies as having a disability under Section 504 should be separated from contact with other persons in school?

   The standard is whether the person is "otherwise qualified" to receive the service or benefit in question. "Otherwise qualified" includes a determination of whether the person's condition creates a substantial risk of transmission to others. This decision is based on accepted medical judgment.

⚡References

Doe v. Belleville Pub. Sch. Dist., 672 F. Supp. 342 (S.D. Ill. 1987).

Family Educational Rights and Privacy Act, 20 U.S.C. § 1232g (2006).

Kohl v. Woodhaven Learning Ctr., 865 F.2d 930 (8th Cir. 1989).

Martinez v. Hillsborough Cnty. Sch. Bd., 861 F.2d 1502 (11th Cir. 1988), *on remand*, 711 F. Supp. 1066 (M.D. Fla. 1989).

Nassau Cnty. Sch. Bd. v. Arline, 480 U.S. 273 (1987).

New York State Ass'n for Retarded Children v. Carey, 466 F. Supp. 487 (E.D.N.Y. 1979).

Ray v. Desoto Cnty. Sch. Dist., 666 F. Supp. 1524 (M.D. Fla. 1987).

Section 504, Rehabilitation Act of 1973, 29 U.S.C. § 794 (2006).

⇉Selected Supplementary Resource

U.S. Department of Health and Human Services Public Health Service, Centers for Disease Control (1989). Guidelines for prevention of transmission of human immunodeficiency virus and hepatitis B virus to healthcare and public-safety workers. *Morbidity and Mortality Weekly Report*, 38 (S-6). Atlanta, GA: Author.

Chapter 18

Free Appropriate Public Education and Equal Opportunity Under Section 504

Chapter Outline

The Regulatory Definition of Free Appropriate Public Education

Free appropriate public education (FAPE) under Section 504 is not defined by statute but by regulation. "Free" education means that the "educational and related services" are provided without cost to the student with the disability, or to his or her parents, except for fees that are charged to students without disabilities and their parents (34 C.F.R. § 104.33(c) (2009)).

"Appropriate" does not have the same meaning as it does under IDEA. "Appropriate" education under Section 504 is defined as "the provision of *regular* or special education and related aids and services that . . . are designed to meet individual educational needs [of persons with disabilities] as adequately as the needs of [nondisabled] persons are met," and that meet the procedural requirements of Section 504 [emphasis added] (34 C.F.R. § 104.33(b)(1) (2009)). This FAPE standard applies to general education students with disabilities as well as to special education students, and suggests a comparison between what is offered to students with disabilities and students without disabilities—with the intent of providing equivalent educational opportunities for both. This has particular significance for non-IDEA students with disabilities, and for IDEA students in matters not covered by their IEPs. According to at least one circuit court case, the definitional difference may also have significance for the availability of money damages under Section 504 when they are unavailable under IDEA (*Mark H. ex rel. Michelle H. v. Lemahieu* (2008). (See chapter 20 under Monetary Damages.)

The term "special education" is not defined by Section 504 or its regulations. Often, OCR rulings borrow the IDEA definition of "special education"—namely, specially designed instruction to meet the unique needs of the student with the disability. Section 504 regulations state that an IEP developed in accordance with IDEA is one way to meet the Section 504 definition of appropriate education (34 C.F.R. § 104.33(b)(2) (2009)). Commentators advise against the development of IEPs for non-IDEA students, however, because it creates confusion in the minds of parents and educators as to whether the student is an IDEA student or a Section 504 *stand-alone* student (one without IDEA coverage). Instead, schools are better advised to develop Section 504 plans, also frequently referred to as Individual Accommodation Plans (or something similar) for stand-alone students.

Comparing Recent IEP Requirements Under IDEA and Related Aids Under Section 504

The requirements for delivery of related aids and services under Section 504 and program modifications in regular classrooms under IDEA may be confusing. Initially, the reach of FAPE under Section 504 was clearly broader than that of FAPE under IDEA because the former extended to nondiscrimination and comparable program quality with respect to regular classroom instruction, while IDEA was limited to special education, conceived initially as separate from regular classroom instruction. Since IDEA '97, however, the IEP requirements in IDEA have overlapped Section 504 nondiscrimination requirements in regular classrooms. The IEP must now include program modifications, support for school staff, and supplementary aids and services to facilitate inclusion in general education instructional and extracurricular settings. Conjoining IDEA's additional IEP requirements with the related aids and services requirements of Section 504, however, should not be seen as allowing the union of IDEA and Section 504 when a stand-alone student is claiming that FAPE under Section 504 has been denied.

It is interesting that the Section 504 regulatory definition of FAPE does not include the term "reasonable accommodations," a phrase that is used in the context of employment discrimination cases brought under Section 504 and ADA. Courts, however, sometimes introduce the term in special education cases,† which adds confusion to the situation. It seems to be used more or less synonymously with the phrase "related aids and services." Nonetheless, OCR, which is responsible for enforcement of Section 504, has reminded school officials that FAPE under Section 504 requires that individual needs be met as adequately as those of nondisabled students are met, which is not necessarily the same thing as simply providing reasonable accommodations (*Letter to Zirkel*, 1993). Although Section 504 does not require extensive affirmative remedies (unlike IDEA's IEP requirements), and although a simple nondiscrimination standard or, in effect, a comparability standard may often suffice, the implication of the OCR position seems to be that in some cases, more than "reasonable accommodations" may be required. One possibility is the provision of special education (individually designed instruction) for non-IDEA students, in which case it would not be federally subsidized by IDEA funds. In fact, OCR has made this point explicitly although it is difficult to think of cases when a Section 504 student would need special education without being able to qualify under IDEA. Perhaps a student with nontraumatic brain injury or Asperger syndrome (if not covered by a school district under the category of autism) might be an example of such a student.

> † The court in *Martinez v. Hillsborough County School Board*, 861 F.2d 1502 (11th Cir. 1988) commented on the need for "reasonable accommodations" to reduce the risk of transmission of AIDS. In *Oberti v. Board of Education*, 801 F. Supp. 1392 (D.N.J. 1992), the court found a failure to provide "reasonable accommodations" to enable a young student with Down syndrome to benefit from inclusive education. More recently, the court in *Molly L. v. Lower Merion School District*, 194 F. Supp. 2d 422 (E.D. Pa. 2002), discussed the usefulness of the term "reasonable accommodations" in a FAPE stand-alone case. Compare *Lyons v. Smith*, 829 F. Supp. 414 (D. D.C. 1993), in which the court determined that Section 504 stand-alone students may be entitled to "substantial accommodations," but only to the extent necessary to prevent discrimination. Note that the *Lyons* decision does not use the term "reasonable accommodations."

It is important to recognize that the Section 504 FAPE requirement is triggered only by the first prong of the definition of disability (*OCR Staff Memorandum*, 1992). Under the second and third prongs, the regulations require only that students with past or perceived disabilities not be discriminated against, not that they receive special services or aids to address the disability. The distinction makes sense because, under Section 504, one is not obligated to provide program adaptations to someone who, in fact, does not have a disability.

The Meaning of Related Aids and Services

No definition of "related aids and services" appears in the Section 504 regulations. The term appears only as part of the Section 504 definition of FAPE. OCR does not utilize the IDEA definition of related services because, under IDEA, related services can only accompany special education and cannot be provided independently. This is clearly not what is meant by related aids and services under Section 504. This is confirmed by the fact that evaluation is required prior to placement of a student who is believed to need either special education or related services (34 C.F.R. § 104.35(a) (2009)). Use of the word *or* indicates that related services can be severed from special education under Section 504.

OCR rulings variously describe the meaning of "related" aids and services as aids and services necessary (a) to meet individual needs as adequately as the needs of the nondisabled are met, or (b) for the student to benefit from either regular or special education in a way that provides equal opportunity. When OCR invokes the first description, it is using the Section 504 FAPE definition. When it invokes the second description, it is using the more general Section 504 regulation prohibiting discrimination that denies an "aid, benefit, or service" to an otherwise qualified individual with a disability (34 C.F.R. § 104.4(b)(1) (2009)). Either explanation produces virtually the same result.

Regular Classroom Program Adaptations

Many kinds of program adaptations to meet a student's educational needs can be made without significantly interfering with a general educator's curriculum or orderly approach to instruction. Thousands of teachers have always tried to accommodate individual student needs, and others are learning that program adaptations which help a child with a disability often help others in the class as well. Among the kinds of classroom program modifications currently in use with Section 504 students are the following:

1. Changing the seating arrangements to accommodate a student with a visual or hearing impairment, or a child with ADD/ADHD. Seating a child in the front of the room can make a positive difference, as can allowing an ADD/ADHD student to work for periods of time at a stand-up desk or in a private study carrel. Similarly, arranging seats in a circle instead of rows can be a significant help to a student with a hearing impairment, as can positioning the teacher so that the sun's glare is not behind the teacher.

2. Using a multisensory approach to teacher instructions so that instructions are given both orally (auditorily) and in writing (visually).

3. Using cooperative learning and peer tutoring strategies so that students with disabilities (and other students) can learn from each other and receive structured individual attention from someone in addition to the teacher.

4. Reducing the length or difficulty level of homework assignments but still requiring mastery of the material before a child moves on.

5. Allowing extra time in which to complete homework assignments.

6. Permitting a child with a visual-motor impairment to copy work from his or her desk instead of from the blackboard or classroom walls.

7. Allowing a child who has trouble with mathematical abstractions to use his or her fingers in doing math calculations if this works for the child.

8. Allowing a child with a math disability to use a calculator during math tests if the ability to produce the correct answer is what is being tested and not, say, the ability to demonstrate the correct steps in generating the answer, or to demonstrate memorization of the multiplication tables.

9. Teaching a child with spatial problems how to find his or her locker, the cafeteria, the gym, and so on, rather than assuming all children can teach themselves how to find their way around the school building.

10. Allowing an extra rest period for a student with an acute or chronic health impairment that limits vitality and alertness.

11. Teaching the other children when and how to ignore the involuntary outbursts of children with Tourette syndrome.

12. Providing advance organizers before introducing a new lesson.

13. Sending home weekly progress reports to parents so they can monitor and reward their child's improvement at school.

14. Allowing a student with a writing disability to have a note taker and to submit test answers through a tape recorder or a computer if handwriting is not what is being measured by the test.

If, to be effective, classroom adaptations require the use of different materials, a different instructional method, or the introduction of new behavioral management techniques, the general educator should be able to call on the special educator or the school psychologist for collaboration in these efforts. The possibilities are multiple, frequently limited only by the creativity of the staff rather than by budgetary shortages. Although adaptations take time to incorporate, they frequently save time in the long run.

When teachers balk at requests for program modifications, it is usually in the belief that all students should be measured according to the same standards, and that students with disabilities must learn this sooner or later. Although it is true that the essential content should be mastered by all children in the general classroom and expectations should remain high, it is also true that children (not to mention adults) have multiple ways of learning and of showing what they have learned. Refusal to acknowledge this fact subjects some children to school failure who should never have to fail.

OCR Approach to Enforcement

As school districts are well aware, OCR regional offices across the country investigate allegations of discrimination and issue findings, sometimes inviting specific remedial action. Usually, OCR limits its investigation to a determination of whether the agency has complied with the procedural requirements of Section 504 and is not excluding students with disabilities or evidencing discriminatory practices (34 C.F.R. app. A, Analysis of Final Regulations, Subpart D (1984)). In other words, except in extraordinary circumstances, OCR does not attempt to second-guess school district decisions about eligibility or placement, as long as they are procedurally compliant. In cases of sustained, deliberate noncompliance with its findings, however, OCR will refer the situation to the Justice Department, which will initiate a lawsuit to terminate all federal funding. Although most investigations result in findings in favor of school district policies or practices, examples of the types of services that OCR has found not to be comparable to those provided to children without disabilities are numerous and will be described next.

Academic Standards and Test Accommodations

OCR has frequently determined that failure by LEAs to consider whether or how to make accommodations to standardized tests is a Section 504 violation. The dilemma for educators becomes how to adapt academic assessments without destroying their validity or impairing the inferences to be drawn from them. This requires a clear understanding of the purposes of the test and whether certain accommodations can still allow those purposes to be realized. (See the High-Stakes Testing section of chapter 6.)

OCR has repeatedly ruled that students with learning disabilities are entitled to individual consideration in determining whether instructional evaluation standards and test-taking procedures require accommodations to meet the students' needs.†

> † In *Hawaii Department of Education*, 17 EHLR 360 (OCR 1990), failure to consider whether a student with a learning disability was entitled to a reader to administer portions of the graduation exam violated Section 504; the portions in question were not intended to measure reading competency. In *Fordland (MO) R-III School District*, 14 EHLR 353:127 (OCR 1988), refusal to allow students with disabilities an opportunity to be on the honor roll violated Section 504. In *Lowell (MI) Area School District*, EHLR 352:574 (OCR 1987), denial of credit to students whose absenteeism was related to their disability violated Section 504.

Blanket denials of all requests for accommodations without an individual assessment are an invitation to trouble. Furthermore, OCR has ruled that a student may not be evaluated against a standard that is impossible to attain because of clear limitations related to a disability—for instance, a handwriting grade for a student whose cerebral palsy precludes the ability to write (*Harrison County (WV) Sch. Dist*, 1988). On the other hand, OCR has indicated that procedures such as weighted or coded grading systems that reflect actual differences in difficulty of courses or grading standards are not discriminatory per se.[1]

Transportation

OCR has made many findings about transportation deficiencies. Certain widespread problems in providing comparably for the needs of Section 504 students with disabilities were addressed in a 1992 letter to public school administrators from then OCR Director Michael Williams. The provision of nondiscriminatory transportation services was singled out as a special challenge. The letter included the following statement:

> Transportation schedules must not result in [Section 504] students spending appreciably more time on buses than nonhandicapped students, and transportation schedules must be designed to ensure arrival and departure times that do not reduce the length of the school day for students with handicaps for whom a shorter school day has not been prescribed on an individual basis (*Williams' Letter to Colleagues*, 1992).

---

[1] *Metropolitan (TN) Pub. Sch. Dist.*, 18 IDELR 971 (OCR 1991); *Letter to Ickes*, 14 EHLR 305:50 (OCR 1989). See also *Pueblo (CO) City Sch. Dist. No. 60*, 17 EHLR 535 (OCR 1990) (holding that excluding students from competing for honors at graduation when their IEPs and course work did not satisfy graduation requirements did not violate Section 504).

The Williams letter also mentioned three specific incidents illustrating discriminatory transportation services: (a) the denial of bus transportation to students with disabilities during bad weather, (b) a five-month lack of bus service to students with mobility impairments, during which time an accessible bus was not available, and (c) a discriminatory 4¾-hour bus trip to school for students with disabilities.

One can see that Section 504 is the vehicle (no pun intended) for ensuring that the length of bus rides for special education students (and sometimes a concomitant shortening of the school day) is not discriminatory.[2] The LEA should be prepared to demonstrate how it has attempted to minimize transportation problems, how it has provided for the transportation of its special education students as adequately as it has provided for its students without disabilities who require busing, and how any shortening of a school day continues to meet the individualized needs of the students affected.

If, in order to meet the Section 504 FAPE requirements, transportation is required to a program not operated by a school district, then the district must ensure "that adequate transportation to and from the program is provided at no greater cost than would be incurred by the person, or his or her parents or guardian, if the person were placed in the program operated by the recipient" (34 C.F.R. § 104.33(c)(2) (2009)).

Administration of Medication

Administration of medication is considered a related service under Section 504 when it is necessary to enable a student to benefit from the education program. This can occur in a number of circumstances—for instance, when failure to administer prescribed medications results in physical illness at school due to asthma or other allergies, or when it results in high levels of distractibility, out-of-seat misbehavior, and impulsivity for ADD/ADHD students.[3] Under these circumstances, the school district must see that medication is administered at school if prescribed by a physician and requested by the parent. The increasing need to administer prescription drugs at school has necessitated the adoption of formal, systematized procedures in school districts across the country.

Examples of Other Related Aids and Services

Among other kinds of related aids and services that have been seen as necessary under Section 504 in specific situations are special dietary accommodations at school for students with diabetes,[4] use of a service dog for a student with cerebral palsy (*Sullivan v. Vallejo City Unified Sch. Dist*, 1990), provision of FM wireless hearing sets for classroom teachers and their students with hearing impairments; provision of large-print books for students with certain kinds of visual impairments, and provision of in-class word processors for students with writing problems. The latter three are also examples of assistive technology devices.

[2] See, e.g., *Santa Rosa Cnty. (FL) Sch. Dist.*, 18 IDELR 153 (OCR 1991); *Lincoln Cnty. (NC) Sch. Dist.*, 17 EHLR 1052 (OCR 1991); *Lafayette (IN) Sch. Corp.*, 16 EHLR 649 (OCR 1990); *Caddo Parish (LA) Sch. Sys.*, 16 EHLR 326 (OCR 1990); *Stafford Cnty. (VA) Pub. Sch.*, 16 EHLR 896 (OCR 1990).
[3] See, e.g., *San Ramon Valley (CA) Unified Sch. Dist.*, 18 IDELR 465 (OCR 1991) (administering allergy medication); *Pearl (MS) Pub. Sch. Dist.*, 17 EHLR 1004 (OCR 1990) (administering ritalin for ADHD); *Berlin Brothersvalley (PA) Sch. Dist.*, 14 EHLR 353:124 (OCR 1988) (same).
[4] See, e.g., *Digest of Response to Veir*, 20 IDELR 864 (OCR 1993) (stating that schools providing food to regular education students must provide special food to students with special dietary needs, the food to be determined on a case-by-case basis).

Administering Ritalin at School: An Interesting Twist

In *Davis v. Francis Howell School District*, 138 F. 3d 754 (8th Cir. 1998), a school nurse refused to administer a prescribed dosage of ritalin to a student with ADHD. The student's treating physician had prescribed 360 mg of the drug, and a second doctor had concurred that the dosage was required to control the boy's ADHD symptoms. The school nurse was concerned because the dosage far exceeded the recommended maximum of 60 mg listed in the *Physicians' Desk Reference* (PDR). The nurse coordinator and consulting psychologist agreed with her, and she notified the parents that she would not administer the medication. The assistant superintendent supported her position but offered to let the parents (or their designee) come to school and administer the medication.

The parents' lawsuit alleged that the nurse's refusal to administer the prescribed dosage of ritalin violated Section 504 and Title II of the ADA. The lower court found no evidence of discrimination, because requests by students without disabilities for administration of drugs exceeding the PDR standards were also denied, and because requests by students with disabilities for administration of drugs within PDR standards were honored. The court also ruled that the school had offered a reasonable accommodation to the student by allowing the parents to administer the drug.

On appeal, the U.S. Court of Appeals for the Eighth Circuit upheld the lower court opinion that the PDR was a nondiscriminatory basis for the nurse's decision. If a reasonable accommodation was required (and the court declined to make such a determination), the parents had been offered one. The Eighth Circuit concluded that it would be an administrative and financial burden for the school district to have to determine the safety of usage and likelihood of future liability when a prescription exceeded PDR standards.

A similar ruling was issued a year earlier in *DeBord v. Board of Education of the Ferguson-Florissant School District*, 126 F.3d 1102 (8th Cir. 1997).

A Special Case of Discrimination?

Do Not Resuscitate (DNR) Orders

Some children with disabilities who are being educated at school have such severe life-threatening conditions that their parents have requested schools to honor medical DNR orders. This has caused extreme concern among school officials, who have argued that they are not medical personnel and should not be asked to behave as if they were. Whether a district chooses to honor a DNR order or not, it is of utmost importance to communicate effectively with the family and let the family know in advance what protocols will be followed in the event that the child stops breathing at school.

A particularly well-known case in Lewiston, Maine, resulted in a caution from OCR that honoring the requested DNR order would be viewed by OCR as discrimination on the basis of disability. In response to the controversy, the school district carefully drafted a policy that made no distinction between students with disabilities and students without disabilities, and that allowed school-based multidisciplinary teams to develop individually designed medical resuscitation plans in appropriate circumstances. OCR determined that this policy did not violate Section 504 or Title II of the ADA. The individual medical resuscitation plan for the particular student was also upheld. See *Lewiston (ME) Public School*, 21 IDELR 83 (OCR 1994). More information about the health care needs of medically fragile students is found in chapter 11.

Nonacademic Services

Section 504 requires that students with disabilities be provided with an equal opportunity to participate in nonacademic services and extracurricular activities (34 C.F.R. § 104.37 (2009)). Such an opportunity encourages social interaction between students with disabilities and students without disabilities, and ensures that students with disabilities are not denied access to various activities or services offered regularly to other students. Among the possible services specified in the regulations are counseling services, physical recreational athletics, transportation, health services, recreational activities, special interest groups or clubs sponsored by the school, referrals to appropriate outside agencies, and student employment opportunities. Part of the reason for specifying such services is to remind educators to see the whole child and not to set expectations that are too low, for instance, by neglecting to provide vocational counseling and employment referrals for students with disabilities.†

> † The IDEA regulations contain similar language at 34 C.F.R. § 300.107 (2009). The only difference is that IDEA refers simply to "athletics" rather than to physical recreational athletics.

Cases challenging the provision of equal opportunity in nonacademic services have been brought mostly under Section 504 rather than IDEA, because IDEA merely echoes Section 504 unless nonacademic services are specifically included in an IEP. The legal standard does not require equal participation in all nonacademic activities but rather an equal opportunity to participate in such activities.

Sports Issues in the Courts

The most common nonacademic issue is competitive athletic eligibility. Although separate physical education and athletic activities may be created under specified conditions, and may serve a valuable purpose for some students with disabilities, Section 504 regulations specify that no qualified student with a disability can be denied the opportunity to compete for athletic teams or, more broadly, the opportunity to participate in physical education and athletic activities that are not separate or different. The regulations make clear that student athletic ability cannot be prejudged on the basis of a disability (34 C.F.R. § 104.37(d) (2009)).

Many disputes over athletic participation have ended up in court. Courts generally rule in favor of allowing the participation of qualified student athletes with a disability such as a visual impairment, hearing impairment, or loss of a limb or organ (e.g., a kidney) if medical opinion supports their participation.[5] Of course, it is important that the athletes understand the risks and be able to participate with little or no greater threat to health and safety than is the case with their teammates.

In *West Virginia ex rel. Lambert v. West Virginia State Board of Education* (1994), a state court held that an eleventh-grade deaf girl receiving interpreter services in academic classes was entitled to receive them as a member of the basketball team so that she could understand the directions of her coach. The court stated that failure to do so would be discriminatory.

Several circuits of the U.S. Court of Appeals have considered whether enforcement of an age ceiling (typically the nineteenth birthday), or an eight-semester rule for high school athletes, violates Section 504 when applied uniformly to all students, including students with disabilities. Student athletes

---

[5] See, e.g., *Grube v. Bethlehem Area Sch. Dist.*, 550 F. Supp. 418 (E.D. Pa. 1982); *Poole v. So. Plainfield Bd. of Educ.*, 490 F. Supp. 948 (D. N.J. 1980); *Kampmeier v. Nyquist*, 553 F.2d 296 (2d Cir. 1977).

with disabilities have asserted that they are older or in school longer solely as a result of their disability (e.g., they have started school at an older age or have been held back) and should not be penalized for that fact. The response of the courts has been mixed. A number of state and federal district courts have adopted a case-by-case approach that analyzes whether granting an exception to the age and eight-semester requirements would frustrate the underlying safety and fairness purposes of the requirement.[6] If it would not, then the age and semester ceilings could be waived for a student with a disability whose presence on the team was not due to red-shirting (in this context, deliberately holding a high school student out a year to increase athletic prowess), and did not create a physical threat to other players because of size or strength related to the student's advancing age. In contrast, a number of other courts have ruled that an even-handed, neutral application of the rule to all students is not discriminatory, and that schools do not need to undertake burdensome case-by-case determinations.[7]

The approach in the latter cases may have been halted by the Supreme Court's decision in *PGA Tour, Inc. v. Martin* (2001), an ADA case in which the Court ruled that individual consideration of a pro-golfer's disability was necessary to determine whether his requested waiver of the no-cart rule was reasonable and necessary for his participation in a PGA tournament. Even if it were, however, the waiver was not required if it constituted a fundamental alteration in the competition. The Court stated that the underlying purpose of the rule must be weighed, and that "an individualized inquiry must be made" (p. 688).† The no-cart rule was waived for Martin.

> † Applying this same approach, a state court in Baisden v. West Virginia Secondary School Activities Commission, 568 S.E.2d 32 725 (W. Va. 2002), nonetheless observed that a disability would not automatically guarantee a waiver to the age rule. The plaintiff was 6'4" tall and weighed 280 pounds, and the court determined that his physical maturity would give him an unfair competitive advantage over younger football players. Waiving the rule in this case would fundamentally alter its underlying purpose.

Unresolved in some jurisdictions is whether students with disabilities who are denied athletic participation because of insufficient academic credits are being discriminated against because of their disability.[8] Texas's "no-pass, no-play" statute, however, has been upheld by the Texas courts.[9]

---

[6] *Washington v. Ind. High Sch. Athletic Ass'n*, 181 F.3d 840 (7th Cir. 1999) (preliminary injunction upheld); *Dennin v. Conn. Interscholastic Athletic Conf.*, 913 F. Supp. 663 (D. Conn. 1996) (preliminary injunction granted), *vacated as moot*, 94 F.3d 96 (2d Cir. 1996); *Johnson v. Fla. High Sch. Activities Ass'n*, 899 F. Supp. 579 (M.D. Fla. 1995) (preliminary injunction granted), *vacated as moot*, 102 F.3d 1172 (11th Cir. 1997; *Univ. Interscholastic League v. Buchanan*, 848 S.W.2d 298 (Tex. Ct. App. 1993), (injunction granted) *Cf. Cruz by Cruz v. Penn. Interscholastic Athletic Ass'n*, 157 F. Supp. 2d 485 (E.D. Penn. 2001) (permanent injunction, based on ADA); *Bingham v. Or. Sch. Activities Ass'n*, 37 F. Supp. 2d 1189 (D. Or. 1999) (waiver of eight-semester rule, based on ADA).

[7] See, e.g., *Sandison v. Mich. High Sch. Athletic Ass'n*, 64 F.3d 1026 (6th Cir. 1995), (upholding the age ceiling for track and cross country); *Pottgen v. Mo. St. High Sch. Activities Ass'n*, 40 F.3d 926 (8th Cir. 1994) (upholding the age ceiling for baseball); *Cavallaro v. Ambach*, 575 F. Supp. 171 (W.D.N.Y. 1983) (upholding the age ceiling for interscholastic wrestling). See also *Frye v. Mich. High Sch. Athletic Ass'n*, 121 F.3d 708 (6th Cir. 1997) (upholding the eight-semester rule) and *McPherson v. Mich. High Sch. Athletic Ass'n*, 119 F.3d 453 (6th Cir. 1997) (ruling that waiver of the eight-semester rule would create an undue financial and administrative burden).

[8] See *Hoot by Hoot v. Milan Area Sch.*, 853 F. Supp. 243 (E.D. Mich. 1994) (allowing the case to go to trial to determine whether waiver would be reasonable).

[9] *Texas Educ. Agency v. Stamos ex rel. Class of All Pub. Sch. Children*, 817 S.W.2d 378 (Tex. Ct. App. 1991) (upholding against a Section 504 claim the Texas statute requiring all students to meet academic eligibility standards prior to participation in extracurricular activities).

Program Accessibility

Not specifically a part of FAPE but also required under the Section 504 regulations is program accessibility: Educational programs, when viewed in their entirety, must be physically accessible to persons with disabilities. OCR differentiates a "program" from a physical facility; it is the program within a facility that must be accessible, not necessarily the entire facility. In the late 1970s, OCR issued a policy memorandum clarifying that carrying a student with a mobility impairment was an unacceptable means of providing the student with access to a program (*OCR Policy Interpretation No. 4*, 1978). More recently, it has ruled that a playground on school premises that is not accessible to students who use wheelchairs is a violation of Section 504 (*Hazelton (PA) Area School District*, 1991).

One case of particularly extensive failure to make programs accessible to students with mobility, vision, and hearing impairments was reported in 1993, when OCR found the following (among other things): excessive pressure required to open classroom and entrance doors; no raised letter or number signage to identify classrooms; safety hazards in restrooms and physics and home economics classrooms; parking spaces improperly marked; and stages inaccessible to persons in wheelchairs (*Uxbridge (MA) Public School*, 1993).

Cost Issues

Readers will recall that federal funds are not available under Section 504 to help pay for related aids and services. Of course, school districts are free to tap whatever sources are available to them, but if the Section 504 student is not IDEA-eligible, and if no other outside sources of funding are available, the cost of the related aid or service must be absorbed by the LEA's regular education budget.

Some commentators worry that OCR's FAPE definition, because it does not employ the concept of reasonable accommodations, allows for no cost limitations on what may be required. This contrasts with Section 504 employment regulations, in which an accommodation can be deemed unreasonable if it constitutes an undue hardship on the recipient of federal funds. Arguably, however, the Section 504 requirement that FAPE must provide an education that is comparable to ("as adequate as") what is offered to students without disabilities introduces its own cost cap, which is pegged to achievement of nondiscrimination and equal educational opportunity. In other words, if facilities or services are inadequate for general education students, then presumably the facilities or services for students with disabilities need be no better. Although the cost implications are sometimes minor, and sometimes more substantial, they are linked, according to this view, to what is being offered to general education students.

Unfortunately, various OCR regional offices across the country do not always use the same language in their rulings. Sometimes, the comparability standard seems paramount; at other times, an assessment of individual need independent of comparability seems to have been used. In the latter type of rulings, it appears that OCR has used the IDEA FAPE standard rather than the Section 504 FAPE definition. In addition, some courts ignore the Section 504 definition and continue to borrow the concepts of reasonable accommodation and undue hardship, introducing cost factors into the equation by that means.

↳Reminders and Tips

1. The purpose of nondiscrimination under the Section 504 ED regulations is to provide equal educational opportunity, that is, to level the playing field, not to provide an unfair advantage to students with disabilities. Neither a student's abilities nor disabilities should be prejudged, but individualized aids and services should be willingly provided when necessary.

2. General education teachers need training to understand the import of Section 504. To meet the nondiscrimination requirements, often all that is required is a change of attitude, a change in aspects of the classroom environment, or a fairly simple modification in instructional programming. Teachers are not expected to lower their standards for mastery of the curriculum.

3. In general, education agencies should explore less expensive ways to deliver Section 504 services effectively before turning to more costly alternatives. Materials and textbooks using universal design technologies can help students with disabilities as well as general education students.

4. When more expense is involved, school districts constrained by limited budgets should search for cost-effective ways to meet individual needs. Use of paraprofessionals and volunteers is one way that has been systematized in many districts. The use of in-school assistive technology devices is another. Devices such as computers, tape recorders and audiotapes, digital voice recorders, headphones, and VCRs, DVDs, CDs, and videotapes are already widely available in classrooms and can be adapted to serve the individual needs of students with disabilities while also being used to serve overall classroom needs.

5. Students who perform satisfactorily academically but who need high-tech, personalized assistive technology (AT) devices and services can be IDEA-eligible if, under state law, AT devices and services can be considered special education. High-tech items like personal computers and reading machines could then be paid for out of the special education budget but, of course, should be saved for those students who really need them. Low-tech devices and services often suffice for stand-alone students.

↳Review

1. What are the basic differences between the Section 504 FAPE definition and the IDEA FAPE definition?

   The Section 504 definition applies to the provision of regular education as well as special education. Also, Section 504 utilizes a comparability standard (requiring that the needs of the student with a disability be met as adequately as the needs of nondisabled students), whereas IDEA uses an individualized standard (identifying and meeting the student's unique special education needs).

2. What is the difference between related services under Section 504 and under IDEA?

   Unlike IDEA, related services under Section 504 are not limited to those required to assist a child to benefit from special education. They can include those aids and services needed to help a child receive a regular education that meets individual needs as adequately as the needs of nondisabled children are met—in other words, that provides equal educational opportunity.

⚡References

Harrison Cnty. (WV) Sch. Dist., 14 EHLR 353:120 (OCR 1988).

Hazelton (PA) Area Sch. Dist., 17 EHLR 907 (OCR 1991).

Individuals with Disabilities Education Improvement Act, 20 U.S.C. § 1400 *et seq.* (2006).

Individuals with Disabilities Education Improvement Act Regulations, 34 C.F. R. § 300.1 *et seq.* (2006).

Letter to Zirkel, 20 IDELR 134 (OCR 1993).

OCR Policy Interpretation No. 4, EHLR 132:02 (OCR 1978).

OCR Staff Memorandum, 19 IDELR 894 (OCR 1992).

PGA Tour, Inc. v. Martin, 532 U.S. 661 (2001).

Section 504 of the Rehabilitation Act of 1973, 29 U.S.C. § 794 (2006).

Section 504 ED Regulations, 34 C.F.R. Part 104 (2009).

Sullivan v. Vallejo City Unified Sch. Dist., 731 F. Supp. 947 (E.D. Cal. 1990).

Uxbridge (MA) Pub. Sch., 20 IDELR 827 (OCR 1993).

West Va. ex rel. Lambert v. West Va. St. Bd. of Educ., 447 S.E.2d 901 (W.Va. 1994).

Williams' Letter to Colleagues, OCR, May 27, 1992.

⇉Selected Supplementary Resources

Rose, T. E., & Huefner, D. S. (2005). High school athletic age-restriction rules continue to discriminate against students with disabilities. *Education Law Reporter, 196*, 385–401.

Sullivan, K. A., Lantz, P. J., & Zirkel, P. A. (2000). Leveling the playing field or leveling the players?: Section 504, the Americans with Disabilities Act, and interscholastic sports. *Journal of Special Education, 33*, 258–267.

Zirkel, P. A. (1996). The substantive standard for FAPE: Does Section 504 require less than the IDEA? *Education Law Reporter, 106*, 369–375.

Chapter 19

Placement and Discipline Issues Under Section 504

Chapter Outline

Placement Requirements for Public Schools

Background

As you will recall from the from the previous chapter, if a student in public school is suspected of having a Section 504 disability and is believed to need special education or related services, then an evaluation must precede the initial placement, even if the setting for the delivery of those services turns out to be a general education classroom. Of course, if the student is suspected of needing special education, in most circumstances that student would be referred for an IDEA evaluation. If the student is thought to need only related services (which are not defined in Section 504, but which do not have the same meaning as under IDEA), a Section 504 evaluation must occur. Placement decisions then must be made by a knowledgeable group of persons who consider information from a variety of sources, including aptitude and achievement tests, teacher recommendations, physical condition, social or cultural background, and adaptive behaviour (34 C.F.R. § 100.35(c) (2009)).

Placement With Students Who Do Not Have Disabilities

The Section 504 regulations are written to cover all Section 504 students and, like IDEA, require that students with disabilities be educated with students who do not have disabilities "to the maximum extent appropriate to the needs of the . . . person [with disabilities]" (34 C.F.R. § 100.34(a) (2009)). Public schools must place a student with a disability in the general educational environment unless education in that environment cannot be achieved satisfactorily with the use of supplementary aids and services.† Furthermore, if the school district places a student in another setting, it must take into account the proximity of the alternate setting to the person's home. In all these ways, the placement requirements under Section 504 parallel those of IDEA, although the IDEA requirements are more extensive and detailed.

> † Note that the Section 504 placement language uses the term supplementary aids and services (IDEA LRE language) rather than related aids and services (Section 504 FAPE language)— indicating what may be appropriate in general education settings. Related aids could perhaps be needed outside the general education classroom.

Participation in nonacademic and extracurricular services and activities (e.g., meals, recess, clubs, student employment opportunities, counseling, recreational activities, health services, and transportation) must, to the maximum extent appropriate, also be with students who do not have disabilities (34 C.F.R. § 100.34(b) (2009)).

A re-evaluation is required prior to "any subsequent significant change in placement" (34 C.F.R. § 100.35(a) (2009)). Readers may wonder what constitutes a "significant change of placement." OCR found that a change from a regular school to an alternative school was a significant change, triggering the need for re-evaluation of the student (*Hillsborough County (FL) School District*, 1997). Changes from self-contained settings to inclusive, integrated settings, or vice versa, usually constitute a significant change of placement. On the other hand, OCR found that a change from one self-contained classroom to another within the same school was not a significant placement change (*Seattle (WA) School District No. 1*, 1997). OCR also found that no significant placement change occurred when a school required a suicidal student to be accompanied by an escort at all times when the student was not attending a class (*Harlowston (MT) Public Schools*, 1997).

A suspension of more than ten school days also constitutes a significant change of placement. Suspensions are discussed in the Discipline Issues section of this chapter.

Removal from regular classrooms and schools.

Because essentially all Section 504 students who are not also IDEA students receive their supplementary aids and services (such as program modifications and accommodations) in general education settings, placement issues for stand-alone students do not raise the same kinds of complexities that arise with IDEA students. Nonetheless, OCR has recognized the need for removal of Section 504 students from the regular classroom in one particular type of situation: "[W]here a [disabled] child is so disruptive in a regular classroom that the education of other students is significantly impaired, the needs of the [disabled] child cannot be met in that environment. Therefore regular class placement would not be appropriate to his or her needs" (34 C.F.R., Part 104, app., para. 24 (1984)).† This position has been important in allowing a placement change from the general education classroom when the behavior of children with disabilities cannot be managed, even with the help of supplementary aids and services.

> † OCR's position was incorporated into an OSEP comment in earlier IDEA LRE regulations to indicate that it was applicable to IDEA students as well as to other students covered by Section 504. Courts have relied on this provision in determining the LRE for IDEA students. See chapter 12. The comment did not appear in the 1999 and 2006 IDEA regulations, perhaps because all comments were eliminated in those sets of regulations, and because IDEA now has its own set of discipline provisions.

OCR has also recognized the need for removal from regular elementary and secondary schools in three kinds of situations. In at least the first two of these situations, it is difficult to imagine that the student could be anyone but an IDEA student. First, the Section 504 regulations provide that if a placement in a residential program is necessary to provide FAPE as defined under Section 504, the program, including nonmedical care and room and board, must be provided at no cost to the person and his or her parents (34 C.F.R. § 104.33(c)(3) (2009)). Second, OCR states that if a recipient of federal money places a student in a program other than the one it operates, it remains responsible for ensuring that the Section 504 requirements are met in the other setting (34 C.F.R. § 104.33(b)(3) (2009)). Finally, several OCR rulings have addressed school-district homebound instruction policies. In each situation, OCR has ruled that individual need, not administrative restrictions on number of hours of homebound instruction per week, must dictate the hours provided to each Section 504 student.[1]

Neighborhood school placements.

A Tenth Circuit decision, in *Urban v. Jefferson County School District R-1* (1996), held that no greater right to neighborhood placement exists under Section 504 and ADA than exists under IDEA. To the authors' knowledge, as of 2011, no court decision in another circuit has explicitly ruled on the neighborhood placement issue under Section 504 and ADA, although many have ruled on the issue under IDEA (see chapter 12).

Comparable Facilities

If the school district operates a separate facility for students with disabilities, this facility must be comparable to the district's other facilities (34 C.F.R. § 104.34(c) (2009)). In other words, the quality of the separate facility must approximate that of the regular education facility, and the services and activities available in the separate facility must be comparable to those offered in inclusive facilities.

---

[1] See, e.g.,*Boston (MA) Pub. Sch.*, 21 IDELR 170 (OCR 1994); *Greensville Cnty. (VA) Sch. Bd.*, 14 EHLR 353:118 (OCR 1988); *Lee's Summit (MO) R-VII Sch. Dist.*, EHLR 257:629 (OCR 1984).

Establishing classes in storage rooms, home economics rooms, partitioned offices, and other areas not conducive to learning will constitute a violation of Section 504 (*Wayne Co. (WV) School District*, 1990); so will classroom sizes that are not adequate to accommodate specific educational, physical, and/or medical needs of students with disabilities. School districts should be certain to allocate resources fairly across staff and not deny special education teachers access to adequate supplies, clerical staff, a classroom telephone, and so forth if they supply general education teachers with such supplies and services. Special education teachers and students can be asked to share in sacrifices made by an entire building staff but should not be singled out for a disproportionate share of such sacrifices; otherwise, such actions will be discriminatory under Section 504.

Discipline Issues

Overview

Traditional definitions of school discipline refer to enforcing school rules and punishing or otherwise controlling student misbehavior in order to ensure order and safety at school. (See chapter 14 for a broader definition.) Discipline typically encompasses such sanctions as suspension and expulsion, school detention, restriction of privileges, restitution, and even corporal punishment in some states.† In recent years, schoolwide disciplinary options have also included the use of positive behavior supports for all students. In using any of these methods, educators must be careful that discipline is not imposed in a fashion that discriminates against Section 504 students. Among other things, such students must not be treated more harshly or prejudicially than students without disabilities. Furthermore, no child should be disciplined arbitrarily or with unreasonable severity.

> † Twenty states, a majority of them in the south, continue to allow the use of corporal punishment, although school districts within those states can bar its use. See The Center for Effective Discipline, <http://www.stophitting.com> for detailed information and statistics. African American students receive a disproportionate amount of corporal punishment compared to their white counterparts. By way of contrast, corporal punishment is not allowed in prisons.

Suspension and Expulsion Policy

The Supreme Court has ruled that all children who are suspended or expelled must be provided with notice of the impending action and a chance to provide their own version of the events leading to the disciplinary action (*Goss v. Lopez*, 1975). This is required by the constitutional concept of due process of law, and it avoids the likelihood of an error in the application of the intended discipline.

In addition, OCR has interpreted the meaning of nondiscriminatory suspension and expulsion under Section 504 in a number of specific situations. In general, ten consecutive school days is seen as the maximum number of days that a student may be suspended without invoking procedures that go beyond notice and a chance to respond.† After ten days, the suspension constitutes a significant change of placement, triggering the re-evaluation requirement, which to OCR includes the need to determine whether the misbehavior is a manifestation of the disability.†† No procedures are specified for making such a determination. If the misbehavior is a manifestation, however, it would be discriminatory for the placement change to be continued solely as a means of discipline, unless that placement is determined to be the setting closest to the general education classroom in which an appropriate education can be delivered. Although this does not foreclose the possibility of removing a disruptive child from the general classroom, it means that the setting must deliver appropriate educational services. Therefore, long-term suspension or expulsion without any services to such a child would be a violation of Section 504.

> † OCR has borrowed the Supreme Court's ruling in *Honig v. Doe*, 484 U.S. 305 (1988) that 10 days or fewer of suspension do not constitute a change of placement under IDEA and, therefore, do not invoke additional due process procedures. For instance, in *Broward County (FL) School District*, 27 IDELR 850 (OCR 1997), OCR concluded that a 3-day suspension did not constitute a change of placement.

> †† In *Roane County (TN) School District*, 27 IDELR 853 (OCR 1997), OCR found a violation for a 12-day suspension imposed without conducting a manifestation determination.

Follow-up issues.

One troubling question that arose after manifestation determinations were introduced was whether an expulsion or a suspension of more than ten consecutive school days could be imposed if the misbehavior did not relate to the disability. OCR has taken the position that, when this is the case, long-term suspensions and expulsions for misbehavior may proceed on the same basis as they would for students without disabilities (*OCR Senior Staff Memorandum*, 1988). This means that expulsion or long-term suspension of a student with a disability may include the cessation of all educational services to the student with a disability, as long as students without disabilities are treated similarly.[2] In other words, all educational services to the student may cease if that is the practice with respect to students without disabilities, as long as state or federal law does not prohibit cessation of services for all students or a given student. This position is in contrast with the statutory requirement for IDEA students that services to allow the student to participate in the general curriculum and continue to progress toward achievement of IEP goals must continue, even if the services are delivered, as a last resort, in the student's home.

Another issue that has arisen is whether multiple (serial) suspensions together totaling more than ten school days in a given school year are permitted under Section 504, or whether ten school days is the cumulative annual total permitted before a school must re-evaluate a student when imposing a longer suspension. The OCR position is that a series of short-term suspensions that together total more than ten school days do not automatically constitute a significant change of placement. Instead, a case-by-case decision is required to determine whether a pattern of discriminatory exclusion exists. Factors in determining such a pattern include "the length of each suspension, the proximity of the suspensions to one another, and the total amount of time the child is excluded from school" (*OCR Senior Staff Memorandum*, OCR 1988). If there is a pattern, then it constitutes a significant change in placement, requiring a re-evaluation to determine whether the misconduct was caused by the student's disability, in which case a team must determine what the appropriate placement should be. Of course, if the law of a given state or a school district policy has established a strict maximum of ten school days of cumulative suspension per year, then it must be followed.

---

[2] *OCR Senior Staff Memorandum*, 14 EHLR 307:05 (OCR 1988); See also *Policy Guidance—Gun-Free Schools Act of 1994*, 21 IDELR 899 (ED 1994).

Another issue relates to the use of alcohol or illegal drugs. With or without any causal link, those whose misconduct involves alcohol or illegal drugs may be suspended or expelled for use or possession in the same manner as students without disabilities, without the need for the procedural safeguards of Section 504. In short, misconduct based on alcohol or current illegal drug use is not protected by Section 504 from ordinary discipline procedures (29 U.S.C. § 705(20)(c)(iv) (2006).[3] In contrast, violations of the code of student conduct such as these would not prevent an IDEA student from receiving the benefit of IDEA safeguards (*Letter to Uhler*, 1992).

Alternatives to Suspension and Expulsion

An extensive range of alternative disciplinary methods in addition to suspension and expulsion remains available to school officials. Among the traditional tools used both for students with disabilities and students without disabilities are the separation of misbehaving students into private study carrels, detention, restriction of privileges, time-out, and in-school suspension. All but in-school suspension were mentioned in the Supreme Court's decision in *Honig v. Doe* (1988, p. 325) as ordinary, acceptable alternatives to suspension and expulsion. According to OCR, however, time-out procedures need to have reasonable controls and limits, or be implemented in accordance with a student's IEP or behavioral intervention plan.[4]

A question that has arisen about in-school suspension is whether long-term in-school suspension would be considered a significant placement change that triggers the need for procedural safeguards. Without evidence to the contrary from OCR or the courts, logic would dictate that in-school suspension for more than ten school days could constitute a significant change of placement—just like out-of-school suspension—if Section 504 FAPE requirements are not being implemented during the in-school suspension periods. At least one state court has so held.[5]

Corporal punishment is also an alternative disciplinary method in some states. OCR rulings approach corporal punishment from two perspectives. Reasonable corporal punishment administered to children with disabilities may be acceptable if administered similarly to children without disabilities who exhibit the same misbehaviors. On the other hand, corporal punishment solely because of the disability is discriminatory—that is, the student with the disability should not be subject to more severe punishment than a student without disabilities. Moreover, if the misbehavior is caused by the disability, then any use of corporal punishment should be subject either to Section 504 FAPE requirements (meeting the student's individual needs as adequately as the needs of those without disabilities are met) or to an IDEA student's IEP requirements concerning discipline and behavior intervention strategies (*West Las Vegas (NM) School District*, 1993; *Nash County (NC) School District*, 1985). Of course, if a state or school district has prohibited the use of corporal punishment, educators in that state or district need not be concerned about these rulings.

---

[3] See also *OCR Staff Memorandum*, 17 EHLR 609 (OCR 1991).
[4] See, e.g., *Lyon Cnty. (NV) Sch. Dist.*, 35 IDELR ¶ 226 (OCR 2000); *East Baton Rouge (LA) Parish*, 29 IDELR 247 (OCR 1998); *Marion Cnty. (FL) Sch. Dist.*, 20 IDELR 634 (OCR 1993); *Sanger (CA) Unified Sch. Dist.*, EHLR 257:02 (OCR 1978).
[5] See *Big Beaver Falls Area Sch. Dist. v. Jackson*, 612 A.2d 806 (Pa. Commw. Ct. 1993) (holding that continued in-school suspension interfered with a student's right to FAPE).

An Example of Discriminatory Corporal Punishment

In one ruling, OCR determined that delays in administering punishments to a first grader with a behavioral disability produced a denial of FAPE under Section 504 because the child had difficulty linking cause and effect. The youngster was difficult to manage and engaged in fights on the playground. He also swore at his teacher and, on one occasion, threw a rock and hit one of the playground instructors. He was spanked by the principal on more than one occasion and spent a good deal of time waiting outside the principal's office for the principal to discipline him. He had also had his recess periods taken away.

Because of the nature of his disability, which included a short attention span and limited impulse control, psychologists testified at his hearing that spankings, long periods of punishment, and time-outs waiting for the principal were ineffective. What was needed instead was a behavioral management plan that imposed immediate consequences for misbehavior, and punishments of short duration that the student could link to the misbehavior (*Central Valley (WA) District No. 410*, EHLR 257:166 (OCR 1979)).

Other disciplinary methods that actually inflict physical discomfort, such as the administration of bad-tasting substances (like the old technique of washing the mouth out with soap), have been challenged occasionally. Although generally disfavored educationally, they have been upheld by OCR if the treatment is nondiscriminatory in its application. For instance, in *Salina (KS) Unified School District No. 305* (1986), administering alum to a student with serious emotional disturbance for the student's use of vulgar language did not violate Section 504 when the rest of the class was treated the same way. Educators must be extremely careful, however, when they use such aversive techniques or physical restraints. Section 504 complaint findings or a court decision will usually be based on an analysis of the facts in each situation. Considerations such as the IEP for an IDEA student, the child's evaluation data, and the ability to successfully implement less aversive techniques will be important to the outcome. Then too, some states outlaw the use of aversive interventions and/or allow administrative dismissal of teachers who use them.

The Gun-Free Schools Act of 1994

The Gun-Free Schools Act of 1994[6] prohibits any state from receiving federal funds under the Improving America's Schools Act of 1994 (major ESEA amendments) unless the state enacts a law requiring the expulsion from the current school setting (not necessarily exclusion from all educational services) "for at least 1 year" of any student who brings a "weapon"† (including an unloaded gun) onto the school grounds. In addition, the LEA must have a policy requiring referral of such a student to the state's criminal justice or juvenile delinquency system. Exceptions to the expulsion requirement may be made by the school superintendent on a case-by-case basis.

> † A weapon under the Gun-Free Schools Act means a firearm, as that term is defined at 18 U.S.C. § 921 (a)(3) (2006): "(A) any weapon (including a starter gun) which will or is designed to or may readily be converted to expel a projectile by the action of an explosive; (B) the frame or receiver of any such weapon; (C) any firearm muffler or firearm silencer; or (D) any destructive device. Such term does not include an antique firearm."

---

6 Sec. 14601-14602 of Improving America's Schools Act, Pub. L. 103-382, 108 Stat. 3907, as amended (codified at 20 U.S.C. § 7151 (2006).

During the enactment of these provisions, a question arose as to their application to students with disabilities who bring a gun to school. Allowing the superintendent to make exceptions to the expulsion requirement was seen by ED as a way to honor Section 504. (See chapter 14 for the provisions of IDEA that, in effect, supersede the Gun-Free Schools Act for IDEA students.)

Application of Section 504 in Private Schools

The general nondiscrimination requirements of Section 504 also apply to recipients of federal funds who operate private elementary or secondary schools.† More specifically, a student with a disability may not be excluded from a private elementary or secondary school if the person can, "with minor adjustments," be provided with an appropriate education by the private school (34 C.F.R. § 104.39(a) (2009)). The private school must provide FAPE (as defined under Section 504) and nondiscriminatory nonacademic services. Only if there is a substantial cost increase to the school may an additional charge be levied for the education of the student with a disability (34 C.F.R. § 104.39(b) (2009)).

> † Recipients of federal funds who operate preschool or day-care programs, or adult education programs, are also prohibited from excluding a "qualified handicapped person" from their programs or activities (34 C.F.R. § 104.38 (2009)).

If the private school operates special education programs, then it also must follow the evaluation, placement, and procedural safeguard provisions applicable to public schools—for instance, placement in the general education environment, unless that setting is unsatisfactory even with the use of supplementary aids and services (34 C.F.R. § 104.39(c) (2009)).

Is A Scent-Free Private-School Environment a Minor Adjustment?

Providing a mandatory, scent-free environment for a girl with asthma was considered more than a minor adjustment in *Hunt v. St. Peter School*, 26 IDELR 6 (W.D. Mo. 1997). In response to the mother's concerns, the private parochial school had adopted a voluntary scent-free policy, and had allowed the mother to provide information to the class about her daughter's severe asthma and the threat to her breathing caused by various scents. In response, the teacher and students in the child's fifth-grade class had agreed not to wear perfumes and colognes. When her daughter reached sixth grade, the girl's mother asked for a mandatory scent-free policy, which the school thought it could not enforce, among other reasons because the girl's classes were held in four separate rooms, not always with the same students, and the sixth grade used six other classes during the week for other activities and Catholic mass. The court noted the difficulty of imposing a "sniffing test" on the school, commenting that "sniffing may be appropriate in the wild kingdom but not in an elementary school."

The standard for public schools is higher than for private schools; public schools are expected to do more than make minor adjustments. Depending on a student's environmental allergies, reasonable adjustments might include air filters, a restroom free of certain chemicals, and an outdoor physical education area free of pesticides or fertilizers. Dictating to students and staff what scents they can wear, however, would be problematic in the public as well as the private school context.

In the first reported case of its kind, a student at a private school obtained an injunction prohibiting her expulsion during her senior year for shouting expletives. Susceptible to life-threatening bleeding as a result of a serious autoimmune disorder, the girl reacted fearfully and emotionally, even hysterically, when she cut herself with an X-Acto® knife in art class. When the school nurse dismissed her fears peremptorily, the girl became even more upset and swore at her. As a recipient of federal funds, the school was subject to Section 504; as a public accommodation, it was also subject to Title III of ADA. The court concluded that the school was not entitled to discriminate against the student on the basis of her physical disability. The failure to take her disability into account and reasonably accommodate it in determining whether or how to punish her emotional outburst was sufficiently likely to be discriminatory under Section 504 and ADA, so as to justify the injunction to stop her expulsion (*Thomas v. Davidson Academy*, 1994). This case puts private schools on notice of their obligations not to impose discipline that does not consider the effect of a student's disability on the misconduct.

Reminders and Tips

1. Stand-alone Section 504 students can be removed from general education classrooms if their behaviors prove unduly disruptive to their teacher and fellow students.

2. When disciplining children with disabilities, it is wise to consider the possible relationship of the disability to the misbehavior. This is a good idea in all cases even though OCR does not require a manifestation determination until after the first ten days of suspension or removal to another setting. It is a good idea because a disciplinary method ideally should be selected and designed so that it will not only be nondiscriminatory but also be effective in changing the behavior.

3. Although it is not a violation of Section 504 to cease services to a stand-alone student if serious misbehavior is determined not to be a manifestation of the disability, school officials need to know whether cessation of services is allowed under state law or district policy. In any event, such a disciplinary action must be comparable to the discipline that would be imposed for the same infraction on a student without disabilities.

4. School disciplinarians must be sure that any serial suspensions that accumulate to more than ten school days do not create a pattern suggesting that the intent of the suspensions was to sidestep the need to re-evaluate and conduct the manifestation determination that must accompany a change of placement.

5. Discipline of IDEA students is usually handled under IDEA requirements, but any Section 504 student (including an IDEA student) can ask for an OCR review or a Section 504 hearing using Section 504 standards. This overlap can be confusing because when it comes to pursuing a Section 504 claim in court, an IDEA student must first exhaust IDEA administrative remedies (the IDEA hearing process). (See chapter 20.)

↳Review

1. In what educational settings should Section 504 students be placed?

   They should be placed in general education settings unless education cannot be achieved satisfactorily there even with the use of supplementary aids and services.

2. When must an evaluation or re-evaluation of a Section 504 student take place?

   An evaluation must occur before the student's initial placement/classification as a Section 504 student in a general or special education program if the student is believed to need either special education or Section 504 related aids and services. A re-evaluation is required before any subsequent "significant change in placement" for such a student.

3. What must be included in a re-evaluation?

   According to OCR, it must include a determination of whether the misbehavior is related to the disability.

4. According to OCR, may students with disabilities be disciplined like students without disabilities?

   Generally speaking, they may, with the following exceptions:

   (a) If expulsion or suspension is for more than ten consecutive school days, the Section 504 student must be re-evaluated and a determination made as to whether the misbehavior was related to the disability. If it was, then the placement must be in the setting closest to the general education classroom in which the student can be educated appropriately. If it was not, then the student may receive the same disciplinary placement as a student without a disability would receive for the same kind of misbehavior.

   (b) If a child receives other kinds of discipline, such as in-school suspension, time-out, corporal punishment, or other methods that cause pain or discomfort, they must not be discriminatory or interfere with the student's receiving an appropriate education that is designed to meet the student's individual needs as adequately as the needs of students without disabilities are met.

⚡References

Goss v. Lopez, 419 U.S. 565 (1975).

Harlowston (MT) Pub. Sch., 26 IDELR 115 (OCR 1997).

Hillsborough Cnty. (FL) Sch. Dist., 27 IDELR 730 (OCR 1997).

Honig v. Doe, 484 U.S. 305 (1988).

Letter to Uhler, 18 IDELR 1238 (OSEP 1992).

Nash Cnty. (NC) Sch. Dist., EHLR 352:37 (OCR 1985).

OCR Senior Staff Memorandum, 14 EHLR 307:05 (OCR 1988).

Policy Guidance—Gun-Free Schools Act of 1994, 21 IDELR 899 (ED 1994).

Section 504, Rehabilitation Act of 1973, 29 U.S.C. § 794 (2006).

Section 504 ED Regulations, 34 C.F.R. Part 300 (2009).

Salina (KS) Unified Sch. Dist. No. 305, EHLR 352:204 (OCR 1986).

Seattle (WA) Sch. Dist. No. 1, 28 IDELR 763, 10-98-1005 (OCR 1997).

Thomas v. Davidson Academy, 846 F. Supp. 611 (M.D. Tenn. 1994).

Urban v. Jefferson Cnty. Sch. Dist. R-1, 89 F.3d 720 (10th Cir. 1996).

Wayne Cnty. (WV) Sch. Dist., 16 EHLR 1261 (OCR 1990).

West Las Vegas (NM) Sch. Dist., 20 IDELR 1358 (OCR 1993).

⇉Selected Supplementary Resources

Dagley, D. L., McGuire, M. D., & Evans, C. W. (1994). The relationship test in the discipline of disabled students. *Education Law Reporter, 88*, 13–31.

Lohrmann-O'Rourke, S., & Zirkel, P. A. (1998). The case law on aversive interventions for students with disabilities. *Exceptional Children, 65*, 101–123.

Zirkel, P. A. (2008). Suspensions and expulsions under Section 504: A comparative overview. *Education law Reporter, 226*, 9-13.

Chapter 20

Due Process, Conflict Resolution, and Remedies Under Section 504

Chapter Outline

Due Process Safeguards Under Section 504

Public elementary and secondary schools and private special education schools receiving federal money must establish a set of procedural safeguards under Section 504 that can be used by parents or guardians who believe that their children are being discriminated against on the basis of disability. The safeguards parallel the basic due process safeguards of IDEA but are less extensive and detailed. They apply to actions regarding "identification, evaluation, or educational placement" of students whose disability creates a need, or perceived need, for special instruction or related services (34 C.F.R. § 104.36 (2009)). Note that the safeguards do not extend to actions regarding FAPE under Section 504.

The safeguards include the following:

- Some kind of advance notice
- An opportunity for the parent or guardian to examine relevant records
- An impartial hearing
- A review procedure

These safeguards are not fleshed out like they are in the IDEA regulations. The contents and nature (oral versus written) of the notice are not specified, nor is the extent of the access to relevant records. The impartial hearing must allow for participation by the student's parents or guardian, and for representation by counsel, but no other details are provided. The nature of the review procedure also is not spelled out.

An Example of Acceptable 504 Hearing Procedures

A parent of a student in the Houston, Texas school district challenged Houston's Section 504 hearing procedures because the district would not allow the parent to cross-examine witnesses or bring a court reporter to the hearing. Instead, the district's procedures provided for an informal, nonadversarial, impartial hearing, and the hearing officer allowed the parent to ask follow-up and clarification questions. The parent was given an audiotape of the hearing. OCR noted that Section 504 required neither cross-examination of witnesses, nor a court reporter, and concluded that the hearing was conducted properly. *Houston (TX) Independent School District*, 25 IDELR 163 (OCR 1996).

Numerous safeguards that are included in IDEA are excluded from Section 504. Among the exclusions are the following:

- Provision for an independent educational evaluation (IEE)
- Surrogate parent provision when the child is a ward of the state, the parents are unknown, or the parents cannot be located after reasonable efforts
- Stay-put placement provision when placement is being challenged
- Exceptions to stay-put placement in cases of disciplinary placement changes
- Provisions soliciting parental input into the evaluation process and into eligibility and placement decisions

- Provision soliciting parental input into the development of the student's individualized educational services
- Provisions for mediation and resolutions sessions
- Explicit private right of action (right to litigate). (Nonetheless, court cases have established an implicit private right of action under Section 504.)

Compliance with the more complete IDEA safeguards, however, is viewed as automatically meeting the Section 504 requirements.

Also not explicitly mentioned in the Section 504 safeguards, although included among the IDEA safeguards, is a consent requirement for initial evaluation and initial services as a student with a disability (34 C.F.R. § 104.36 (2009)). Commentators have speculated about the absence of a consent requirement. In 1997, OCR offered policy guidance on the subject, concluding that although the regulations were silent, they should be construed to require parental consent prior to initial evaluation for purposes of identification, diagnosis, and prescription of specific educational services but not for subsequent evaluations. The stated rationale for the policy was that "parental discretion" with regard to these matters was an "appropriate and necessary policy component" (*Letter to Durheim*, 1997).

OCR also has taken the position that when a parent refuses to give consent for initial evaluation or initial placement as a Section 504 student, a school district may use the Section 504 hearing procedure to override the lack of consent but is not required to do so (*Letter to Zirkel*, 1995). Instead, presumably, it could simply maintain the status quo.

Sometimes, it is the parent who seeks a Section 504 evaluation—over the objection of the school district. If school officials have no reason to suspect a disability, they need not agree to the parental request. If this happens, the district must provide the parent with notice of the procedural safeguards, including the right to a hearing to challenge the school district's refusal to evaluate (*OCR Memorandum*, 1993).

Avenues for Conflict Resolution

Section 504 Coordinator

Under Section 504 regulations, each school district (or other recipient of federal money) that employs fifteen or more persons must establish grievance procedures that provide for prompt and equitable resolution of complaints alleging violations of Section 504 (34 C.F.R. § 104.7 (2009)). An employee must be designated as the district's grievance coordinator (Section 504 coordinator). Sometimes, the coordinator is used only to resolve employee complaints of discrimination on the basis of disability, but the coordinator also should be the person to whom a parent turns if the parent thinks a child has been subject to discrimination in school, assuming the parent cannot resolve the issue with the teacher directly.

School officials may be tempted to ask a special educator to serve as the Section 504 coordinator because they think the special educator will be more knowledgeable about Section 504. This may or may not be appropriate, and school officials should consider seriously who in the school district is in the best position to gain the cooperation and support of the entire staff. The hope is that, with the help of the Section 504 coordinator, all parties can understand the law, and disputes can be resolved amicably.

Complaints to OCR

Grievances can also be reported directly to the OCR office in the appropriate region (see Table 20.1 at the end of this chapter). The complaint can be brought by either an individual or a group but usually must be initiated within 180 days of the date when the complaining party learned of the allegedly discriminatory action. The confidentiality of the complainant will be protected to the extent allowed by law.

After screening the written complaint for merit and the appropriateness of an OCR review, OCR will invite and facilitate early complaint resolution between the parties if they wish to cooperate on reaching an agreement. If not, OCR will investigate the complaint, typically by asking for documents from the school and, if necessary, by interviewing school officials. If a violation is found, OCR will seek an agreement to correct the violation. It can also issue Letters of Findings (LoFs) when violations are found that the school does not willingly remedy or when LoFs would have important value as precedent (even if a violation is not found). In cases where a violation has not been remedied, OCR will seek a written corrective action agreement by the school. Monitoring will occur in all cases except where the parties reach a resolution agreement. OCR can also punish a school that retaliates against or intimidates those who engage in a protected activity under Section 504.†

> † OCR has the authority to punish retaliators through incorporation of the standards of Title VI of the Civil Rights Act of 1964. See 34 C.F.R. § 100.7(e) (2009).

Frequently, as a result of an OCR investigation, the school will voluntarily undertake to change its procedures to comply with Section 504 requirements, and the complaint will be closed. If a school refuses to comply with an OCR ruling, OCR can begin administrative enforcement proceedings to terminate federal funds, or can refer the matter to the Justice Department for enforcement in court. Regardless of OCR's findings, an aggrieved party can file a court action.

Except in extraordinary circumstances, OCR investigates only for procedural compliance, including implementation of Section 504 plans (or IEPs) and avoids second-guessing the substance of a school district's determinations (e.g., evaluation results, placement decisions, the extent of related services or special instruction).† If a due process hearing has been initiated under IDEA, OCR will defer automatically to the IDEA hearing decision.

> † In *Manteno (IL) Community Unit School District #5*, 27 IDELR 960 (OCR 1997), OCR made clear that it does not resolve educational disputes over the content of the IEP and related aids and services, and that such issues should be resolved at a due process hearing. Comparably, in *Virginia Beach City (VA) Public Schools*, 26 IDELR 27 (OCR 1996), OCR stated that a dispute over a Section 504 plan should be resolved at a due process hearing.

Section 504 Hearings

As an alternative to filing an OCR complaint, parents who feel that their child has been incorrectly denied disability status, placed in an inappropriate setting, or discriminated against in academic or nonacademic activities may request a Section 504 hearing to challenge the school district's action. State law or policy will dictate whether Section 504 claims that are combined with IDEA claims can be handled in an IDEA due process hearing, or must be resolved in a separate Section 504 hearing. Obviously, it is convenient to combine IDEA and Section 504 issues in one hearing although the SEA does not have responsibility for enforcement of Section 504 as it does for IDEA issues. In some states, separate Section 504 hearing officers are trained, whereas in others, IDEA hearing officers are trained to hear 504 disputes as well. Regardless of the specific procedure in a given state, Section 504 regulations do not require plaintiffs to first hold a Section 504 hearing before going to court to remedy Section 504 violations. On the other hand, some federal courts have required Section 504 plaintiffs to hold an IDEA hearing before having their claim heard in court. (See the following section.)

Litigation

Litigation is an alternative to both the OCR complaint and the Section 504 hearing. For many years, parents of IDEA students have attached Section 504 claims to their child's IDEA claims. The courts typically resolve the IDEA issue first, which often precludes the need to resolve the Section 504 claim because the IDEA rights are more specific and extensive than those of Section 504. If the issues are independent of one another and IDEA does not provide a remedy, however, then the courts will also resolve the Section 504 claim.†

> † In an important recent case, even though relief had been awarded to the plaintiffs for denial of FAPE under IDEA, the Ninth Circuit held that money damages could be available under Section 504. The court remanded the case to allow the plaintiffs to plead discrimination and a denial of FAPE under Section 504 (separate from IDEA), observing that the definitions of FAPE under Section 504 and IDEA are not the same. Nonetheless, in order to receive monetary damages, the court indicated that the plaintiffs ultimately would have to prove that the relevant Section 504 regulations did not impose obligations that went beyond the intent of Section 504 and that the school district was deliberately indifferent to the relevant Section 504 requirements (*Mark H. ex rel. Michelle H. v. Lemahieu*, 513 F.3d 922 (9th Cir. 2008)).

If a civil action is filed under Section 504 seeking relief that is available under IDEA, the claim must first be subject to an IDEA due process hearing (20 U.S.C. § 1415(l) (2006)), a requirement that is also true for an IDEA claim alone. In addition, even if the Section 504 claim is for monetary damages unavailable under IDEA, most federal appellate courts require exhaustion of IDEA administrative remedies if any IDEA relief is available that addresses the injury alleged (*S.E. v. Grant County Board of Education*, 2008; *Charlie F. v. Board of Education*, 1996). The courts disapprove of parents trying to evade the hearing process by claiming only monetary damages when other relief is available.

An example of an independent Section 504 issue is found in *McKay v. Winthrop Board of Education* (1997).[1] In *McKay*, a teenager with a chronic connective tissue disorder (Marfan syndrome) who needed a power wheelchair or scooter to move around her high school alleged that the school violated Section 504 by failing to make the school's activities, programs, and facilities accessible. The federal district court held that a due process hearing was unnecessary because no IDEA issues were raised in the complaint, and the monetary damages sought by the student for her alleged pain, suffering, humiliation, and embarrassment were not available under IDEA but could be available under Section 504. The parties subsequently settled the case, and the township paid the student $50,000 and agreed to renovate its schools. It also paid $30,000 to Maine Advocacy Services for the plaintiff's attorneys' fees and costs.

---

[1] See also *Randolph Union High Sch. Dist. No. 2 v. Byard*, 22 IDELR 617 (D. Vt. 1995).

Two Questionable Section 504 Decisions

One appeals court has required an IDEA hearing for Section 504 stand-alone students, that is, those who are not covered under IDEA, which is arguably an incorrect result. Section 504 itself does not specify that a Section 504 hearing must precede litigation, so a court requiring such a hearing is borrowing from IDEA and applying it to non-IDEA students. In *Babicz v. School Board of Broward County*, 135 F.3d 1420 (11th Cir. 1998), two siblings with chronic asthma and other severe allergies that led to multiple absences from school alleged that the school failed to implement their Section 504 plans. The Eleventh Circuit cited cases involving IDEA students for the proposition that Section 504 students who are not covered under IDEA must use IDEA administrative hearing procedures. The court in *Babicz* did not recognize that these other cases were not analogous but involved IDEA students who were seeking to skirt IDEA hearings by asking for monetary damages when some other kind of relief was potentially available under IDEA, which is quite a different proposition. See *Charlie F. v. Board of Education*, 98 F.3d 989 (7th Cir. 1996); *Hope v. Cortines*, 69 F.3d 687 (2d Cir. 1995); *Waterman v. Marquette-Alger Intermediate School District*, 739 F. Supp. 361 (W.D. Mich. 1990). Nonetheless, parents of Section 504 stand-alone students in the Eleventh Circuit must be aware of the *Babicz* decision.

Another questionable decision was handed down in *N.L. v. Knox County Schools*, 315 F.3d 688, (6th Cir. 2003), in which the Sixth Circuit misinterpreted decisions in other cases as standing for the proposition that "a student who does not qualify under the IDEA also does not qualify under Section 504" (p. 696, n. 5). This poorly worded statement appears to reject the existence of Section 504 stand-alone students, and the decision negated the possibility that a student could be eligible under Section 504, even though not eligible under IDEA. The Sixth Circuit cited several other cases in support, but in reality those cases all dealt with IDEA students whose 504 claims were based on the same allegations as the IDEA allegations. See *Urban v. Jefferson County School District*, 89 F.3d 720 (10th Cir. 1996); *Monahan v. Nebraska*, 687 F.2d 1164 (8th Cir. 1982); *Doe v. Arlington County School Board*, 41 F. Supp. 2d 599 (E.D. Va. 1999).

Remedies for Section 504 Violations

The same kinds of equitable relief available under IDEA are available under Section 504, namely, an order to stop violating a student's rights, an order requiring specific changes in the child's educational program, and other forms of equitable relief such as compensatory education. These remedies can be ordered by a hearing officer as well as by a court. In addition, in some situations, reimbursement of a parent's out-of-pocket costs can be ordered when the parent paid for aspects of the child's education that should have been provided for publicly (*Board of Education of Palmyra Borough v. F.C.*, 1998). Attorneys' fees for parents who prevail on a disputed issue are also available.

The Supreme Court has not yet ruled explicitly on whether Section 504 provides a monetary damage remedy against recipients of federal aid. Its decision in *Franklin v. Gwinnett County Public Schools* (1992), however, allowing monetary damages under Title IX for sex discrimination, implies that damages would also be available under Section 504 for intentional discrimination.† Most lower courts have held that monetary damages for pain and suffering are available if the violation results from intentional discrimination (deliberate indifference or "bad faith") or gross misjudgment.[2] Mere failure to provide accurate evaluation, appropriate placement, instruction, and services, or to provide equal opportunity to participate in nonacademic activities under Section 504 is insufficient.

---

[2] See, e.g., *Sellers v. Sch. Bd. of Manassas*, 141 F.3d 524 (4th Cir. 1998); *Hoekstra v. Indep. Sch. Dist. No. 283*, 103 F.3d 624 (8th Cir. 1996); *Monahan v. Nebraska*, 687 F.2d 1164 (8th Cir. 1982); *K.U. v. Alvin Indep. Sch. Dist.*, 991 F. Supp. 599 (S.D. Tex. 1998).

† In 1996, the Supreme Court ruled that monetary damages are not available against the federal government under Section 504 because statutory language does not explicitly waive federal governmental immunity as it does state governmental immunity (*Lane v. Pena*, 518 U.S. 187 (1996)). Of note in *Lane* was the Court's reference to *Franklin v. Gwinnett County Public Schools*, apparently taking as a given that monetary damages were available under Section 504 against parties other than the federal government.

In separate action, the Supreme Court ruled in *Barnes v. Gorman* (2002) that punitive damages were not available under Section 504 or the ADA in private suits against a municipality. The reasoning in the case would extend to educational agencies as well.

Retaliation Can Get School Officials and Their Boards Into Trouble

An itinerant adapted physical education (A.P.E.) teacher expressed concerns about the lack of suitable equipment, materials, and facilities for children with disabilities whom she was instructing in various schools in the district. After she wrote letters to her supervisors complaining about the problems, her evaluations became much more negative. Her IEP writing was criticized, and her probationary contract was not renewed. She sued for damages under Section 504 and also Section 1983 of the Civil Rights Act of 1871 (see chapter 15), alleging unlawful retaliation under Section 504 and violation of her First Amendment free speech rights. The Ninth Circuit ruled in her favor and reinstated a jury award of $952,000 against the school board under Section 504. Applying the damages provision of Section 1983, it also upheld $50,000 in punitive damages against the two supervisors. The court observed that the teacher had complained through proper channels. Moreover, no evidence was introduced that any of her IEPs were revised or discarded. The court stated:

> [The plaintiff's] speech may have had important effects for the disabled students in the district and their parents. Teachers are uniquely situated to know whether students are receiving the type of attention and education they deserve, and in this case, are federally entitled to . . . This is particularly so with respect to disabled children, who may not be able to communicate effectively that they lack appropriate facilities. (*Settlegoode v. Portland Public Schools*, 371 F.3d 503, 514 (9th Cir. 2004), *cert. denied*, 2004 U.S. LEXIS 7419 (2004))

↳Reminders and Tips

1. The best way to avoid legal liability is to take seriously the mandate not to discriminate against a student with a mental or physical impairment that is substantially limiting a major life activity, including learning. This means finding a way to provide a comparable opportunity for such a student to learn and participate in school activities.

2. Although the issues surrounding the judicial and administrative remedies can be technical and complex, what is important to remember is that a court can assess monetary damages against school districts for deliberate or bad-faith refusal to honor Section 504 requirements. Gross misjudgment of a student's eligibility and needs also opens up the possibility of monetary liability.

↳Review

1. What is the difference between the procedural safeguards under Section 504 and IDEA?

   The safeguards under Section 504 are fewer and more general. If a student is an IDEA student, the safeguards under IDEA will supersede Section 504.

2. Is there a certain sequence to the options that one should use in resolving Section 504 conflicts?

   Generally speaking, one may select from several options, each of which may be chosen without regard to sequence. A Section 504 coordinator, an OCR complaint, a Section 504 hearing, or litigation may be used at one's discretion. Plaintiffs should check the case rulings in their own circuits, however, with respect to going to court without a hearing first, especially when suing for monetary damages under Section 504. In most circuits the case will be dismissed if a potential remedy is available under IDEA.

3. What kinds of remedies are available for violation of Section 504 by educational agencies?

   The same kinds of equitable relief are available under Section 504 that are available under IDEA: declaratory and injunctive relief, compensatory education, and even out-of-pocket costs in a few situations. Attorneys' fees can also be awarded. The general rule is that monetary damages are available only in cases of intentional discrimination, deliberate indifference, or gross misjudgment, and that punitive damages are unavailable.

⚡References

Barnes v. Gorman, 536 U.S. 181 (2002).

Bd. of Educ. of Palmyra Borough v. F.C., 2 F. Supp. 2d 637 (D.N.J. 1998).

Charlie F. v. Bd. of Educ., 98 F.3d 989 (7th Cir. 1996).

Franklin v. Gwinnett Cnty. Pub. Sch,, 503 U.S. 60 (1992).

Letter to Durheim, 27 IDELR 380 (OCR 1997).

Letter to Zirkel, 22 IDELR 667 (OCR 1995).

McKay v. Winthrop Bd. of Educ., 26 IDELR 1100 (D. Me. 1997).

OCR Memorandum, 19 IDELR 876 (OCR 1993).

Section 504 of the Rehabilitation Act of 1973, 29 U.S.C. § 794 (2006).

Section 504 ED Regulations, 34 C.F.R. Part 104 (2009).

S.E. v. Grant Cnty. Bd. of Educ., 544 F.3d 633 (6th Cir. 2008).

Table 20.1

OCR Offices and Addresses *(as of February 2011)*

National Headquarters:

U.S. Dep't of Education, Office for Civil Rights
400 Maryland Ave. SW
Washington, DC 20202-1100

Tel 1-800-421-3481 Fax 202-453-6012   TDD 877-521-2172   Email: OCR@ed.gov

Regional Offices and Addresses:

Eastern Division	Midwestern Division
Connecticut, Maine, Massachusetts, New Hampshire, Rhode Island, Vermont OCR, Boston Office: U.S. Dep't of Education 5 Post Office Square, 8th Floor Boston, MA 02109-3921 Tel 617-289-0111 Fax 617 289-0150 TDD 877-521-2172 e-mail: OCR.Boston@ed.gov	**Illinois, Indiana, Iowa, Minnesota, North Dakota, Wisconsin** OCR, Chicago Office: U.S. Dep't of Education Citigroup Ctr. 500 W. Madison St, Ste. 1475 Chicago, IL 60661-7204 Tel 312-730-1560 Fax 312-730-1576 TDD 877-521-2172 e-mail: OCR.Chicago@ed.gov
New Jersey, New York, Puerto Rico, Virgin Islands OCR, New York Office: U.S. Dep't of Education 32 Old Slip., 26th floor New York, NY 10005-2500 Tel 646-428-3900 Fax 646-428-3843 TDD 877-521-2172 e-mail: OCR.NewYork@ed.gov	**Kansas, Missouri, Nebraska, South Dakota, Oklahoma** OCR, Kansas City Office: U.S. Dep't of Education 8930 Ward Parkway, Suite 2037 Kansas City, MO 64114-3302 Tel 816-268-0550 Fax 816 823-1404 TDD 877-521-2172 e-mail: OCR.KansasCity@ed.gov
Delaware, Maryland, Kentucky, Pennsylvania, West Virginia OCR, Philadelphia Office: U.S. Dep't of Education 100 Penn Square East, Ste. 515 Philadelphia, PA 19107-3323 Tel 215 656-8541 Fax 215 656-8605 TDD 877-521-2172 email: OCR.Philadelphia@ed.gov	**Michigan, Ohio** Office for Civil Rights, Cleveland Office: U.S. Dep't of Education 600 Superior Ave. East, Suite 750 Cleveland, OH 44114-2611 Tel 216 522-4970 Fax 216 522-2573 TDD 877-521-2172 email: OCR.Cleveland@ed.gov

Southern Division	Western Division
Alabama, Florida, Georgia, Tennessee OCR, Atlanta Office: U.S. Dep't of Education 61 Forsyth St. S.W., Ste 19T70 Atlanta, GA 30303-8927 Tel 404-974-9406 Fax 404-974-9471 TDD 877-521-2172 e-mail: OCR.Atlanta@ed.gov	**Arizona, Colorado, New Mexico, Utah, Wyoming** OCR, Denver Office: U.S. Dep't of Education Cesar Chavez Memorial Bldg. 1244 Speer Blvd., Suite 310 Denver, CO 80204-3582 Tel 303-844-5695 Fax 303-844-4303 TDD 877-521-2172 e-mail: OCR.Denver@ed.gov
Arkansas, Louisiana, Mississippi, Texas OCR, Dallas Office: U.S. Dep't of Education 1999 Bryan St., Suite 1620 Dallas, TX 75201-6810 Tel 214-661-9600 Fax 214-661-9587 TDD 877-521-2172 e-mail: OCR.Dallas@ed.gov	**California** OCR, San Francisco Office: U.S. Dep't of Education 50 Beale St., Suite 7200 San Francisco, CA 94105 Tel 415-486-5555 Fax 415-486-5570 TDD 877-521-2172 e-mail: OCR.SanFrancisco@ed.gov
North Carolina, South Carolina, Virginia, Washington, D.C. OCR Washington DC Office: U.S. Dep't of Education 400 Maryland Ave., SW Washington, D.C. 20202-1475 Tel 202-453-6020 Fax 202-453-6021 TDD 877-521-2172 e-mail: OCR.DC@ed.gov	**Alaska, Hawaii, Idaho, Montana, Nevada, Oregon, Washington, Pacific Region** OCR, Seattle Office: U.S. Dep't of Education 915 Second Ave., Room 3310 Seattle, WA 98174-1099 Tel 206-607-1600 Fax 206-607-1601- TDD 206-607-1647 e-mail: OCR.Seattle@ed.gov

Afterword

Law is a tool of society, providing order and setting expectations for our behavior. Although it is meant to provide stability, it is not static. It evolves over time to reflect changing needs and aspirations. Sometimes it gets it right; sometimes it gets it wrong. Sometimes we cannot agree on whether it gets it right or wrong. This is no less true for special education law than for any other body of law.

Judges, in court decisions, will continue to interpret ambiguity in federal statutes and regulations. Legislators will continue to amend statutes, and agency personnel will continue to write regulations that reflect those amendments. Although state special education rules must conform to federal laws, state legislatures can go beyond the federal law to serve children with disabilities even better than the federal law requires. All of this means there is a need for continuous learning, training, reflection, assessment, and involvement in policy formulation on the part of teachers and parents.

IDEA '97 and IDEA '04 both represent considerable shifts from their predecessors. In these statutes, Congress was more interested in results for children with disabilities, and so these statutes are far more prescriptive than earlier versions. Some would say they represent a great deal of micromanagement by the federal government, with the disciplinary and IEP provisions leading the way. Whether the shift is wise is not the most important question. In general, a retreat to earlier positions does not provide a good solution for the more than 6.8 million children with disabilities currently being served, or for those who will come after them.

The level of federal funding has not kept pace with the level of government mandates. More resources are needed to meet the expectation that the individualized needs of the vast majority of children with disabilities can be met in general education classrooms with supplementary aids and services. More resources are needed to reduce pupil-teacher ratios in key areas, to recruit and train teachers who understand functional behavioral assessments and behavior intervention plans, to train and supply related service providers, such as school nurses or health care aides, to work with children who are medically fragile, and so on.

More than financial resources are needed, however. As expectations mount and the law continues to evolve, we need to invest more of our personal resources in the education of children with disabilities if we want to achieve good results. There are many ways to invest. We can be constructive critics as well as supporters of the law. We can share our insights with government policy makers. We can improve our skills in working collaboratively with one another. We can improve our behavior management skills or our skills in given curricula, especially reading and math. We can improve our understanding of a particular disability or a particular child. Any one of these investments is worthwhile.

Like all of us, children with disabilities are a diverse group; like all of us, they can learn and grow. Public schools are a good place for this to happen, but growth requires continuing efforts on our part. Laws and regulations cannot make this happen alone; students with disabilities need dedicated educators and parents to convert their legal rights into educational realities.

Appendix A

Glossary of Legal Terms

adversary process—the method courts use to resolve disputes in which each side presents its case, subject to rules of evidence; an independent fact finder (judge or jury) determines which side's evidence is most persuasive.

affirm—to uphold the opinion of a lower court on appeal.

allegation—an unsupported assertion made in a legal proceeding by a party who expects to prove it in court.

alternative dispute resolution—procedures for settling disputes by means other than litigation; e.g., by arbitration or mediation. Such procedures are usually less costly and faster.

appeal—a party's request to a higher court to review a decision by a lower court. In cases where the right exists, the appeal must be made according to certain procedures and limitations.

appellant—the party bringing a court appeal.

appellate court—any state or federal court empowered to review and amend the judgments of a lower court over which it has jurisdiction.

appellee—the party responding and defending against the appeal.

arbitrary—without rational basis, underlying reason, or guiding principle; nonrational, capricious, whimsical.

case law—a primary source of law or legal authority formed by the body of reported court cases.

certiorari (abbreviated as cert.)—a petition for a superior court to review the decision of a lower court. Review may be granted or denied at the discretion of the superior court.

citation—in legal writing, a notation that directs the reader to a specific source of authority, such as a court case, statute, regulation, or journal article.

civil action—a lawsuit, as opposed to a criminal prosecution, commenced in order to recover a private or civil right, or to obtain a remedy for the violation of such a right.

civil rights or **civil liberties**—personal, natural rights guaranteed and protected by the Constitution or state constitutions, e.g., freedom of speech and the press, freedom from discrimination.

class action—a lawsuit commenced by one or more members of an ascertainable class who sue on behalf of themselves and others having the same complaint and seeking the same remedy.

code—a written collection of laws or regulations arranged according to an elaborate subject-matter classification scheme (e.g., the U.S. Code and Code of Federal Regulations).

color of law—generally, the semblance, without the substance, of legal right; misuse of power made possible because the wrongdoer is clothed with the authority of the state.

common law—law deriving its authority not from legislative enactments, but from ancient and continuing custom or from the judgments and decrees of courts enforcing those customs.

complaint—the original pleading that initiates a lawsuit and that sets forth a claim for relief.

consent decree—a judgment entered by consent of the parties whereby the defendant agrees to stop alleged illegal activity without admitting guilt or wrongdoing.

counsel—a lawyer or team of lawyers; both parties to an administrative hearing or lawsuit in special education disputes are entitled to counsel.

court—a governmental body authorized to decide disputes concerning the law. Judges are often referred to impersonally as "the court."

damages—the monetary compensation awarded by a court to the prevailing party in a lawsuit for injury, loss, or other harm done to their rights, their property, or their person through the illegal or wrongful conduct of another. **Compensatory damages** are meant to pay for the actual and projected harm (loss of wages, hospital expenses, etc.). **Punitive damages** are in addition to compensatory damages and are used to punish a defendant for intentional wrongdoing and to deter the defendant (and other potential wrongdoers) from committing the same wrong again.

declaratory relief—a judgment or opinion of the court that merely sets forth the rights of the parties without ordering anything to be done.

defendant—the defending party in a civil action who must answer the complaint; the plaintiff's opponent.

de minimis (Latin)—a matter that is small, unimportant, not worth a court's attention

dictum (pl., dicta)—any statement in a judge's opinion that is not essential to the determination of the case; conclusions on which the decision does not turn. Dictum, unlike the holding, is not binding in subsequent cases.

discrimination—unfair treatment or denial of normally available privileges to individuals because of their race, age, color, sex, national origin, religion, disability, or veteran's status.

dissenting opinion—a court opinion, written by a judge or minority of the judges sitting on a court, setting forth views that contradict and often criticize the judgment and reasoning of the majority opinion. Only the majority opinion has the force of law.

due process of law—a phrase from the Fifth and Fourteenth Amendments of the United States Constitution that generally refers to the reasonable, fair, and equitable application and administration of the law. **Procedural due process** refers to constitutionally guaranteed rights to fair notice, fair hearing, and other fair procedures in any legal proceedings that might jeopardize one's life, liberty, or property.

enjoin—to command, especially a court's command or order forbidding certain action; the word also can be used to mean require certain action.

equal protection of the laws—the constitutional guarantee that no person or class of persons shall be denied the same protection of the laws that is enjoyed by other persons or other classes in like circumstances.

equitable relief—court relief in the form of an injunction, a declaratory judgment, or some other form of redress other than money damages.

evidence—information in oral testimony or written documents presented to persuade the fact finder (judge or jury) of the correctness of a party's point of view.

finding—a conclusion or decision upon a question of fact reached as a result of a judicial examination or an investigation by a court or jury.

good faith—a term referring to a party's honest intent. A good faith undertaking is one devoid of any fraud or any motive to take unfair advantage. **Bad faith** is the opposite.

hearing—a proceeding with definite issues of fact or law to be resolved, in which witnesses are heard, the parties confront each other, and an impartial officer presides.

holding—a judge's binding decree upon a particular issue of law in a case. (Compare with dictum.)

informed consent—consent based on knowledge of what action(s) will result from giving consent; informed consent requires full disclosure by the person seeking to obtain consent.

injunction—a court order requiring a party to refrain from engaging (or to engage) in some particular conduct.

judge—a government official with authority to decide lawsuits brought before courts.

jurisdiction—(1) the legal authority of a court to hear and decide a case (e.g., federal courts have jurisdiction to decide issues that involve federal law but not to decide issues that involve only state law); (2) the geographic area within which the court has authority to decide legal issues.

liability—a party's legal obligation, duty, or responsibility.

liberty interest—an interest protected through the due process clauses of state and federal constitutions. Although defying precise definition, liberty interests have been declared by courts to include the liberties guaranteed by the first eight amendments of the U.S. Constitution as well as such rights as the right to one's good name and the right of individuals to contract; to engage in any of the common occupations of life; to acquire useful knowledge; to marry, establish a home, and bring up children; and to worship God according to the dictates of their own consciences. More generally, it is the right to enjoy those privileges long recognized as essential to the orderly pursuit of happiness by free people.

litigation—a civil action of an adversary nature; a lawsuit.

majority opinion—a court opinion, usually written by one judge, in which the decision is set forth and in which the reasoning behind the decision is agreed to by a majority of the judges on the case.

moot case—a case that no longer rests upon existing facts or rights and in which a judgment would be without practical effect; also an abstract or pretended case.

negligence—conduct that either (1) breaches the standard of care that a reasonably prudent person would exercise in the same situation, (2) falls below a standard of care fixed by law, or (3) falls below a standard of care fixed by a profession or trade and about which the allegedly negligent party knew or should have known. If a person owes a legal duty of care to another, breaches the standard of care, and is the direct or "proximate"cause of injury to person or property, negligence will become a tort. Otherwise, it remains careless behavior.

parties—the plaintiff(s) and defendant(s) to a lawsuit.

plaintiff—the party bringing suit in a court of law by the filing of the complaint.

precedent—any decided case that may be used as authority in deciding subsequent similar cases.

privacy, right of—the right to live without unwarranted interference by the public in matters with which the public is not necessarily concerned; the right of a person to be free from unwarranted publicity. The term encompasses a number of rights recognized as inherent in the concept of "ordered liberty." The right is not absolute.

private right of action—the legal right of a private person to file a lawsuit and seek a remedy for a violation of a law; some statutes do not create a private right of action but allow some other remedy such as withholding funds for noncompliance.

procedural due process—(See **due process**.)

property interest—an interest protected through the due process clauses of state and federal constitutions. It safeguards the interests that a person has acquired in specific benefits. Property interests are created by statutes that support individual claims of entitlement to specific benefits. A property interest includes far more than ownership and possession of tangible property. For instance, state statutes entitling youth to a public education have been held to establish a property interest in the education.

qualified immunity—an affirmative defense that shields public officials from liability for damages if their conduct does not violate clearly established statutory or constitutional rights of which a reasonable person would have known.

quasi—"nearly, almost, like"; a modifying prefix used to designate a resemblance or similarity to the object or conduct modified. For example, administrative hearings under special education law are "quasi-judicial" in nature; they resemble judicial hearings in many respects but are not conducted by a judge and lack some of the formalities of the courtroom.

question of fact—any question in a lawsuit that relates to the factual context out of which the controversy arose, such as conduct, time, place, duration, physical cause or effect, i.e., that gave rise to the adversary proceedings. Questions of fact traditionally have been left for the jury to determine, although in special education suits, the judge is both judge and jury. (Compare with question of law.)

question of law—any question in a lawsuit relating to the meaning, relevance, interpretation, or application of any law. Questions of law are for the court to decide. (Compare with **question of fact**.)

reasonable—having a rational basis; fair; not arbitrary.

regulation—a rule or direction written by an administrative agency or department in order to implement a statute, and having the force or authority of law.

remand—an appellate court's return of a case to a lower court for further proceedings there.

remedy—the means by which a right is enforced.

restraining order—a temporary order issued by the court, sometimes without notice and without hearing, commanding the party or parties to maintain a certain status until a more certain judicial remedy can be determined.

settlement—an agreement wherein the parties to a lawsuit resolve their differences without having a trial or hearing.

statute—a law enacted by a state or federal legislature.

statute of limitations—a law that fixes the period of time in which a party may commence an action in court.

stipulation—an agreement made between parties in a lawsuit to accept certain facts as uncontroverted or true or to submit to some proceeding or arrangement; usually the agreement is possible because it is mutually beneficial.

subpoena—a writ issued by a court to a witness commanding the witness to appear and testify in court; failure to obey is punishable by fine or imprisonment for contempt of court.

suit or lawsuit—an action or proceeding brought by one person or persons against another or others in a court of law in order to redress an injury or enforce a right.

summary judgment—a judgment given before the case comes to trial, based on the fact that there is no genuine dispute regarding the material facts and therefore no need for a trial to determine them. On the basis of the preliminary proceedings, the judge abbreviates the full proceedings to avoid waste and inefficiency, and rules as to the law governing the given set of facts.

tort—"a wrong"; any wrongful, noncriminal conduct that causes injury to another's person, property, or reputation; the conduct is wrongful if it is unlawful or amounts to a breach of legal duty existing between the wrongdoer and the injured party.

vacate—to render void; often applied to the action of an appellate court when it sets aside or voids the judgment of a lower court and either substitutes its own judgment or remands the case to the lower court for further proceedings.

waiver—the voluntary and intentional abandonment of a known right.

Appendix B

U.S. Supreme Court Decisions Concerning Services Under IDEA

1982   *Board of Education of Hendrick Hudson School District v. Rowley,* 458 U.S. 176 (1982).

The Supreme Court held that a free appropriate public education (FAPE) meant an education that was provided at public expense for children of school age, met state standards, was delivered in conformity with an IEP, was individualized, and was calculated to provide some educational benefit. The Court held that an appropriate education need not maximize the potential of students with disabilities in a way that is commensurate with the educational opportunities provided to students without disabilities.

1984   *Irving Independent School District v. Tatro,* 468 U.S. 883 (1984).

The Supreme Court held that clean intermittent catheterization (CIC) of a young student with spina bifida was a related service, needed to enable the student to benefit from special education, and that CIC could not be excluded as a medical service.

1985   *Burlington School Committee v. Massachusetts Department of Education,* 471 U.S. 359 (1985).

The Supreme Court held that the "stay-put" provision of IDEA (then EHA) did not preclude parents from removing their child from public school and placing him or her in a private school. In such a situation, if the courts ultimately decide that the student did not have FAPE available in the public setting, then the parents may be reimbursed for the costs of a "proper" private placement. If, on the other hand, FAPE was available, then the parents will not be reimbursed.

1988   *Honig v. Doe,* 484 U.S. 305 (1988).

The Supreme Court held that IDEA (then EHA) did not allow dangerous or disruptive special education students whose misbehavior related to their disability to be suspended from school for more than 10 days or expelled without parental consent, a hearing decision, or a court order. To do so would violate the stay-put provision and constitute a unilateral change of placement. (Congress later amended IDEA to allow for some limited unilateral placement changes by school districts.)

1993   *Zobrest v. Catalina Foothills School District,* 509 U.S. 1 (1993).

The Supreme Court held that the establishment clause of the First Amendment does not prohibit a publicly financed sign language interpreter for a deaf student at a religious school when: (a) the services are part of a general government program that distributes IDEA benefits neutrally to any child who qualifies, (b) the child is the primary beneficiary, (c) the school receives only an incidental benefit, and (d) the school was not selected by the state. The Court also reasoned that the interpreter is merely a transmitter of the instructional material and neither adds to it nor subtracts from it.

1993   *Florence County School District Four v. Shannon Carter*, 510 U.S. 7 (1993).

The Supreme Court held that when a special education student is denied FAPE by a school district, the parents can be reimbursed for the costs of an "otherwise proper," unilateral private placement of their child, even in a school that does not meet state standards.

1999   *Cedar Rapids Community School District v. Garret F.* 526 U.S. 66 (1999).

The Supreme Court held that IDEA requires continuous one-to-one nursing care for a medically fragile student because it is a related service and not an excluded medical service under the IDEA regulations. The Court said that accepting a cost-based standard would require it to create a standard that is not present in the statute.

2005   *Schaffer v. Weast*, 546 U.S. 49 (2005).

The Supreme Court held that the burden of proof in a due process hearing challenging an IEP lies with the party seeking relief unless state law provides otherwise. The parent is typically the party seeking relief.

2006   *Arlington Central School District Board of Education v. Murphy*, 548 U.S. 291 (2006).

The Supreme Court held that parents who prevail in an IDEA lawsuit are not entitled to recover their expert witness fees because IDEA provides no clear notice that such fees are recoverable.

2007   *Winkelman v. Parma City School District*, 550 U.S. 516 (2007).

The Supreme Court held that nonlawyer parents have independent, enforceable rights under IDEA and may represent their own interests in IDEA cases. In other words, they need not hire a lawyer, and may file claims encompassing both procedural and substantive rights (e.g., claims about inappropriate IEPs and denial of FAPE).

2009   *Forest Grove School District v. T. A.*, 129 S. Ct. 2484 (2009).

The Supreme Court held that courts have the authority to award reimbursement in private school cases, even when the student has never received services in a public school setting first. When FAPE has not been made available to an eligible student, parents may bring their claims for reimbursement of their child's private placement.

Appendix C

Hypotheticals for Discussion
With Selected Chapters

Chapter 6 Hypothetical

(IDEA Evaluation)

Fred

As a sixth-grader Fred began to fight with his peers at school. He was suspended briefly for two separate incidents of fighting. Throughout elementary school, he was quite a good student—an able reader, a motivated and active participant in science and social studies—but a poor speller. His math performance was good until he confronted decimals, fractions, and percents. One day in sixth grade he was asked to perform calculations on the blackboard in front of his peers; after missing the answer three times, his teacher criticized him for continuing to get the answer wrong, at which point he fled from the room and ran home crying.

In seventh grade, Fred's school performance deteriorated significantly. He began talking back to his teachers and not doing his homework if he didn't like the teacher. His grades fluctuated from C to F in his academic subjects; he particularly had problems relating to his math teacher. He got an A in his music class. He began hanging out with a peer group that was experimenting with drugs. Fred overdosed at school on No-Doze and had to be hospitalized to have his stomach pumped. He indicated that he had been trying to get high. Later in the year, he was suspended for fighting with a fellow student in P.E. class and refusing to "let it go" when his P.E. teacher attempted to intervene. Teachers began to suggest to Fred's parents that he might need private counseling, a suggestion with which they agreed. They indicated that he was rebelling against their rules and values.

In the fall of eighth grade, Fred continued to do poorly in most of his classes. Unbeknownst to his teachers, he was depressed following his breakup with a girlfriend. One day, he told his peers that he was going to commit suicide by jumping off a freeway overpass, and he left the school premises. Peers reported this information to a counselor, who told the peers to go retrieve the boy. They were able to do so, and upon the boy's return to school, he had an emotional collapse. The hospital and his parents were summoned. Fred then experienced a series of psychiatric hospitalizations over a period of several months. He was diagnosed with severe depression and a drug problem, and was uncooperative in each setting. A private evaluation at a psychiatric institute identified possible residual traumatic brain injury and learning disabilities in addition to clinical depression and the drug problem. The psychiatric institute reported at a subsequent IDEA administrative hearing that it mailed its evaluation to the school, but the school insisted that it never received the report. The institute did not have documentation to confirm that it had mailed the report.

At the end of eighth grade, Fred's parents enrolled him in an out-of-state residential placement, where his condition stabilized and his academic performance improved greatly. His parents sued his former school district for tuition reimbursement, claiming a failure of child-find under IDEA and failure to evaluate when a disability should have been suspected.

1. Should Fred have been referred for an IDEA evaluation? Why or why not? If so, when?

2. What kinds of prereferral interventions might have been appropriate?

3. Assuming he should have been referred, who in junior high school was (or should be) in a good position to make the referral? Do the parents have any responsibility in this regard?

4. Would procedures leading up to referral need to be any different in secondary school than in elementary school?

5. Design an appropriate IDEA evaluation for Fred. What kind of data would you want to collect? Who should collect it? Given the information prior to his hospitalization, what disabilities might you want to check for? What might you want to rule out? What kind of needs might you identify?

6. If Fred were a member of an ethnic minority, would it change your assessment procedures at all? Why or why not?

Chapter 8 Hypothetical

(Due Process Protections Under IDEA)

What might be the most effective and legally appropriate way for (a) a parent and (b) a school to remedy the following situations? (Their choices might not be the same.) Consider all dispute resolution options and relevant procedural safeguards.

1. Parents were not invited to contribute input to their child's IEP before being given a proposed IEP.

2. The LEA evaluation indicated that a child had an intellectual disability, but the parents believe their child has a learning disability.

3. No behavioral objectives were included in the IEP of a student with emotional disturbance.

4. Parents were not notified of their child's change of placement until after it occurred.

5. The school wishes to deliver physical therapy services via a paraprofessional, but the parents object that this person is not sufficiently skilled.

6. A parent believes that IDEA requires written parental consent for each service that the school wishes to provide under IDEA, and the parent does not want travel training for his child with visual-motor deficits. The school believes that it is obligated to provide all services necessary for FAPE, including travel training, once the parent has consented to the child's initial IEP.

7. The parent is seeking $37,000 in attorneys' fees as the prevailing party at an IDEA hearing. The school thinks the request is inflated.

Chapter 9 Hypothetical

(FERPA)[†]

"A school principal is notified that two students are in possession of handguns. Following appropriate procedures, the principal confiscates the weapons and contacts the parents and representatives from law enforcement. When the school liaison from the police department arrives, the principal has a short meeting. During the course of the meeting, the principal indicates that one of the students receives special education services through the school and will require additional hearings at the school regarding educational placement. This information, the principal says, is significant to the county juvenile probation department. The police officer recollects a memorandum requiring school officials to share student information in all cases involving special education students and cases involving criminal activity and requests this special education documentation and specific student information for the appropriate students.

"When the parents arrive, the principal allows for a short meeting between the police and the parents in the conference room at the school. In a spirit of cooperation, the police meet with both parents at the same time and inform them of the legal procedures to take place when the students leave the school. During this meeting, the police allude to the principal's comments about one of the students having additional procedures, necessitating further meetings at the school and indicate that the school administration has cooperated with the police, as provided for by law. Within the day, the school principal is made aware that one of the parents has contacted legal counsel regarding a violation of student rights to privacy under FERPA."

> † Quoted material is excerpted with permission from Decman, J. & Bauer, C. (2003). Student discipline and the sharing of records: FERPA, IDEA, and the duty to ensure safety. *Education Law Reporter, 171*, 407.

Questions:

1. Did the principal commit any FERPA or IDEA violations? Did the police?

2. Did any exceptions to the nondisclosure requirement justify the principal's statements to the police? (Was the situation an emergency? Had a crime been committed? Was there a state law allowing release of confidential information to state and local officials so that the juvenile justice system could effectively serve the student prior to adjudication?)

3. Was the police officer an employee or agent of the LEA? If not, would he be "maintaining" the student's special education classification for law enforcement purposes? (If discipline records are shared with a law enforcement unit, do they lose their status as education records?) If not, and the officer was entitled to know of the student's special education status, is he allowed to redisclose this information?

4. Who actually shared private, restricted information about the special education student with unauthorized persons—the principal or the police officer? Can't one ever orally disclose to parents that a student is a special education student?

Chapter 10 Hypothetical

(FAPE Under IDEA)

Jodi

Jodi is a seven-year-old who is profoundly deaf. Her native language is American Sign Language, and that is her primary means of communication. She is in second grade, and she has not yet learned to read and write. The school district in which she is enrolled relies on total communication methods for its students who are deaf or hard of hearing. The district's total communication program uses oral methods (lip-reading, hearing aids, development of speech) and Signing Exact English (SEE) as methods to teach language and communication in pullout classes. Jodi's parents are also deaf, and they believe that Jodi requires the assistance in all her general and special classes of a sign language interpreter who uses ASL. They believe that ASL must also serve as a bridge to the development of her ability to read and write in English and that, for the time being, SEE will not be useful to Jodi. If the school district does not have access to an ASL interpreter, Jodi's parents want her placed in the state school for the deaf.

Describe the issues and questions that should be addressed at Jodi's IEP and placement meeting. Who should be there? What kinds of IEP goals should be considered? Are language and communication modes legitimate factors in developing her IEP? In determining her placement? Can the LRE be determined on the basis of the above information?

Chapter 12 Hypothetical

(LRE Issues Under IDEA)

Terry

Terry is an eleven-year-old with severe intellectual disability that includes language impairments and some symptoms of autism. The school district proposes to change his placement from a self-contained placement to a program entitled CHOICES, in which Terry will spend part of his day in a resource room and part of his day in the general education classroom. The CHOICES program is designed to promote interaction between students with disabilities and students without disabilities. The proposed placement change will involve a change in school location. School district officials advocate this program because they believe that interaction will allow Terry to model good social habits and acquire more language skills. Terry's parents, however, are concerned that their son needs more intensive intervention with a speech-language pathologist, and believe that Terry's toileting skills are more important than social goals at the present time. The school district is recommending the CHOICES program plus thirty minutes with the speech-language pathologist twice a week. The parents want Terry to remain in his self-contained program with increased speech-language services five times a week for an hour each. They also do not want him to leave his neighborhood school.

1. What relevant information do we have about Terry, and what additional information do we need about his past IEP and his proposed new IEP?

2. What LRE factors should be considered in determining the LRE for Terry?

3. How should the IEP placement team go about seeing if it can reach consensus?

4. Who should attend the IEP placement meeting?

Chapter 14 Hypothetical

(Discipline Under IDEA)

Peter

Peter is a junior high school special education student with a moderate learning disability that primarily affects his performance in mathematics and his social judgment. His self-esteem is low, and his need for acceptance is high (arguably, like most junior high school students). He attends regular classes with the exception of a study skills resource class for one period a day. He was caught selling marijuana on his junior high school campus in violation of the student code and was given a ten-day suspension. He explained that he was not making any money from the sales but was just helping a group of girls, one of whom promised to go to the upcoming dance with him in return for his help.

During the suspension period, school personnel knowledgeable about learning disabilities reviewed his records and determined that his misbehavior was not related to his disability. The school team decided that he should be placed in an interim alternative educational setting (in this case, the district's alternative school for junior high school students who get in trouble in their regular schools) for sixty days—that is, for the rest of the school year—the same amount of time a student without disabilities would be placed in the alternative school for this infraction.

Identify any problems in this scenario as you answer the following questions:

1. Can Peter's parents stop the first ten-day suspension? If so, on what grounds?

2. Can Peter's parents stop Peter's removal to an IAES? Why or why not?

3. Can they challenge the duration of his removal? How, and on what grounds? What arguments should they make?

4. Regardless of how long Peter may be in an IAES, what kind of educational services should he receive there, including services to address his misconduct?

Chapter 18 Hypothetical

(FAPE Under Section 504)

A child in a public school third-grade classroom has a severe, life-threatening allergy to peanut butter. The school has evaluated the allergy and agrees with the parents that the child is covered under Section 504 of the Rehabilitation Act. The parents insist that an education designed to meet the child's individual needs as adequately as those of other children means that no peanut butter can be allowed in the child's classroom or in the cafeteria. Can you forbid the parents of the other children in the child's classroom from allowing their children to bring peanut butter products to school? Can or should you extend the ban to all peanut butter products in the cafeteria? Can you effectively enforce either ban? Would a court that uses the concept of reasonable accommodation as a stand-in for FAPE consider this to be a reasonable accommodation? Are there other options that might meet the child's needs? In any event, what should the school do to minimize the chances of the child's exposure to peanut butter? Consider how the child's privacy rights might be affected by the school's actions. Consider whether or how the cafeteria staff should be trained. Consider what emergency plan should be in effect. Consider how to deal with the issue of whether parents can bring classroom treats to school, and if so, what precautions must be in effect.

Appendix D

Selected Internet Sites With Information on Special Education and Disabilities

These Internet sites are well-established ones of governmental agencies, professional organizations, and advocacy groups. Occasionally, when you try to access a site, you will receive a message that it cannot be located or is temporarily out of service. In either case, try again later because these sites were correct and active as of the date of publication of this book. You will find that many of these sites will link you to other sites as well.

All begin with the prefix http://

Alexander Graham Bell Association for the Deaf and Hard of Hearing	**nc.agbell.or**g (note: no www in url)
American Foundation for the Blind	**www.afb.org**
The Arc of the U.S. (for people with intellectual and developmental disabilities)	**www.thearc.org**
Association for the Education and Rehabilitation of the Blind and Visually Impaired	**www.aerbvi.org**
Autism Society of America	**www.autism-society.org**
Brain Injury Association USA	**www.biausa.org**
Children and Adults With Attention Deficit/Hyperactivity Disorder (CHADD)	**www.chadd.org**
Cornell Law School Legal Information Institute (source for U.S. Code, statutes, regulations, case law, etc.)	**www.law.cornell.edu**
Council for Exceptional Children	**www.cec.sped.org**
Council of Administrators of Special Education	**www.casecec.org**
Council for Children with Behavioral Disorders	**www.ccbd.net**
Council for Learning Disabilities	**www.teachingld.org**
Division for Early Childhood	**www.dec-sped.org**
Developmental Disabilities news	**www.disabilityscoop.com**
Disability Rights Education and Defense Fund	**www.dredf.org**

Federal Register
(first source for final regulations that are
later codified in the Code of Federal Regulations)

www.gpo.access.gov/fr/index.html

Federation for Children With Special Needs
(the Massachusetts parent center, with links
to other parent centers across the country)

www.fcsn.org

Internet Special Education Resources
(a directory of professionals serving children with learning
disabilities and other disabilities)

www.iser.com

Iris Center for Training Enhancements
(free online training materials for program
development)

www.iris.peabody.vanderbilt.edu

Learning Disabilities Association of America

www.ldanatl.org

National Association for the Education of
Young Children

www.naeyc.org

National Information Center for Children
and Youth With Disabilities

www.nichcy.org

Parentpals, a division of Ameri-Corps Speech
and Hearing

www.parentpals.com

Special Ed Law

www.specialedlaw.net/index.mv

United Cerebral Palsy

www.ucp.org

U.S. Department of Education
   Office for Civil Rights
   Office of Special Education Programs
   IDEA site

www.ed.gov
www.ed.gov (under ED Offices)
www.ed.gov (under ED Offices)
http://idea.ed.gov
(no www in the url)

   IDEA Data

www.ideadata.org

Wrightslaw

www.wrightslaw.com

Index

Index of Court Cases

Index

2

General Index

accommodations

    appropriate, 117, 130, 137

    reasonable, 64, 75, 81, 289, 292–93, 298, 301, 344

    testing, 116–19, 282

ADD/ADHD, 68, 81, 95, 97, 214, 222–23, 248, 257, 280–83, 294, 297

adequate yearly progress (AYP), 114–16, 184, 187

Administrative Procedure Act, 50

administrative remedies, exhaustion of, 262–69, 272

AIDS. *See* HIV/AIDS

alcohol. *See* drug and alcohol use

alternate assessment

    alternate achievement standards, 49, 115–16

    modified achievement standards, 115

    See also standardized testing

American Academy of Child and Adolescent Psychiatry, 95

American Sign Language (ASL). <u>See</u> sign language

    Americans With Disabilities Act (ADA)

    American With Disabilities Amendments Act (ADAAA), 74–75

    court cases under Titles II and III, 76–82, 186, 298, 313

    enforcement, 77

    major life activities and, 74, 280, 282

    mitigation of disability, 74

    public accommodations, 75

    reasonable modifications, 75, 82

    scope of, 54, 74–76

Asperger syndrome, 69, 96, 293

assessment, 47

    See also evaluation

assistive technology, 197–201, 302

attorney's fees, 150, 269–72, 341

autism, 46, 101

average per-student expenditure (APSE), 44, 204

behavior problems, 181–82, 244, 246–47, 253, 255–57, 309

behavioral intervention plan (BIP), 47, 131, 249–50, 252–54

blindness, 43, 197

brain injury

non-traumatic, 96–97

traumatic, 46, 88, 92, 96–98, 102

bullying. See harassment

burden of proof, 149, 337

See also due process; parents; specific cases and statutes

Bush, George W., 48

case law (definition), 32

Centers for Medicare and Medicaid Services, 206

charter schools, 47, 185

child find provision, 106, 218–20, 340

civil rights

ADA and, 65, 74

IDEA and, 42

influence on disability law, 30, 65, 119

Section 504 and, 61, 66

See also Office for Civil Rights (OCR)

Civil Rights Act of 1964, 42, 112

Civil Rights Restoration Act, 66

Clinton, William, 46

comparable facilities, 308

compensatory education, 264–65, 272

complaints, 69–70, 77, 113, 134, 142, 148–53, 166, 184, 219, 268–72, 280, 288, 311, 319–21

conduct disorder, 95, 99–100

conflict resolution, 319–21

See also due process; Individuals With Disabilities Education Act (IDEA); Section 504 of the
Rehabilitation Act

Congressional Research Service (CRS), 255

consent (parental), 156, 169

contagious diseases, 286–90

Controlled Substances Act, 194

corporal punishment, 255–56, 308, 310–11

correctional facilities, 131, 185–86

Council for Children with Behavioral Disorders (CCBD), 255

crimes (reporting of), 166, 168, 215–16, 256–57, 311

dyslexia, 93

early intervening services, 91
early intervention program, 45, 51, 91
educability (definition), 44
Education for All Handicapped Children Act
    See Public Law 94-142
Education of the Handicapped Act (EHA), 42–43, 45, 50, 52, 140
education record
    See FERPA
Elementary and Secondary Education Act (ESEA), 46, 48–50, 52, 114–16
Eleventh Amendment, 54, 76
eligibility
    ADA and, 74
    IDEA and, 48–49, 62, 88–91, 95–99, 107, 114
    Section 504 and, 62, 279–81
emotional disturbance, 43, 88, 92, 94–95, 98–101, 184, 311
English language learners
    See limited English proficiency
Equal Employment Opportunity Commission (EEOC), 74
establishment clause, 236–37
evaluation
    IDEA and, 106–16, 143–45, 231, 340
    Section 504 and, 279–81, 313–14, 318–19
expert witness fees, 272
expulsion. *See* suspension and expulsion
extended school year (ESY), 179–80, 263

Family Educational Rights and Privacy Act of 1974 (FERPA)
    access rights and, 145, 162, 169–70, 172, 341
    "education record," 160-169, 171-72, 288, 342
    privacy rights and, 53, 160, 163–64, 173, 287–88
    remedies for violations of, 166
Family Policy Compliance Office, 166
federal court system, 33–35
    See also specific cases

IDEA and, 106, 134, 147, 150, 152–53

    Section 504 and, 319

Medicaid, 81, 206

medically fragile students, 203–4, 208

medical services, 193, 204–5

medication (administration of), 194, 297

mental health services, 79, 204–5

mental retardation, 101, 110

    See also intellectual disabilities

misclassification

    based on LEP status, 111–13

    based on race, 109–10

monetary damages. *See* damages

multiple disabilities, 46, 81, 88–89, 97, 101, 216, 224

National Disability Rights Network (NDRN), 255

National Instructional Materials Accessibility Standard (NIMAS), 197

neighborhood schools, 78, 222–23

No Child Left Behind Act (NCLB)

    alternate assessment and, 115–20

    IDEA and, 90, 111, 114

    IDEA '04 and, 48–49, 116

    IEP and, 114, 129–30

    January 2004 regulations of, 115

nonacademic services, 207, 299–300

notice (parental)

    FERPA and, 160, 163–64, 180

    IDEA and, 90, 141–43, 180

    Section 504 and, 278, 318

    See also parents; prior written notice

Nursing Practice Acts, 204

nursing services. See school nursing services

Obama, Barack, 44, 116

occupational therapy, 195, 264

Office for Civil Rights (OCR)

    ADA and

    complaints to, 320

list and definitions of, 192–97, 208

reimbursement for, 207–8

religious schools, 236–37

residency requirements, 46

residential placement, 205, 214, 231–33, 238, 280

resolution sessions, 50, 63, 148, 150, 156, 166–67, 172, 270, 319–21

response to treatment intervention (RTI), 93–94

restraints. *See* physical restraints

risk pool, 50, 204

ritalin, 194, 248, 282, 297–98

Roncker standard, 217, 220, 222, 224

Rowley standard, 135, 176–78, 180–84, 189

school health services, 196, 202–3

school nursing services, 193, 196

Section 1983 of the Civil Rights Act of 1871, 265–67, 272, 323

Section 504 of the Rehabilitation Act

ADA and, 77

conflict resolution and, 319

contagious diseases and, 286–90

definition of "disability" under, 278

discipline and, 64, 308–12

due process and, 308–10

employment discrimination and

enforcement of, 295–302

evaluation procedures in, 279–81

FAPE and, 63, 176, 292–302, 310, 312–13, 344

hearings under, 318, 320–21

history of, 42, 52, 60

IDEA and, 66–68, 89, 321, 323

notice and consent requirements in, 278

"otherwise qualified recipients" and, 64–65, 67, 286–87, 289

placement requirements of, 223, 305–16

private schools and, 312–13

remedies under, 69, 319–24

scope of, 61, 278

serious bodily injury, 248–50, 252

suspension and expulsion
   alternatives to, 242, 310
   bus suspension and, 247
   FAPE and, 186, 256
   OSEP and, 246, 248–49
   Section 504 and, 308–9

Telecommunications Act, 266
terminology change (disability vs. handicap), 45–46
testing accommodations. See accommodations; standardized testing
Title IX of the Education Amendments of 1972, 42, 65, 67, 265, 322
Tourette syndrome, 68, 97, 102, 222, 280–81, 295
transition services, 201–2
transportation, 197, 296
   See also free appropriate public education (FAPE); suspension and expulsion
tuition reimbursement. *See* reimbursement

U. S. Department of Education (ED)
   enforcement of IDEA by, 50–51, 77, 80, 116
   IDEA '04 and, 50–51
   See also specific office names
U. S. Department of Health, Education, and Welfare, 60
U. S. Department of Health and Human Services, 206
U. S. Department of Justice, 80

visual impairment, 88, 102, 131, 223
visual-motor impairment, 294
weapons, 152, 215, 242, 245–50, 257, 311, 341

zero-reject, 44, 97-8, 236, 242
zero-tolerance, 242, 252